PRAISE FOR GRANTLEE KIEZA'S BOOKS

'Engagingly written ... one of the most nuanced portraits to date'
The Australian

'Vivid, detailed and well written'
Daily Telegraph

'A staggering accomplishment that can't be missed by history buffs and story lovers alike'
Betterreading.com.au

'A free-flowing biography of a great Australian figure'
John Howard

'Clear and accessible ... well-crafted and extensively documented'
Weekend Australian

'Kieza has added hugely to the depth of knowledge about our greatest military general in a book that is timely'
Tim Fischer, *Courier-Mail*

'The author writes with the immediacy of a fine documentary ... an easy, informative read, bringing historic personalities to life'
Ballarat Courier

ALSO BY GRANTLEE KIEZA

Annette Kellerman: Australian Mermaid

Mr and Mrs Gould

Sister Viv

Flinders

Knockout: Great Australian Boxing Stories

The Remarkable Mrs Reibey

Hudson Fysh

The Kelly Hunters

Lawson

Banks

Macquarie

Banjo

The Hornet (with Jeff Horn)

Boxing in Australia

Mrs Kelly: The Astonishing Life of Ned Kelly's Mother

Monash: The Soldier Who Shaped Australia

Sons of the Southern Cross

Bert Hinkler: The Most Daring Man in the World

The Retriever (with Keith Schafferius)

A Year to Remember (with Mark Waugh)

Stopping the Clock: Health and Fitness the George Daldry Way (with George Daldry)

Fast and Furious: A Celebration of Cricket's Pace Bowlers

Mark My Words: The Mark Graham Story (with Alan Clarkson and Brian Mossop)

Australian Boxing: The Illustrated History

Fenech: The Official Biography (with Peter Muszkat)

MARY PENFOLD

Bestselling author of *Annette Kellerman: Australian Mermaid*, *Mr and Mrs Gould*, *Sister Viv*, *The Remarkable Mrs Reibey*, *Flinders*, *Hudson Fysh*, *Banjo*, *Banks* and *Mrs Kelly*

GRANTLEE KIEZA

ABC BOOKS

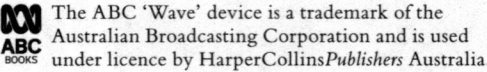 The ABC 'Wave' device is a trademark of the Australian Broadcasting Corporation and is used under licence by HarperCollins*Publishers* Australia.

HarperCollins*Publishers*
Australia • Brazil • Canada • France • Germany • Holland • India
Italy • Japan • Mexico • New Zealand • Poland • Spain • Sweden
Switzerland • United Kingdom • United States of America

HarperCollins acknowledges the Traditional Custodians of the lands upon which we live and work, and pays respect to Elders past and present.

First published on Gadigal Country in Australia in 2025
by HarperCollins*Publishers* Australia Pty Limited
ABN 36 009 913 517
harpercollins.com.au

Copyright © Grantlee Kieza 2025

The right of Grantlee Kieza to be identified as the author of this work has been asserted by him in accordance with the *Copyright Act 1968*.

All rights reserved. Apart from any use as permitted under the *Copyright Act 1968*, no part may be reproduced, copied, scanned, stored in a retrieval system, recorded, or transmitted, in any form or by any means, without the prior written permission of the publisher. Without limiting the exclusive rights of any author, contributor, or the publisher of this publication, any unauthorised use of this publication to train generative artificial intelligence (AI) technologies is expressly prohibited. HarperCollins also exercises its rights under Article 4(3) of the Digital Single Market Directive 2019/790 and expressly reserves this publication from the text and data-mining exception.

HarperCollins*Publishers*
Macken House, 39/40 Mayor Street Upper
Dublin 1, D01 C9W8, Ireland

A catalogue record for this book is available from the National Library of Australia

ISBN 978 0 7333 4327 8 (hardback)
ISBN 978 1 4607 1700 4 (ebook)

Cover design by Louisa Maggio, HarperCollins Design Studio
Jacket images: *Feby [i.e. February]* 1841 by Samuel Thomas Gill, courtesy National Library of Australia (134354667); *Vitis vinifera, Germany's Wild Medicinal Plants* by Johann Gottlieb Mann, courtesy Loyola University, New Orleans Special Collections and Archives; Penfolds Vineyard, Magill Estate by Chronicle / Alamy
Endpaper images: *Grapes Against White Wall*, 1883, by Edwin Deakin, courtesy National Gallery of Art, Gift of William and Abigail Gerdts (2004.165.4); *Still Life with Grapes*, 1888, by Edwin Deakin, courtesy Smithsonian American Art Museum, Museum purchase (1989.102)
Author photograph by Steve Pohlner
Index by Garry Cousins
Typeset in Bembo Std by Kirby Jones
Printed and bound in Australia by McPherson's Printing Group

For Lachlan McLaine, with my eternal gratitude

Prologue

MARY PENFOLD[1] SAT side-saddle upon her stunning white mare[2] and gazed through the soft glow of a winter sunset towards the masterpiece she had spent thirty years creating. Mary was approaching the twilight of her extraordinary career as a winemaker, and the fading light of dusk all around her vineyard flowed gently over horse and rider, and across the khaki green of the rolling Adelaide Hills behind her. It almost seemed that the towering splendour of distant Mount Lofty was looking over her work with silent approval.

By the winter of 1874 Mary was a widow in her late fifties. Dressed in a long, dark, high-necked dress, she looked more like her small, stout sovereign, Queen Victoria, with each passing year. She had an imperious presence too, as the commander in chief of her booming wine company,[3] which she had overseen from infancy. In a male-dominated industry, Mary Penfold had become one of Australia's most important vintners, taking what was a backyard vineyard at her whitewashed cottage called 'The Grange', and turning it into a world-renowned brand.

Mary had become one of the great drivers of the Australian wine industry – which, like her own vineyard, had the humblest of beginnings. Wine had been an important provision for sailors on the *Endeavour* when it reached Botany Bay in 1770, and when the First Fleet arrived in 1788, grapevines accompanied the convicts to their new prison home. Grapevines were nurtured and cherished from the first day of European settlement in

Australia; wine was seen as a civilising influence in the harsh prison settlement.

In front of the Widow Penfold at her Magill vineyard, just outside Adelaide, were what seemed like endless rows of vines, spaced more than two metres apart and stretching far into the distance. She had spaced the vines in such a way to promote the free circulation of air and for easier harvesting, allowing plenty of room for horses and carts to be taken between the rows.[4]

Mary and her assistant, Ellen Timbrell[5] – whose grandfather had befriended the great mariner Captain James Cook 100 years earlier – had planted many of the vines long ago, and now they were thick, old and tangled, having produced fine vintages year after year from soil that had never grown grapes before. Other vines were new arrivals to Mary's estate, bare twigs that in a few months would put forth delicate white buds, which would eventually grow into grapes for the production of fine wines. The gentle slopes of Mary's vineyard would be resplendent in shades of green, red and purple.

Mary was justifiably proud that the recent autumn harvest had produced three tonnes of grapes per acre for her family business, Penfolds, a growing enterprise that had started on her kitchen table. She had since turned it into one of the most respected winemakers in the Australian colonies.

Three decades earlier, Mary, her husband Christopher[6] and their baby daughter Georgina,[7] along with Ellen Timbrell, had braved wild seas on a terrifying voyage to an unfamiliar land thousands of miles from their English home, a world away from the cossetted middle-class lives they had known. In fact, overcoming obstacles was something Mary's family had done for centuries. In the late 1700s her grandfather had escaped war-ravaged Germany to build a new life for himself in London, and his brother had gone even further, becoming the richest man in America.

Full of curiosity, passion and an unquenchable thirst to sculpt lasting treasures from the red, loamy soil[8] around Adelaide, Mary had spent thirty years teaching herself to be a master winemaker and entrepreneur, all at a time when opportunities for women

Mary Penfold in 1869 just as her wine business was becoming a major commercial enterprise. *State Library of South Australia, B 22970RGB*

in such roles were almost non-existent, as they were generally consigned to lives as homemakers, looking after their husbands and children. Always in the shadow, never the spotlight. By 1874 Mary was sending Penfolds wines to markets not just in the Australian colonies but overseas, and she was confident that demand for the wines she was crafting would continue to grow long after she was gone.

As the sun sank lower, bathing the Adelaide Hills in the glow of a cool winter's evening, Mary encouraged her white mare to walk further on through the rows of vines, which were drinking in the remaining drops of sunlight. Now and then she used her spyglass to survey the more distant parts of her property and to gaze on the growing gas-lit city of Adelaide in the distance, with its spectacular Town Hall, ornate General Post Office and new sports ground, known as the Adelaide Oval, where an English cricket team of eleven players had just beaten South Australia's finest twenty-two.[9]

Mary and Christopher had purchased around 200 hectares of the 'choicest land' that made up the Magill Estate in 1844.[10] She began planting the grenache[11] and other vine cuttings that she and Christopher had sourced from the south of France and Portugal, which they had brought to South Australia dipped in wax and wrapped in canvas. The cuttings had thrived and grown thick and bountiful in the rich earth between the ocean and the hills, nurtured by Mary's tender care and by the Mediterranean climate, with its south-westerly winds, hot summers and cool winters. Mary had first planted the vines to make tonics, which Christopher supplied to weary patients through his medical practice – and from little things, big things had grown.

Almost everything Mary knew about wine she had taught herself.[12] Now she sat astride her horse as it walked slowly through her flourishing estate. She breathed in the quiet, still evening air and looked about the surrounding hills. Not only were her own vines abundant, she was also making large purchases of grapes from her neighbours and blending the juice to produce smooth, fine wines of even quality.[13]

The great French microbiologist Louis Pasteur, in this time when water was often unsafe because of polluted rivers, had recently described wine as possibly 'the most healthful and hygienic of all beverages'.[14] His endorsement certainly did not hurt sales for the fruit of Mary's vines.

From her most recent season Mary had crushed 400 tonnes of grapes and produced almost 200,000 litres of wine, sweet and dry reds and sweet and dry whites, which were now undergoing the process of natural fermentation. She had procured a sophisticated wine press capable of crushing 40 tonnes of grapes a day, and her workmen had built three large stone warehouses with galvanised-iron roofs.

In her cellars, Mary's casks and vats of South Australian redgum and English oak contained about 100,000 litres of wine that was at least four years old and now ready for market. Her total stock was more than 400,000 litres.[15]

Mary had built her international wine business at a time when women were all but invisible in the corporate world and seen mostly through the lens of their husbands' lives. While Dr Christopher Rawson Penfold had encouraged Mary's first experiments with wine for use in his medical practice, it was Mary who oversaw the expansion of the family business into a wine producer that would become a global icon. She had a small army of workers on her estate, but the wines were blended under what newspaper reports said was 'Mrs Penfold's personal supervision, not in conformity with any fixed and definite rule, but entirely according to her judgement and taste'.[16] Within a decade, Penfolds would be producing a third of South Australia's wine.[17]

From her vantage point, Mary could look down on Penfolds Road, a gravel track along which her beloved husband's funeral procession had travelled four years before. After his death, some of those close to Mary had advised her to leave the vineyard and allow others to run the business. It was too big and too stressful a concern for a woman, they said. But the commander in chief wouldn't budge.

Mary's struggles had mirrored the battles of the Australian wine industry as it grew from infancy. She too had walked a long road of hard work, sacrifice and heartbreak to reach this point. Winemaking in Australia had been dominated by men ever since vines arrived with the First Fleet at Botany Bay almost a century before. But Mary Penfold had broken the mould.

Chapter 1

IN 1844, MARY PENFOLD arrived in the mosquito-riddled, swampy wasteland that was Adelaide's international port, her husband by her side and a crying ten-month-old baby on her hip. In her trunk were European grapevine cuttings that she planned to plant in South Australia's rich soil.

It had been more than four months since Mary had heard the anguished goodbyes of her beloved parents, as their only daughter sailed off into weeks of raging storms. Mary's father had been so stressed by her departure that she feared he would soon die. When she left, Mary was afraid she would never see her parents again.

For more than four months, as the little ship carrying the young Penfold family to the frontier town of Adelaide was tossed about by nature's fury, Mary had prayed for the life of her little daughter, Georgina, as she breastfed her and tried to keep her alive in the middle of vast, deadly seas that had claimed the lives of so many thousands of travellers before. When Mary finally stepped onto the dock at Port Adelaide and swatted away at the swarms of bloodthirsty mosquitoes that descended on her and her baby, she was twenty-seven years old and ready for any challenge.

Mary had been born beside the Kent Road in South London in 1816, as the world's weather patterns were thrown into chaos by rapid, cataclysmic climate change. London had lost its lustre and become an ugly, overcrowded metropolis that was cold, broke and in despair. It was also perpetually dark, as a freak weather event had plunged much of Europe into blackness, ruining crops and wrecking lives. But the wrinkled, crying baby was the product of generations of ambitious, adventurous people who had grown strong through facing difficulties and had triumphed over hard times.

Mary's astonishing story of enterprise, hard work and daring began four decades before her birth, when her German grandfather, Georg Astor,[1] jumped off a sailing vessel from Hamburg in 1770[2] and strode boldly onto the London docks and into a new world. Georg was a butcher's son[3] looking for a chance at a better life in the English capital.

London, then a city of about 700,000 people,[4] was the busiest port in Britain, a wealthy, fast-growing centre of international trade that was a melting pot of aspirational, hardworking immigrants with new ideas. It offered the ambitious young German a far better future than his homeland after the ravages of the Seven Years' War.[5]

While crime was rife in London, and growing worse as masses of rural poor were being forced into cities to find work, it was also becoming the scientific and cultural capital of Europe. The wealth being generated by merchants, bankers and a new wave of industrialists and business owners allowed art and fashion to flourish. Theatres, music halls and ornate coffee houses abounded, and teams of workmen were erecting spectacular mansions and churches.

Georg had been raised in the town of Walldorf, near Heidelberg, a place synonymous with enchanting wines. Riesling, often called Rhine riesling, had been made on the steep slopes of the Rhine near his family home for hundreds of years.[6] Mary would one day learn of the long, slim strip of vineyards of her grandfather's homeland, nestled between the hills of the Black Forest and the magnificent river. She would also hear of the 'Heidelberg Tun', an enormous wine barrel built at that city's castle in 1751 to store more than 220,000 litres of wine.[7]

In England, Mary's grandfather lived with an uncle who worked for Shudi & Broadwood, craftsmen who had created some of the most exquisite musical instruments in the world.[8] Handel and Mozart had played Burkat Shudi's harpsichords, while John Broadwood made pianos for Beethoven, Haydn, and Bach's son Johann Christian Bach.[9]

Georg Astor anglicised his name to George, the name of Britain's king, and quickly began assimilating to British life. The teenager had arrived in Britain in the same year that London's wealthy young botanist Joseph Banks set foot on the east coast of the land that in time would be known as Australia.

The 27-year-old Banks was one of the richest young men in Britain and one of its foremost scientists. He was also a tall, burly ladies' man with a ponytail, an endlessly enquiring mind and a well-stocked wine cellar at his Soho mansion. He had helped to finance the greatest scientific expedition mankind had known until that time, a three-year voyage around the world on a converted coal transport vessel, His Majesty's Bark *Endeavour*, which was under the command of an imposing Yorkshireman: Lieutenant James Cook.

Shortly before the voyage began in 1768, a merchant friend in Lisbon had sent Banks a huge hogshead – about 240 litres – of sweet, rich Portuguese Carcavelos wine as a gift.[10] During the voyage, Banks took no chances about contracting scurvy – a disease caused by a lack of vitamin C that results in bleeding, swollen gums, loose teeth, listlessness and, in the worst cases, loss of life. Scurvy had been responsible for more deaths during the 'age of exploration' than all the storms, shipwrecks, wars and other diseases combined.[11]

Most of the sailors on the *Endeavour* were fed oranges, lemons and fermented cabbage – sauerkraut – to guard against scurvy, but Banks also carried a concoction of citrus juices preserved with brandy, given to him by Dr Nathaniel Hulme. 'Oenotherapy' – the use of wine for medicinal purposes – had been practised in Europe for centuries, and it would have a huge bearing on the life of Mary Penfold.

In the 1700s, many drugs prescribed by physicians could not be made without wines such as sherry, madeira, port or tokay.[12] Port was recommended to treat fevers and anaemia, astringent red wines for diarrhoea. White wines worked as a diuretic, champagne for nausea and catarrhal conditions. Claret and burgundy were used in tonics for loss of appetite, and sherry and madeira were recommended to help patients who were convalescing.[13]

James Cook had also ensured a plentiful supply of wine for his *Endeavour* crew, both as a tonic for the sick and as an emergency replacement if fresh water became scarce as they traversed 50,000 kilometres of largely unchartered territory on their global expedition.

For Banks and his influential friends in science, the aristocracy and government, wine was a foundation pillar of civilisation, both as a medicine and as a way of celebrating God's bounty for mankind. But almost all the wine consumed in Britain in the late 1700s was imported and expensive, and British politicians, facing increasing crime and the other ill-effects of poverty and drunkenness in their overcrowded cities, blamed much of the lawlessness on 'poisonous liquors'[14] – by which they meant cheap beer, ciders and spirits such as rum and gin. Wine, by contrast, was linked with temperance and good manners. It was a drink to be sipped and appreciated in moderate amounts, as a civilising influence that gave its drinkers a touch of class.

HUMANKIND HAS ENJOYED an extraordinary love affair with wine for thousands of years. Indeed, grapevines are one of the earliest recorded cultivated crops. The Egyptians recorded the harvest of grapes on the walls of their tombs; clay jars of wine were even buried with pharaohs in order that they might entertain guests in the afterlife.[15] The Bible contains more than a hundred references to wine, both for medicinal purposes and simply to make hearts glad.[16] Jesus turned water into wine at a wedding feast; the apostle Paul advised his ailing fellow missionary Timothy to 'take a little wine for the sake of your stomach'.[17] Red wine has been used by Christians for almost 2000 years to represent the blood of Christ.

For the British upper classes of George Astor's time, wine was associated with the birth of modern civilisation. It was a drink of the elites in ancient Greece, immortalised by the philosopher Plato and the Greek poets, who paid homage to Dionysus, their god of wine. The popularity of wine had increased during the Roman era, as major wine-producing regions across Europe, which still exist today, were established. The Romans worshipped Bacchus, their god of wine, and vintners developed grape varieties and improved cultivation techniques. Wine bars and taverns were commonplace in Roman cities, and the Romans exported both wine and winemaking techniques to the ends of their empire.

By the Middle Ages, the science of winemaking had advanced further thanks to monasteries across the continent producing wine for Christian sacraments. Wine became an alternative drink in places where fresh water was hard to find, and gradually more and more people across Europe developed a taste for wine with their meals. Around 1600, Shakespeare could write that 'good wine is a good familiar creature, if it be well used'.[18]

Some of the finest vineyards in Europe emerged, and the wealthy maintained well-stocked cellars. In the 17th century the invention of the corkscrew made it possible to more effectively seal glass bottles with corks.[19]

Three weeks after the *Endeavour* commenced its global voyage in 1768, James Cook had steered the ship to the impoverished Portuguese-controlled island of Madeira, 700 kilometres west of the North African coast, and taken on large supplies of wine, along with water, green vegetables, fruit and beef. There, Joseph Banks watched men squeezing grapes with their bare feet and elbows, and suggested that Noah would have had a 'more sophisticated method before the flood'.[20]

Though its production was rudimentary, madeira wine was fortified with a distilled spirit, usually brandy, to preserve it, and unlike many other wine styles, which quickly soured when stored on hot boats, it seemed to age well in the bottle during long voyages. Devotees grew to love the variety, and madeira wines were among the most popular in London in the 1700s. There was also a huge market in the British colonies on the east coast of the Americas.[21]

During the *Endeavour*'s voyage, Cook mapped a large section of the world, including a huge tract of land west of New Zealand which he named New South Wales. He and Banks first set foot on it in 1770 at a place Cook named Botany Bay in honour of

Banks' botanical studies. Banks later remarked that he thought the area would be ideal for producing wine, as it was 'mild and moderate ... similar to that about Toulouse, in the south of France'.[22]

THE *ENDEAVOUR* RETURNED to England in 1771, and Banks regaled the scientific community with tales about the discoveries of exotic peoples, otherworldly animals and vast lands ripe for exploitation by the British Crown.

Meanwhile, Mary Penfold's grandfather George Astor was more interested in exploring business opportunities in the narrow, crowded lanes of bustling London than he was in the discovery of exotic and mysterious new lands on the far side of the world.

George was prospering in his new home, and in 1779, at the church of St George the Martyr in Southwark,[23] in London's south, he married Elizabeth Dorothea Wright.[24] He wrote home to Walldorf, inviting his sixteen-year-old brother, Johann Jakob Astor,[25] to leave their father's sausages and pigs' livers behind and join him and his new wife in London. Together, the hard-driving brothers built an admirable company in London as 'George and John Astor' – first in Holywell Street, off the Strand, and then in Wych Street, off Drury Lane[26] – selling flutes and other woodwind instruments.[27]

While the Astor brothers enjoyed business success, Britain was fighting to protect its territories across the Atlantic. American patriots had started an armed rebellion when thirteen colonies broke free from the rule of King George III and his high taxes on Chinese tea and madeira wine. The founding fathers of the 'United States of America' had declared their break from Britain on 4 July 1776, toasting their independence by raising glasses of madeira when they signed their document in Pennsylvania a month later.[28] General George Washington, the leader of the American forces in the war that followed, stocked the first mobile headquarters for his newly formed Continental Army with at least 1900 bottles of madeira.[29] He knew the positive effect the sweet, fortified wine would have on his men's morale.

A square piano made by Mary's grandfather George Astor. The Met, New York, 1980.82

As American pirates roamed the Atlantic, British shipping was severely disrupted, and lawlessness reigned in London, which was already intolerably overcrowded. The thousands of sex workers touting for business in Covent Garden, Soho and Drury Lane reflected unprecedented levels of poverty. Child labour gave rise to a world of bleak workhouses and starvation.

Under what became known as 'the Bloody Code', the number of crimes in Britain that carried the death penalty increased during the 18th century to well over 200. Most were tied to poverty, such as stealing a rabbit from a warren or taking goods from a shipwreck. Even chopping down a tree for firewood during winter became a hanging offence.[30] More humane judges had preferred to send convicts and prisoners of war to work in penal servitude on the plantations in North America, but the Revolutionary War had made this impossible, causing massive overcrowding in British jails. Ships left over from the Seven Years' War crowded the Thames as floating prisons, but even these 'hulks' could not cope with the flood of offenders.

War with the Americans raged until 3 September 1783, when three representatives of the United States of America signed the Treaty of Paris with Great Britain at the Hôtel d'York in the French capital. One of the delegates was America's ambassador to France, Benjamin Franklin, who had earlier declared that wine was 'a constant proof that God loves us, and loves to see us happy'.[31]

WHILE THE MUSIC BUSINESS had produced a good living for George and John Jacob Astor, the Revolutionary War split the brothers apart.

George's wife, Elizabeth, was pregnant with their first child, and he continued to run his London business with a team of craftsmen, expanding his woodwind manufacturing to include pianos and organs.[32] But John Jacob Astor was restless, and convinced that the world had much more in store for him.

John took the cessation of hostilities with America as his cue to explore new opportunities in this bold new nation. In 1783 he sailed for Baltimore, taking a bagful of George's flutes with him to sell in the United States. As John's ship, the *North Carolina*,[33] lurched and rolled amid the grey waves, he befriended a fur dealer, who told him of the riches that could be made exporting pelts from North America.[34]

John soon moved to New York, where he explored the fur business and real estate investments, while also acting as the American agent for George Astor and other British manufacturers of musical instruments. He regularly placed advertisements in the American press advertising 'German Flutes, Of a Superior Quality'.[35] In 1785 he ran this advertisement multiple times:

> JACOB ASTOR. No. 81, Queen-Street [New York], near the Friends Meeting-House. Has just imported, in the ship *Triumph*, an elegant assortment of musical instruments, such as Piannaforte's [*sic*], German-flutes, Violins, Clarinets, Hautboy's, Guitar's, &c.[36]

The musical instruments sold well, and John Jacob Astor eventually became the patriarch of one of the world's wealthiest dynasties, and America's first multimillionaire.[37]

Just like her grandfather and great-uncle, Mary Penfold would develop a cool head for business – and a powerful ambition too.

Chapter 2

BY THE TIME MARY PENFOLD arrived in Adelaide in 1844, grapes had been grown in Australia for fifty-six years. The Australian wine industry had started as a project in a backyard garden, but Mary would take their cultivation and production to a new level.

As Mary's grandfather worked to establish a comfortable life for future generations of his family, the British government began considering plans to make wine and wool from the lands of New South Wales, a place the *Endeavour* had visited but which had not yet been colonised.

By the 1780s America was the land of opportunity for go-getters such as John Jacob Astor, but Britain had surrendered much of its wealth with the loss of those fertile North American lands. Britain also had nowhere to ship its thousands of convicts, who were now crammed into hulks on the Thames.

James Matra was an officer who had sailed with Cook and Banks on the *Endeavour*. In 1783 he submitted to the British government 'A Proposal for Establishing a Settlement in New South Wales', saying that the land he'd visited was 'an immense tract of more than 2,000 miles' and that since 'great parts of it were extremely fertile', it had the potential under British rule to 'cause a revolution in the whole system of European commerce'. He saw wine, wool and timber as potentially valuable exports from there.[1]

In consultation with Sir Joseph Banks, Prime Minister William Pitt and his government put into action on 21 August 1786 a plan to settle Botany Bay. The Secretary of State at Britain's Home Office, Lord Sydney,[2] sent a letter to the Treasury saying that King George III had approved the voyage. Included in his missive was a document prepared by Sydney's undersecretary, Evan Nepean,[3] which described 'a plan for effectually disposing of convicts, and rendering their transportation reciprocally beneficial both to themselves and to the State, by the establishment of a colony in New South Wales'.[4] Sydney bypassed James Matra[5] and appointed a friend of Nepean, the naval captain Arthur Phillip,[6] to lead an expedition to New South Wales, establish a penal colony there and become its first governor.

Phillip, a small, olive-skinned former spy with a pear-shaped head, a fleshy nose and a smile that was missing a front tooth,[7] was given command of eleven ships to transport prisoners, jailers, guards from the Royal Marines and supplies on an eight-month, 24,000-kilometre voyage to Botany Bay.

Wine would be one of the vital supplies carried on the fleet for the protection of the voyagers. Sir Joseph Banks – effectively the minister in charge of the new colony – instructed Phillip to plant vineyards when they arrived.

Thirty-one-year-old John White[8] was appointed chief surgeon for the First Fleet, with another eight surgeons[9] under him who were assigned to various vessels. White advised Lord Sydney that he considered wine a 'necessary'[10] for convalescence for those on the voyage. William Balmain,[11] the surgeon assigned to the *Alexander*, pleaded that as well as fresh vegetables, 'a small quantity of wine would also be a powerful restorative to the sick'.[12]

Marine guards aboard the six convict transport ships petitioned their officers to ensure that they were supplied with wine and spirits for the voyage, with the men assigned to the *Scarborough* asserting that a 'moderate distribution' of liquor or wine was 'indispensably requisite for the preservation of our lives, which change of climate and the extreme fatigue we shall be necessarily exposed to may probably endanger'.[13]

On 10 May 1787, sauerkraut and malt were taken on board the ships to ward off the effects of scurvy. A 'pipe' of wine –

about 500 litres – was distributed among the vessels as medicine too.[14]

To prevent unrest among the marines, Nepean asked the Treasury that the fleet be authorised to spend £200 purchasing thirty pipes, or 15,000 litres, of wine at Tenerife, in the Canary Islands off north-western Africa, when the voyage reached there.[15] Wine from the Canaries had been popular in Britain since even before Shakespearean characters drank it.[16] Phillip said the wine that he procured there would also be issued as rations to the marines when they reached New South Wales.

Banks instructed Phillip to take trees and seeds of all descriptions to plant in the new colony, so that the settlers could develop a self-sufficient agricultural community. Among them were grapevine cuttings packed in camphor to stop them spoiling from heat.[17] Banks knew that grapevines had to be propagated from cuttings to ensure the new plants retained the characteristics of the parent vine. Spain, Portugal and the Netherlands had all set up vineyards in their colonial territories and Banks did not want Britain to miss out on the enormous export potential of Britain's new land.

GEORGE ASTOR, now the father of a son and two young daughters, read in the newspapers that a fleet carrying 750 convicts and 550 military personnel and free settlers had left Portsmouth on 13 May 1787, bound for Botany Bay.[18] George Worgan, the surgeon aboard the fleet's flagship, the *Sirius*, had packed a small 'square piano' – actually rectangular in shape – which was built in London by one of George Astor's rivals.[19] Smaller than a modern piano, Worgan's instrument was fitted with 'campaign legs' that could be folded for storage.[20]

When the fleet arrived at Tenerife, Captain Watkin Tench of the Royal Marines noted: 'Dry wines, as the merchants term them, are sold from ten to fifteen pounds a pipe; for the latter price, the very best, called the London Particular, may be bought: sweet wines are considerably dearer.'[21]

Phillip's purchase of sweet, fortified Canary Islands wine allowed him to allocate the marines a daily ration of a pint of wine (473 millilitres) per man, to go with their pound of bread and pound of beef (about 450 grams each). Convicts were given three-quarters of a pound of beef and bread (about 340 grams of each) but no wine, unless they were ill and a doctor recommended it for therapeutic purposes.[22]

When the ships reached Rio de Janeiro, in Brazil, and were anchored there for a month, George Worgan played his piano for some of his officers on the *Sirius*.[23] More plants and seeds were loaded for New South Wales, including grapevines,[24] coffee, cocoa, cotton-seed, bananas, oranges, lemons, guava, tamarind and prickly pear.[25]

Arthur Phillip could not purchase wine except from retailers, which made it more expensive. Although thirty pipes of wine had been ordered for the fleet's hospital, the high prices in Rio meant that 'only 15 pipes [had] been purchased' – 7500 litres.[26] Phillip dined with old friends in Rio, while the captain of a Brazilian fort entertained Arthur Bowes Smyth,[27] the surgeon from the ship *Lady Penrhyn*, bringing out 'a bottle of excellent port wine'.[28]

The fleet sailed on, but as it rounded the Cape of Good Hope, on the southern tip of Africa, the crew aboard the *Sirius* were taken with scurvy. A day out from Cape Town, many on board had blood running out of their mouths from teeth loosened by the disease. When the ship docked, its captain, John Hunter, ordered the men be served with the best provisions that the Cape could provide, and for 'as much wine' as was needed to make the men 'well and hearty'.[29]

In Cape Town, the convicts languished for weeks on their prison transports while Phillip and his officers embarked on a tour of the lush region, where Dutch and French settlers had established vineyards that produced some of the world's favourite wines. Phillip wrote of the beauty of Cape Town, and of Constantia, 'a district consisting of two farms, wherein the famous wines of that name are produced'.[30]

One of Phillip's officers, David Collins,[31] wrote that the Constantia dessert wine had 'a very fine, rich, and pleasant flavour, and is an excellent cordial'. Over time, Constantia's 'excellent cordial' would win praise from such diverse characters as Giacomo Casanova, George Washington, Napoleon Bonaparte, Jane Austen and Charles Dickens.

Constantina wine was developed from a blend of Muscat de Frontignan, pontac, red and white muscatel and a little chenin blanc, grape varieties that thrived at the Cape, along with groendruif (semillon) and hoenpoten (known then by the British as 'muscat of Alexandria').[32]

David Collins went from vineyard to vineyard, sampling the produce, and loving every minute and mouthful of it. He noted that 'wines of their own growth' formed a considerable part of trade at the Cape, and the 'neatness, regularity, and extent' of the vineyards and wine vaults 'were extremely pleasing to the eye'. 'But a stranger should not visit more than one of them in a day,' he warned, 'for almost every cask has some peculiarity to recommend it, and its contents must be tasted.'[33]

Constantina remained a popular wine in London for decades, and Mary Penfold would become familiar with its taste and fame.

Taking advice from Colonel Robert Gordon, the commander of the Dutch troops at the Cape, and from the botanist Francis Masson, who was sending plants back to London for Joseph Banks, Arthur Phillip also gathered farm animals and 'a vast number of plants, seeds and other garden articles', including fig trees and sugarcane, to take to Botany Bay. Vines 'of various sorts' were loaded onto the ships.[34] Collins recalled that the officers of the fleet obtained not only 'a great variety of the best seeds and plants' at the Cape, but also information about 'the culture, the soil, and the proper time of introducing them into the ground'.[35]

As the fleet sailed across the Indian Ocean and into the Southern Ocean, Surgeon-General John White wrote that 'scurvy began to show itself in the *Charlotte*, mostly among those who had the dysentery to a violent degree; but I was pretty well able to keep it under by a liberal use of the essence of malt and some good wine'.[36]

In the cabin of Surgeon Arthur Bowes Smyth aboard the *Lady Penrhyn*, some of the grapevines prospered. As the ships approached Van Diemen's Land in the first week of 1788, the officers drank two 'bumpers' of claret each: 'one, [saluting] success to the undertaking in general, the other to their safe anchoring in Botany Bay', which was still a fortnight's sailing away.[37]

On 9 January the fleet was dispersed by a massive storm, 'with a greater swell than at any other period during the voyage'. The sky appeared black, broken only by lightning that was the most vivid Bowes Smyth had ever seen. Then hail battered everything within sight; much of the fleet's livestock, housed on the decks, was killed. During the storm, the convict women on the *Lady Penrhyn* were so terrified that most were on their knees at prayer. With the heavy rolling of the ship, the tubs containing the grapevines broke from their fastenings; the cuttings were thrown out and 'much hurt'.[38]

In time, Mary Penfold would know just how they felt, trying to stay alive on a ship at the mercy of the angry elements.

THE FIRST FLEET BEGAN arriving at Botany Bay on 18 January 1788. The doctors on board had done a sterling job, using wine and other medicines. Despite the generally poor state of health of many convicts, all but forty-five of them made it to Australia alive after eight months at sea – an extraordinary survival rate for the times.

With all his ships anchored, on 20 January Captain Phillip and a small group of marines boarded two small boats and explored the land around Botany Bay, trying to communicate with the Eora people they encountered as they went. They carried wine as a refreshment. Phillip was under instructions from the British government to use 'every possible means' to make friendly relationships with 'the natives' and 'to conciliate their affections, enjoining all our subjects to live in amity and kindness with them'.[39]

Whenever Phillip and his men met the Eora, they offered gifts of beads and cloth. Philip Gidley King, the second lieutenant on the *Sirius*, noted that the Eora weren't keen on wine but wanted 'ye great coats & Cloathing … hatts was more particularised by them, their admiration of which they expressed by very loud shouts, whenever one of us pulled our hatts off'.[40]

Phillip then took his group to one side of the bay, while King went exploring another of the inlets. King 'soon perceived that the natives were following us' and grew afraid. Some Eora men waded out to King's boat. 'I was apprehensive,' King wrote, 'that they might find means to surprize us as every one of them were armed with lances, & short bludgeons.'

He gave two of them a glass of wine as a sign of friendship, but 'they had no sooner tasted [it] than they spit it out'.[41] Wine was an acquired taste that the Eora had not yet acquired; sadly, European alcohol would blight many Indigenous lives in the years that followed.

AFTER HIS EXPLORATIONS, Governor Phillip deemed Botany Bay unsuitable for a settlement because of its sandy soil, mangroves and scarce fresh water, and decided to explore more of the coastline. The fleet left Botany Bay and sailed a few kilometres north, soon reaching what Surgeon White called 'without exception, the finest and most extensive harbour in the universe'.[42]

At sunset on 26 January 1788, at a place Phillip named Sydney Cove, he and his principal officers assembled round a newly hewn flagstaff, drank toasts with wine to the health of King George and the success of the settlement, and raised the union flag.[43] George Worgan soon unfolded the legs of his square piano to entertain Phillip and the free settlers.

Many of the grapevines had been badly damaged on the stormy seas, but there were enough hardy survivors. Phillip ordered they be carried to a clearing of the bush beside the grand harbour, near the present-day Botanic Garden.

David Collins wrote that 'a portable canvas house, brought over for the Governor, was erected on the east side of the cove'.

Some ground having been prepared near His Excellency's house on the east side, the plants from Rio de Janeiro and the

Cape of Good Hope were safely brought on shore in a few days and we soon had the satisfaction of seeing the grape, the fig, the orange, the pear and the apple, the delicious fruits of the Old, taking root and establishing themselves in our New World.[44]

Phillip was hopeful that the grapevines would grow strong and healthy in the warm climate of Sydney Cove, and produce a fine vintage.

IN LONDON, MEANWHILE, George Astor's family was also growing strong and healthy. In 1788 he and Elizabeth welcomed a third daughter, named Elizabeth after her mother.[45] Twenty-eight years later she would become the mother of Mary Penfold.

Chapter 3

AS LITTLE ELIZABETH ASTOR was learning to walk around her father's London home, Governor Arthur Phillip was closely watching the progress of his vines under the warm Australian sun on the southern side of Sydney's grand harbour. Phillip saw the cultivation of grapes and the making of wine as evidence that Britain had brought civilisation to this rugged infant colony, thousands of miles from the gentrified world he and his officers had left behind.[1]

Although he expressly forbade convicts from touching alcohol, Phillip was certain that the land around Sydney Cove would produce wines equal to anywhere in the world. He considered the climate the equal of the most idyllic locations in Europe, and wrote gushingly of the warm sun and fine soil as he watched the settlement's freshwater stream flow past his newly planted grapevines and into Sydney Cove.

Just as Mary Penfold would discover at her Adelaide vineyard decades later, Phillip observed that the rains in his new domain were never of long duration, and there were seldom fogs. 'The soil, though in general light, and rather sandy' around the settlement, he wrote, was as good as any he had found 'so near the sea-coast'. All the surviving plants and fruit trees brought from Brazil and the Cape of Good Hope were soon thriving. His convict gardeners were growing excellent cauliflowers and melons. Vegetables – both the European varieties and those native to his new home – had become plentiful.[2]

'The orange trees flourish,' Phillip wrote, 'and the fig trees and vines are improving still more rapidly.' He was looking forward to seeing the white buds on the vines turn into grapes. 'In a climate so favourable,' he declared, 'the cultivation of the vine may doubtless be carried to any degree of perfection; and ... the wines of New South Wales may, perhaps, hereafter be sought with avidity, and become an indispensable part of the luxury of European tables.'[3]

Four months after the fleet's arrival at Sydney Cove, Surgeon George Worgan joined Captain John Hunter and Lieutenant William Bradley on an expedition,[4] travelling by boat along what would become known as Sydney Harbour and then upriver for about 16 kilometres. Worgan thought the surrounds looked like 'a Beautiful Park', and observed that 'the Soil was extremely rich, and produced luxuriant Grass'.

> Having extended our Excursion as far as we wished, we returned to the Place where we landed and after regaling Ourselves with a cold Kanguroo [sic] Pie and a Plum Pudding, a Bottle of Wine &c, all which Comforts we brought from the Ship with Us, We returned on Board.[5]

Two days later, convict workers laid the foundation stone for Arthur Phillip's Government House,[6] situated beside the harbour near today's Bennelong Point. Before long William Bradley sketched the first two-storey structure built on the continent, complete with a path from the harbour flanked by two rows of grapevines growing like bushes without the support of trellises.

At about the same time as those vines were planted, the crew on another British ship, the *Bounty* – bound for Tahiti and destined to experience a mutiny – planted the first grapes on the island that became known as Tasmania. Under the command of William Bligh, the *Bounty* arrived at Bruny Island in August 1788 and anchored in Adventure Bay. On 30 August, Bligh recorded in his log that he and his gardener, David Nelson, planted a variety of fruits and vegetables, including 'nine vines'.[7]

Bligh was aware, however, of the way the Indigenous people burnt the countryside to reinvigorate the soil, and so was pessimistic about the prospects of his grapes. He was correct; on his return to Adventure Bay in 1792, on a voyage that also included the young midshipman Matthew Flinders, he found just a single apple tree growing, and no sign of the vines or any of his other plantings.

WINE BECAME A STAPLE at Arthur Phillip's dinner table, enjoyed by all the officers who benefited from his hospitality, but the governor noted that most of the area's First Peoples treated alcohol with disgust.

When young Eora man Arabanoo dined at a side table at the governor's house, Watkin Tench reported, he 'ate heartily of fish and ducks, which he first cooled. Bread and salt meat he smelled but would not taste.' And he would drink nothing but water, turning his nose up at the liquor and wine that was offered.[8] A month later Arabanoo was still refusing those drinks, treating them with 'disgust and abhorrence'.[9]

According to Tench, Bennelong – a Wangal man from Manly Cove who had been kidnapped by Phillip's men and taken to Government House as a reluctant guest – 'was the only native we ever knew who immediately showed a fondness for spirits ... nor was the effect of wine or brandy upon him more perceptible than an equal quantity would have produced upon one of us, although fermented liquor was new to him'.[10]

In September 1790, Phillip found Bennelong again, among a group of Wangal men feasting on a whale carcass on the beach at Manly. Bennelong was wary of Phillip, but he began speaking cordially with him in English. Tench said that Phillip decided to see if Bennelong's 'love of wine ... still subsisted', so he 'uncorked a bottle, and poured out a glass of it'. Bennelong drank the wine with his former 'relish and good humour, giving for a toast, as he had been taught "the King"'.[11]

But not all of Bennelong's companions wanted to toast Phillip's arrival or the King's health, and one of them drove a spear into the governor's shoulder, apparently as payback for Bennelong's previous capture and confinement. Dr William Balmain,[12] now the colony's surgeon, drew out the pointed shaft and the governor recovered. Phillip later wrote to Banks that there were no hard feelings. 'Many of these people,' he told the celebrated botanist, 'are now as much at home at Sydney as they are in their woods, but in bringing this about they treated me rather roughly.'[13]

At the same time, on the new settlement of Norfolk Island, almost 1700 kilometres north-east of Sydney, the perpetually 'disagreeable'[14] lieutenant-governor, Major Robert Ross,[15] was positively jubilant over the vineyard he had planted on the windswept outpost. He had seen ten grapevines brought from England multiply into 600 cuttings, while Phillip had sent another 250 cuttings from Sydney. Ross waited in eager anticipation for fine homegrown vintages bearing his name. In a report back to Evan Nepean in London in 1790, Ross declared that all the cuttings were:

> ... thriving equally well with the others, and some of the old stocks have fruit this year, nor have I any doubt but the whole will bear fruit this year; and in the course of two or three years I can see no reason why we may not have as much wine made upon this island as will supply New Sh. Wales and this place, and I think it very probable that in a short time they may export wine from this island.[16]

TWO GOOD SUMMERS eventually produced the first two good bunches of grapes in Phillip's garden, which he declared 'may be mentioned, as being the first this Country has produced'.[17] The colony's chaplain, Richard Johnson, described by Watkin Tench as 'the best farmer in the country',[18] wrote to a friend that the soil of the new colony seemed ideal for agriculture. 'I promise you if ever wine be made here & not prohibited from being exported,' he declared, 'I will send you a specimen & perhaps may drink your health in a bumper of New Holland wine.'[19]

Partly because of their proximity to the waters of Sydney Harbour, however, Governor Phillip's vines fell victim to a blight infection called anthracnose.[20] Phillip wrote to Sir Joseph Banks in the middle of 1790 to say that while the best of the vine cuttings he had brought to Sydney had 'decayed on the vine'[21] because of the absence of 'a well-studied gardener', he had directed convicts in November 1788 to plant 2000 vines at a new government farm at Rose Hill, about 20 kilometres west of Sydney Cove. This was an area he soon renamed Parramatta,[22] after an approximation of the Darug people's word for 'place of eels'. He was keenly awaiting the arrival of the first grapes there.

The vineyard at Rose Hill was planted in a fertile crescent area above the Parramatta River, and soon more vines were added. At Phillip's suggestion, the British government recruited nine farmers and others to be sent to Sydney: they were to be superintendents of convicts, but their knowledge would improve the colony's agricultural prospects.

One of the men sent to Sydney was German-born widower Philip Schaffer, who had been a lieutenant in a Hessian rifle corps that had fought for the British against the American rebels in the Revolutionary War.[23] Schaeffer, who was 'accustomed to farming',[24] and his ten-year-old daughter, Elizabeth, sailed for Sydney aboard the *Guardian*, along with supplies and grapevines

Vine cuttings were planted on the side of a hill at Parramatta that Governor King said was 'formed like a crescent, facing the north, which is the best exposition'. View at Rose Hill Port Jackson c1791. *SLNSW [a1528525 / DG SV1A/24] (Dixson Galleries)*

organised by Banks for the infant colony. But the ship was wrecked when it hit an iceberg off the Cape of Good Hope.[25]

The Schaffers made it back to land and were taken aboard the *Lady Juliana*, a convict ship full of female prisoners that became known as the 'Floating Brothel', and reached Sydney in June 1790. In March the following year, Schaffer was granted 57 hectares on the northern bank of the Parramatta River, on land where the Wallumettagal people had held corroborees.[26] Schaffer named his property 'The Vineyard', built a fine brick home[27] and planted an acre (around 4000 square metres) under vines. The German had grown up on a small estate on the banks of the Rhine, where his father grew grapes; when Watkin Tench visited Schaffer in December 1791, he described him as 'a man of industry and respectable character'.

Tench observed that in Sydney and Rose Hill, 'vines of every sort' seemed to do well. He was convinced that the grapes of New South Wales would 'in a few years, equal those of any other country. That their juice will probably hereafter furnish an indispensable article of luxury at European tables, has already been predicted in the vehemence of speculation.'[28]

Schaffer told the marine officer that he had always been fond of assisting in his father's labours. Tench noted that Schaffer had 900 vines 'flourishing',[29] though as they walked through the rows of his vineyard, the German farmer shook his head more than once and made 'some mortifying observations' about the soil and his present domain, compared with the fertile banks of the Rhine.

Even so, Schaffer assured Tench that hardly any difficulty could arise which 'vigour and perseverance' would not overcome.[30] This was the philosophy Mary Penfold would bring to her winemaking as well. Schaffer is likely to have made Australia's first homegrown wine at The Vineyard in 1792.[31]

SHIPS BRINGING CONVICTS and supplies to Sydney delivered more grape seeds and vine cuttings from England and from the various ports of call along the route, including Madeira, Tenerife, Rio de Janeiro and Cape Town. Verdelho was mostly sourced from Madeira and grew successfully, especially on the banks of the Parramatta River.[32]

Within three years of the First Fleet's arrival, David Collins could note that at Parramatta there were 350 acres (142 hectares) of maize being cultivated, 'also 44 in wheat, six in barley, one in oats, two in potatoes, and four in vines',[33] including the 1.2 hectares of grapes growing at a new but temporary Government House, a small, single-storey cottage of lath and plaster, near the river in Parramatta.

At the end of 1791, Watkin Tench described how he:

> ... went round the crescent at the bottom of the [governor's] garden, which certainly in beauty of form and situation is unrivalled in New South Wales. Here are eight thousand vines planted, all of which in another season are expected to bear grapes ... Although the soil of the crescent be poor, its aspect and circular figure, so advantageous for receiving and retaining the rays of the sun, eminently fit it for a vineyard.[34]

Governor Phillip wrote to Sir Joseph Banks that, despite a long dry spell and grubs,[35] which had disheartened some of the settlers, he now had 'many thousand young vines' in Sydney and on Norfolk Island, growing from the few cuttings he had brought from Rio and the Cape. 'I had two or three bunches of grapes the year before last, and last year several good bunches,' he reported, '[and] at present the old vines in my garden are loaded with very fine fruit.'[36]

Tench described Phillip's grapes as 'handsome; the fruit of a moderate size, but well filled out; and the flavour high and delicious'.[37]

Surgeon George Worgan gave lessons on his now battered piano to a young mother named Elizabeth Macarthur.[38] She had arrived in Sydney on the *Scarborough*, part of the Second Fleet of convicts and settlers, in June 1790, along with her pugnacious husband, John,[39] an ambitious army officer, and their infant son Edward. Worgan told Elizabeth she had done 'wonders in being able to play God save the King and [Foote's] Minuet' and that she was 'reading the Notes with great facility'.[40]

When Worgan returned to England the next year, he left the piano with her. Arthur Phillip liked Elizabeth, despite the prickliness of her husband, and sent her grapes that were 'as fine' as any she ever tasted.[41] Elizabeth wrote home to England to tell her mother that 'there was little doubt but in a very few years there will be plenty'.[42] She, John and their sons would play a huge part in growing them.

ELIZABETH ASTOR, who would become Mary Penfold's mother, grew up in a comfortably middle-class world surrounded by music, art and the latest fashions.

George Astor & Co. had become one of the most respected retailers of musical instruments in London, at a time when there were thirty other manufacturers of pianos in the city.[43] The British music business boomed. *The Times* reported that 'England, instead of importing her instruments as formerly from Holland, Germany, and Italy, is now become the greatest manufactory for musical instruments in Europe'.[44]

The creations that Elizabeth's father marketed were often exquisite organs and ornate pianos made of mahogany, with ebony and ivory keys and tapered legs finished in gilt brass.[45] He continued to turn out 'square pianos' like the one that had been taken to Sydney Cove on the *Sirius*, and this style of piano became the instrument of choice for many middle-class families – much like the upright piano of future generations. George's work graced parlours and drawing rooms on both sides of the Atlantic. As he became the king of piano dealers in Britain, he began using a logo featuring a charging lion and a dancing white unicorn separated by a crown.[46]

With his rich brother pushing sales across the Atlantic, George Astor's customer base extended to those with vast wealth, including the third president of the United States, Thomas Jefferson.[47] George Astor instruments survive to this day in museums and collections around the world, including the Music

School at the Australian National University, Canberra; the Metropolitan Museum of Art, New York; the National Museum of American History at the Smithsonian Institution, Washington DC; and the Astorhaus in his hometown of Walldorf, Germany.[48]

Years after her grandfather retired from the music business, Mary Penfold would make her own lasting contributions to cultural life.

Chapter 4

WHEN MARY PENFOLD began to turn her backyard grapevines into a commercial enterprise, it was obvious that she had inherited much of her business acumen from her German grandfather. Success, in his view, depended on turning out a top-quality product that was the envy of the competition.

By the mid-1790s, George was looking to supply the British military with equipment for marching bands, using advertisements such as this from London's *Morning Chronicle*:

> MILITARY BANDS OF MUSIC
> OFFICERS of the ARMY and NAVY may be immediately supplied with complete sets of Instruments for a Band, with good Musicians to play the same, at GEORGE ASTOR's, Musical Instrument-maker, No. 26 Wych-street, St. Clement's, who keeps always ready for their inspection an Assortment of well-tuned and properly-seasoned Instruments; consisting of Clarionets [sic], Hautboys, Flutes, Fifes, Bassoons, Serpents, Tamborines, Drums, Trumpets, French-horns, Bugle-horns, Triangles, and Cymbals equal to those made in Turkey.
>
> Several good Masters for teaching Bands to be heard of as above. Likewise some capital French Harps.[1]

It was a happy time for George and his growing family, and on 14 October 1795, a quarter of a century after he arrived in

London from Germany, his naturalisation as a British subject was confirmed in the House of Commons.[2]

George moved his wife and children from the decidedly working-class area around Wych Street to a much grander residence and 'Instrument Manufactory' at 79 Cornhill Road, where he also branched out into music publishing.[3] He succeeded in wooing the military, because the next year he was advertising from his new premises as 'musical instrument makers to His Majesty's army':

> MANUFACTURE and sell Wholesale, Retail, and for Exportation, Organs, Harpsichords, grand and small Piano Fortes, Violincellos, Violins, Drums, Tambourines, and Wind Instruments of every description. Music sold, printed, and published. Importers of Pedal Harps, Roman Strings, and German Wire.
>
> Regiments supplied with complete Setts of Military Instruments, and Musicians provided
>
> Instruments let on hire, repaired, and tuned in Town and Country.[4]

WHILE GEORGE ASTOR was making friends in high places in London, John Macarthur was establishing himself as one of the most powerful and divisive figures in New South Wales. He held combined roles as paymaster of the New South Wales Corps – the unit that had replaced the Royal Marines as the colony's military guards – and Inspector of Public Works, which gave him almost total control of the colony's captive workforce, materials and machinery. In 1793, Macarthur and his wife had established 'Elizabeth Farm', named after her, at Parramatta on a 40-hectare land grant that she called 'some of the best ground that has been discovered'.[5] By the following year, when their third son, John Macarthur, was born the farmhouse was surrounded by 'a vineyard and garden of about 3 acres [1.2 hectares], the former full of vines and fruit trees, and the latter abounding with most excellent vegetables'.[6]

Over the subsequent years, the prickly Macarthur would become the bane of one New South Wales governor after another as he lived by his own set of self-serving rules. Arthur Phillip no longer had to worry about him, though, as he had sailed for England in late 1792 to seek medical attention for kidney stones that caused him excruciating pain. He took with him Bennelong and another Wangal man, Yemmerrawanne, to show the people of Britain the First Peoples of their new colony.

One of Phillip's great fears as he sailed past the immense sandstone cliffs guarding Sydney's harbour to begin his journey home was that the increasing number of merchant ships reaching Sydney were bringing liquor for sale. While he prized wine as a symbol of an enlightened society, Phillip was aghast at the effect other forms of alcohol were having on his infant colony.

Only a few weeks before he departed, Phillip had allowed shops to sell a dark beer called porter, which had arrived on the ship *Royal Admiral* from London. The decision was a disaster, as an alcohol-fuelled madness afflicted the settlers at both Sydney and Parramatta. A licence was given for the sale of porter, but spirits also found their way among the people. Several of the settlers conducted themselves 'with the greatest impropriety', beating their wives, destroying their flocks, and trampling on and damaging their crops and each other's property.[7] Some of the men were arrested and one spent an hour in the stocks for drunkenness. David Collins reported that the generosity and indulgence of the governor in allowing the sale of porter had been 'most shamefully abused'.[8]

John Macarthur watched the mad frenzy for liquor with a calculating eye.

IN 1794, THE GERMAN scientist Johann Friedrich Blumenbach wrote to his collaborator, Sir Joseph Banks, in London:

> Yesterday I received from a friend of mine [a clergyman] ... a curious present of a small bottle of a strong red wine from Rosehill near Sydney Cove and a specimen of biscuit from

Norfolk Island ... (as he says) he had received from a friend in London. He adds that the wine was brought over by Cptn Phillips [sic] in '92.⁹

This may have been wine made by Philip Schaffer from grapes growing at Parramatta.

By 1795, Captain William Paterson,¹⁰ second in command at New South Wales, wrote to Banks to tell him that Schaffer – or 'old Chiffer', as he called him – had made 'this year from a small vineyard ninety Gallons [405 litres] of wine. In about two years more I expect we will not want to purchase either wine or Brandy for common use. The vines I think produce better than at the Cape.'¹¹

Paterson did not figure on disease, farm mismanagement or the settlers' conflicts with the local Indigenous people, but Thomas Fyshe Palmer, one of the Scottish Unitarian 'martyrs' banished to Sydney as political prisoners, wrote that the wine being produced in Sydney – presumably by Schaffer – was 'tolerably good'.¹² 'The climate is delicious,' he recorded, 'the air so salubrious ... The grape vine thrives with the utmost luxuriance ... This will be the staple article of commerce.'¹³

BY 1797, THERE WERE 3.4 hectares of vines under cultivation in New South Wales,¹⁴ but the settlers' cruel treatment of Indigenous groups was a precursor to the Battle of Parramatta, when the Bidjigal man Pemulwuy led a group of about 100 warriors in an attack on the settlers. Several dozen lives were lost and agricultural pursuits were severely disrupted.

Disease and harsh weather conditions caused Philip Schaffer to abandon his grapes. The government granted him more land at the Field of Mars – modern-day Marsfield. Schaffer sold The Vineyard to Henry Waterhouse, who had been a midshipman on the *Sirius* with the First Fleet and had just returned from the Cape of Good Hope with the first Spanish-bred merino sheep to be landed in New South Wales. Waterhouse kept the name of the property but chose not to pursue viticulture.

A year later, in 1798, during their circumnavigation of Van Diemen's Land in the small but hardy sloop *Norfolk*, Matthew Flinders and George Bass saw the potential for winemaking along the banks of the River Derwent, reporting to David Collins that 'the land around Prince of Wales Cove is ... perhaps better adapted to the growth of grape vines, than of grain'.[15]

Without the encouragement of Arthur Phillip, however, grape growing and wine production in New South Wales floundered. To Phillip's great regret, rum – a generic term for distilled beverages – had flooded New South Wales after his departure and the colony was now awash with the troubles it caused.

Phillip's temporary replacement, Francis Grose, relaxed Phillip's ban on the trading of rum, and with the colony having a shortage of coins, liquor soon became the currency. The officers of the New South Wales Corps used their power to monopolise the liquor trade, earning them the nickname 'the Rum Corps'. At the forefront of this was John Macarthur, who was happily growing grapes but cashing in on the popularity of spirits.

Attempts by subsequent governors John Hunter and Philip Gidley King to curtail the power of the rum traders were largely ineffective. By 1800, mismanagement and a lack of expert knowledge about viticulture meant that all the vines in the colony now did not cover a single hectare. King wrote with regret to the British Home Office in 1801 that, except for a couple of unsuccessful attempts at making wine by one or two individuals, grapes were now only being grown as fruit, and then in very small quantities.[16]

On the advice of William Paterson, Sir Joseph Banks organised for more vine cuttings, fruit trees, plants and seeds to be sent to Sydney. He also arranged for a 23-year-old London gardener named George Suttor[17] to care for the plants on the voyage, in return for £30 and free passage to the colony for himself, his wife and their baby son, and the promise of land to farm when he arrived. Included in Suttor's eighteen boxes for the colony were tea plants, fruit trees, vegetables, mulberries for silkworms, cider apples, brewing hops and grasses for livestock fodder. There were also fifteen varieties of vine cuttings, sourced from Hugh Ronalds, a nurseryman of Brentford, in outer London. Suttor's cargo included cuttings of tokay, white frontignac, white muscadine, black frontignac, Constantia and muscat of Alexandria, plus two sorts 'unknown' that he bought at the Cape.[18]

The ship *Porpoise* set sail with the precious cargo on 6 September 1799, amid considerable doubt about her seaworthiness, as it had earlier been fitted with a plant cabin on the quarterdeck according to Joseph Banks' specifications, which made the vessel unbalanced. The ship was forced to return to Spithead, but in November 1800 a second refitted vessel, also known as the *Porpoise*, finally reached Sydney. Only a few plants survived the journey, though, because they were 'constantly exposed … to the washing of the sea'.[19]

The young man settled his family on seventy-five hectares at what is now Baulkham Hills. In time he established his own vineyard, though his grapes suffered from what he said was 'want of labour and the requisite time to pay proper attention to them' as he was 'too much occupied with the raising of the necessaries of life'.[20] Ultimately he would concentrate on growing oranges.

Two weeks after Suttor's arrival,[21] the ship *Royal Admiral* arrived in Sydney again. As well as carrying 257 male convicts, it bore two French prisoners of war, Antoine L'Andre[22] and his cousin Francois de Riveau, both of Nantes. The two had been languishing on a prison ship moored at Portsmouth when they managed to convince the authorities that they had a 'perfect knowledge of the cultivation of a vineyard and the whole process of making wine',[23] having been brought up in the business from their 'infancy'.[24] Britain's Home Secretary, the Duke of Portland,[25] ordered the Admiralty to liberate them[26] and wrote to Governor Philip Gidley King at Government House in Sydney that, 'as it appears that the soil and climate of New South Wales are favourable to the culture of the grape', the Frenchmen would be invaluable for 'the purpose of superintending the cultivation of the vine'.[27]

I trust the employment of these men will enable you in a very short period to cultivate a vineyard for the Crown of such an extent as to allow of your producing, on the spot, whatever wine may be wanted on the public account; and this circumstance will, of course, be the means of promoting, on the part of individuals, the cultivation of the vine and the making of wine throughout the settlement at large.

One of the men is also a cooper, a circumstance which will render him very useful to the colony.[28]

L'Andre and de Riveau were to be paid £60 a year each, for three years.[29]

Governor King had seen the corrosive effect of liquor on the infant colony and had turned back trading vessels bringing it from around the world, including an American vessel with more than 100,000 litres of spirits and wines.[30] He had high hopes for the two French vignerons and regarded them as 'intelligent men' who seemed 'conversant in the business' of wine. He provided them with six convict workers, a large supply of cuttings and land at Parramatta, and he looked forward to some fine table wine by 1803, which he believed would be a great 'benefit to the inhabitants' of New South Wales.[31]

L'Andre and de Riveau had brought a huge array of tools for cultivating vines and detailed instructions in French for producing wine and brandy.[32] By October 1802 there were 'upwards of 12,000 vine cuttings' planted on the side of a hill at Parramatta, 'formed like a crescent, facing the north, which is the best exposition',[33] and five months later Governor King had the first batch of the winemakers' instructions translated from French into English and reprinted in the very first edition of Sydney's first newspaper, in the hope that it would encourage settlers and emancipated convicts to plant their own vineyards.[34]

Alas, the Frenchmen had overstated their abilities and Governor King realised they 'knew very little of the business'. In late 1804 he told Britain's Secretary of State for War and the

Colonies: 'They attempted last year to make wine from some of the best grapes that could be collected, but it has turned out so bad that I shall not trouble your Lordship with the sample I intended sending.'[35] Most of the colony's grapes had perished with blight, and de Riveau returned to England. King was pleased, though, that L'Andre had 'made some very good cyder [sic] from peaches'.[36]

Still others planted vineyards. Nicholas Devine, another superintendent of convicts, planted a vineyard of 1.2 hectares on his property in what became the Sydney suburb of Newtown, but like Schaeffer and the two Frenchmen he found the conditions unsuited to his vine types and abandoned his attempts at winemaking.[37] Reverend Samuel Marsden, a magistrate known as 'the Flogging Parson' for the severe sentences he imposed on convicts, was granted land at St Marys, between Parramatta and the Blue Mountains, a steep range that had so far proved impenetrable to the European settlers. He called his property 'Mamre' and established a vineyard from cuttings grown on one of his Parramatta farms. Nearby, Mary Putland, the widowed daughter of William Bligh, who had replaced Philip Gidley King as governor, started her own vineyard, which she called 'Orange Grove'.

WHILE THE INFANT COLONY around Sydney was still finding its feet as a prison settlement in a world of hardship and frequent cruelty, and without homegrown wine to ease the discomfort, Elizabeth Astor was growing into an elegant young woman in a well-to-do household. George Astor's business continued to attract wealthy customers, including James Monroe, one of the Founding Fathers of the United States. Monroe was the American minister to Great Britain from 1803, and he took one of George's pianofortes with him when he returned to New York four years later.[38] He likely took the piano with him to the White House when in 1817 he became the United States' fifth president.[39]

Elizabeth Astor's life was one of middle-class comfort and privilege, of music and of a level of education that was unavailable to most young women of the time in London, a city that was often crowded with soldiers. A revolution across the English Channel had devoured the French aristocracy, and a new French leader, Napoleon Bonaparte, had set Europe afire. Now he threatened to make Britain the crown jewel of his empire.

One in six British males over the age of fourteen entered military service, and soon the Kent Road, leading from London to Britain's ports and battlements along the south-east coast, was crowded with troops either marching off to war or limping home to recuperate. The taverns overflowed, and discharged soldiers, many missing limbs or with other traumas, swelled the numbers of beggars on every corner.

The war with France was still raging in 1809, when at the age of twenty-one Elizabeth Astor married a young doctor named Tom Holt[40] at the grand Anglican church in London known as Saint Bartholomew the Great.[41] Tom was the son of an eminent Westminster surgeon,[42] Thomas Glover Holt,[43] who was a pillar of the London establishment and who had also been a church warden at Westminster Cathedral.[44] The newlyweds began building a happy life together in a smart London home, against a backdrop of continued turmoil.

A few weeks after their wedding, the Royal Navy destroyed five warships of the French Atlantic fleet in the Battle of the Basque Roads. Then, on the night of 5 July 1809, Napoleon's troops kidnapped Pope Pius VII from his private apartments in Rome.

In September 1811 Elizabeth gave birth to a boy, paying homage to her ailing father when she named him George William Astor Holt.[45] Two years later she had a second son, who was christened Alfred Astor Holt.[46] Elizabeth's father, George Astor, died that same year, but his family still ran the music business, which was renamed Astor & Horwood.[47]

Three years later, in 1816, Elizabeth prepared to deliver her only daughter, Mary. Her birth would take place during one of the darkest times in British history.

Chapter 5

ON 6 NOVEMBER 1816,[1] in her fashionable home at Southwark, in South London, Mrs Elizabeth Holt, wife of a prosperous doctor, niece of a fabulously rich American and mother of two young boys, was giving birth for the third time.

Outside on the Kent Road, there was the constant muffled murmur of horse hoofs as riders and carriages passed along the main link between London and England's south-east coast. Pedestrians rugged up against the cold and walked briskly. The waters of the Thames, whipped up by the cold winds, were icy.

Winter was coming, but the English capital was already freezing. It had been the coldest decade on record in England,[2] and the foul weather added further discomfort as Elizabeth gave birth. Her husband, Dr Tom Holt, stoked the fireplace for his wife and their new daughter, Mary.

There were very real fears for mother and child at every birth in the early 19th century. The nature of infections was not fully understood, and one in three British children did not reach their fifth birthday.[3] Midwives and doctors were always prepared for mother or child, or sometimes both, to perish in childbirth.

The year 1816 was an especially bleak one in Britain. Napoleon had met his match at Waterloo in the form of the Duke of Wellington in June 1815, but any prosperity that the peace brought was short-lived. Trading vessels sailed to British ports with their crews undisturbed by French warships, but an economic depression had brought Britain to its knees. Government coffers were bare after years of fighting, and hundreds of thousands of unemployed and unskilled soldiers and sailors were looking for work in the cities and often sleeping rough.

Half a world away, in what was then the Dutch East Indies and is now Indonesia, the eruption of the volcano Mount Tambora in April 1815 had sent thousands of tonnes of ash into the sky above the Java Sea. Plumes of smoke miles high had blocked sunlight around the planet. Global cooling was quickly followed by widespread crop failures and food shortages. Food prices skyrocketed and there were long periods of famine. In London in 1816, hunger and chaos swirled around the city on cold, angry winds in what became known as the 'Year Without a Summer'.

But the baby who would become Mary Penfold arrived as a little ray of sunshine. Tom Holt signed the birth registry as a witness to her delivery, noting that Mary Holt had been born at No. 2 York Buildings on the Kent Road, Southwark, in the parish of St George the Martyr, in the county of Surrey. Her parents identified as 'non-conformists', which signified that they were Protestants who, while professing to be Christians, did not put themselves under the jurisdiction of the Church of England.

ON THE DAY OF MARY'S BIRTH, wine merchants around England were charging premium prices for a product that was in short supply because of the long period of cruel weather. More than ever, those who could afford it felt that wine enriched their lives even on their darkest days.

French claret had once been immensely popular throughout Britain, but its sale had slowed to a trickle due to the wars with France, followed by heavy tariffs. While there were a few small vineyards in Britain, most wine was imported in huge quantities from Spain, Portugal, Germany and the Cape of Good Hope.

As Elizabeth and Tom Holt marvelled at the wonderful new addition to their family, Thorpe's, the wine merchant in London's Haymarket, was advertising its latest shipment of the finest Spanish wines, claiming they were superior to the best Portuguese ports and all the white wines coming from the Cape.[4]

Prices were sky-high: the effect of the freak cold weather in Europe was compounded by a recent storm over Portugal, which had seen flooding rains rotting vast areas under grape. Fine wines, the merchants informed their customers, were bound to be a rarity for some years.[5] Spanish white wine was going for twenty-eight shillings for a dozen bottles, and reds for four shillings more. That was a substantial amount of money in an age when most workers in Britain were earning five shillings for a six-day working week.[6]

In the great room of Christie's auctioneers in London, meanwhile, more than 2000 bottles of port, as well as some of sherry and madeira, were going under the hammer.[7]

IN 1816, AS MARY DREW her first breaths, the Society for the Encouragement of Arts, Manufacturers and Commerce in London — later known as the Royal Society of Arts — offered a medal for 'the finest wine not less than 20 gallons [ninety-one litres] of good marketable quality made from the produce of vineyards in NSW'.[8] The offer was designed to stimulate the development of an Australian wine industry as a possible export commodity for the Crown. After a promising start, winemaking had faltered in New South Wales because of disease and a lack of knowledge about viticulture in a climate beset by droughts and flooding rain.

Gregory Blaxland,[9] a mercurial and often melancholy farmer on the Parramatta River, resolved to win the medal. The son of the mayor of Fordwich, in Kent, and part of Britain's landed gentry, he had been in the colony for ten years. The ageing Sir Joseph Banks, a family friend, advised Blaxland about the farming potential around Sydney and the potential in planting vines. Banks encouraged him to create an empire in a new territory. So in September 1805 Blaxland had sailed for Sydney on the *William Pitt*, along with his wife, three children, two servants and a farm overseer.

On the voyage, the Blaxlands stayed at Madeira and, just like Banks on the *Endeavour* almost four decades earlier, watched the 'gathering and the pressing of the grapes'. Gregory then collected vine cuttings at the Cape of Good Hope and observed 'full

The mercurial adventurer and farmer Gregory Blaxland was the first Australian winemaker to gain international acclaim, winning medals from London's Royal Society of Arts. *Mitchell Library, SLNSW, SAFE/R 266*

management of the grapes out of the cellar'.[10] After arriving in Sydney, he planted the vines on 184 hectares at his new property, 'Brush Farm', north-west of the original settlement in what is now Eastwood.

Elizabeth Macarthur, whose husband was exiled in Britain after leading a coup against Governor Bligh in 1808, loaned Blaxland a book by the Swiss winemaker John James Dufour,[11] which detailed his attempts to build America's first commercial winery near Nicholasville, south of Lexington,[12] Kentucky, and then in an area called New Switzerland, on the Ohio River in Indiana.[13] Dufour had great expectations for his grapes and eventually sent his brother to Washington DC with a horse-drawn cart carrying two five-gallon (22-litre) barrels of wine for America's most popular connoisseur, President Thomas Jefferson.[14]

Blaxland planted black Constantia (muscat noir) from the Cape and claret-style grapes,[15] and eventually built an imposing two-storey brick home in the colonial Georgian style. He conducted exhaustive but unsuccessful experiments with tobacco and hops, but was much more successful with his vines.

Blaxland's older brother, John,[16] arrived in Sydney in 1807, and together they prospered as merchants and cattle dealers. In 1813, Gregory was part of the first European expedition across the Blue Mountains, with William Lawson and William Charles Wentworth, which opened up the vast grazing lands of the New South Wales interior to European settlement.

Two years later he had set aside 1.2 hectares of a 'well chosen' situation at Brush Farm to grow year-old vines, and another 0.8 hectares for two-year-old vines. The colony's government newspaper reported that 'as every possible care is bestowed on its cultivation, the most flattering expectation may be formed of an ample remuneration for the trouble, and expence [sic] which an experiment in this delicate branch of husbandry must necessarily require'.[17]

Gregory Blaxland selected wine varieties from old gardens and vineyards that had been planted by both seed and cutting, and he initiated both the madeira practice of training the young vines and the Cape practice of trenching, or breaking up, the ground to better keep the roots moist in summer.[18] His experience and experiments with winemaking would help generations of winemakers to come, including Mary Penfold.

In 1818 Blaxland wrote to Governor Lachlan Macquarie about the challenges he had encountered growing grapes in the harsh Australian climate:

[T]he vines in general are subject to two different diseases of blight in the colony; one destroys the young shoots and leaves in the early part of the season, which stops their growth and destroys their blossom; they appear as if burnt or scalded; the other affects the grapes as soon as they are grown to the size of small peas; it appears as a black speck on the berry with a small puncture in the centre after which they remain hard and sour and never fill with juice, nor ripen and if the speck extends far the berry entirely dries up and perishes.[19]

Blaxland raised 200 new vines from seed and planted two varieties of what he called 'Claret grapes' – probably burgundy (pinot noir) and Miller's burgundy (pinot meunier).

He had sent a barrel of wine to Macquarie in 1816. It was virtually undrinkable. Realising his error in selecting grapes from abandoned vineyards and gardens, Blaxland pulled out most of his early plantings, except for the pinot noir and pinot meunier, and developed a species that was resistant to blight.[20] He had now collected 'three or four good bearing sorts, which appear to me fit to make wine, and have acquired some further knowledge of their culture which induces me to persevere in my attempt, which render me more sanguine in my hopes of ultimate success'.[21] The contents of a second barrel sent to Macquarie were far more pleasing.[22]

Macquarie knew his wine. As a young army officer, he had resolved to restrain himself and never to drink more than one bottle of wine at dinner,[23] even though he once left the vineyards of Constantia with 273 litres of their finest produce.[24] Macquarie also knew that wine in moderation could be strong medicine. He had asked his personal physician, Dr William Redfern, a former convict, to investigate the ill-fated 1814 voyage from London to Sydney of the prison ship *Surrey*,[25] on which fifty men – convicts, sailors and even the skipper – had died from typhoid fever.[26]

Redfern reported that, as well as having confined the men for too long in crowded, dark spaces, the *Surrey*'s captain had further weakened them by withholding rations, including their wine allocation, in order to sell them for his own pocket. Redfern's report included eleven major recommendations to Macquarie regarding the convicts' diet, clothing, cleanliness and need for improved medical attention, as well as for regular periods of fresh air on deck to repel disease.

He recommended the prisoners' ration of wine for the voyage from England be lifted from nine litres to twenty-seven, so that they could each have a quarter of a pint (150 millilitres) a day as a tonic. He told Macquarie:

> This quantity would be amply sufficient and would be attended with the most beneficial consequences, as it would, by assisting to maintain the Vigor of the System, Counteract debility arising from bad weather, confinement below, and despondency. It ought to be diluted with an equal quantity of Water, to which might be added a small portion of lime juice and sugar, and served out, and drunk at the tub by each individual, that was able to come up on deck.[27]

The cocktail of wine, lime juice and sugar would, he said, be a powerful weapon against scurvy.

Not long after making his recommendations, Redfern became the first Australian medical vigneron, establishing his Campbellfield vineyard in present-day Minto, fifty-five kilometres south-west of Sydney.[28] His aim was to make wine as a tonic.

Redfern's recommendations saw convict death rates drop during transportation from one in three in 1790 to one in twenty by 1833.[29]

MARY PENFOLD WOULD come to know all about the medicinal benefits of wine. It was an important tonic for the patients who saw her father, Dr Tom Holt. His work not only helped his community but provided a comfortable home for his wife and three children. Mary's childhood was spent in a close, loving family environment, in which she was cherished. Her mother said that Mary's smile was 'sunshine' for her parents, who doted on her.[30]

By the time Mary was walking, her older brother Alfred had become utterly mesmerised by the shiny scales of what he thought were the coats that fish wore. Mary and Alfred would closely study the fish that the Holt family cook prepared for their dinner table, and the boy became captivated by everything to do with fishing. Mary would watch her brother heading off to the bend of the Thames near their home in South London, carrying his fishing rod with him to catch dinner for the family, whether they wanted something from the murky, malodorous waterway or not.[31] Alfred would spend hours by the great river, baiting his hooks and hauling in seabass or sole, learning everything possible there was to catching fish. It became his great passion in life.

Dr Holt, meanwhile, was earning a reputation as one of the best medical practitioners in London,[32] but when he wasn't saving lives or mending wounds, he relaxed with a paintbrush and easel. The tinkling of a piano built by George Astor was often in the background as he caressed the canvas. Mary always thought that one of the most beautiful gifts her father ever gave his children was a painting of Jesus walking on water – a painting Tom Holt named 'The Divine Fisherman'. Alfred considered it a precious heirloom all his life.[33]

London in the 1820s, when Mary began her schooling, was the largest city on Earth, with a population of 1.4 million people.[34] It was the financial centre of the world too, a bustling port and the base for Britain's colonial expansion around the globe.

Mary was growing up in the Regency era, named for King George IV, who had first ruled as Prince Regent when mental illness left the reigning monarch – his father, George III – incapacitated. The period ushered in new styles of art, opulent fashion and culture, but that was only for the wealthy.

Despite the British Empire's presence in every corner of the globe, the effects of war, economic depression, mass unemployment and the bad harvest of 1816 exaggerated the glaring social divide between the haves and have-nots. Mary's fine home was only a few miles from the stinking Thames and the teeming, filthy slums of Stepney and Bethnal Green, where typhoid and scarlet fever lurked amid polluted water and rotting waste.

While the destitute residents there were often clothed in rags, Elizabeth Holt and other wealthier women of the time favoured long, brightly coloured bell-shaped pleated skirts with corseted waists, padded bustles and big sleeves. They wore linen caps indoors, while outdoors they donned wide-brimmed hats decorated with feathers and ribbons. Girls such as Mary often had their hair teased in ringlets.

Men's clothing changed dramatically in this era, with jackets designed around the contour of the body, with high collars and waistcoats buttoned high on the chest. Mary's father and his generation now wore trousers with fabric to the ankle rather than to the knee, as their parents and grandparents had.

For most girls in London in the 1820s, even those from wealthier families, schooling was limited compared to what boys had. But along with reading, writing and basic arithmetic, Mary was taught practical skills for homemaking and family life: sewing, knitting and music – she learnt to play one of her late grandfather's pianos. Girls also studied languages, especially French. Mary learnt to dance, and was coached in social graces and deportment, all the better to appeal to a suitable husband when the time came. Mary's parents wanted her to have enough education to make her fascinating but not daunting for a suitor from a successful family. She was also exposed to the business her grandfather founded, which was still flourishing as one of the main manufacturers of musical instruments in Britain.

BY THE EARLY 1820s, grapevines had been growing with limited success for more than thirty years in New South Wales, with more and more settlers establishing vineyards on their estates. The rumbunctious John Macarthur continued to educate himself in the art of winemaking, and now had two major vineyards operating.

Macarthur was at the forefront of the Australian agricultural industry, even though it had been his long-suffering wife, Elizabeth, who shouldered the workload on his properties, while he spent years in England doing his best not to get hanged for acts of insubordination.

Back in 1801, Governor Philip Gidley King had sent Macarthur home in disgrace to face a court martial, reporting how this cunning, troublesome man – a 'rich Botany Bay perturbator' with a 'diabolical spirit' – had blown away part of William Paterson's shoulder in a duel.[35] Macarthur returned to Sydney emboldened and swaggering four years later, after escaping penalty and having courted powerful friends while in London.

Despite protests from Sir Joseph Banks, Macarthur had obtained a small number of rare merino sheep from the prized royal flocks to add to those he and Elizabeth were already breeding, and he had secured a grant of 2024 hectares of the best pastureland in the colony. It was about seventy kilometres southwest of Sydney, and Macarthur called it Camden Park.

Macarthur had only been back in New South Wales for two and a half years when he led the Rum Corps in a coup against Governor William Bligh, a night after Macarthur and his supporters had secured a pipe of wine – about 500 litres – for a large party. The result was that Macarthur spent another decade away from his wife, leaving her to run their estates while he fought to clear his name in Britain. He took with him two of his sons, James and William, so they could be schooled in Britain.

Macarthur also advanced his business interests in England, networking with political and aristocratic contacts. The Napoleonic wars had limited European travel, but almost as soon as those restrictions were eased Macarthur and his sons set about gaining firsthand experience of wine growing in Europe.

In 1814, they travelled to France and witnessed Napoleon's triumphal return to Paris after his dramatic escape from Elba. The three looked on in astonishment as the returning emperor appeared at a window of the Tuileries Palace. Macarthur thought the indefatigable Frenchman was a 'pest of the human race',[36] but the huge crowds were in raptures, shouting, '*Vive l'Empereur, vive Napoleon!*'[37] From Paris, the Macarthurs travelled south, often by foot, through the celebrated wine region of Burgundy and on to Lyon and Geneva, collecting grapevine cuttings as they went.

In Switzerland, Macarthur sought out John Dufour, who had returned home after his investors in the infant American wine industry withered on the vine because of slow returns exacerbated by mildew and black rot.[38] Dufour told Macarthur that the vines in America had 'at first failed in the way they had done' in New South Wales, but that 'by dint of perseverance he had at length made them succeed'. Macarthur found this information 'of so much consequence that he resolved to make a long stay in this part of the country'.[39] Dufour and his family were about to begin pruning, so Macarthur was able to study the methods of an experienced vigneron.

Macarthur wrote to Elizabeth, telling her that the slow journey through France and Switzerland had given him 'ample opportunity to acquaint myself with the mode of pruning, planting and preparing the soil to receive the Vine so that pleasure and business went hand in hand'.[40]

James Macarthur was struck by the realities of the winemaking process:

[T]he vintage, which I expected to find a very beautiful sight ... is however very much the reverse. The grapes, when gathered, are put into large tubs, where they are pounded until they have much the appearance of hogs wash. They are then carried away to the house and before they are pressed, undergo another pounding with men's feet. In short no process can be in appearance more dirty ...[41]

The Macarthurs also travelled for a time with a team of skilled workers, including two vignerons from Montreux, and studied winemaking closely wherever they went, 'in order to give greater facilities for acquiring agricultural information'. They returned to London through the Rhône Valley and the south of France.[42] A Swiss pony carried the baggage, cuttings and plants collected on the way,[43] including vine cuttings from Tain-l'Hermitage[44] and what William said were about 'thirty of the best varieties of the vine' from other regions.

On the family's return to London, the Macarthurs entrusted the collection of cuttings to a nurseryman, while a convict ship, the *Lord Eldon*, was fitted with a special greenhouse in which to transport them to New South Wales.⁴⁵ They also bought vines at Madeira on their voyage south, and after arriving back in Sydney in September 1817, they planted the cuttings at Camden Park and later at another Macarthur farm at the base of the Blue Mountains, near present-day Penrith.

When the vines yielded their first crop, though, Macarthur realised that their valuable collection of cuttings had been stolen: most of the vine-stock material they had so carefully conveyed to Sydney was not what they had collected on their long trek through Europe. Much of it was sweetwater, a variety freely available in Britain.⁴⁶ Most of the Macarthurs' vine types were already growing in New South Wales.⁴⁷

AS THE MACARTHURS TRIED to build up their estates with the flavour of European wines, and enjoyed the cultural associations of wealth and sophistication that brought, another prominent Sydney identity, Reverend Samuel Marsden, was spreading the word of God and his own ideas about harsh justice on a missionary visit to New Zealand.

Marsden had imported Miller's burgundy (pinot meunier) to New South Wales in 1817,⁴⁸ and probably took the first European vine cuttings to New Zealand in 1819,⁴⁹ planting about a hundred of them at Kerikeri, in the Bay of Islands on the North Island.⁵⁰ Marsden had his doubts about Australia ever becoming a wine country, given the extent of the blight's destruction, but felt New Zealand promised to be 'very favourable to the vine, as far as I can judge at present of the nature of the soil and climate. Should the vine succeed, it will prove of vast importance in this part of the globe.'⁵¹

Marsden's vineyard was poorly fenced and his vines were soon eaten by goats, but the pastor's prophecy about New Zealand viticulture would prove true. His experiments with wine were inspired to some degree by a friend named Ambrose Serle,⁵² a British naval officer who had become a leading figure at the Transport Board. 'Your vines can only succeed in dry or gravelly Soils,' Serle told Marsden. 'Either Springy Land or Clays will never suit them. The Slope of a Hill towards the Sun, with a proper soil, surely would give you as fine grapes as you have Oranges in other Situations.'[53]

Even so, Serle cautioned Marsden that winemaking was a highly specialised craft and that 'without intelligent industry nothing can be expected'.[54]

Mary Penfold would prove to be a woman of both intelligence and industry.

Chapter 6

IN MARCH 1822, when Mary was six years old and still unaware of the role grapevines would play in her life, Gregory Blaxland sent a quarter of a pipe (about 120 litres) of red wine from his Brush Farm vineyard to the august gentlemen of the Royal Society of Arts, on John Adams Street in Westminster, just across the river from Mary's home. The president of the Royal Society was Prince Augustus Frederick, the Duke of Sussex and a brother of King George IV.

Blaxland was making great strides in viticulture and had compiled one of the most important documents in the early history of the Australian wine industry. 'A Statement on the Progress of the Culture of the Vine'[1] was a journal that would assist many Australian winemakers in later years, including Mary. In careful detail he described anthracnose, which he described as 'disease or blight'.

Blaxland was proud of his vintage and had fortified the wine with about 10 per cent brandy so it could 'bear the voyage'.[2] The prince and his committee members sniffed Blaxland's offering, swirled it around in their glasses and sipped it with raised eyebrows of approval, though with some reservations.

They pronounced that Mr Blaxland's offering:

> ... appeared to be a light but sound wine with much of the odour and flavour of ordinary claret, or rather holding an intermediate place between that wine and the red wine of

Nice. The general opinion seemed to be, that although the present sample, from the in-expertness of the manufacturer and the youth of the vine, is by no means of superior quality, yet it affords a reasonable ground of expectation that by care and time it may become a valuable article of export.[3]

The society awarded Blaxland its silver medal for colonial produce.

In 1826 Blaxland succeeded in introducing a species of small black grape that resisted blight, and a year later, on 5 February 1827, he sent the society a shipment of three half-pipes (720 litres) of his most recent pressing, a tawny red wine made from a small black cluster grape – pinot noir – 'supposed to be a seedling from the claret grape', which he grew on the side of a steep hill. The society declared that this wine was better than Blaxland's previous attempt and 'wholly free from the earthy flavour which unhappily characterises most of the Cape wine'.[4]

This time Blaxland received the society's gold 'Ceres' medal for wine, named after the Roman goddess of agriculture. He had finally achieved international recognition for wine being grown in a land Britain was now officially calling 'Australia'.

Along with the shipment of his wine, Blaxland also sent the society 'two copies of a work published in the colony on the culture of the vine, &c., which I beg may be placed in the library of the Society'.[5] This was written by Scottish-born James Busby,[6] who had arrived in Sydney as a 23-year-old in 1824 with a collection of cuttings. Busby had obtained a land grant of 800 hectares in the Hunter Valley, beside the Hunter River, about 150 kilometres north-west of Sydney, and he took a short-lived job as farm manager, teaching viticulture to boys at the Male Orphan School in what is now the outer-Sydney suburb of Bonnyrigg.

To promote the fledgling Australian industry, in 1825 Busby published *A Treatise on the Culture of the Vine and the Art of Making Wine*, which began with a quote from the Roman writer Pliny: '*Tot vina, quot agri*' – 'As many wines as there are fields'.[7]

The book was essentially a scientific textbook translated from French writings Busby had gathered, and it made little impact

James Busby planted a vineyard in the Hunter Valley of New South Wales and wrote important books on winemaking. Alexander Turnbull Library, NON-ATL-P-0065

among the settlers of the time. But five years later he marketed a more successful publication, *A Manual of Plain Directions for Planting and Cultivating Vineyards and for Making Wine in New South Wales*.[8] The book sold for three shillings and sixpence, and Busby distributed more than 20,000 vine cuttings among those who showed an aptitude for winemaking.[9]

Busby's writings would still be popular when Mary Penfold grew her first grapes in South Australian soil two decades later.

The vines Busby planted eventually produced a wine that he took to Europe in 1831,[10] as he set out to source richer and more diverse vine stock for the Australian settlers. Busby's voyage was partly financed by John Macarthur's sons, James and William, whose Camden nurseries and vineyard were already important sources of grapevines for the colony. Busby spent four months touring France and Spain, and spent time in London campaigning for a high-paying role in the colonial government. His Australian wine 'was highly approved'[11] wherever he took it.

Busby had transported half his wine in pint bottles and half in a small cask. Some of the bottled wine spoiled, but the cask wine remained 'perfectly sound'. A Bordeaux merchant bought most of it and pronounced it 'like Burgundy, and most promising'.[12] It was displayed as a novelty from Britain's far-flung colony.

Busby toured many vineyards and gathered a large variety of vines, including 437 from the botanical gardens at Montpellier, in France; 133 from the Royal Nursery at the Luxembourg Gardens, in Paris; and forty-four varieties from the lavish Syon House, near Kew Gardens, west of London on the Thames. He also compiled a collection of vine stock while touring Spain, but it perished while at sea.

John Macarthur was one of the prime movers behind the formation of the Australian Agricultural Company in 1824, which involved investment of a million pounds to develop a million acres (about 405,000 hectares) 200 kilometres north-west of Sydney for farming and grazing. The company planned to produce fine wool, beef cattle and goods worthy of a wealthy, sophisticated colony: 'Wine, Olive-Oil, Hemp, Flax, Silk, Opium, etc as articles of export to Great Britain'.[13] The AA Company crest featured symbols of wealth and prosperity: an olive branch, a woolly sheep, a royal crown and bunches of fat, juicy grapes.

All around Sydney, wealthy landholders were planting vineyards as symbols of their success and sophistication. One was Robert Townson,[14] a gentleman scientist who had often visited the London home of Sir Joseph Banks and who had graduated as a doctor from Germany's University of Göttingen in 1795, a year after Banks' collaborator at that institution, Johann Friedrich Blumenbach, had tasted what he believed was a bottle of 'Rosehill wine' sent by Arthur Phillip.

Before arriving in Sydney in 1807 as the most eminent scholar in the young colony, Townson had spent close to a decade on a study tour through Europe, observing among other things the nature of tokay grapes and the business of winemaking. Townson had supported John Macarthur in the coup against Governor Bligh, and it wasn't until 1811 that he was able to settle on about 800 hectares of land at Minto, south-west of Sydney. He named his property 'Varro Ville' after the Roman writer on agriculture, Marcus Terentius Varro.

Townson died at Varro Ville in 1827. By that time the property, which eventually passed into the hands of the explorer Charles Sturt, was 'a show place for its beauty, abundance and variety in orchard and garden' with the 'colony's second most extensive vineyard'.[15]

WHILE AUSTRALIAN wine was enjoying its first international exposure, the colourful and cunning former convict Bartholomew Broughton[16] was busy planting the first commercial vineyard on Tasmanian soil.

Broughton was a junior naval officer and the son of a respected solicitor practising in the bankruptcy courts of London.[17] But he was convicted in March 1819 of a series of burglaries – at the White Horse Hotel in London's Fetter Lane, and the Swan with Two Necks in Lads Lane, 'where he had at different times slept'.[18] At a time when the theft of twelve pence was enough to get a culprit hanged, Broughton had made off with £165 in banknotes pilfered from the rooms of his fellow guests. The 27-year-old was fortunate to face his trial at a time of growing compassion in British courts, and although he was sentenced to death, there was a recommendation for mercy. He was sentenced to transportation for life.

Broughton spent time as a prisoner in Sydney, but after he earned his ticket of leave in 1822[19] he set out to make his fortune in Van Diemen's Land, by hook, by crook or by the barrel. Broughton was a hard worker, and a fast worker too. Within eighteen months of his arrival in Hobart, he had purchased a house in Bridge Street and was working both as treasurer of the Police Fund and as a clerk in the Naval Office. He also opened a general store in Liverpool Street,[20] and advertised his wares in *The Hobart Town Gazette*.[21]

Not long after arriving in Hobart, he formed an attachment to the family of Colonial Surgeon Edward Luttrell and his son Alfred, the owner of the 40-hectare 'Prospect Farm' on the banks of the Derwent River, in New Town. Edward's daughter,

Malvina Hobson, had arrived in Hobart Town from Sydney in 1821 with her husband and two children. But by October 1823, Malvina had left her family and was living with Broughton at Prospect Farm,[22] which Broughton now owned. This was where he planted Tasmania's first vineyard.

By the summer of 1823, grapes were among the most productive fruits in Van Diemen's Land,[23] and the following year growers eagerly awaited the best harvest 'since the formation of the Colony'.[24] While he waited the three necessary years for his grape vines to bear enough fruit to make wine, Broughton sold raspberry and currant wine, made from the previous year's fruit.[25]

As a businessman starting out after a period of incarceration, Broughton raised many eyebrows with his property purchases and the money he spent developing Prospect Farm. Lieutenant-Governor George Arthur was suspicious about the source of his income. When he wasn't tending to his grapes, Broughton worked as a clerk for Dr Edward Foord Bromley, the colonial treasurer.

In 1824 Governor Arthur reported to Earl Bathurst in London that £4665 had gone missing from government funds; the true amount was later calculated to be more than £7000. The colonial treasurer was ultimately responsible, but Governor Arthur was greatly suspicious of Broughton's role, asking how a clerk 'living in open adultery' on a salary of a shilling a day and £60 a year in fees could afford 'not only to live expensively but to purchase an estate and erect a good house upon it with every comfort and convenience' with a value exceeding £3000.[26]

Broughton was charged with embezzlement and tried over two days in October 1826, but found not guilty.[27] Despite this, the stress, he said, caused him to suffer a ruptured blood vessel and endure 'a mind worn out by Anxiety and a Body by Weakness and Disease'.[28] Before long he was toasting his escape, though, with his own bottles of bubbly, advertising them in *The Colonial Times and Tasmanian Advertiser*:

FOR SALE, at MR BROUGHTON'S at Newtown, 200 Gallons [909 litres] of GRAPE WINE, made in imitation of Champaigne, from the last year's Grapes, in Casks of 20 Gallons [ninety-one litres] each ... Wanted to Purchase from 50 to 60 Dozen of Wine Bottles.[29]

Broughton's vineyard had already received the plaudits of a 'gentleman from the Cape', with the same newspaper reporting:

> GRAPES – We have been informed by a Gentleman who has just come from the Cape, which is considered a wine country, that the grapes in this Colony grow far more luxuriantly than they do in that; and expressed his great surprise at seeing so fine a vineyard as at Mr Broughton's, at Newtown ... Mr Broughton has several hundred gallons of Tasmanian wine, part of which he intends to send home, to the Society of Arts and Sciences, so soon as he can procure the Lieutenant Governor's certificate of its being the produce and manufacture of this Colony.[30]

A week after Broughton's 'Champaigne' went on sale, the *Colonial Times* reported:

> TASMANIAN WINE – The first attempt to make wine from the grapes in this Colony, to any extent, has been made by Mr. Broughton of Prospect, Newtown ... Several Gentlemen, among whom are Mr. Colonial Secretary Burnett, Dr Sherwin, Mr. Bryant, the Wine Merchant, and several others, have tasted this wine and all pronounce it very little inferior to Champaigne; and have recommended him to distribute the produce of one Vintage throughout the two Colonies, and in England, in order that various opinions might be formed upon it. Dr. Sherwin, who tasted Mr. Blaxland's Australian wine ... declared, that Mr. Broughton's was far superior ...'[31]

A month later, Broughton sent a case of stone bottles and a wooden cask of his wine to England on the *Hugh Crawford*.[32] He bought more land, but his grand ambitions were brought to a halt by another ruptured blood vessel, and he died the following year aged just thirty-five.[33]

IN GRECO-ROMAN TIMES, wine was an important therapeutic agent, used as an antiseptic and anaesthetic, as a diuretic and sedative, as an appetite stimulant, and as a tonic and an ingredient in poultices.[34] In the 16th century, a doctor was said to have saved the life of Mary, Queen of Scots, by using wine to treat her bleeding stomach ulcer.[35] During the Plague of London, which began in 1665, doctors fortified themselves with wine before entering the homes of patients; Dr Nathaniel Hodges recommended they drink sack, a type of sherry, 'to warm the stomach, refresh the spirits and dissipate any beginning lodgement of the infection'.[36]

After visiting London in 1821 as part of a delegation to argue for the rights of emancipated convicts such as himself, Dr William Redfern had spent time at Madeira, recuperating from an illness he suffered on his way home to New South Wales. He collected vines and fruit trees, and he invited a husband-and-wife vigneron team – Emmanuel Serrao[37] and Ana De Freitas[38] – to move to Sydney to plant them at his Campbellfield property.

Another colonial doctor, Sir John Jamison, established a terraced vineyard on a steep hill beside the Nepean River at Regentville, near present-day Penrith. Jamison was the first president of the Agricultural Society of New South Wales,[39] founded in 1822. The society's original prospectus noted: 'We are just in the latitude of the finest parts of Europe where the vine, the olive, the fig and the mulberry grow ...' Jamison added:

> No body of men can more effectually assist us than the Merchants and their Captains, by bringing us from foreign countries what is adapted to our climate. Vessels, touching in the winter months at the Madeira, or the Cape, and other countries noted for their wine, their figs, or their olives, might bring what, in a few years hence, may constitute the grand sources of the wealth of this Colony. The foundation

of a fine vineyard, for instance, may be brought in cuttings of the vine from the Madeiras, the Canaries, or the Cape, in a rejected empty water cask.[40]

Jamison's vigneron, F.A. Meyer, had learnt his trade in the Rhine Valley. Before long he was offering his services not just to Jamison but to any cultivator 'for winter pruning on moderate charges', and recommending grape growing for all farmers as the Australian climate 'was particularly favourable for it'.[41]

Meyer claimed that in several places where he had established vineyards, 'the produce of Grapes, of which has been made a very promising wine, has been so abundant in the second and third year, that he is convinced every cultivator of the Vine will gain a great profit by it'.[42]

The hardiest grapes he recommended were the 'Burgundy, both varieties, the black Hamburgh (known under the name of Black Portugal, or Oporto,) the white Gouais, the Tinta and Madeira' — but he noted that 'the two latter are still very scarce in the Colony'.[43]

He had done an outstanding job tending the vines for Dr Jamison. He told *The Sydney Monitor* in 1833 that he was growing four varieties of grape: 'the white Gouais, a French grape; the Oporto, or black Portugal, the Xeres or Sherry grape; and the small black clustering, or Burgundy grape'. The vineyard's soil, he said, which consisted of 'sand, mixed with a great quantity of pebbles, slate, with more or less of clay ... would not be fit for any other agricultural purpose'.[44]

Over time, other medical men would follow the example of Redfern and Jamison, establishing vineyards with an eye to promoting wine's medicinal benefits as well as the cultural benefits of having quality vineyards on Australian soil. They would have a profound effect on the development of the Australian wine industry.

In London, meanwhile, Mary Holt, now a young woman, had fallen hard for a medical student named Christopher Penfold, whose family was also well versed in wines. Their meeting would change her life forever.

Chapter 7

AT SEVENTEEN, MARY was a bright, attractive young woman with long, dark hair tied back off her face and large, enquiring eyes. She had been raised in a fine home, surrounded by books and music, and her social graces made her the centre of attention in London's most fashionable drawing rooms. She was a 'beloved child' for her parents, Tom and Elizabeth Holt, who gave her the nickname 'Toots'. To them Mary was a 'much loved dearest girl', a 'dearest angel', their 'idolised Mary'.[1]

King William IV had succeeded his late brother George IV to the throne of Great Britain in 1830, ushering in a more restrained era that was at odds with the reign of his spendthrift predecessor. Sixty-four when he took the throne, William was a man of the people and often walked among his subjects both in London and at the emerging seaside resort of Brighton – a town that would soon be Mary's home.

While the British authorities still transported more than 7000 convicts a year to the Australian colonies, and rogue elements murdered many Indigenous people for their land, Britain was advancing in areas of social justice. Public outcries against the slave trade grew louder in Britain and eventually led to the *Slavery Abolition Act* (1833), although it was staunchly opposed by Viscount Melbourne, who became British prime minister the next year.

It was a time of great advancements in medicine, with early experiments in the use of chloroform as an anaesthetic for surgery, and research showing a direct connection between poverty and epidemic fevers.[2] Through their medical practices, both Mary's father and grandfather had an association with St Bartholomew's Hospital – commonly known as 'Barts' – which was one of the most prestigious teaching hospitals in Britain.

Only 500 metres from the domed magnificence of St Paul's Cathedral, Barts had been a cornerstone of British medicine since its foundation in 1123, and was a world leader in medical discoveries. It was at Barts in the 1600s that William Harvey made his essential breakthroughs about the human circulatory system – which doctors now agreed could be assisted by the moderate use of red wine.

In 1830,[3] a handsome vicar's son from the small town of Steyning, in Sussex, had travelled to the venerated hospital from his country home to begin four years of medical training. Christopher Rawson Penfold – his family often called him Chris[4] – had started studying the art of making medicines as an apprentice apothecary, following in the footsteps of his brother, Dr Richard Penfold,[5] who had died in 1829 aged just thirty-one. From the outset Chris was coached in the therapeutic value of wines, either used alone or in a variety of concoctions.

The terms of Christopher's apprenticeship saw him promise 'to keep his Master's secrets, and to obey the Master's lawful commands'. He would not waste the goods of his master, nor lend them unlawfully to anyone. He would not commit fornication, nor contract matrimony during his apprenticeship; he would not play cards or gamble with dice, nor engage in any other unlawful games. He would not buy or sell. He would not 'haunt taverns or playhouses nor absent himself from his Master's service day or night unlawfully', but would conduct himself 'in all things as a faithful apprentice' towards his master during the term of his indenture.[6]

Christopher Penfold was an ambitious and handsome young man with soft features, a friendly face, a mass of thick, wavy hair and wide, expressive eyes that seemed to glisten in the light. With his crisp, high-buttoned waistcoat, frock-coat and high white collar, he could have been the hero in a Regency-era romantic novel.

It was Mary's father who introduced this young man of promise he knew from Barts to his precious daughter, and before long the two became inseparable.

The end of 1833 was a time of even greater celebration for the Penfold and Holt families, with newspapers reporting three days after Christmas that the Court of Examiners from Apothecaries' Hall had issued a 'certificate of qualification' to eight young medical students, among them 22-year-old C.R. Penfold of Steyning, Sussex.[7] Chris had now received his Licence of the Society of Apothecaries as a 'general practitioner' under Britain's *Apothecaries Act* (1815).[8]

Apothecaries were increasingly the doctors of Britain's poorer classes. Under the act, they had to be at least twenty-one years of age and had to have served an apprenticeship of five years before sitting for the licence examination.[9] The standard required for the licence was gradually raised over the years, and studies of midwifery and the diseases of women and children were added to medicine and pharmacy in the examination for Christopher's class.[10] Now that he could practise medicine, Chris decided to stay on for another year's training at Barts to qualify as a surgeon.

Over the next few months, the young medical graduate and the doctor's daughter grew extremely fond of each other, taking romantic walks by the Thames, where Mary's brother Alf was still casting his fishing line. Chris felt as though Mary was family already. He liked the name Mary Penfold, he said. It was his sister's name too.[11]

Christopher Penfold was an eternal optimist, a dreamer who longed for a life not mired in debt.[12] He had seen money woes and disputes over borrowings weigh down members of his family. As the young couple fell in love, Christopher told Mary all about his life and the struggles of growing up as the son of a country vicar with a big, hungry family in rural England.

Steyning, a charming village by the River Adur, six kilometres inland from the southern coast of England, was home to a thousand or so people. It had been a Saxon port before the 11th century, but silt had made the river too shallow for large vessels.

Christopher's grandfather had been a medical man too; an apothecary and 'man midwife'[13] who could trace his roots in Sussex back almost 400 years to the reign of Britain's King Henry VI.

Christopher's ageing parents – the Reverend John Penfold[14] and Charlotte Jane Penfold (nee Brooks)[15] – had married in Steyning in 1792. Over the next nineteen years, Charlotte gave birth to thirteen children. The Reverend Penfold had a Master of Arts degree from St Alban Hall at Oxford,[16] and became a pillar of the Anglican faith as the personal chaplain to Prince Augustus Frederick, Duke of Sussex – the man who, as the head of the Royal Society of Arts, had given his nod of approval to Gregory Blaxland's wine.

The Penfolds had been bulwarks against the spread of smallpox in the previous century, advocating for vaccinations,[17] a relatively new procedure in England adopted from the Chinese[18] and Turks.[19] Still, childhood remained dangerous across Britain. Among the sermons, weddings, christenings and funerals the Reverend Penfold performed, he also had to bury three of his own children.[20] Chris was never allowed to use a swing as a child because when he was two years old his brother Robert, then seven, had died in an accident involving one,[21] horrifying his parents and plunging the family into a long period of despair.

Beside the vicarage where he raised his enormous family, the Reverend Penfold preached in the Parish Church of St Andrew,[22] with its a stunning 12th-century nave featuring grand columns, archways and carvings of biblical accounts.[23]

The Steyning church had a long, colourful history, with Saint Cuthmann building a wooden Saxon-era church on the site at the beginning of the 9th century. It was said that Ethelwulf, King of the West Saxons and father of the famed King Alfred, was buried there in 857. As a small boy, Chris watched his father host meetings in Steyning's National School Room for 'Promoting

Christian Knowledge, and for the Propagation of the Gospel in Foreign Parts'.[24]

Christopher's childhood surrounds were steeped in history, but were certainly not as opulent as Mary's London home, although his mother, Charlotte, kept it as happily as she could. Charlotte Penfold was an extraordinary woman, and much of Christopher's interest in medicine derived from her studies of home remedies and the use of wine in them. She was the eldest child of a wealthy London property owner, Thomas Brooks, and grew up on Great George Street, Bedford Square, in London's Bloomsbury district.

Bedford Square was developed when Charlotte was a small child, as an exclusive neighbourhood, with 'houses only as are fit for the habitation of persons of fortune and distinction'.[25] Charlotte's formative years were a pleasant time of beautiful clothes, genteel friends, polite society and fascinating excursions to attractions such as Christchurch in Hampshire and boating trips to the Isle of Wight and Gosport, although the latter underwhelmed her as 'rather a dirty town'.[26]

Since she was seventeen, Charlotte had kept a journal in which she made whimsical entries, detailed lists pertaining to her domestic life and careful, clever sketches of her family. On 4 October 1792, on the day of her wedding to the charismatic and good-looking Reverend John Penfold at St Giles in the Fields, Holborn, in London, Charlotte jotted down all the furniture in her huge room at Bedford Square as well as the cartloads of furniture given to her by 'my dear Father and Mother' for her new home at the vicarage in Steyning.

There was 'a good mahogany four-post bedstead with handsome purple and white furniture complete and fringe', '2 feather beds, 2 blankets, 1 under blanket, 1 counterpane bedspread, 2 pillows and a bolster, a wash handstand with bason [sic], a mahogany wardrobe and double chest of draws, dressing table, 6 chairs horsehair, and 2 horsehair armchairs, bookcase, large carpet, black ebony clock'. There was also a painted work table, a mahogany dining table with six chairs, and new white window curtains.

Her clothing inventory included a white satin gown trimmed with lace for her wedding day, a fine calico gown, blue striped Canterbury gown, straw-coloured gown and a dark Irish gown, six nightshirts, '12 cotton stockings, 12 purple bordered handkerchiefs, 4 flannel coats and 6 under dainties'. She had a long list of fans, too, as well as a black satin bonnet and fine black lace veil, and a brown beaver hat with feathers.[27]

For the next four decades, Charlotte would copy poems from newspapers and magazines into her journal. By the time she met Mary Holt, Charlotte was entering poems into her journal written by her brother Octavius Brooks, which had appeared in a new magazine called *The Spectator*. She dedicated what she thought were the most beautiful poems to her husband, and wrote out his sermons in full to preserve them for future generations.

Soon after beginning her new life in Steyning, Charlotte practised her elegant cursive signature, 'Charlotte Jane Penfold'. She also visited the graves of her husband's ancestors, the naval officer Hugh Penfold and his grandson Richard, in the churchyard at the nearby Sussex village of Angmering, making sketches of the tombs to show the rest of her family.

Charlotte took out a subscription to the St James's Library and Reading Room, in nearby Brighton, when it opened in 1827, and she encouraged Chris Penfold to read widely. She also encouraged his medical studies as he followed his late brother Richard's example, and she jotted down all sorts of remedies she found that she could share with him.

At about the time that Chris Penfold met young Mary Holt, his mother showed him a cure she had found for a bad cough in children: ten drops of ipecacuanha wine after every meal in a wine glass with cold water. The tonic was made by soaking the root of the Brazilian ipecacuanha plant and mixing it with wine or syrup. Charlotte noted that the ipecacuanha wine would create gentle perspiration, which was useful in eliminating the cold. She told Chris that children with a cough should be kept out of cold winds.[28] He already knew that.

As well as recipes for cakes and stews, and even a homemade waterproof cement to fix household cracks, Charlotte also showed Chris and Mary a cure for malaria using red Peruvian bark, black pepper, brown sugar and poppy syrup.[29]

CHRISTOPHER RAWSON PENFOLD told Mary he had been named in honour of the family's wealthy benefactor. Despite John Penfold's lofty status within the Anglican church, his large family was often beset by financial woes.[30] Fairly early in John and Charlotte's marriage, they met Christopher Rawson,[31] a former naval officer with the British East India Company who had become chairman of his family business, an institution in northern England known as Rawson's Bank.[32] Rawson lived with opulence at Hope Hall in Halifax, almost 400 kilometres to the north of the Penfold vicarage.

In 1807[33] Rawson married Mary Anne Brooks,[34] the much younger sister of Chris Penfold's mother, and the marriage forged a strong bond between the battling Penfolds and the wealthy Rawsons, even though the Penfolds' constant stumbling in financial matters almost drove Rawson spare. To honour their rich and generous relative, the Penfolds named their two youngest boys after him: George Rawson Saxby Penfold,[35] born in 1808, and Christopher Rawson Penfold, their last child, born three years later. The elderly Penfolds saw their thirteenth child as a little miracle, born at the vicarage of Steyning's ancient Norman church.[36]

Christopher's older brother, Thomas Brooks Penfold,[37] was fifteen when Christopher was born and was about to embark on a naval career with the East India Company, then the largest business in the world, with its own private military force numbering more than a quarter of a million men.[38] Tom returned from India in 1834 and would forever claim that almost immediately Reverend Penfold started tapping him for money to pay the mounting bills the care of his siblings incurred.[39] In time Tom would argue savagely with his family over money.

All this meant there was not a lot of money for Christopher's expensive medical books and living expenses in London, and the young man could not afford to support himself on his earnings as an apprentice physician.

When Mary met Chris, he was a young man already well versed in the world of wine. One of his father's cousins, Richard Penfold, ran Hopkins & Penfold, wine and spirit merchants at Worthing, a coastal town a short carriage ride to the south of Steyning. Richard Penfold sold 'superior wines and spirits', and at various times advertised 'Port, Cape Madeira, Fine Old Sherry, Fine Old Teneriffe, Fine Old Lisbon, West India Madeira, East India Madeira, Mount Etna Madeira, Bronti Madeira, Claret, Champaigne [sic], Old Jamaica Rum, Cognac Brandy, Brown Stout, Edinborough [sic] Ale, Hertfordshire Cider and the Best English Gin'.[40]

As well as fine wines, the Penfold family of Steyning could also educate young Mary about the harshness of Australia as a penal colony. Back in 1828 at the West Sussex Quarter Sessions held in the Petworth County Hall, a middle-aged farm labourer named Daniel Daniels was convicted of stealing from Reverend Penfold's vicarage four cock turkeys, five hen turkeys and three hen fowls.[41]

The full bench of magistrates had a packed caseload on the day his matter was heard, dealing with 44 prisoners, male and female, on various felony charges. One man, James Hayler, was found guilty of stealing a hive and bees and was given three months' hard labour, after being publicly whipped. Others found guilty were given similar sentences. Daniel Daniels was spared a flogging, but for stealing from a reverend he was sentenced to be transported to New South Wales for life.[42]

THE AUSTRALIAN COLONIES were still places of torment for numerous convicts, many of whom had been sentenced to exile with hard labour for what later societies would regard as minor offences. Many free settlers, though, were trying to recreate the finest European culture from Australian soil.

In 1834, Dr John Jamison's new cellar at Regentville contained 6400 litres of wine in casks. The new governor of New South Wales, Sir Richard Bourke, was proud that many visitors to the colony's vineyards claimed the wines 'fully equalled if they did not surpass anything of the kind they had ever witnessed in any of the wine countries they had visited'.[43] A year later, Jamison's vineyard had expanded to nearly four hectares, with 'upward of 200 varieties' and as many as 40,000 vines.[44]

James Busby had returned to New South Wales from his European journey with 362 vine cuttings[45] still alive, which he had procured from the best vineyards of France, Spain and Germany.[46] These were divided into three parts and planted at Busby's property, 'Kirkton', in the Hunter Valley, at John Macarthur's Camden Park and at Sydney's Royal Botanic Garden in what he called a 'national collection'. Busby's vines included pinot noir, shiraz, Mataro, grenache, carignan, pinot gris and chardonnay. Soon colonial vignerons were able to source a wide range of varieties for their soil, leading eventually to much improved wines.

Busby published two more books in 1833 and 1834, documenting his European tour and an update on winegrowing in the colony.[47] When he left New South Wales soon after with his new wife and some more European vine cuttings, to become the British representative in the emerging territory of New Zealand, his brother-in-law William Kelman extended his Kirkton vineyard, while other winemakers settled nearby in the Hunter Valley.

One of the new neighbours was the young and adventurous George Wyndham,[48] a former first-class cricketer for Cambridge University who had travelled through Canada and then studied winemaking on a grand tour of Europe. Wyndham had arrived in Sydney on Boxing Day 1827 with his wife, Margaret, a team of servants, sheep, cattle, horses, pigs and hounds. He bought 800 hectares of fine grazing country near the village of Branxton, about six kilometres south of the Busby vineyard, and started growing crops. Soon he had a large family of twelve sons and two daughters.

With cuttings supplied by Busby, Wyndham planted Australia's first commercial shiraz vineyard,[49] and before long he was planting cuttings from other budding winemakers in the Hunter Valley: muscatel, black Hamburg, red Portugal, green malaga, Constantia and black cluster or pinot noir. Then there was also oporto and gouais, and by 1836 his hectare or so of vineyards produced about 7500 litres of a wine he called 'Dalwood', the name he had given to the Wyndham estate.

In time, Dalwood would occupy a huge place in the winemaking legacy of Mary and Christopher Penfold.

Chapter 8

AS THEY WALKED hand in hand by the Thames, Chris Penfold told Mary that money had been so tight at the Steyning vicarage when he was a boy that one of his sisters was more or less adopted out.

Fanny Penfold[1] had moved to Halifax at a young age to live with her rich uncle and aunt, the Rawsons. The Rawsons had no children of their own, Chris said, and felt this act of charity would take a financial burden off the Penfolds. It did. Mary Anne Rawson doted on her niece and treated her as a daughter. In turn the young Miss Penfold treated Mary Anne like a mother, and her uncle Christopher Rawson like a 'father, guardian, trustee and friend'.[2] Rawson, though, said his wife went too far with her kindness and generosity, and he accused her of 'idolatry'. He believed she was spoiling the child and making an ingrate of her.[3]

As Fanny grew older, the Rawsons introduced her to many of the Rawson Bank's clients, including some of the wealthiest young bachelors in Halifax. One was the rich landowner John Walker, whose ghostly complexion suggested his life would likely be short. Friends suggested to Fanny that while a marriage with Walker might not be a match made in heaven, it would certainly make her very wealthy,[4] and the two became engaged. Rawson, so rich that he printed his own banknotes,[5] paid for his wife to accompany Fanny, Walker and various Penfold relatives on a luxury holiday to Brighton on England's south coast. He also gave Fanny a large cash advance ahead of her wedding.[6]

Chris Penfold was eighteen when his proud father performed the wedding ceremony for the new Mr and Mrs Walker at Steyning's Church of St Andrew.[7] Witnesses included the Rawsons and two of Chris Penfold's older sisters, Catherine[8] and Charlotte.[9] The newlyweds left on their honeymoon in August 1829, accompanied by a female friend and the 30-year-old Catherine Penfold.

Over the next few months the four young travellers did the grand European tour in style, visiting Paris, Basel, Geneva, Livorno, Florence and Milan, with young John Walker spending copiously.[10] Catherine wrote home to Steyning to say it was the holiday of a lifetime. Florence was divine and Livorno so beautiful. Everyone was having a delightful time – except John Walker, who seemed to grow paler despite the sunny climes.[11]

Fanny became pregnant on this lavish honeymoon, but John Walker came down with a severe lung complaint and was desperately ill by the time their carriage reached Naples late in December 1829. Despite the careful attention of five physicians, Fanny's husband died in a hotel there the following month, aged just twenty-five.[12] He did not leave a will.

Late in February 1830, Fanny, now a pregnant widow, left Naples with her friend and Catherine Penfold. Another member

St Andrew Holborn where Mary married Chris Penfold in 1835. *The Trustees of the British Museum / Creative Commons*

of the Penfold family, their brother James,[13] a solicitor, made part of the journey back to England with them, as did Catherine's new Florentine fiancé, Giovanni Baroncelli,[14] a much older man who would soon become her husband.

Christopher Rawson met the group in Calais to take Fanny back to Steyning,[18] where Fanny delivered a stillborn son[15] only two weeks after her sister's joyful marriage to Signor Baroncelli in London.[16] Devastated by the death of her husband and child, Fanny moved back to Halifax, along with her sister Charlotte, and eventually settled into a fine house there, bought for her by Christopher Rawson. That arrangement would not end well, either.

CHRIS PENFOLD FOUND his medical studies fascinating, and he regaled Mary with tales of the unexpected while training to be a surgeon at Barts. His classmates included Henry Lindeman,[17] another young doctor with a keen interest in wine.

Born at Egham, Surrey, about thirty kilometres west of central London, Lindeman had grown up in Hythe, now a suburb of Southampton, where his father worked as a doctor. Lindeman had become an apprentice physician at just thirteen, working with his father for the next five years under the mentorship system that was common for aspiring medical men at the time.

It was a remarkable time for medical development in Britain. Decades of war with France had produced major breakthroughs in the study of pathology, and the focus on individual organs. The French doctor René Laennec had invented the stethoscope to investigate chest infections, and two other Frenchmen, Antoine César Becquerel and Gilbert Breschet, were conducting experiments which ultimately established that the mean body temperature of a healthy adult was 37 degrees Celsius. The fiery London surgeon Thomas Wakley had founded the influential weekly medical journal *The Lancet*.

The continuous overcrowding of British towns and cities accelerated the spread of infectious diseases, and Chris and his fellow students became well versed in dealing with epidemics. They also studied anatomy and physiology, as Barts offered one of the most comprehensive surgical courses in London, with daily ward visits and crowds of students gathered around the beds of patients.[18]

There was also the close examination of the dead, and Barts stressed the importance of dissection in understanding disease. The chance to dissect a cadaver became a powerful lure for many students, as it offered a new way of looking at the body. Early in Chris Penfold's tenure at Barts, more merciful judges in the British criminal courts meant that the legal supply to science of bodies from the gallows was limited to just a few every year. As a result, Barts and other flourishing medical schools found they simply did not have enough cadavers for the adequate instruction of their students in anatomy and surgical skills. Barts and many other hospitals made secret arrangements with 'resurrection men' – grave robbers who worked in gangs in the dead of night, exhuming newly occupied plots. Some of these 'body snatchers', such as the notorious William Burke and William Hare in Edinburgh, created their own cadavers through murder and then sold the bodies for dissection.

The more sociable corpse salesmen employed at Barts, having dug into the mass graves at public cemeteries or unguarded churchyard burial places, would bring their treasures to the Fortune of War pub, opposite the hospital. The freshly disinterred deceased were displayed on benches in a room set aside for the purpose. Surgeons from Barts would peruse the offerings and buy the most suitable, while the sweaty body snatchers revived themselves with refreshing ales.[19]

Mary reeled in horror at some of Christopher's stories, but he pointed out that some of the body parts he studied at the hospital – including amputated limbs and surgically removed growths – had been taken with consent from the living. These were collected and stored in spirits.

In Chris's last year at Barts, 1834, he and Henry Lindeman were joined by twenty-year-old student James Paget, who had already served a four-year apprenticeship with a general practitioner and would go on to detail the bone condition that became known as Paget's disease.

After Chris graduated as a physician, he entered a partnership with an older doctor, Henry Sanders,[20] and began seeing patients from a medical practice in fashionable Sloane Square, in London's Chelsea. Like many of the Penfolds, Dr Sanders had been buffeted by economic headwinds throughout his life, and a decade before going into business with Chris he had been working as a surgeon and 'accoucheur', delivering babies from his premises in Beaumont Street, Marylebone, when he was effectively declared bankrupt as an 'insolvent debtor'.[21]

By the time he went into business with Chris Penfold, Sanders was thirty-five years old and trying to rebuild his finances as a father of three.

MEANWHILE, BACK IN her new home at Halifax, Christopher's older sister Fanny became embroiled in a fierce fight over her late husband's estate with his sisters, the Walkers, who claimed to be his rightful heirs.

Fanny's claims to her husband's fortune had been diluted by the absence of a will. Had Fanny's son lived, the vast fortune of John Walker would have gone to him in trust, but the death of both father and son left Fanny in a precarious position. But just like her future sister-in-law Mary, the former Fanny Penfold was not about to give in. With the help of the Rawsons and her lawyer brother, James, Fanny eventually received a settlement of £16,642 – equivalent to about $A8 million in 2025.[22]

Fanny married a well-to-do Irishman in Halifax before settling in Dublin, where she gave birth to a son and a daughter. The protracted battle over John Walker's inheritance, though, and Fanny's eventual second marriage exacerbated tensions between her and her uncle Christopher Rawson, who was angry that the money he had advanced her before her first marriage and the house he had bought for her in Halifax were not returned, despite the fortune she eventually inherited.

Indeed, Rawson was aghast at the way so many members of the Penfold family seemed to mismanage their money. He once exclaimed that they were an 'unfortunate' bunch and demanded that Fanny '[l]ook at every member of your own family. Where is there one individual that is not in dire affliction and distress?'[23] Rawson claimed that despite Fanny and other Penfolds receiving 'so splendid a fortune', they had still taken advantage of his wealth and generosity for many years.

He declared that his wife's 'enthusiasm' for Fanny had 'been the ground work of all my unhappiness ... when my comforts and my property have so often been sacrificed on her account'.[24] He barred Fanny and the rest of the Penfolds from ever setting foot in Hope Hall again – or at least he did until she named her daughter after Mary Anne Rawson. There were no hard feelings toward Chris Penfold's mother, Charlotte, either, as she gave pride of place in her recipe book to 'Mrs Rawson's chicken curry'.[25]

Fanny moved for a time to Penzance, on England's Cornish coast, for the clean air, but sadly she would die there,[26] just six months after the passing of the four-year-old daughter whom she had named for her favourite aunt.

AMID A SEA OF FAMILY turmoil and personal tragedy, the handsome young doctor Christopher Rawson Penfold, twenty-three, prepared to marry his beautiful eighteen-year-old fiancée, Mary Holt.

Given that Mary was still so young, Chris needed the express permission of her father, Tom Holt. The *Marriage Act* (1753) stipulated that anyone under the age of twenty-one – the age of 'majority' – needed parental consent in order for their marriage to be valid.

Tom and Elizabeth Holt knew that their 'dearest angel' and 'idolised Mary'[27] had met the love of her life, but they were concerned about how Chris would react to the pressures of life – and they were aware of the Penfold family's money woes. But after much pleading from Mary, Tom Holt gave his permission for Christopher to marry her. Tom and Elizabeth were growing old, and their two boys, George and Alfred, were talking about moving to America to chase opportunities there. Mary's parents prayed that Chris would keep their beloved daughter close to them for the rest of their days.

Marriages in England at the time could take place after publication of the 'banns' (the public announcement of an impending marriage) or by the granting of a special and hard-to-obtain licence.

Charlotte Penfold wanted more than anything for her youngest child to find happiness in his marriage, and she shared all the advice and recipes she could think of to help Mary when she became a wife. Charlotte had all sorts of remedies she thought Mary might find useful: everything from preventative measures against consumption to advertisements for Dixon's Antibilious Pills – 'Patronized by the Royal Family', no less, and given ringing endorsements from all around Britain and from ships' captains sailing around the globe.

She showed Chris and Mary an article she'd saved outlining the famous Dr Robert Thornton's remedy for scarlet fever: twenty-five drops of tincture of foxglove.[28] Charlotte also had recipes for ginger wine, orange brandy and an 'excellent orange wine' made with twelve Seville oranges, a lemon and '4 pounds of good moist sugar to a gallon of water'.[29] She showed Mary how to make gooseberry vinegar, with nine litres of the ripe fruit to fourteen litres of water.

Charlotte also shared with Mary her recipes for everything from beef stew to stewed eel, French flummery, strawberry jam, lime juice marmalade, orange marmalade, orange jelly, apple jelly, calves foot jelly, 'plumb' cake and 'plumb' pudding.[30] She gave Mary advice on how to make her almond cake, and ginger beer, new milk whey, caramel pies, soup of rhubarb and onion sauce. Pudding was always a treat at the Steyning vicarage, and Charlotte showed Mary her recipes for baked apple pudding, raisin pudding and 'Spong' pudding, and for a 'succulent lemon pudding' that started with beating four egg yolks.[31]

Charlotte made a delicious blancmange, and her son-in-law Signor Baroncelli had given her marvellous tips for a lemon-flavoured Italian cream. Charlotte shared with Mary the advice from Baroncelli on the best way to cook macaroni, declaring that 'the water must boil fast before being salted'.[32]

If all that food was too much to bear, Charlotte swore by a concoction made from camomile flowers and ginger that was a cure-all for heartburn, indigestion and that bane of Regency-era dinner parties, flatulence.

Charlotte's recipe book was eclectic and multicultural. From his time in Calcutta, her surly son Tom Penfold had sent his mother a recipe for 'Indian Pickle' using cucumber and French beans, and another for an East India 'currey', using coriander, turmeric, black pepper, cayenne pepper and cumin seed.

The Penfolds were partial to a curry, and Charlotte's friend Harriet Timbrell[33] had given them a recipe she loved for curried rabbit. Harriet was a widow who had moved to nearby Brighton with her daughters Elizabeth[34] and Ellen, after the death of her husband, a sea captain with the East India Company. Ellen Timbrell and Mary would become firm friends. In fact, Ellen would follow Mary to what was then considered the ends of the Earth.

MARY'S WEDDING WAS to take place at the ancient Anglican church St Andrew Holborn, a place of worship that had gained national attention.

Both Mary and Chris knew the church well, as it was only a stone's throw from the front door of St Bartholomew's Hospital. A few years earlier, on the church steps, another young doctor, William Marsden, had found a homeless girl suffering from hypothermia. Marsden had sought help for her from one of the nearby hospitals, but not one of them would admit her. The poor girl breathed her last in Marsden's arms.

The overwhelming distress Marsden experienced inspired him to establish a medical centre to help London's poor in 1828. It was an institution revered for its charity, and it became known as the Royal Free Hospital, paving the way for free hospital care in other parts of the world.

In March 1835 Christopher dissolved his partnership with Henry Sanders[35] so that he could start his own medical practice. He and Mary had plans to begin their new life together in the Sussex countryside, while Sanders was about to start a new life with his family in New York.

Chris's father, now aged seventy-one, was in poor health, with breathing difficulties, and Charlotte had to beg off invitations in Steyning as she felt it would be wrong to 'leave the house on any pleasant visit of my own'.[36] But Reverend Penfold wanted to see the new bride and groom with clear eyes, and in readiness for the big day he bought three pairs of spectacles from William Harris and Co., manufacturers of optical instruments on London's High Holborn Street. He also wore his 'very elegant gold watch and chain'.[37]

And so it was that Gilbert Beresford,[38] church rector of St Andrew Holborn, wrote in a neat cursive hand for entry number 1086 in his marriage register:

Christopher Rawson Penfold of this Parish, bachelor, and Mary Holt, of the Parish of Saint Mary Magdalene Bermondsey in the County of Surrey, spinster and minor, were married in this church by licence and with the consent of Thomas Holt, the natural and lawful father of the said minor, this Twenty fourth Day of May in the Year One Thousand eight hundred and thirty Five By me …[39]

Mary kissed her beaming young husband. She looked forward to a life of romance and wonderful adventure with a boyish-looking man who had big dreams and passion in his big, soft eyes.

As the young husband and wife toasted each other with fine wine at their wedding feast, Mary did not suspect that the adventure ahead would take her about as far from her beloved parents and her comfortable life in London as humanly possible.

Chapter 9

TEENAGE BRIDE Mary Penfold navigated a whirlwind of emotions when she and Chris settled down to married life. She wanted desperately to stay close to her parents while being with her young and romantic husband.

Mary and Chris lived together in London for a short while, before making their home near the Penfold family's base in Steyning, where Chris briefly set up his practice as a surgeon.

Mary's mother-in-law, Charlotte Penfold, showed her a myriad of household hints – how to make furniture oil, transparent varnish, boot cleaner, a green wash for colouring the rooms of their marital home, and how to turn a black powder into ink by mixing it with vinegar and rainwater.[1] She told Mary all about a moisturising cream she used called Pomade Divine, which was advertised as a restorative cream to treat all sorts of pains, swellings, bruises, stiff necks, injuries from falls, piles, gangrene and even cancer.

The sea air of the Sussex coast agreed with Mary and soon the young couple were planning a permanent move to the bigger and more fashionable beachside town of Brighton, about 20 kilometres to the south-east. Brighton was within a day's travel of London, so Mary could still see her mother and father regularly.

It had been a settlement for 5000 years.[2] In the late 1700s it became one of Britain's favourite places when its beachside spas transformed it from a run-down fishing town to a health retreat for the rich and famous.[3] The chalk cliffs around its beach were spectacular and the cold, salty air spraying off the English Channel was a perpetual burst of invigoration.

Under the patronage of George IV, Brighton became one of the most fashionable and expensive locations in Britain, its reputation and image enhanced by the construction of the King's exquisitely furnished Royal Pavilion, a magnificent oriental-style palace that showcased his wealth and extravagant lifestyle. King William IV had stayed at the Pavilion after his brother's death, but his entertaining was on a far more modest level.

Brighton's star rose even higher with the patronage of the new young queen, Victoria, who had made her first visit to the Royal Pavilion in 1837, when she was just eighteen and still planning her coronation. Victoria's delight at the coastal town and its surrounds ensured it remained a fashionable destination for the well-heeled.

Her five-hour coronation ceremony in London on 28 June 1838 was a lavish extravaganza of a kind Britain had never experienced. After a succession of aged and infirm kings, the public was captivated by their radiant new queen, who was three years younger than Mary Penfold. Of her crowning, Victoria wrote:

> It was a fine day & the crowds of people exceeded what I have ever seen ... There were millions of my loyal subjects, assembled in every spot, to witness the Procession. Their good humour & excessive loyalty was beyond everything. I really cannot say how proud I felt to be the Queen of such a nation.[4]

The ceremony culminated with Victoria, adorned in sumptuous red and gold robes,[5] taking the oath of the British monarch at Westminster Abbey with the Archbishop of Canterbury, William Howley, presiding.

Charlotte Penfold later copied a report of the oath into her journal to show Mary and everyone at Steyning:

Archbishop: Madam, is your majesty willing to take the oath?

The Queen: I am willing.

Archbishop: Will you solemnly promise and swear to govern the people of this United Kingdom of Great Britain and Ireland and the dominions thereto belonging according to the statutes in parliament agreed on and the respective laws and customs of the same?

The Queen: I solemnly promise so to do.

Archbishop: Will you to your power cause law and justice in mercy to be executed in all your judgments? ...

The Queen: All this I promise to do. The things which I have here before promised I will perform and keep. So help me God.[6]

To celebrate the coronation, 5000 children paraded in Brighton's green space, called the Steine, where fishermen dried their nets, and a huge fair was held beside the Chain Pier, which jutted out over 300 metres into the sea towards France. An ox and several sheep were roasted whole and the meat distributed to the crowd.[7]

The fresh-faced teenage Queen set the fashion trend, arriving in Brighton that year for her seaside vacation wearing a smart hat like a man's top hat and adorned in a flowing green velvet gown that clung to her slim frame.[8] Mary and other stylish young women of the time followed Victoria's lead. They also took advice from the British fashion bible of the time, *La Belle Assemblée*, which advocated bodices cut low and off the shoulder.

Young Mary Penfold now favoured skirts that were long and full and sometimes trimmed with a flounce of lace. Open robes over a full petticoat of Indian muslin were popular, with a 'low corsage and square behind'. For evening wear, when she and

Christopher visited friends, there were 'pelisse': coat-like robes, which fastened down one side in a series of ribbon knots.[9]

Mary and Chris arrived in Brighton in 1838 with loaded trunks and bursting ambitions to make their mark on the world. They moved into a smart house at 110 Western Road, about 500 metres from the western end of the town's long, narrow strip of pebbled beach.[10]

That same year, work started on the construction of the London–Brighton railway, which was good news for Mary and her parents, Tom and Elizabeth. A mail coach started running between Brighton and London daily, and the steam packet *Belfast* made its first crossing of the English Channel to Dieppe with nineteen passengers. To coincide with Queen Victoria's Christmas holiday in Brighton in 1838, work had begun on the building of the Victoria Wing of the town's Royal Sussex County Hospital.

Chris Penfold had started his own private medical practice. Just like the First Fleet doctors, he had become a great believer in the medicinal benefits of wine in moderate amounts, and was convinced of its curative power in treating anaemia.[11] He had found it to be beneficial for other patients needing a restorative elixir. Sometimes wine was just good for the soul.

Mary and Chris were very much in love and Brighton was replete with romantic vistas. The Royal Pavilion gave them both a sense of awe and grandeur, even though Queen Victoria wasn't so impressed with her late uncle's building, decrying George IV's showpiece as 'a strange, odd Chinese-looking thing'.[12]

Brighton's Steine parkland became the stylish centre of town, and a library was opened on its east side. On their evening strolls along Brighton's Esplanade, Mary and Chris would pass the newly built Brighton Town Hall, the Coast Guard House and the Old Ship Hotel, at one time a meeting place for smugglers.[13] They could take a short carriage ride north of town to the Dyke House Hotel, which overlooked the vast, rolling, misty forests and hills of the Weald. The owners boasted that there was no view in England to exceed it: it was 'a view ... most enchanting ... the spectator being able to distinguish ... six counties'.[14]

THE YOUNG PENFOLDS had moved to Brighton at a time when thousands of other Britons were looking for coastal homes thousands of miles away. The colonisation of the Australian continent continued apace, as mostly British migrants saw endless opportunities to establish businesses there and procure land grants to build their own colonial kingdoms as the original inhabitants were displaced. New settlements were taking root across the vast landscape – and many of the settlers were planting grapevines.

In 1829 cuttings sourced from Gregory Blaxland, William Macarthur and Sydney's Botanic Garden were sent on a 5000-kilometre ocean voyage from Sydney to the newly established Swan River colony in Western Australia.[15] Botanist Thomas Waters, who had been a botanical collector in South Africa, established a market garden and planted grapevines on land adjoining the Swan River at South Guildford, twelve kilometres north-east of present-day Perth.[16] Waters made his own wine and used it to barter with local shopkeepers. Olive Farm continues to produce wines today from the same soil.

In 1830, Charles McFaull, who would become the Perth postmaster and a newspaper publisher, arrived from England and also planted vine cuttings, sourced from the Cape, at his Hamilton Hill property.[17] And, four years later, a syndicate featuring three British Army officers – Richmond Houghton, Ninian Lowis and Thomas Yule – planted vines in the Swan River Valley and established the Houghton winery.[18]

At the same time, the pastoralist Edward Henty established the first permanent European settlement in what is now the state of Victoria, at Portland Bay, and planted grapevines there beside the sea. A few hundred kilometres to the east, John Batman, a grazier and bounty hunter from Launceston, in Van Diemen's Land, looked over the countryside around Port Phillip Bay and declared it '[l]and of the best description, equal to any in the world … the most beautiful sheep pasturage I ever saw in my life'. He claimed he had signed a treaty with the local Aboriginal people, the Wurundjeri, for land beside the Yarra River, which he said would be 'the place for a village'.[19] It became the site of a town named for the British prime minister of the day, Viscount Melbourne.

Not long after, William Ryrie drove his sheep and cattle from the Braidwood district, south of Sydney, to his new property, Yering Station in the Yarra Valley, and took with him vine cuttings from the Macarthur family's Camden Park estate to establish the first commercial vineyard in Victoria.[20]

CHRIS PENFOLD YEARNED for the chance to have his own estate and his own vineyard. At night, as Mary lay in her husband's arms and thought about the family life that lay ahead for them, she and Chris talked about what was happening in the emerging colony known as South Australia. The newly settled region was all the talk in England, and there were enticing invitations for British immigrants to buy cheap land. A naval officer had told Chris about the endless opportunities South Australia was offering.[21]

The European settlement there had started as an idea in the mind of a wealthy diplomat and convicted kidnapper named Edward Wakefield.[22] While in prison, Wakefield had formed the opinion that, if they were to develop faster, the Australian colonies needed an emphasis on more free settlers with farming skills and business ambition, rather than convict labourers.

British commander Matthew Flinders and French naval skipper Nicolas Baudin had both charted the southern coast of the Australian continent in the first years of the 19th century, and in 1830 Charles Sturt had explored the Murray River. Sturt reported to Governor Ralph Darling: 'All who have ever landed upon the eastern shore of the St. Vincent's Gulf agree as to the richness of its soil and the abundance of its pastures.'[23]

The idea of having a large farm with their own rows of grapevines played on Chris's mind. He knew Tom and Elizabeth Holt were aghast at the thought of their daughter starting afresh in a new land when they had a comfortable life in England,[24] but still Chris let the notion germinate.

Promoters of the idea that British free settlers should move to South Australia had formed the South Australian Association in 1833 and started lobbying the British government to create a colony there. While New South Wales and Van Diemen's Land had been established as penal colonies, the planners of a South Australian settlement foresaw a more enlightened beginning.

Edward Wakefield proposed the sale of Crown lands in smaller units, rather than the granting of large tracts of land for free, as had been done in New South Wales. Money raised from the sales would then pay for poor labourers to migrate from Great Britain. This would provide South Australia with a workforce that did not depend on the often dangerous criminals who were being assigned as labourers in other Australian colonies. For many Britons contemplating a new life in the Great Southern Land, South Australia was starting to seem like the most inviting destination.

In 1834, public notices – or 'broadsides', as they were known – had started circulating throughout Britain, advertising the 'New Colony of South Australia'.[25] An initial public meeting about settlement there was held in Exeter Hall, on the Strand in London, chaired by William Whitmore, the member of parliament for Wolverhampton and an anti-slavery campaigner. Whitmore was opposed to the use of convict and slave labour everywhere. Colonies built by free settlers, he said, would provide new opportunities for Britain's working class through emigration. Other public meetings were organised to give the British public the chance to hear politicians and others discuss the principles for South Australia and the opportunities migrants could expect.

Whitmore introduced to the House of Commons what became the *South Australia Act* (1834). Unusually, the letters patent establishing the Province of South Australia two years later promised land rights for the Indigenous people of the colony, so that the arrival of the Europeans would not 'affect the rights of any Aboriginal Natives of the said Province to the actual occupation and enjoyment in their own Persons or in the Persons of their Descendants of any Lands therein now actually occupied or enjoyed by such Natives'.[26] It sounded wonderful in theory.

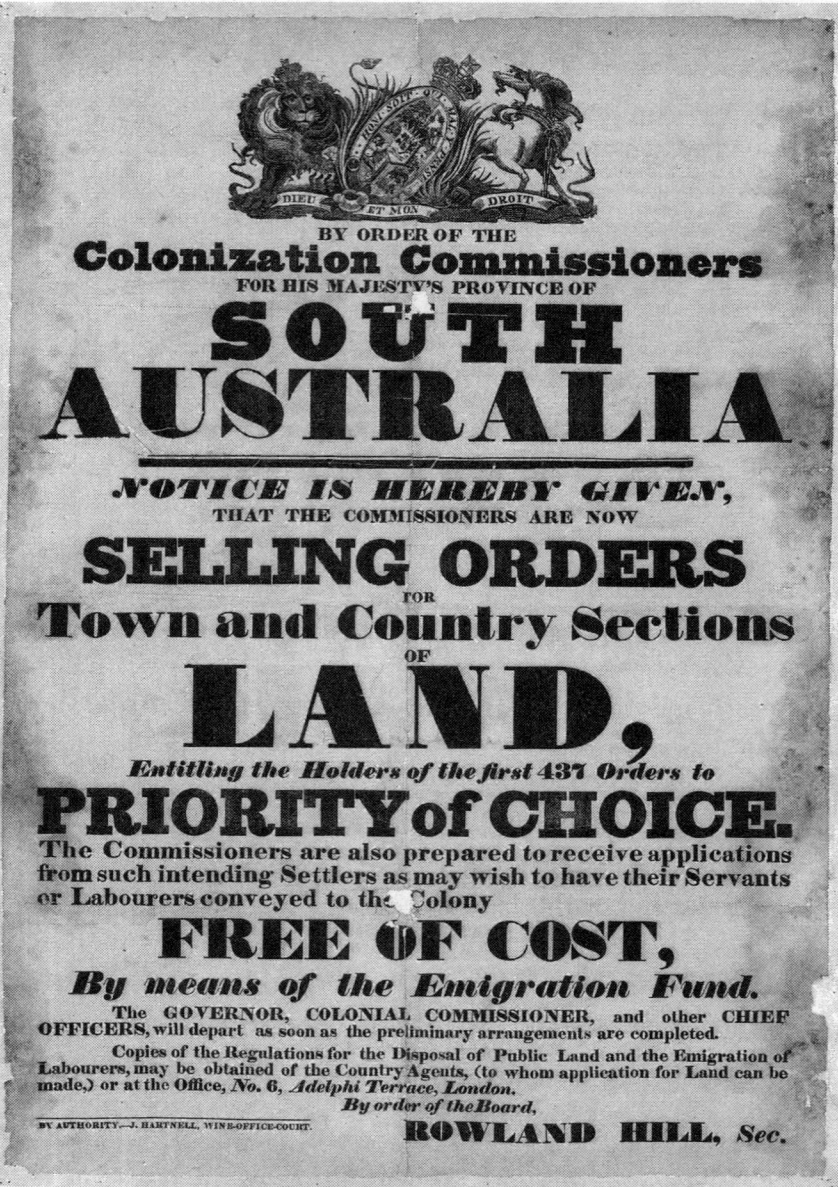

Posters such as this encouraged Mary and Chris Penfold to emigrate to South Australia with their daughter Georgina and friend Ellen Timbrell. *National Library of Australia obj-3461876908*

The first edition of the first South Australian newspaper was published in London, on 18 June 1836, before the first vessel carrying settlers had departed England for the South Australian coast. In a front-page editorial, editor George Stevenson[27] declared that it was his intention 'to print the first number of the *South Australian Gazette and Colonial Register* in the capital of the civilized world, and the second number in a city of the wilderness, of which the site is yet unknown'.[28]

The first free settlers arrived in South Australia in 1836, with the colonial government sworn in on 28 December near what became known as the 'Old Gum Tree',[29] at a site in present day Glenelg North. British governor John Hindmarsh, conscious of the atrocities against Indigenous peoples committed in the frontier wars in New South Wales and Van Diemen's Land, had George Stevenson read out a proclamation: it was his resolution 'to take every lawful means of extending the same protection to the native population as to the rest of His Majesty's Subjects'. The proclamation also made clear Hindmarsh's 'firm determination to punish with exemplary severity, all acts of violence or injustice which may in any manner be practiced or attempted against the natives, who are to be considered as much under the Safeguard of the law as the Colonists themselves, and equally entitled to the privileges of British Subjects'.[30]

The capital for the new colony was established on land that the traditional owners, the Kaurna people, called 'Tarndanya';[31] King William IV named it after his German-born wife, Adelaide of Saxe-Meiningen. Before long, grapevines were growing thick and fruitful in the loamy soil. The climate was Mediterranean, with hot summers, cool winters and caressing south-westerly winds.

Hindmarsh had arrived on the HMS *Buffalo* as one of 176 colonists. Another was an Englishman named Frank Potts,[32] who many years later planted shiraz and verdelho grapes at his property, 'Langhorne Creek', about fifty kilometres from Adelaide. Also on board were two hardy Scots, Robert Cock[33] and William Ferguson,[34] who pooled their resources and bought land in the new colony.[35] Cock and Ferguson also started a carting business and became the first auctioneers in the colony. In 1838, they bought 210 hectares in the lower reaches of the Adelaide

Hills from the new colonial government. They named their estate 'Makgill', after Robert Cock's family trustee, David Maitland Makgill of Fifeshire, Scotland.[36]

Before long, Chris and Mary Penfold would learn all about that beautiful estate. It was perfect country in which to make wine.

Chapter 10

EACH NIGHT, WHEN Chris Penfold returned to Mary after his working day in Brighton, he would hold her spellbound with his stories of babies he had delivered, potions he had prescribed and, occasionally, the awful business of amputating limbs when the need arose. Sometimes, as Mary listened to his news, they would be interrupted by a breathless messenger arriving and exclaiming, 'Pray, sir, please come!' Another medical emergency had arisen.

Late one cold winter's night, Chris was called out to the newly built Egremont Arms Hotel, about three kilometres from their Western Road home. Chris rushed there on a galloping horse.[1] He later described for Mary the distressing scene that had greeted him.

A young baker named George Salter, who also lived in Western Road, had arrived in the hotel parlour at about 9 p.m. Soon after, Captain William Bulbeck, an ageing maritime pilot, shuffled in for an ale. The old man smoked all the tobacco in his pipe as he listened to the small group of musicians who served as the pub band, and then refilled it for a second round.

The musicians packed up their instruments and left, leaving the door ajar. The captain rose to shut it, but the pipe fell from his left hand as he seemed to lose all strength in his body. Captain Bulbeck said it was nothing; it happened every now and then. He'd survived worse things than that. He showed George Salter his left hand, which was missing two fingers from an accident with a gun.

The captain filled his pipe for a third time. He was about to light it once more when the pipe fell from his hand again and this time broke on the floor. Salter was suffering a stroke; his mouth was drawn harshly to the left side, distorting his face.[2] Bulbeck's speech had 'faltered very much and fast', and he had spat up some phlegm.

The landlord rushed over with a glass of ale for Captain Bulbeck and helped him to a chair. The stricken man sipped some of the beer, and in barely a whisper asked the landlord to help him to his nearby home in Chalybeate Street. Bulbeck had lost the use of his left leg. His right hand was paralysed too but, Chris told Mary, the captain appeared 'perfectly sensible' and said he could go home under his own steam, provided the others walked behind him just in case. But he collapsed again and three men carried him to his house and sat him in a chair in the back parlour.

Bulbeck's wife, Martha, was aghast. She thought perhaps he'd been drinking too much or that his gout was tormenting him.[3]

Chris helped Bulbeck take off his waistcoat and jacket. He then took a scalpel and cut open the old man's arm to bleed him – this was thought to be the best treatment. The idea was to relieve the captain's blood pressure by draining some blood away. But the situation was hopeless. Looking gravely at the others in the room, including the old man's wife, Chris told them to keep Bulbeck in bed in an upright position. Chris departed, saying he would leave Bulbeck in peace, but he knew the captain would not last much longer.

Mary listened with rapt attention as Chris finished the story.

Two men stayed in the room with the captain and his anguished wife. They bathed Bulbeck's temples with a cloth steeped in vinegar and water. The treatment gave the old man a little comfort, but he died about ten minutes later. The next day, Chris gave evidence to a coroner's court, telling them Bulbeck had died from paralysis. The coroner returned a verdict of death 'by the visitation of God'.[4]

IN SOUTH AUSTRALIA, farmland in the shadow of the Adelaide Hills quickly became prized among the first European settlers in the colony, and the Third Creek, rising in the foothills of the Mount Lofty Ranges, provided water for the extensive orchards being planted.[5] At the time, the area was mostly woodland, with widely spaced gums over native grasses and some small shrubs.

Not long after arriving in the colony, William Ferguson and Robert Cock found themselves short of cash and decided to subdivide and sell a section of a little over thirty-two hectares at the northern end of their farm.[6] They took out a display ad in the colony's first newspaper:

> MAKGILL VILLAGE.
> THIS VILLAGE is situated about four miles from Adelaide, in one of the most beautiful and fertile locations in the district, about a quarter of a mile on this side [of] the third stream to the north-east of the town, and near the foot of the mountains; one of the best roads from the Stringy Bark Forest is through the same property, which makes this location most desirable for woodsmen and carriers in the timber trade.
>
> A plan of the Village may be seen by applying to Robert Cock, and blocks of from two acres [0.8 hectares] and upwards may be had on reasonable terms.[7]

This 'most beautiful and fertile location' would become crucial to the lives of Mary and Chris Penfold.

WHILE SOUTH AUSTRALIA became an enticing destination for emigrants leaving Britain in the late 1830s, others saw different vistas in their future. Mary's brother Alfred, who had grown into a tall, thin man with small, keen eyes and wavy hair,[8] arrived in New York in May 1837, two years after Mary's wedding.

His departure was sad for his family, and Tom and Elizabeth Holt felt the wrench of losing a child to distant shores. But their middle child had made up his mind to see the world, and he told them America was the land of opportunity. Alfred took with him his father's painting of 'The Divine Fisherman' walking on water, a treasured item that he kept all his life in the sitting room of his home near the East River, in the Bedford-Stuyvesant section of Brooklyn, off Kosciuszko Street.

When Alfred arrived in New York, the stock markets were in turmoil, but even though the markets deeply affected his cousins, the New York Astors, money issues were of no concern to him. On his first day in New York, Alfred went fishing at Macombs Dam on the Harlem River between Manhattan and the Bronx, and came away with a haul of bass and sweet-tasting crabs.[9]

Although he had rich relatives, Alfred was determined to make his own way in the world and found a job as a tailor with the clothing firm Brooks Brothers, in the company's first premises on Catherine Street, Manhattan. He would work for Brooks Brothers off and on for the next fifty-five years, until he was almost eighty.[10] He also worked as a tailor for August Belmont, the financier and racehorse owner who gave his name to the Belmont Stakes, the third leg of the Triple Crown of American horse racing. Alfred called Belmont 'a profuse spender' who insisted that his staff and servants be outfitted in the most splendid liveries.[11]

Mary's brother married a New York girl named Matilda Rhodes.[12] They were together for fifty-one years and raised a large family, although Alfred would often joke that the second-best catch he made in his life was a bass weighing 12.5 kilograms, which he took from the East River, at the foot of South Fourth Street in Brooklyn,[13] when it was still 'an abundant fishing station'.[14]

IN THE MIDDLE OF 1839, Chris Penfold arrived home to Mary one evening ashen-faced. He had just come from a horrifying incident at the Brunswick Hotel in Hove, a few hundred metres from their home.

William Hebden, a local bootmaker, had undressed on the beach for a Saturday-afternoon dip in front of the imposing row of magnificent homes facing the sea along Brunswick Terrace. The surf was rough and there were few people braving the pounding waves – only Hebden and Henry Goode Elborne, a holidaying student from Cambridge University.

The student later told Chris that he had spent about twenty minutes in the water, but that when he came out, there was no sign of the bootmaker, although he had observed him several times while leaping into the foaming spray. Elborne wondered if the bootmaker was a good swimmer and had challenged himself by going further out to sea.[15]

Elborne looked up and down the beach and out at the water, but there was no sign of the bootmaker for some time. When his body was finally spotted floating at a distance offshore, Elborne and two other men battled the waves and dragged him back to the beach. Hebden was deathly pale and there were no signs of life. The men carried him into the taproom of the Brunswick Hotel, startling the patrons there.

Elborne and his companions placed the bootmaker's body on a hotel table, but were startled to see his jaw moving. One of the men later told Chris that the mouth of the drowned man moved twice as they stood back to look at him on the table. No one knew what to do to revive him, and before long Hebden made no further movement.[16]

Chris was called to examine the body. The following day he told a coronial inquest held at the same hotel:

> I was called yesterday afternoon to view the body of [the] deceased at the top of this house ... I examined the body ... The motion of the jaw might have taken place from spasmodic action after the vital spark had fled. In cases of drowning it may take place for ten, fifteen or twenty minutes. It is, in some cases, symptom of life not being wholly gone.[17]

Being a doctor's wife prepared Mary for any type of stress or sudden tragedy.

Chris dispensed his medical theories among all his family as well as his patients. As well as advocating a little wine for the stomach, he gave his mother, Charlotte, a recipe for 'tooth powder', using '1 dram of gum myrrh finely pulverised, 1 dram of chalk [and] 3 or 4 drops of oil of cinnamon'.[18] Mother and son also collaborated over a formula to cure rheumatism using 'gum ammoniacum and garlic', and an elixir made from the plant guaiacum, liquorice root, coriander, rhubarb, raisins, saffron and gin.

Chris's moody big brother, Tom Penfold, also gave Charlotte a recipe for a cough syrup made from horehound, clarified honey and crushed poppies, to be drunk in a wineglass full of hot water.[19] Everyone thought he should take some sort of tonic for his moods.

And from *The Morning Post* newspaper, Charlotte had jotted down a cure for 'tic douloureux', also known as 'trigeminal neuralgia', a chronic pain disorder causing sudden, intense shooting pain in the face, typically on one side. The treatment was devised by Dr Alexander Turnbull, who advised sufferers to take five grains of aconitine and make it into an ointment with five drams of waxy cerate. They should then place a small amount of the greasy mixture on their forefinger and track it along the painful nerve for half a minute once or twice a day.[20]

MANY OF THE FIRST colonists around Adelaide could have done with nerve tonics as well.

In June 1839, when the world's pre-eminent bird expert, John Gould, visited Adelaide, he described it as not so much a city but 'a chaotic jumble of sheds and mud huts, with trees growing here and there in the newly marked-out streets and squares'.[21] Parrakeets of various kinds and honeyeaters filled the sky and trees, searching for food as road makers levelled the ground and workmen rushed about in construction. Here and there, Gould noted, were groups of newly arrived emigrants, 'both English and Irish, who had chosen this distant country for their future home; groups of Germans, too, whose fatherland no longer offered opportunities for enterprise, were dotted about the country busily engaged in constructing their little villages and getting their gardens under cultivation'.[22]

Gould noted that South Australia's surveyor-general, Colonel William Light, had been busy realising his grand vision for the town, pegging out sites along the River Torrens while leaving large parcels of verdant land for parks and public buildings, such as Government House, botanical gardens, a hospital and a cemetery. In his visionary concept for the colony's capital, Light had created a grid pattern of streets, with wide terraces to the north, south, east and west, all surrounded by trees and grass to ensure fresh air and open spaces in urban areas.[23]

Then Light came down with a fatal dose of tuberculosis and Charles Sturt took his place.

Gould wrote to his secretary:

> People live in tents, and customs are so different from what they have been used to, that I really wonder how they reconcile themselves to their new mode of life. On the whole, however, I think South Australia may be considered as flourishing, and its condition will ultimately be prosperous.[24]

The birth pangs of the colony would be intense for some time, but Chris Penfold's enthusiasm for wine and its benefits for health were shared by the many budding vignerons among its first colonists.

John Barton Hack,[25] a banker's son from Chichester, had built up a successful leather business in England, but because of an illness affecting his lungs he was told to seek a warmer climate. With his wife, six children and younger brother, he took to farming in Adelaide, arriving in February 1837; soon he was serving on the committee that was naming the streets.

Hack planted vines at his home, Chichester Gardens, between Melbourne and Stanley streets in North Adelaide, and later bought a property of some 1600 hectares that he called 'Echunga

Springs'. This was at Mount Barker in the Adelaide Hills, and he planted more wine grapes there.

George Stevenson, editor of *The South Australian Gazette and Colonial Register*, grew grapes in his 1.6-hectare garden at Melbourne Cottage, between Melbourne and Finniss streets. The first locally produced issue of his newspaper was printed in the tent of publisher Robert Thomas, and soon after the editorial office was upgraded to a mud hut.

Progress was rapid in the colony. In a speech on horticulture at Adelaide's Mechanics' Institute in 1840, Stevenson predicted that the grapevine would 'flourish abundantly' in South Australia in coming years:

> I am glad to say that there are at present upwards of sixty fine varieties growing in the colony. Among them I may enumerate as the sorts which appear to be the most flourishing – Black Hamburgh, Black Cluster, Damascus,

John Barton Hack planted vines at his farm at Echunga Springs at Mount Barker in the Adelaide Hills. *From a sketch by Col. Gawler [picture] / drawn on stone and printed by J. Hitchen, PIC Drawer 1837 #U1228 NK254, State Library of South Australia.*

Tokay, Chasselas (two varieties), White, Sweet-water, White Muscat, Verdelho or the Madeira grape, Muscadine (black and common), besides a number of others, evidently of different sorts, more recently obtained from Sydney and the Cape, the varieties of which will not be correctly ascertained till they bear fruit. Looking at the peculiar adaptation of our climate, and considering that the soil between Adelaide and the mountains, especially on the sides of the numerous gently rising slopes so admirably fitted for the purpose, is a moderately light loam with a sub-soil of decomposed limestone, I cannot doubt that the grape will, at no distant period, become one of the staples of South Australia, and that another season will witness the formation of many vineyards in this district.[26]

Stevenson's head gardener, George McEwin, sourced many grapevines from the vineyards of James Busby and William Macarthur in New South Wales, and he later wrote South Australia's first text on grape-growing and winemaking, *The South Australian Vigneron and Gardener's Manual*.[27]

At seaside Glenelg, Richard Hamilton,[28] a tailor from Dover, in Kent, bought thirty-two hectares and settled there with his wife and seven children. By 1840 his 'Ewell Farm' included a two-hectare vineyard planted with vine cuttings from the Cape of Good Hope.

And at Moore Farm at Fulham, now a western suburb of Adelaide, Abraham Davis,[29] a publisher of books and religious tracts back in London, planted a small vineyard among his fifty hectares of wheat, barley, oats, potatoes and fruit trees.

In October 1840 a meeting chaired by Charles Sturt was held to form an Association for the Introduction of Vines to South Australia.[30] It attracted thirty subscribers, including Sturt and the new governor, George Gawler, which funded the purchase of a shipload of cuttings from South Africa.[31]

In May 1841, the association's secretary, Henry Watson, a North Adelaide chemist, sent an order to the South African office of the London trading company Borradaile & Co. Writing from his home, 'Vine Cottage', in Adelaide's Pennington Street, Watson advised the association that the cuttings would likely reach Adelaide in about two months:

> I would earnestly impress upon the subscribers the importance of preparing the ground for their reception. The Vineyard should be well trenched, two spades deep, and well manured. If this be thought too expensive to be undertaken at once, it should be done in lines six feet apart, the cuttings planted in these lines, and the intervals trenched at leisure. If neither of these projects be adopted, at least let a piece of ground be prepared large enough to hold the cuttings, let them strike root there, to be transplanted next season. By this last mode a year is lost. Should these cuttings be allowed to perish for want of preparation it would be a public calamity.[32]

The cuttings took longer than expected to arrive, but on 21 October 1841 the barque *Elizabeth Moore* sailed into Adelaide. It was late in the planting season – but better late than never.[33]

There were 57,200 cuttings, of which 30,000 were madeira,[34] but only about two-thirds of the cuttings arrived alive.[35]

MARY AND CHRIS PENFOLD hoped for children, though perhaps not as many as the thirteen who grew up at the vicarage in Steyning. But for a long time they remained childless.

Still, the young Penfolds of Brighton made the most of their life together in one of the most picturesque and desirable neighbourhoods in Britain. Mary was married to an eternal optimist, a charming and convincing dreamer, and Brighton was just the place to be perpetually cheerful.

Two years after Mary and Chris Penfold settled there, Brighton turned on a grand ball to commemorate the wedding of Queen Victoria, and – despite opposition from anti-monarchy political groups – a grand time was had by all. A new rail line was opened between Brighton and Shoreham, and the Earl of Chichester chaired a meeting of the auxiliary of the Society for the Extinction of the Slave Trade and for the Civilisation of Africa. The opera singer Adelaide Kemble performed at the Old Ship pub. The Queen and her husband, Prince Albert, visited the Chain Pier, and Albert had a hit at the Brighton Tennis Court. At Brighton's Royal cricket grounds, there was a benefit match for the celebrated wicketkeeper Thomas Box, with an All-England team beating Sussex.

The bracing sea air at Brighton was almost as powerful a tonic as red wine, but Chris remained enthusiastic about the idea of trying their luck in Australia. He kept on about the possibilities there, not just for them but for future generations of the Penfolds. Chris was making a comfortable living as a surgeon in Brighton, but he spent money as fast as he made it. Like so many of the Penfolds before him, he was often broke and in need of financial assistance. If he were ever to realise his dream of owning a large property with a vineyard and fields of crops, it would be after emigration. And with pastureland so fertile and no convicts on the roads, South Australia sounded like an idyll.

But there were many storms and detours on the way from Brighton to Adelaide. Mary's father-in-law, Reverend John Penfold, the vicar of Steyning for almost half a century, died in 1840. As he had left no last will and testament, he instead bequeathed to his heirs a financial war that would last for years. As Chris saw it, getting away from the internecine bitterness couldn't hurt. He was growing ever more determined to chase his dreams on the far side of the world.

But in 1843 he had to park his ambitions – for a very good reason. After eight years of marriage, Mary Penfold discovered that she was finally pregnant.

Chapter 11

AS MARY BECAME FULL and round with her first child, Chris spared no expense to make her as comfortable as possible. He had gone into a partnership with fellow Brighton surgeon W.S. Watson,[1] but was spending more than he was earning before he and Mary moved from Western Road into a bigger house called 'Norfolk Lodge', on Norfolk Square, near the home Harriet Timbrell shared with her daughter, Ellen.[2]

The huge Norfolk Lodge had been fitted up as a wealthy army officer's residence and the landlord claimed no expense had been spared. Outside there was a coach house, a three-stall horse stable and a large loft. On the ground floor there was a portico entrance, two parlours and a small library. A few steps up to the first landing there were two good bed chambers and a water closet with an indoor toilet. On the first floor there was a drawing room and back bed chambers, and on the second floor were two more 'excellent bed chambers'.[3]

Norfolk Lodge had space for domestic servants, with a housekeeper's room, a butler's pantry, a good size kitchen, a scullery, a knife house, and vaulted wine and coal cellars.[4] Mary and Chris hired Ellen Timbrell, not as a maid so much as a personal assistant. She would be kept very busy, as the Penfold family was about to grow.[5]

After eight years of trying to have a baby, Mary Penfold gave birth to a daughter at Norfolk Lodge on Sunday, 13 August 1843. Dr Christopher Penfold helped deliver his new daughter.

The delighted, beaming parents named their pride and joy Mary Georgina Anne Penfold, though she would be known as Georgina throughout her life.

Publicly, Mary's role in Georgina's arrival was all but ignored as, following the custom of the time, her local newspaper, *The Brighton Gazette*, referred to the mother who had endured nine months of pregnancy and the pain of labour merely as 'the lady of C.R. Penfold Esq.'.[6] A lack of recognition for her efforts was something Mary Penfold would become used to during her lifetime.

But the absence of public acknowledgement did not diminish Mary's euphoria at the miracle she and Chris had created, even though Dr Penfold's eternal optimism and carefree spending was starting to bury the young family in debt.

All around Brighton it was a joyful summer of sunshine and heat. When Georgina was just six days old, Brighton's thermometers registered the temperature as 82 degrees Fahrenheit (28 degrees Celsius) in the shade, and 112°F (44°C) in the sunshine.

The Brighton Races had just been held and steam packets were now making daily crossings between Brighton and France. Georgina was barely a month old when Queen Victoria, along with the Prince of Wales – the toddler who would become King Edward VII – the three-year-old Princess Royal, Victoria, and the baby Princess Alice arrived in Brighton under the care of the royal governess, the Dowager Lady Lyttleton.

Ellen Timbrell became Mary's constant companion, helping her care for little Georgina. Ellen was twenty-six, the same age as Mary, and she was the daughter and granddaughter of captains commanding vessels for the British East India Company. Her grandfather, Thomas Timbrell, knew Captain James Cook well. He offered Cook assistance at Table Bay, off Cape Town, during the great mariner's final voyage, when Cook led an expedition of two ships looking for a North-West Passage, an ice-free sea route through the Arctic that would link the Atlantic and Pacific oceans. At the time, Timbrell was commanding the 499-ton merchant vessel *Hampshire* on a voyage returning from Bombay. On 6 November 1776 Cook wrote in his journal:

> [T]he *Hampshire* India ship sailed for England. In her I sent home an invalid, whom Captain [Timbrell] was so obliging as to receive on board. I was afterwards sorry that I had not availed myself of this opportunity to part with two or three more of my crew, who were troubled with different complaints; but, at this time, there was some hope of their health being re-established.[7]

Cook was killed three years later in Hawaii, and Ellen's grandfather died soon after, while returning from a council of East India Company skippers in Calcutta. On the Atlantic island of Saint Helena, where his ship, the *True-Briton*, anchored to take on supplies, Timbrell went sightseeing on an especially hot day. After climbing to a high point to take in the ocean view, he suddenly expired, and 'although every means was taken to recover him to life, they proved ineffectual'.[8]

Ellen's father, James Timbrell, commanded his brother Andrew's ships – the *Lord Hawkesbury*, the *Taunton Castle* and the *Exeter* – on voyages to India and China, and was being considered as a future director of the East India Company when Ellen was born, the youngest of his three daughters. Ellen arrived into the world in October 1816, three weeks before Mary Penfold's birth. Hers was a comfortable, affluent home in leafy Hampstead, but Ellen was only five months old when her father died. The family finances would never recover.

Ellen's older sister, Elizabeth Timbrell,[9] married a captain of the 12th Royal Lancers[10] in Brighton in 1841, and Ellen's work with the Penfolds became an enjoyable job with good friends. Tom and Elizabeth Holt worried about her becoming part of the young Penfold family, though. To them, Ellen was not particularly hardworking and treated her job more as a paid friend than an employee.[11]

For her part, Ellen wondered what opportunities might present themselves for her in the far-off land of South Australia, of which Mary and Chris spoke so often.

NOT EVERY COLONIST leaving Britain was sold on South Australia. There had been much fanfare and publicity about the fertility of the soil and the warmth of the sun around Adelaide, but reports about the infant colony were mixed. Landholders trumpeted the potential of a convict-free settlement to entice more workers from England. But they usually had a financial interest; many wanted to sell or lease their land, or needed people to work on it.[12]

The initial landing site, at Port Adelaide, was situated on a low bank of sandhills at the southern end of what is today known as 'Old Port Reach' on the Port River.[13] The short sail up the river was picturesque, with both sides thickly lined with mangrove trees and shrubs, but the tidal water could be so shallow that vessels from England generally cast anchor a mile or two offshore. Some stayed out in St Vincent Gulf because they were too heavy to cross the sandbars.[14]

One new arrival on the barque *Alice Brooks* wrote that Port Adelaide was a 'nasty place':

> [A]ll goods are landed by lighters or boats, and have to be lifted out by sheer strength. There is not a single crane to hoist them up, as the land is low. If the goods be not delivered above high water mark, they will be floating by next tide. Such was the case this morning. The wharf officers appear to be careless for I see by yesterday's paper, a complaint of dogs and pigs unmolestedly eating away at some sugar, lying on the wharf in bags …[15]

The South Australian Register printed the observations of another disgruntled visitor, who wrote of his arrival by ship to the shallow entrance of the port and his vessel striking the sand and mud of the Port Adelaide bar as it ran aground:[16]

> The shore is an uninhabitable swamp and the few people who are living in the wigwams at Port Adelaide are too busily engaged in landing boards and rolling up casks, to

> take any notice of a party of ladies and gentlemen up to their knees in mud trying to reach the shore ... Arrived on the dry land – the party wash the mud off their legs, and put on their shoes and stockings, then carrying their trunks as well as they can ... they all walk up the side of a little canal, as it is called, which brings them to the only spot of land at the creek free from inundations, which is called the sand hill, where one or two grog shops, made of branches of trees, are seen, a few native blacks stark naked, and a large iron store painted white belonging to the Commissioners. This is Port Adelaide! Port Misery would be a better name; for nothing in any other part of the world can surpass it in everything that is wretched and inconvenient.[17]

Packages of goods and 'heaps of merchandise' lay about in every direction, as if they had cost nothing.

> Stacks of what were once beautiful London bricks crumbling away like gingerbread, and evidently, at each returning tide, half covered with the flood; trusses of hay, now rotten ... iron ploughs and rusty harrows – cases of door frames and windows that had once been glazed – heaps of the best slates half tumbling down – winnowing machines broken to pieces – blocks of Roman cement now hard as stone ... Sydney cedar and laths, and shingles from Van Diemen's Land in every direction – whilst, on the high ground, are to be seen pigs eating through the flour sacks and kegs of raisins ...[18]

Mary Thomas,[19] a 53-year-old poet and the wife of the *Register* newspaper's publisher, Robert Thomas, was just one new Australian who had a hard time adjusting to life thousands of miles from her family home in Southampton. She had arrived at Holdfast Bay, off Adelaide, in November 1836 and was present when Governor Hindmarsh's proclamation was read on 28 December.

In what could have been a warning to Mary Penfold as well, she had written to her younger brother George in March 1840 to say that she had not altered her opinion 'respecting this Country, for I dislike it more than ever, or at least the Climate':

> [W]e have had a very hot Summer the Thermometer frequently at 90 or 100 in the House and even more and is now while I am writing upwards of 80 [26.7 degrees Celsius] at 8 o'Clock in the Evening ... our Cottage contains two sitting Rooms, three Bed Rooms and a Kitchen, on the ground floor, with two Attics above, and is altogether very neatly fitted up, quite in the english stile [sic], and indeed is the envy of almost every body who has seen it, but for my part <u>I would exchange it for a Cow pen</u> in England, admitting I could have those comforts which are incompatible with this Country, or at least be free from the Annoyances which this Climate subjects us to ... If I were now in England with the experiences I have had and recollecting the dangers and difficulties I have undergone nothing would induce me to return to South Australia.[20]

Mrs Thomas made her complaints despite her husband's newspaper declaring that negative remarks about South Australia's potential were 'the false, distorted, garbled, and in some cases ... the manufactured statements of ignorant emigrants published by interested and injudicious parties at home', and that his newspaper was 'a journal of safe reference to all persons who may be on the eve of seeking in this distant land that comfort and independence which they may toil for in vain in England or elsewhere'.[21]

Negative press had its impact, though, and the flood of migrants encouraged by the promoters of South Australian land sales slowed to a trickle. By the early 1840s, the low immigration rate and the resultant lack of demand for land had pushed the infant colony to the brink of bankruptcy.[22] Merchants, retailers and land speculators were forced to offload assets cheaply, including a huge amount of property, to honour their debts.[23]

CHRIS PENFOLD STILL had his heart set on South Australia, even if some of his circle looked elsewhere.

Henry Lindeman, his former classmate at Barts, had already made his move. After graduating as a member of the Royal College of Physicians, Dr Lindeman spent time practising medicine in Southampton and toured through vineyards in France and Germany. He and his new wife, Harriet, had sailed for New South Wales in 1840 aboard the barque *Theresa*, with Lindeman acting as the ship's surgeon. His growing fascination with wine was enhanced with stops at Madeira and Cape Town.

When they reached New South Wales, the Lindemans settled in the remote village of Gresford, 200 kilometres north of Sydney, in the Hunter Valley. Two years later Lindeman bought 330 hectares from the owner of the 'Trevallyn' station, George Townshend, who had been forced to sell due to the drought and depression.[24] Townsend was a friend of the Hunter Valley vintner George Wyndham. Lindeman called his estate 'Cawarra', and in the rich soils of the Paterson River flats he planted riesling, verdelho and shiraz vines and set about building a cottage, a winery and a cellar in which to age his wines until they were ready for release.[25] He eventually had sixteen hectares under vines,[26] and grew a large family too, with five sons and five daughters.

A century and a half after going their separate ways, the names Penfold and Lindeman were reunited in Australia in a business takeover.[27]

Mary's parents, Tom and Elizabeth Holt, became increasingly worried about losing their daughter and baby granddaughter after seeing their eldest child swallowed by the same great siren call of America that had taken Alfred. Mary's eldest brother, George William Astor Holt, had worked in the family's piano-making business following his grandfather's death,[28] but in 1842 he followed Alfred to New York,[29] where he lived to the age of seventy-nine.[30] George's family money did not follow him, though, and he abandoned the music business to become a daguerreotypist, using a pioneering photographic technique invented by Louis Daguerre.

George experimented with other photographic methods throughout his life, but while he made a reputation as a skilled photographer, he did not enjoy the financial success of other Astors or Holts – or of his little sister Mary Penfold, who was about to risk everything she held dear in the biggest challenge of her life.

Chapter 12

MARY'S PARENTS WERE heartbroken and in tears when she broke the news to them that she, Chris and Georgina would be sailing for South Australia in February 1844. Chris could not be dissuaded in his determination to start a new life for his family on the other side of the world.

Tom and Elizabeth Holt had hoped and prayed that something would change the mind of their flighty son-in-law, but nothing could. They told Mary that, to them, her smile was sunshine. With her in their lives, they were rich; without her, they were poor. No matter what else could be taken from their lives, nothing was more precious to them than Mary and little Georgina.[1]

By 1844 Chris had run up heavy debts in Brighton, and his parlous financial situation had damaged the young couple's reputation.[2] He now poured what money he had left into moving his family to South Australia. Chris's mother, Charlotte Penfold, had died in October 1843, bringing an end to her whimsical notes, favourite recipes, medicinal tips and the sketches that decorated her fascinating journal. Both his parents were gone now, and what remained of his family were skirmishing over money. He would be glad to leave all that behind.

Chris's brother, Tom Penfold, feuded with just about all his siblings except his brother James, the solicitor.[3] He remained on the warpath with his brothers and sisters over his father's will, but Chris and Mary were desperately short of cash. Chris had to settle some debts and pay a deposit to the Colonial Land and Emigration

Commission ahead of the planned move to Adelaide.[4] He was so determined that a fresh start would be a lifesaver for them that Tom agreed to lend him £200.

Tom made his younger brother sign a contract for the loan, which was witnessed by a Brighton solicitor, George Dempster, and one of the Holt family's friends, Ann Guillod,[5] who was also migrating to South Australia. Chris would later dispute the terms of the arrangement, leading to even more friction within the family.[6]

Chris dissolved his partnership with Dr W.S. Watson,[7] then he and Mary bought four cabin berths on a 350-tonne barque named the *Taglioni*, on which they planned to sail to Port Adelaide with Georgina and Ellen Timbrell. The ship was just thirty metres long and a mere eight metres wide.[8] It was tiny in comparison with the massive East Indiaman trading ships that Ellen's father and grandfather had commanded.

Mary was utterly torn over the choice between her old life and the new. Both her brothers had started afresh in New York, and now Mary was about to deprive Elizabeth and Tom Holt of their 'idolised' daughter and granddaughter, whose company they were so looking forward to sharing in their twilight years.

Although Chris was mired in debt, he remained an optimist. He told Mary and her parents that all would be well when they reached Adelaide. Still, Elizabeth fretted that Christopher was taking Mary and the little child to their doom.[9]

Tom and Elizabeth continued to plead with Mary to change her husband's mind, but Chris would listen to no one but the agent for the Colonial Land and Emigration Commission,[10] who was promising vast tracts of fertile land and the prospect of wealth beyond what Chris could make in England.

Mary began packing up the family's belongings for the 20,000-kilometre voyage to what was then the end of the Earth. Her parents had given her expensive wedding presents: the Penfolds owned Wedgwood and Sèvres porcelain, handsome mahogany furniture and a pianoforte made by her grandfather George Astor's company.[11]

Even though they had no real experience as vignerons, Chris knew wines, and with an eye to building his own vineyard for his medical practice, he sourced vine cuttings from the Rhône region[12] of southern France and from Portugal.[13] Most of the vines were grenache.[14] Chris believed the cuttings could help the Penfolds establish themselves in a distant land far from the comforts of home and that they could build something great and long-lasting.

He and Mary dipped the roots of the vines in wax and covered them with canvas to prevent them from drying out on the journey to their new home, which would take at least four months.[15]

MARY'S EXCITEMENT ABOUT the voyage mixed with the fears and heartbreak she felt at leaving her parents and all that she had grown close to in England.

The *Taglioni* was a sturdy vessel built four years earlier at Ramsey, on the Isle of Wight. It was under the command of its Scottish skipper and owner, William Black,[16] and moved beautifully through the water – as it should, having been named in honour of Marie Taglioni, the Swedish-born ballet star who was gracing Her Majesty's Theatre in London at the time.

But no matter the reputation of the ship, sailing the world's vast oceans for months was a hazardous endeavour, especially for a baby just six months old. How would Mary care for a baby at the breast with the many distresses she knew an ocean voyage in a small ship would cause? How would she protect or even comfort Georgina in storms if the *Taglioni* was being hurled from side to side by huge waves? What would happen if the ship struck trouble? What would happen if it started leaking hundreds of miles from shore?

Mary knew that many emigrants who sailed for Australia never made it there – and that of those who did, few returned to their old country.

With that in mind, Mary was adamant that if anything happened to Georgina, the child would be known to God. So, six days before the *Taglioni* was due to sail from the ominously named Kent port of Gravesend, Mary Georgina Anne Penfold was baptised at the Holt family's church, St Botolph-without-Bishopsgate, in the heart of London on 7 February 1844.[17] The same day, Mary and Chris deposited £100 with the Colonial Land and Emigration Commission to buy, sight unseen, some fertile land being offered for sale just outside Adelaide.[18]

MARY'S FATHER WAS SO stressed that he began to suffer heart palpations. In the Holts' home at Edmonton, in London's north, he told Mary that he feared he would never see her or the precious baby again. Mary was just twenty-seven, and her parents had hoped to have her in their lives for many more years than that.

Tom and Elizabeth pleaded again with Chris and Mary to reconsider, but Chris – as always – was carefree and confident, just as he was with money. He assured Mary's parents that everything would work out well in the end.

On 10 February,[19] Captain Black left the port of Deal, in Kent, and sailed the *Taglioni* upstream in the Thames to load cargo and passengers for the long voyage south, which was set to depart Gravesend on 13 February.[20] Despite Christopher's assurances that Tom and Elizabeth would see Mary again soon, the young couple were not preparing to return to England in a hurry. Dockworkers loaded an immense cargo for the young family: twenty-two cases, fifteen casks, four bundles, two packages, two crates, a keg and a tub.[21]

It was a tearful and anguished goodbye between father, daughter and granddaughter. As Mary, Chris and Georgina left the house, Tom called pathetic goodbyes after them from his sick bed and prayed that there might somehow be a postponement, or even that Chris might have a care for the distress his decision was causing. Later, as he tried to rest in his darkened room, Tom Holt waited in anxious expectation for news that Chris had changed his mind.[22]

Finally the day of departure arrived. Tom Holt's heart was behaving so wickedly that Elizabeth insisted he should not leave his sick bed to see Mary off at the docks, and even in his sickened condition he remonstrated with his wife. Tom said he would ride down to Gravesend and take Mary and Georgina home by force if he had too. To hell with what Christopher Rawson Penfold wanted![23]

Instead, Elizabeth travelled in a carriage the fifty kilometres to Gravesend. All the way she was ashen-faced and desolate. When she reached the docks, the *Taglioni* was moored in the Thames: it looked small and frail, helpless to challenge the roaring seas that waited ahead.

MARY WAS STRUCK BY the busyness of the scene around the *Taglioni* as dockworkers loaded cargo and helped passengers on board. Including the Penfold party of four, there were eleven voyagers travelling as cabin passengers in the more luxurious part of the ship. Thirty-four other passengers made their way below deck, where they would travel in the claustrophobic confines of steerage. They included John and Mary Ann Frost and their nine children.[24]

Mary's fellow cabin passengers included the shipping agents John Newman and George 'Captain' Hall, who had been prominent in bringing migrants to Adelaide. Captain Hall was carrying home his patented salting machine, a device of his own design, with which he planned to establish a salt-curing business in the beef market.[25]

Two other cabin passengers were Robert Norman, another Brighton medical man, who listed his profession as surgeon–dentist, and George Heseltine, a businessman looking for new opportunities in Adelaide. Both would become pioneers of the photographic trade in South Australia.[26]

The *Taglioni* was also carrying the latest British newspapers to South Australia – this was the quickest way colonists could keep abreast of happenings on the other side of the globe. Captain Black loaded into his cabin multiple reports of an earthquake hitting the English Channel island of Guernsey: 'persons out of doors felt the earth heave under them, in some cases so violently as to oblige them to lay hold of the nearest object for support …

the vane of the town church was violently agitated, and the bell struck twice'.[27]

With such catastrophe in the news, Mary and her mother prayed for divine protection for the voyage ahead. Workmen, rugged up against the teeth-rattling wind coming off the Thames, loaded large bales and crates of cargo for Adelaide merchants. The new stores along Hindley and High streets[28] were about to be flooded with everything from cross-cut saws, mattocks and nails to saucepans, kettles, augers, taps, corkscrews, iron pots, pitsaws, boilers, metal spoons, tacks and teapots, moleskin and cloth trousers, ladies' gloves, lace cuffs and collars, ball dresses and crepe shawls.[29]

The *Taglioni* was also carrying twelve purebred merino rams – worth an astonishing £18 each – to nourish South Australia's emerging wool industry, which was being promoted by the brothers John and Alfred Hallett.[30]

Finally, Captain Black had been entrusted with delivering the commission from Britain's Board of Ordnance for South Australia's surveyor-general, Charles Sturt, to finance and mount a three-year expedition into the interior,[31] looking for an inland sea.

THE SKIES OVER GRAVESEND were leaden, and there were oceans of tears as Mary said goodbye to her mother for what she suspected in her heart would likely be the last time.

'Please, please, Mary,' Elizabeth begged, her eyes wide and yearning, 'promise me you'll come home if things go wrong out there and it's not what you want.'[32]

'Yes, yes, mother,' Mary gushed, 'we will see you again no matter what. I promise.'

Elizabeth then gave Christopher a hard look of disappointment, and grabbed him by the arm. 'Christopher,' she demanded, 'promise me you will protect my child and Georgina.'

'I will, I will,' he stammered.[33]

Mary's mother wasn't entirely convinced. She gave a final farewell hug to Georgina as though it was the last time she would gaze into the innocent eyes of that unsuspecting babe, given the breadth of the oceans and the growing infirmity she and Tom Holt were feeling. Had they been younger, perhaps they might have sailed with the Penfolds to see out their days in their daughter's care, but Tom's health meant that was out of the question.

Then, finally, as the wind whipped the river water all around the little ship, Mary gave Elizabeth a forlorn wave and a half-smile of regret as Captain Black steered the *Taglioni* through the choppy waves of the Thames and towards the English Channel. In the funereal air, Elizabeth Holt watched the ship move slowly down the river and disappear.

Even before the *Taglioni* reached the channel, Mary and Georgina were terrified. Night fell and the ship was enveloped by rolling, rocking winds that tossed the vessel around as though it were weightless. Mary wrote a letter to her mother and father telling them not to worry, and she had the crew deliver it to the river pilot who was guiding the *Taglioni* to the open waters.[34] Mary promised her parents that God would protect them all and that she would write home again as soon as they reached their first port.

Heavy waves thumped against the ship's wooden hull like great mallets, and all about the Penfold cabin furniture and their possessions – including the wax-sealed vine cuttings from France and Portugal – were hurled about like marbles. Mary held Georgina close and tried to calm her screams.

When Elizabeth Holt returned to her husband in Edmonton, he had somehow convinced himself that, at the last moment, Mary would pull out of the voyage on that 'horrid vessel', as he called it.[35] So when Elizabeth broke the news that they were gone for good, Tom's 'anguish of mind' was so extreme, his grief so palpable, that Elizabeth could not accurately describe it.[36] She worried he would die of a broken heart.

It was not 'a selfish sorrow', Elizabeth explained later. Mary's father was missing his daughter, but most of his sorrow was because he 'deplored the hardship' Mary and little Georgina would endure on that little ship.

Five days later, the wind around Edmonton blew in gales. Tom and Elizabeth spent the next few days and nights saying constant prayers for the safety of the ship, unsure how their precious child and grandchild were faring out on the ocean. There was no way of knowing their condition.

Elizabeth was so distressed that even though she felt she was 'unfit to be seen out', she put on a thick veil and went to her local chapel to ask for the 'united prayers of the congregation and the pastor' and to beg for the protection of 'Him who could alone stay the winds and waves'.[37]

But the foul weather was unremitting, unrelenting. For almost three weeks Captain Black found the English Channel impenetrable. He tried to keep an even keel as the wind worked hard to push the *Taglioni* onto its side.[38] Then, once the ship was clear of the channel, the notorious storms of the Bay of Biscay seemed intent on tearing its three masts from their fastenings. As the vessel was blown across the raging whitecaps, one of the crewmen fell overboard and drowned.[39] A deathly pall fell over the rest of the ship.

As Georgina wailed at the horror of her new watery surrounds, there were angry skies above, surging waves below and terror all about. Mary wondered if her little family would live to see the promised land of South Australia.

Chapter 13

AFTER 127 DAYS AT SEA, many of them spent in fear for the lives of her family and companions in the cramped cabin quarters of their ship, Mary finally reached the safe harbour of Port Adelaide[1] on Tuesday, 18 June 1844.[2] The journey of 20,000 kilometres on a small sailing vessel had been an ordeal, as Captain Black steered the *Taglioni* across the Atlantic, Indian and Southern oceans. Seasickness and terror were Mary's constant companions.[3]

Confined for much of the time to their close quarters even in the more expensive realms of cabin class, Mary had months to ruminate on the life and loved ones left behind and the uncertainty ahead for her family. Finally, as the ship sailed along the spectacular limestone coast of South Australia, a sense of calm resolve came over Mary. More than ever, she felt a determination to make the most of her new circumstances.

The *Taglioni*'s arrival was greeted with joy by many of the more than 17,000 settlers who called South Australia home, as it was the first ship to arrive at Port Adelaide from London in months, bringing news and mail from loved ones.[4] But while the arrival of the ship had Adelaide in a festive mood, Mary initially found her new home underwhelming, to say the least. Port Adelaide was living up to its 'Port Misery' description. Mary spent her first hours there swatting away ravenous mosquitoes from Georgina's pale and delicate skin, but at least the landing place once derided by the colony's second governor, George Gawler, as 'inconvenient, disreputable, and injurious to the colony' now had a wharf.[5]

At a civic ceremony in 1840, with 'wines in every variety in profusion'[6] and toasts to the young Queen Victoria, Queen Adelaide's niece, Gawler had declared open a wooden pier some 102 metres long, built in water that was 4.6 metres deep at low tide.[7] Gawler described the wharf as 'sufficiently commodious for all [of South Australia's] present commercial wants, and capable of extension commensurate with the future demands of the colony'.[8] One of the workmen who constructed the pier was a Bavarian farmer named Johann Gramp,[9] who, like the young Penfolds, had a great interest in winemaking.

The opening of the pier meant that Mary and other ladies on the *Taglioni* could walk to shore along the wooden pier, rather than be carried through the mangrove mud 'slung like sacks of potatoes over the shoulders of burly sailors', which had been standard for female arrivals at the colony before then.[10]

Some of the Penfolds' luggage had been damaged, but eventually the beautiful piano and the crockery was carried ashore. The Penfold party of four boarded a carriage and made their way to their Adelaide lodgings, fifteen kilometres to the south-east. While the parklands surrounding the infant city had been designed as verdant areas to beautify the growing settlement, Mary was startled to see that they were little more than desolate paddocks. Towering trees had been cut down and these areas set aside for the beauty and health of the capital were now unprotected by their original forests. They were at the mercy of ferocious dust storms in summer, and likely to be muddy quagmires after winter rains.[11]

Adelaide was growing fast. Mary learnt that two more ships, the *John Hayes* and the *Yare*, would soon be arriving. And the American liner *George Washington* had been chartered at Bremen and was bound for South Australia, carrying 200 Germans who wanted to enjoy a religious liberty denied them in their own land.[12] Many were skilled winemakers.

There was already a strong German presence in the colony, thanks to the sponsorship of George Fife Angas, the chairman of the South Australian Company, a collection of wealthy British merchants tasked with developing this new territory. Angas, who had been a member of the original South Australian Association which had lobbied the British government to form their new colony, knew that bringing Germans to the colony would ensure a supply of skilled farmers and keep the price of labour under control. In all, 596 Germans escaping sanctions on their Old Lutheran customs left their country on four ships at the end of 1838. Led by Pastor August Kavel, they established communities at Klemzig, near Port Adelaide, at Hahndorf, in the Adelaide Hills, and at Glen Osmond, near Makgill.

THE INDIGENOUS KAURNA PEOPLE, known as the 'Adelaide tribe' by the early settlers, camped regularly along the banks of the River Torrens, hunting, fishing and digging for the tubers and roots and the yam daisy herb that were staples in their diet. But their culture was being swamped by mass immigration.

For the most part, by the time the Penfolds arrived in Adelaide the relationship between the Europeans and the Kaurna was peaceful, but in preceding years there had been bitter skirmishes between settlers and the First People of South Australia. The British government had given the colony's governors – Hindmarsh, Gawler and then George Grey – specific instructions to extend the full protection of British justice to the Indigenous groups in South Australia, including their property. But violence had erupted nevertheless.

Tensions escalated after about twenty-five survivors from the small Irish vessel *Maria* were shipwrecked off Cape Jaffa in June 1840 and tried to walk 300 kilometres north to Adelaide. They were all hacked to death, and the massacre was blamed on men from the Milmenrura Indigenous people. Retribution by the settlers was swift. At least five Indigenous men – but probably more – were shot dead, and many more wounded as a posse of Europeans hunted the perpetrators. In violation of the laws giving Indigenous people equal rights under British law, two Milmenrura men accused of having a role in the massacre were hanged without trial, after they were handed over to the posse of colonists by their own people.[13]

In Adelaide, the Kaurna were helpless against the encroaching tide of colonial settlement. They had managed their lands carefully for generations, and were especially skilled in the careful use of fire to rejuvenate open stretches of country for hunting and to control the thick undergrowth that might otherwise fuel wildfires.

But their use of fire to burn scrub in the Adelaide Hills – as a way of attracting emus and kangaroos to the new grass – led to fatal conflicts with colonists, who accused them of deliberately burning fences. The Europeans did not initially understand the importance of fire in land management. Nor did they understand the need to tread lightly on the land, conserving food and plant resources; this was a skill that Mary Penfold would later learn.

Two months before the Penfolds arrived, mounted police had intervened in a dispute between the Kaurna and Moorundie people in Adelaide's West Parklands, and smashed the Kaurna's weapons. Over time, the Kaurna lost much of their tribal land and cultural identity, and fell victim to European disease.[14] In their efforts to preserve the Kaurna language, though, two Lutheran missionaries, Christian Teichelmann and Clamor Schürmann, ran a school for Kaurna children in the Adelaide parklands, teaching them to read and write in their native language and recording almost 3000 Kaurna words for future generations.[15]

South Australia saw itself as the most progressive of the Australian colonies when it came to its relationships with the first inhabitants of the land. The Penfolds had arrived in South Australia just as it was about to become the first Australian colony to allow evidence from Indigenous Australians to be accepted in courts.[16]

South Australia's first judge, John Jeffcott,[17] a leading anti-slavery campaigner back in Britain, had proclaimed that 'humanity shuddered' at the treatment of Indigenous people in the convict colonies of New South Wales and Van Diemen's Land, and that he would not allow the same situation in his jurisdiction.[18] Jeffcott, who had once killed a doctor in a pistol duel in England, warned South Australians that 'any aggression upon the Natives, or any infringement on their rights, shall be visited by greater severity of punishment than would be in similar offences committed upon white men'.[19]

AS MARY'S CARRIAGE moved through the growing settlement of Adelaide, she and Chris saw a small but carefully laid out city with wide streets and terraces. The first portion of the opulent Government House on North Terrace had been completed, and next to it the first Legislative Council building. Further along was the new Adelaide Hospital.

One of the shops in Adelaide's Gawler Place was run by 26-year-old Samuel Gill,[20] a native of Somerset and the son of the Reverend Samuel Gill, a Baptist minister who had been the headmaster of a school in Plymouth. The Gills had arrived in Adelaide five years before the Penfolds, and Reverend Gill had become the postmaster in the area called Coromandel Valley. He had also opened a 'Classical and Mathematical Preparatory School' for boys aged under twelve.

The younger Samuel Gill, better known as S.T. Gill, was busy sketching and painting Adelaide life. Advertising himself as 'S.T. Gill late Draftsman and Water Color Painter to the Hubard Profile Gallery of London', he offered his services as a portrait painter to anyone in Adelaide or its surroundings desirous of 'obtaining correct likenesses of themselves, families or friends ... Correct resemblances of horses, dogs, &c., with local scenery, &c. executed to order.'[21]

Gill would become one of the most celebrated of Australia's colonial artists. As Mary arrived in Adelaide with her family, he was documenting some of the most important scenes of the town's early life. One of his early watercolours depicted two vinedressers in South Australia – a woman in a long dress and cotton bonnet, and a man with jacket and cloth cap – pruning vines growing on stakes like shrubs, a practice popular among some of the German settlers.[22]

Mary and Chris moved into temporary lodgings and prepared

to begin the life of colonial farmers, though Chris would earn extra money through his home surgery.

Adelaide, despite its promise and potential, and the enthusiasm of its civic-minded colonists, lacked the grandeur and comfort of Brighton, though it was trying hard to be an ornament to the British empire.

As Mary tended to little Georgina and her other babies – the carefully packed vine cuttings from France and Portugal – she mused over the harshness of life in this new territory, including the poisonous snakes she had been warned about: the eastern brown, the red-bellied black snake, the tiger snake. Mary heard that others might not kill with you with their venom, but they could choke you to death, so she had to be vigilant whenever she left Georgina to sleep. There were huge, sinister-looking monitor lizards called goannas in the Adelaide Hills, as big as large dogs and with enormous claws and cruel eyes. There were colourful exotic birds, of all colours of the rainbow – 'Adelaide parrots', rosellas, galahs, cockatiels and cockatoos. But they screeched instead of warbling like those gentle, more genteel creatures of the Sussex skies. South Australia would take some getting used to for Mary.

Agriculture was already proving a successful endeavour for many settlers, more and more of whom were planting vineyards. The cuttings Mary and Chris had sourced would have many neighbours.

EXACTLY ONE MONTH after they arrived, Chris and Mary bought the remaining 179 hectares of the Makgill estate from the English merchant Edmund Trimmer, who had taken over the property in June 1844 in lieu of the £1259 6s that the cash-strapped Robert Cock and William Ferguson owed him.[23]

The Adelaide Observer reported: 'Mr Penfold, who arrived in the Colony per *Taglioni*, is the fortunate purchaser of the delightfully situate and truly valuable estate of Mackgill [sic], at the sum of 1200 pounds.'[24] The property was about ten kilometres east of the city, in the shadow of the Adelaide Hills, and recent winter rains had beautified the area after a long dry spell,[25] although much of Adelaide was in flood.[26]

When the storm finally passed, the lovely blue gums and native pine contrasted gloriously with the red-brown soil being ploughed for cereal crops. Mary Penfold was not mentioned in the report of the land purchase, but the newspaper, exaggerating slightly the size of the farm, went on to say that the property:

> ... which comprises 500 acres [202 hectares] of the choicest land, 200 acres [81 hectares] of which are under crop, cost its late proprietors several thousands.[27]
>
> The site of the residence is worthy of a noble mansion. The front view embraces a great extent and diversity of scenery, and the uplands in the rear, crested by the mountain range and its woodlands, afford a most agreeable background to this highly picturesque and desirable property.[28]

For just over £2 an acre, Mary and Christopher had bought a sizable, profitable farm that was already yielding large crops of wheat, with the promise of much more to come. They did not have £1200 to pay for the property, but Chris arranged a mortgage of £1000[29] with the vendor, Edmund Trimmer,[30] and used the money Tom Penfold had loaned him to close the deal. Over time, he and Mary would sell pieces of the land and pay off the mortgage early.[31]

Five days after the newspaper report of their purchase, Christopher, Mary, Georgina and Ellen Timbrell moved into William Ferguson's wooden house on the property,[32] as a temporary home. There was a stone cottage there too, that needed work and which would become their permanent home. It certainly was a bucolic location, and far more land for their money than Mary and Chris could have bought in Britain.

But the new Penfold farm was a long way from anywhere. Indeed, some of the early colonists called Makgill 'World's End' because it was situated at the end of the Adelaide plain, at the foot of the hills.[33]

Mary and Chris Penfold had not long arrived in Adelaide when they watched Charles Sturt's Overland Expedition leaving Adelaide, on 10 August, 1844. S.T. Gill, 1844-45, State Library of South Australia Accession number 0.1128

With the help of Ellen Timbrell, Mary and Christopher were still unpacking their belongings at Makgill two days after moving into their wooden house when S.T. Gill took his pencils and watercolours and began documenting Charles Sturt's overland expedition, which left Adelaide in a grand procession on 10 August 1844, one of the most significant days in South Australia's colonial history.[34]

Adelaide was ecstatic, and the Penfolds joined a great crowd of cheering well-wishers as Sturt first hosted a ceremonial breakfast with Governor Grey at a warehouse in Grenfell Street, and then led the 'procession of upwards of 100 horsemen' from the corner of King William and Currie streets, with thirty-two bullocks, 200 sheep, five bullock drays, a light cart and a boat behind.[35]

A long line of settlers followed Sturt and a team of sixteen colonists, which included the expedition's draughtsman, John McDouall Stuart, as they passed along King William Street to the City Bridge, through North Adelaide, and along the North Road as far as the Dry Creek, fifteen kilometres north of the city. The creek, though, was no longer dry. Heavy downpours meant that it flowed strongly, in honour, it seemed, of the grand occasion. There the cavalcade halted, and Captain Sturt rode off to the cheers of the adoring colonists with the slow-moving bullock drays rolling on behind him.

But the intrepid explorer had faked his own departure. After leading the grand procession out of town, Sturt returned to his Adelaide home for a few days to tidy up some personal affairs, before riding off again to catch the rest of the expedition, which included two Indigenous guides.[36]

MARY WROTE HOME to her parents to tell them of the family's safe arrival, but it would be four months before the letter eased the anxiety in the Holts' Edmonton home as it traversed the seas on the return journey to Britain. Mary had kept Tom and Elizabeth abreast of the progress of the voyage and had written an eleven-page epistle about her travels and travails as soon as the *Taglioni* reached the calmer waters of the Atlantic.[37]

But Tom and Elizabeth were beside themselves with worry, wondering about their young family's new life in Adelaide. Two weeks before the *Taglioni* arrived at Port Adelaide, Elizabeth wrote to Mary, hoping that her daughter was still alive and that the letter would somehow reach her, addressing it simply to 'Mrs Penfold, Adelaide, South Australia'.[38]

'Yes, my beloved child,' Elizabeth wrote, 'you have been the subject of many prayers and I trust they have been answered by sparing your valued life with that of your sweet babe & husband. We pray you are in Australia.'[39]

Elizabeth and Tom thought constantly of that 'darling creature' Georgina, and of the big, beautiful eyes that had followed Tom wherever he went. Elizabeth told Mary that she was still disgusted by Christopher's determination to ignore their advice and leave England. She was angry that he refused to listen to them, heeding only the hard sell of the migration agent.[40] Elizabeth feared that Mary's health might have suffered before she reached the end of the voyage, but she told her daughter to stay strong and ensure her family did the same.

Christopher's brother, Tom Penfold, was living in Notting Hill, in London, and was making noises about wanting repayment from Chris for the loan he'd given him, but Elizabeth had heard nothing yet from the couple's Brighton solicitor, George Dempster.[41] Tom Penfold's wife, Emma, who loved Mary, was pregnant and had been too ill to visit the Holts in Edmonton. Elizabeth believed Emma's sickness was stress-related, the result of living with an overbearing husband.[42] 'Tom leads her such a dreadful life,' Elizabeth told Mary.

Emma and Tom had been married for two years, but Tom was furious with her and with the lawyer who'd looked after her affairs when she was single. Tom wanted money left in trust for Emma by her late father deposited into his account.[43] He was thinking of taking Emma's family to court. Mary's mother told her that Emma had 'wished much' to hear of Mary's arrival in Australia, and looked constantly in the papers for news of the *Taglioni* reaching Port Adelaide. She waited and waited in a sea of anxiety. 'I would gladly go and see [Emma],' Elizabeth Holt wrote, 'to tell her I have heard of you.'[44]

Mary's parents had suffered another cruel blow of late, and their stress over Mary's voyage only compounded it. Alfred Holt had been planning to return from New York to London with his wife and two children. Elizabeth had 'lived in daily expectation' of seeing him again. But he wrote to his parents soon after Mary's departure that his tailoring business in New York had taken a sharp uplift and he was now employing six men. He was thinking of his wife and children and, for the time being, had given up all thoughts of coming back to London. Elizabeth told Mary that Alfred's news was another 'undoing' of her life after the fierce blow of losing her daughter to Australia.

But although her world had been all 'mortification and disappointment' of late, Elizabeth was gradually learning not to fix her mind on anything sad. Even though they had been shattered by Mary's departure, her parents 'approved' of her conduct and were 'proud of such a child who has so strictly acted up to her duty as a wife'.

Elizabeth had gone into London just before writing her letter, she continued, but had only been there for a short while when a note was delivered to her to return home quickly, as Mary's father had 'taken worse than ever'. She knew Mary would be stressed by this news, but she had to tell her. 'We did not expect him to live,' Elizabeth wrote. 'Now he is better but I do still think he cannot possibly get through another attack.'

And so Elizabeth signed off, hoping her daughter would receive the letter and write her own soon, with happy news of their safe arrival in South Australia. With all that she had, Elizabeth wished that Mary 'be prosperous on earth', and that if they did not see each other again, that they would both find peace in heaven.

And now[,] my dearest girl, goodbye, your father tells me to say all that is kind and affectionate for him. But he does not know when I write to you as it only renews his grief and I try to avoid this. All relatives and friends send love.
From your affectionate mother, E Holt.[45]

Her mother's letter made Mary's heart ache. The warning that Tom Penfold was making noises about his money made her a little afraid.

Chapter 14

MARY, CHRISTOPHER and Georgina moved from their temporary wooden house into their whitewashed stone cottage, which they called 'The Grange', a word common at the time to describe an English farmhouse. The name would become synonymous with Penfolds Wine.

Mary and Chris planted the cuttings they had brought from England in a gully behind their new house.[1] They made renovations and additions to the cottage and it became a fine, comfortable home, with the rear built into the slope of the land and the crop fields rising gently behind it towards the Adelaide Hills.

The Grange was at the lower end of their property, facing the dirt track that would become known as Penfold Road. From the highest point of the Penfold land, Mary could gaze out at the grand stone buildings taking shape along the wide boulevards of Adelaide. Through her spyglass she could see ships along the coast, such as the *Taglioni*, bringing letters from her parents in London.

The Grange had five small rooms, a gabled roof, wooden floorboards and two fireplaces for the cold Adelaide winters. The porch was made from English bricks that had been used as ballast on ships coming to Adelaide. A passage ran the whole length of the house, and there was decorative red cedar woodwork throughout.[2] Mary had a comfortable sitting room at the front of the house. One of the small bedrooms even had its own privy, accessible through a low, narrow door.

An early drawing of Mary's much loved home The Grange on the Magill Estate just outside Adelaide. From Eve Keane, *The Penfold Story*, Oswald L Ziegler, 1951.

At the end of the passage, at the northern end of the house, was the dining room, and next to it a narrow room that Chris used as his surgery and consulting room. In it was a small wooden desk and a leather bag containing his medical instruments. He made house calls on horseback. The Grange also had long, breezy verandas and high ceilings to battle Adelaide's summer heat. At the rear of the house was a large kitchen with a woodburning stove, while a hand pump was the only source of water for the house. Next to that was a laundry with a low ceiling, built into the slope of the hill. The house was well furnished, and Mary had all the modern conveniences of the time, including wire soap 'jigglers' to make suds in the kitchen.

Summer arrived five months after the Penfolds reached Adelaide, and with it a heat so stifling that the new arrivals from England could never have imagined it. In several days over summer the temperature in Adelaide passed 100 degrees Fahrenheit – about 38 degrees Celsius – and the conditions were debilitating, especially for women, who generally wore long dresses better suited to a cooler climate.

Ellen Timbrell was an important part of the Penfold family as they came to grips with this strange new world. Early in 1845, she was devastated to learn that her older brother, Brevet-Captain William Timbrell of the Bengal Horse Artillery, had died.[3] He too was far from the Hamstead home where they had been raised. In a river of sweat and filth, he had succumbed to a fever at Shikarpur, in the Sindh province of Pakistan, about thirty kilometres west of the Indus River. William was just thirty-one, three years older than Ellen. [4]

NOT LONG AFTER THEY moved into their new home, the Penfolds were stunned to see a local dairyman named John Horsnell[5] stumble onto their verandah gasping for breath. Horsnell, a hardworking but lonely widower in his early thirties, had been gored by a bull while working in his orchard at a picturesque gully just south of Third Creek at Woodforde, about a mile to the north. With his life bleeding out through his hands, he had staggered the agonising journey to Dr Penfold's home.

With Mary and Ellen doing all they could to assist, Chris ushered Horsnell into the dining room and laid him on the ornate table. Mary and Ellen cleaned him up and the wounded man tried to stifle his screams as Chris stitched the gaping hole in his flesh with needle and thread, saving Horsnell's life.

After he had recovered sufficiently, Horsnell walked back to his home, took a glass marble bottle stopper from his stores, placed it into the barrel of his old muzzle-loader and used it as a bullet to shoot the bull.[6]

As it transpired, the ill-fated beast had actually done Horsnell a good turn. Mary and Chris needed a gardener, and Horsnell gratefully took on the task of replanting many of the grape vines in the plot they called 'The Grange Vineyard'.

Horsnell knew that grapes had to be propagated from vine cuttings to ensure new plantings adopted the characteristics of the parent vine, while plants grown from seed were likely to revert to their wild state, with fewer and smaller berries that would not produce enough juice for wine.[7] He also knew how to carefully prune vines to control the number of bunches produced on each cane, and how to regulate the growth of the leaf canopy on the vines to increase or decrease sunlight on the developing bunches.[8]

Mary and Chris also hired Elizabeth Smyth, a twenty-year-old Cornish-born maidservant.[9] Elizabeth was a tall, quietly spoken woman with an unflappable temperament. Before long, John Horsnell was courting Elizabeth and they married soon after,[10] eventually raising seven sons and seven daughters over the next twenty-two years.

Horsnell had not been in the colony long. He had first seen the fertile gully on which he established his dairy farm, 'Woodvale', while working for Governor Gawler as a coachman. Born in Brentwood, Essex, he was two when his older brothers left home to fight in the Battle of Waterloo.[11] His parents were both dead by the time he was seventeen, and his foster parents succumbed to a tuberculosis epidemic. Horsnell contracted the disease as well, and his first wife died of smallpox as they sailed for Port Adelaide in 1839.

Horsnell had reached the mosquito-ridden port with just two shillings and sixpence in his pocket, weakened from smallpox and with breathing problems that were likely due to the long-term effects of tuberculosis. He was alone and broken in this new world, having lost his wife, his biological parents and his adoptive parents. He had collapsed on the side of the road while walking from the port to Adelaide, but was rescued by a stranger. He never looked back. If Mary ever needed an example of resilience to guide her life, she found it in the tireless gardener she hired to help her grapevines prosper.

Together with other eager workmen, such as British migrant Elijah Lovelock,[12] Horsnell also planted the Penfold property with many acres of wheat, a crop that promised great export potential to Britain.

A THRIVING COMMUNITY was growing around Makgill as Mary and her family settled in. Her neighbours included carters, farm labourers, stonemasons, plasterers and carpenters, who had taken up the small farms from Ferguson and Cock's subdivision. Mary found the Makgill village a hub of activity. It already had a blacksmith, tearooms, a chaff mill, hotels, a butchery and a post office.[13] And it was already an important crossroads, as settlers from the Adelaide Hills travelled through there to and from the growing city.

The Penfolds' fellow passenger on the *Taglioni*, Robert Norman, had opened his new dental business and was taking out display advertisements in the Adelaide newspapers, promising to supply '[e]very description of artificial, natural, and mineral teeth, from one to the entire set'.[14] But before long he and George Heseltine would go into partnership as daguerreotypists, capturing photographic images of Adelaide and its people. S.T. Gill would order similar camera equipment and go into business as a professional photographer too.

One of the Penfolds' neighbours at Makgill was Scottish-born Patrick Auld,[15] who had arrived in Adelaide in 1842 with wife Eliza, son William Patrick[16] and daughters Agnes and Georgiana. They had travelled on the *Fortitude*, a British ship that would bring free settlers both to South Australia and to the 'Fortitude Valley' area of New South Wales that would later become part of the colony of Queensland. Auld established himself in Hindley Street as a wine and spirit merchant, and paid a pound an acre for two 93-hectare sections of land at Makgill. There he planted vines that in time would become the 'Auldana' vineyard, next to the Penfold farm.

Most of the buildings in the area were made from stone quarried from John Finlay Duff's property at Woodforde, or from smaller quarries in the south-east of the Adelaide Hills. Duff had previously been owner and captain of the barque *Africaine*, which had carried immigrants to Adelaide as part of South Australia's First Fleet but which was wrecked off the Canadian coast on a voyage from England to Quebec. He would soon volunteer land to build Mary's local church.

AS MARY WATCHED THE PENFOLD grapevines growing in the Adelaide sun, other vignerons had enthusiastically joined the pioneer winemakers of South Australia. Their laborious efforts were starting to bear fruit.

As well as Mary and Chris's vines, the *Taglioni* had carried Spanish vine cuttings; the word was that they were destined for the 'Clarendon' property, on the eastern side of the Adelaide Hills.[17] It was owned by the wealthy, British-based absentee landlord William Leigh, who had told his agent, John Morphett, in 1839 that '[a]s the culture of the vine might be profitable to my South Australian tenantry ... it will be desirable that there should be some hill of a suitable soil for its profitable growth on the estate'.[18]

About thirty kilometres south of Adelaide, in an area that would become known as McLaren Vale, William Oliver[19] was establishing a vineyard on his property, 'Taranga'. Oliver had bought a parcel of land sight unseen, and he left his village on the Scottish border in October 1839, sailing for Adelaide with his wife, Elizabeth, and their two children on the ship *Delhi*.

John Reynell,[20] a well-travelled young man from a Devonshire farming family, had arrived in Adelaide in October 1838 with his cousin Samuel, aboard the ship *Surrey*.[21] Reynell was used to long ocean voyages. At sixteen, after his father's death left his family broke, Reynell had journeyed to Egypt to work in a cousin's counting house. He had then taken work trading in wheat and other goods that allowed him to visit Italy, France and North America.

Reynell was inspired by the vineyards he saw growing in Europe, and was convinced that the South Australian climate would be ideal for growing grapes. He obtained vine cuttings at the Cape of Good Hope on the journey to Adelaide – and acquired his future wife during the voyage, becoming engaged to Mary Lucas, who was travelling with her extended family. After the *Surrey* arrived at Holdfast Bay, near Adelaide, John and Samuel Reynell had rented a house at 81 Rundle Street, but John planted his vine stock and potatoes on the Lucas family's property, 'Surreyville', beside the Field River to the south.

Reynell was one of the fifty settlers who formed the Agricultural and Horticultural Society of South Australia, and when he acquired his own property, about twenty kilometres south of Adelaide near the present township of Reynella, he planted 500 cuttings sourced from Van Diemen's Land and the vine stock he had acquired at the Cape. He went on to establish 'Stony Hill', South Australia's first commercial vineyard, and he also introduced Southdown and Saxon rams from Van Diemen's Land. By 1842 his workers were shearing 4000 sheep.[22] Reynell made his first small batch of wine in 1843 and built a fine home called 'Reynella House'.[23]

But the ambitious newcomer had overextended himself, and in the same year he was declared bankrupt when his pastoral endeavours went belly-up. He complained that he had lost £4000 of capital and five years of time, and that his health had been 'much subverted'. In what could have been a warning for Mary and Chris Penfold, he complained: 'This is the reward, so far, of the pioneer of this really fine country.'[24] He was treated leniently by his creditors, though,[25] and in 1844, the year Mary and Chris arrived in Adelaide, Reynell planted 2000 square metres of vines with cuttings from 'Highercombe', George Anstey's Adelaide Hills vineyard.

Anstey[26] was the son of a Van Diemen's Land pioneer and had planted 2000 cuttings from the Macarthurs' Camden Park estate on his sixty-hectare farm, which was not far from the Grange Cottage. Anstey also took up extensive pastoral leases on the Yorke and Eyre peninsulas.

While the Penfolds and Ellen Timbrell were still waiting for their vines to produce fruit, John Reynell expanded his vineyard, planting 1.6 hectares of shiraz and grenache vines cut from the Macarthur family's Camden Park. He also constructed the Old Cave cellar for temperature control, which today is part of the Hardy's Reynella Winery complex, making it the oldest operational wine cellar in Australia.[27]

MARY WROTE HOME OFTEN, but given the enormous distance between Adelaide and London, it could take almost a year to receive a reply.

Tom Penfold was continuing to throw his weight around in London. As he had threatened, he took his wife's family and legal team to court over her money, which he wanted in his account. In effect, Tom was suing his own wife, Emma Penfold (nee Bouch),[28] in November 1844, in the cloistered majesty of the Vice-Chancellor's Court – part of the Court of Chancery – at London's Westminster Hall, the oldest building in the British Parliament. It was the highest court of equity that heard cases involving trusts, land law and inheritances.

Emma, a dear friend of Mary's as well as her sister-in-law, had just given birth to their daughter, also named Emma.[29] The child's middle name was Mary, in honour of her dear friend and sister-in-law in Adelaide.

But Tom was taking no prisoners. In a case marked as *Penfold v Bouch*, Tom's legal team pressed the case for Emma's money in trust to be paid to Tom – with expenses. London's *Morning Herald* reported:

> His Honour gave judgment in this case, the question being whether parties who had accepted a trust in respect of the separate property of a single lady, and who afterwards married, were liable to the costs of a suit which had become necessary in consequence of their refusal to pay over a portion of the money to the husband, and the residue to the trustees of the marriage.

The judge observed that although the conduct of the trustees was 'in every respect correct up to and until after the marriage', they were not justified in withholding the money until a bill was filed, and they must, therefore, be held liable to the costs of the suit incurred by their refusal.'[30] Tom had won this battle in court, but other members of the Penfold family were waiting to ambush him with lawsuits of their own.

When writing to her parents, Mary put a positive spin on all that was happening in Adelaide. She described how well Georgina was growing. Chris, she said, was working harder than ever to

Grapevines line the path leading to the first Government House at Sydney. *National Library of Australia obj-134781285*

Mary Penfold's father, Dr Thomas Holt Jr.

Christopher Penfold's parents Charlotte and the Rev John Penfold, the vicar of Steyning, near Brighton in Sussex.

Young doctor Christopher Rawson Penfold, Mary's husband for 35 years.

Mary as a young woman.

Christopher Penfold's childhood home, the Steyning vicarage. *Alamy*

Mary and daughter Georgina.

The silver and gold medals won by Gregory Blaxland in the 1820s for producing outstanding colonial wine. *State Library of New South Wales a4754001h, a5292001h*

The Proclamation of South Australia 1836. Painting by Charles Hill. *Art Gallery of South Australia Accession number 0.893*

Vine dressers in Adelaide in the early 1840s as seen by S.T. Gill. *National Library of Australia obj-134354667*

S.T. Gill drew these images of Adelaide at the time Mary Penfold was getting to know her new home. Above: uninviting Port Adelaide, also known as 'Port Misery' looking across Gawler Reach. *State Library of New South Wales 840388*

Rundle Street, Adelaide 1845. *Art Gallery of South Australia Accession number 0.647*

The corner of King William and Rundle Streets. *State Library of South Australia B 60076*

King William Street about 1845 (attributed to S.T Gill or E.L. Montefiore). *State Library of New South Wales 840386*

Pedro Ximénez is a white Spanish wine grape variety Mary used to make dessert sherry from her first experiments with winemaking. Illustration by Alexis Kreyder from *Ampélographie: Traité général de viticulture*, 1910.

The five-room cottage Mary called The Grange is a few kilometres from the centre of Adelaide, and was Mary's home for almost 50 years.

The interior of The Grange cottage as it would have been when Mary lived there. She ran her huge wine business from the small office that had been her husband's home surgery.

The rustic kitchen at The Grange complete with its hand-cranked water pump, the only water source inside the cottage.

Mary and Chris Penfold began building wine cellars almost as soon as they settled at Magill Estate.

Mary and Chris Penfold were among the founding parishioners at St George's Anglican Church near The Grange.

Mary's difficult brother-in-law Thomas Brooks Penfold built the East Torrens Hotel about two kilometres from The Grange.

Queen Victoria made a grand entrance into Paris in 1855 and came to admire the Australian wines which William Macarthur offered her at the Paris Exposition Universelle on the Champs-Élysées. Painting by Eugène-Charles-François Guérard. *Royal Collection Trust*

Adelaide turned out to welcome Queen Victoria's son Prince Alfred in 1867.
National Library of Australia obj-516432208

Christopher Penfold in 1869, a year before his death. *State Library of South Australia B 22969*

Mary was an elderly woman when she finally handed over the reins of Penfolds.

The Penfolds wine cellars and bottling plant in 1917 when Mary's grandsons Frank and Leslie Penfold Hyland were running the business. *State Library of South Australia B 11567*

Mary's son-in-law Tom Hyland took over the wine business from Mary and expanded the operation further.

Mary's Magill Estate in the 1920s.

A Penfold's promotional vehicle of the 1920s as Mary's grandsons made it one of Australia's most recognisable brands.

Max Schubert, Penfolds' chief winemaker, developed the company's most celebrated wine, Grange, named after Mary's long-time home. *Newspix*

give the family the best chance of a good life in South Australia. The wheat was growing splendidly in long fields of waving green stalks, and the grapevines were thriving, although it would be a couple of years before they reaped any rewards from them.

Chris was as carefree as ever. He was practising as a doctor in Adelaide even though he only been approved as an apothecary.[31] It would be more than a decade before he got around to completing the process necessary for him to be registered as a medical practitioner in Adelaide. But he didn't mind. He was building up a successful medical practice, and he was confident that, with The Grange's abundance of sun and good soil, he and Mary could make some decent wines as well.

Chapter 15

MARY'S FIRST SUMMER at Makgill was savage and enervating, but even though it would take years for the small vineyard at The Grange to produce wine, the sun, the soil, the water and the Mediterranean warmth promised some grand vintages ahead.

Mary knew that the Penfolds' winemaking would be on a small scale for many years, but she eagerly awaited the arrival of the grapes so she and Chris could make their first bottles of Penfolds fortified wine. He was the expert on medicinal wines, but she was a fast learner. Other South Australian winemakers had far bigger vineyards than the Penfolds, but the results of their efforts had thus far been mixed. Chris and Mary knew there was an opportunity for them to make wines that were as good as – if not better than – anything else in their colony.

The South Australian Agricultural and Horticultural Society's Exhibition, held in the Adelaide parklands on 14 February 1845, only encouraged the eager Penfolds to press ahead with nurturing their own vines. A crowd of 3000 people attended the exhibition, and amid the lofty gums, hundreds of drays and carts delivered the finest of South Australia's harvests to the big show. Mary and Chris worked their way through the crowds of people who had come to see the best produce from local farms and vineyards.

Admission was a shilling, but a great many patrons waited until later in the afternoon when the gates were thrown open.[1] There were booths and tents established at regular intervals around the exhibition 'for the benevolent purpose of affording shade and refreshment to the expected multitudes'.[2] Also among the crowd was the tireless and ever-enthusiastic S.T. Gill, with his pencils, watercolours and paper, capturing the colour and excitement of this important day in the colony's young history.[3]

Adelaide newspapers were in raptures. The pride of this frontier community was on display, as its citizens showed not only that they could produce food that was the envy of the world, but also that their people were as prosperous and sophisticated as those they had left behind in Britain.

The South Australian newspaper reported that the exhibition pavilion:

> ... became crowded with a gay and gallant assemblage, comprising the greater portion of the youth and beauty of our fair province. In the Australian, as in other sunny climes, the ladies dress well, and tastefully, and we can assure our British readers, that our company would contrast most favourably, in every respect, with those at the best exhibitions of our native land ... everyone was agreed as to the great improvement in the wheat, oats, barley, onions, butter, cheese, bacon, hams, malt, and fruits, even over last year, and certainly these articles were very excellent.[4]

The wines were a different story, although the grapes received 'much notice' and rave reviews – 'and very deservedly so', according to *The Adelaide Observer*, 'the whole being very fine in appearance'. This bolstered the often-repeated predictions at the exhibition that South Australia would soon be in 'the first rank of wine-producing and wine-exporting countries'.[5]

George Stevenson and Abraham Davis were the two front-runners for prizes as grape producers, but Stevenson – with a lot of help from head gardener George McEwin – won both prizes on offer. He received two guineas (£2 2s) for producing the best six pounds (almost 2.7 kilograms) of grapes, with his samples sourced from nine varieties.[6]

Mary and Chris Penfold as well as other budding winemakers were inspired by Adelaide's Agricultural and Horticultural Show in 1845. *State Library of South Australia B 16066*

McEwin was most likely looking for a pay rise after Stevenson collected another two guineas for the best overall collection of grapes, this time representing twenty-nine varieties[7] that McEwin had prospering at Stevenson's new vineyard, now on the Old Botanic Garden site on the River Torrens, below McKinnon Parade, North Adelaide. The wines chiefly came from the French collection of vines at Sydney's Botanic Garden, from William Macarthur at Camden, from the Constantia vineyard at the Cape and from the garden at London's Syon House. They included Pedro Ximénez, described at the time as the 'true Sherry Grape', verdelho and the douro grape, reputedly 'the best variety of Port Wine Grape' from Oporto, Portugal.[8]

Abraham Davis won a great deal of praise for the produce of his vines at Moore Farm, and was judged to have shown the best peaches and nectarines.[9]

There were only two varieties of wine exhibited, one labelled 'Burgundy' from George Stevenson's vineyard, and a 'Hock' – a German-style white wine – made at Echunga.[10]

By this time Stevenson had lost control of *The South Australian Register*, and he was shown no charity by his former publication, which announced that he should have poured his burgundy down the drain rather than embarrass himself at a wine show. The *Register*'s wine critic sniffed that, rather than resembling a fine French wine, Stevenson's foul drop was more like 'the warm water with which a jar of currant-jam had been washed out'.[11]

The other wine, the paper claimed, 'while almost as improperly termed Hock, for it had none of the character of a Rhenish wine; was pleasant in taste, and gave a pleasing promise of really good South Australian wine'.[12] This white wine had been made by Walter Duffield,[13] the ambitious young manager of the vineyard belonging to Jacob Hagen,[14] a member of South Australia's Legislative Council. The *Register*'s wine critic opined:

> We ought not to expect wines resembling those we have tasted in Europe. The climate and the soil are entirely different, and all we can now be sure of is, that we shall be able to make it good. It may not be equal to that of Portugal or of Germany; but it may be better than either. Who knows?[15]

Duffield and Hagen were confident about the quality of South Australian wine, so much so that a week after the Adelaide show, they sent twelve bottles to Buckingham Palace, addressed to Queen Victoria.[16] The wine writer for *The South Australian* reported that he had 'the pleasure of tasting some of [the Hock] and if we may judge from our own sensations, we can confidently state, not only that it does the highest credit, both to the province and to the manufacturers, but that it will give much satisfaction to her Majesty and to her royal consort'.[17]

It did – and Mary and Chris thought they, too, could produce something special from their backyard. The Agricultural and Horticultural Society announced a valuable prize for the best wine at the show in 1846. Although the Penfolds still would not be able to produce wine from their grapes by then, they realised that wine was destined to become a major industry in South Australia.

AFTER A YEAR IN ADELAIDE, Mary and Chris were enjoying their second Southern Hemisphere winter, basking in the mild season in the Adelaide Hills. They watched their vine leaves shimmering in the South Australian sun like waves on the sea that they had crossed on the way to this promised land. As they savoured their freedom from the stresses of a debt-riddled life back in England, Mary and Chris were blissfully unaware of the conflicts surrounding Tom Penfold back in London.

Instead, as Chris did his medical rounds on horseback, Mary and Ellen, with John Horsnell leading the workmen, tended the vines and the vegetable garden at The Grange, and supervised the flourishing wheat. Ellen was proving to be a bit of a loafer at times, though. Despite them being the best of friends, Mary complained about Ellen to her parents.

Dr Tom Holt had recovered well enough from his heart problems to pen his daughter a long letter in March 1845, and he reassured Mary that she was as dear to her family as ever. He addressed this letter to 'Mrs Penfold, Grange, Makgill, near Adelaide, South Australia'[18] and gave the letter to Captain Black to carry on the *Taglioni*'s next voyage.

Elizabeth Holt included a note to tell Mary that Tom Penfold, who was still angry despite his windfall from the court action against his wife, had finally allowed Emma to invite the Holts to see their new baby. Little Emma Mary Penfold was a pretty girl, but Mary's mother was now suffering health problems, and she let Tom Holt, now recovering from his own bouts of ill health, do most of the writing. 'My dearest angel Toots,' Tom Holt wrote:

> ... How truly were your dear mum's and dad's hearts gladdened by every succeeding communication by letter or otherwise of your voyage to the antipodes ...
>
> Your last dear long and very delighting letter was only surpassed in interest by the intelligence it gives of your safe arrival at Adelaide.
>
> I know how much our anxieties have been reciprocated and I thank God I have been granted time to hear of your

perils being at an end, and that you are well and happy. God forever bless you my dearest child and <u>may he ever</u> in life bless you with the same enjoyments is my constant prayer.

I thank you a million times for the trouble and pains you have taken in your journal and letters to describe every particular and circumstance, well knowing you would not curtail us of a pleasure next to beholding you my beloved child.

I have not got over <u>parting with you</u> yet or ever shall I while I live ... but hope still bids <u>me indulge</u> in thoughts of seeing you again in England.[19]

Tom was writing the letter from the same bed in which he was suffering so badly when Mary last saw him. He was much better now, but his heart still gave him concern, and he asked Mary to excuse his scribble because his hand sometimes shook 'most abominably'. He said that Mary's letters had been handed about to a good many friends, who had 'been well pleased' with them. 'It does you credit my dear girl,' Tom wrote, 'in head and heart and <u>I am not a little proud</u> of having so clever a chick as my dear Toots for the author.'[20]

Elizabeth Holt and other relatives were sending Mary news from the British papers – the births, marriages and obituaries – but in this letter Tom conveyed more personal news for his daughter. Mary had sent her parents a sketch that 'conveyed a very good conception' of The Grange and the farm, along with her and Chris's 'grand plans'.[21]

'I fancy I can see all the buildings, pigs, cows, turkeys, fowls, pigeons etc to the minutest detail,' Tom wrote back affectionately. He could also picture that 'little dear darling' Georgina, now eighteen months old, striding in 'awful authority' among the poultry with her red shoes and stockings. He asked Mary to give Georgina fifty-two kisses from him, and as many more from dear 'old Bet' – Elizabeth – and to tell her that he had not forgotten her 'pretty self dancing', just like the real Marie Taglioni.

Tom included a daguerreotype picture of Elizabeth so that the little girl would have an image of the 'dear old granny' who she might never again meet. He also sent a portrait of himself, and was organising pictures of Mary's brothers, George and Alfred. He was proud that George had written to say he had become accomplished in the art of taking images by the daguerreotype process.

Neither Tom nor Elizabeth was in good health, but they made the most of every day. Tom was contemplating a change of scene:

> I am thinking every day of going to some place on the coast and try what sea air will do for me, but the weather has been too severe here from January to the present month [March 1845] that I cannot muster courage to make the attempt. I only wish my dear child that your dear mother and myself had been about 30 years younger. I think you would not have been in Australia without us and we could have enjoyed the beauties of the climate and scenery with you to perfection.
>
> Say in your next whether the river is as close to your farm as it was in the house you temporarily occupied, and what sort of fish you get supplied with and whether there is any game there beside your Cockney cockatoos to shoot at.[22]

The mining industry was booming in South Australia, and Mary had told her parents all about the copper discoveries at Kapunda, a village on the Light River near an area called the Barossa Valley, where English and German settlers had started planting vineyards. Closer to Makgill, silver-lead ore had been discovered on the property of Osmond Gilles back in 1839, and the Glen Osmond Union Mining Company had been established. The ore gave 75 per cent of lead with eighteen ounces (about 500 grams) of silver to the ton. The discovery was followed by two further mines.[23]

Tom said he was 'much amused' with the mining prospects in Australia. Mary had sent him a small specimen of Australian 'lead and silver united', and he had heard wild stories of the untold mineral wealth that was ready to be tapped.

'I suppose you must say "Open Sesame" and the fortune will appear,' Tom told Mary, but he warned her and Chris not to 'neglect the fleece and farm yard to dig a will o' the wisp out of the bowels of the earth'. He knew it would be just like Chris to chase such castles in the air, and Dr Holt was adamant that the Penfolds must knuckle down and build their reputation and their finances. He ended his letter:

God bless you my dear, dear, ever dear child. I must now write adieu and conclude in farewell prayer for your health, happiness and prosperity be where you will and giving my remembrance to all.
You will believe me my beloved child,
your affectionate father
T. Holt[24]

Separately, Elizabeth Holt wrote directly to Chris Penfold, reminding him of the promise he had made to protect her daughter. He was to stay focused:

My dear Christopher, I am glad to hear you like Adelaide and sincerely hope you may realise your expectations. Many thanks for your promise to take care of my idolized Mary and I place implicit confidence in your promise and will do my best to be happy. You can judge of my affection by your own for your lovely darling Infant. God bless you all. Adieu. E Holt[25]

THE SOUTH AUSTRALIAN weather was proving to be a blessing for Mary and Christopher, but not so kind to Charles Sturt and his expedition. They had left Adelaide in mid-1844, just days after the Penfolds had taken over their farm.

Sturt and his team had gone north, following the Murray River to its junction with the Darling, and had then travelled over the Barrier Range, 500 kilometres from Adelaide. They travelled north-east for another 270 kilometres to Preservation

Creek, where they took the last water they could find. Instead of an inland sea, the bedraggled, desperate men were surrounded by a vast, stony desert and enveloped by a drought that lasted for six months. Sturt would abandon the boat he'd towed for almost a year. Between January and July 1845, Sturt's team were trapped in that harsh country, and Sturt's lieutenant, James Poole, died of scurvy. Mercifully, the rains came – but by the time Sturt finally made it back to Adelaide,[26] his health had suffered terribly.

It was a different story among the lush greenery of Mary Penfold's Grange. The Penfolds planted more vines in September 1845, probably from locally sourced cuttings.[27] A reporter from *The Adelaide Observer* noted:

> We lately saw a remarkably fine bed of asparagus in the garden of Dr Penfold, at Makgill. The plants, one year old, were unusually vigorous. The variety and excellence of this gentleman's collection of English esculents afford equal proof of the goodness of the soil and the judicious care of the cultivator. The Doctor has also a large number of vines and fruit trees, which promise, 'ere long, amply to repay his spirited outlay.[28]

Mary and her workers had done an outstanding job with the crops, vines and garden, but publicly it was always Dr Penfold who received the credit – at least for now.

At about the same time as this gushing tribute to Chris's horticultural skills, Mary received another loving letter from her parents.

'My dearest Mary,' Tom Holt wrote.

> I do most sincerely regret any distress that I may have caused you through not writing sooner if you have not received four letters before this. It is because I have sent them to the post office; for the future, all shall go to [a shipping agent].
>
> I well know the joy your letters give us and can believe our feelings to be reciprocal although my letters can contain

very little to amuse, in news to tell you. I will write every two months [even] if it is only to tell you that you are still as dear to us and as much loved as ever you were.[29]

Mary had talked up the success she and Chris were having in Adelaide, and with good reason. They were about to enjoy a bumper wheat crop and the vines promised so much. Her parents were delighted and in a combined letter told Mary:

> How different everything turns out to be in Adelaide to what we anticipated but you know it was contemplated that you should go to the Bush, and you must have endured many hardships from which you are now exempt. Indeed, I hear nothing that should induce you to wish to leave Adelaide (excepting to be with those dear to you) and I can say with truth that all our happiness is in yours. Therefore, I cannot wish your return at present if I love you or those near and dear to you, because it must be to poverty. I have made up my mind to be happy and know that my dear girl will do the same. 'Tis very, very gratifying to hear that Chris likes the change and is so determined to put his shoulder to the wheel. You say he works so very hard, I trust he will reap the benefit and that your crops will turn out very profitable that for the future we may indulge the cherishing hope of your success. I do hope that [Chris] will see not only his profits but think as well of the losses he may meet with as I attribute all his failures in life to have arisen from his being too sanguine.[30]

Tom and Elizabeth were still upset that Chris's 'sanguine' nature — his carefree confidence, especially in financial matters — had caused them to be separated, perhaps forever, from their daughter and granddaughter. Mary had told her parents that a prospector tried to sell her husband the location of a motherlode for £50 but had been rebuffed. Tom Holt was pleased to hear this.

You cannot think my dearest one how you are enquired after. I could never have believed my child had so many friends. I cannot tell you <u>who</u> has not read your journal and letters. Of course I do not disclose family affairs. All of us are in raptures with the darling babe. Anything you tell of her is interesting. How I do rejoice that you have this loved one. She must have been such a swell case on your voyage. What a clever duck she is ...[31]

Sadly, both Tom and Elizabeth still had pressing health issues: 'Your mother ... has had two most desperate attacks. I have had much palpitation in my heart and cannot bear as much fatigue as I could when you were here.'

The Holts had now abandoned thoughts of moving from Edmonton to the coast because of the expense involved. Regarding Mary's complaints about Ellen Timbrell, Tom said: 'I am not surprised [she] will not work. If I could have had any influence, she should not have gone [to South Australia].' He suggested, however, that Tom Penfold might be an even bigger problem for Mary and Chris.

Dr Holt had gone to Tom's home in the affluent Notting Hill area of London to visit him, Emma and their new baby – and had found Tom as prickly as ever. He had shown Dr Holt a copy of the 3 August 1844 edition of *The Adelaide Observer*, which featured an account of Mary and Christopher's purchase of the Makgill farm, and the glowing report of the property and its value.[32] The same issue had also featured an advertisement for the sale of a 'splendidly worked Christening Robe and Cap, and two Dressing Cases, suited for lady or gentleman'.[33] Dr Holt presumed the dressing cases were Mary's, and the christening robe and cap the ones that had adorned Georgina at her baptism in London.

Tom Penfold had been intrigued by the reports of Adelaide's potential, and was talking about emigrating to the land of opportunity as well – and of getting back the money Chris owed him.[34] In contrast to her husband, Emma Penfold was a joy to be around, Tom Holt said, and was 'all life and spirits with the expectation' of seeing Mary and Chris again. It seemed likely to happen soon enough. Tom Penfold told Mary's parents that he was ready to make a start for Adelaide on 1 June 1845.

Mary's father was glad his daughter would have Emma's 'society' again, to compensate in some measure for the vast distance she was from the rest of her family. 'But I do not know what to say [about] Tom,' he warned.

> He says he is forgetting all that has passed and with a good feeling towards Christopher and would be willing to lend him money again if he will but pay the interest – this Emma tells me – but I would advise you to have nothing to do with <u>his</u> money however advantageous it may appear to you. Do pray strive to overcome all difficulties and be independent of him. Remember his irritability he will always take with him and although I would say we must forgive and forget all injuries, you must avoid having your reputation injured as it was at Brighton... There must be something wrong in the man who is at variance with all his brothers and sisters (excepting James) as Tom is ...[35]

Emma had been quite well despite the constant stress of living with Tom, and in the months since her pregnancy and the court case she could now walk four or five miles and eat and drink anything she wanted. Her 'babe', Emma Mary, was pretty, sure enough, but not 'near as pretty', Dr Holt reckoned, as his own darling granddaughter, Georgina.

In her addition to her husband's letter, Elizabeth Holt pointed out that the mail from South Australia to London cost only eightpence for the receiver, which was not much more than the postage from nearby Brighton. Elizabeth was disappointed that their family friend Ann Guillod, who was also now in Adelaide, had not kept in touch with the Holts as she had promised, but the Holts were determined to keep their daughter abreast of everything that was happening at home.

'We go to dine with Tom and Emma on Sunday next and tell them what you say – not to bring out more than they want,' Elizabeth explained to Mary. 'I tell them to take only one servant, she wants two. I have told them to take feather beds.'[36] Elizabeth had heard a lot of gossip about bush remedies, and told her daughter that 'if the mosquitoes bite you must put a bit of honey on, as this almost instantaneously cures wasp stings'. She too warned Mary of Tom Penfold's bite.[37]

It was the last warning Elizabeth gave her beloved daughter, the 'idolized Mary'. Only a few weeks after her letter arrived in Adelaide, Elizabeth Holt died suddenly at her family home in London. She was fifty-six. It would be months, though, before Mary opened a letter at The Grange and read her father's terrible news.

Chapter 16

WHILE THE LAST LETTER from Mary's mother was making its way across three oceans to reach the Penfolds at The Grange, Tom Penfold was fighting for his freedom in a London courtroom against other members of the Penfold clan.[1] Not only did the 47-year-old Tom assert that his brother Chris was ripping him off over his loan to set up the young doctor's family on a magnificent property in South Australia, but in June 1845 two other members of the Penfold family conspired to have Tom, a former officer of the East India Company, thrown into debtors' prison. Tom had hoped to leave for Adelaide with his young family in June 1845 – but that was before others in the Penfold family broadsided him with a blast he didn't see coming.

The war over his late father's will had taken an ugly turn five years after Reverend Penfold had died. In the middle of June 1845, another Penfold brother, Reverend William Penfold, the curate of St Mary's, Marylebone, and Catherine Penfold's husband, John Baroncelli, brought a civil action against Tom. So it was that in the Vice-Chancellor's Court in Whitehall – the same court where Tom had sued to gain the money from his new wife's trust account – he was now forced to stage a costly and emotionally draining fight for his liberty.

On 24 June 1845, as the court hushed and the three judges asked Tom's counsel to present their case, one of England's most expensive barristers – Richard Bethell,[2] a future attorney-general of the United Kingdom – moved to discharge a writ of *ne exeat regno*, an order that would prevent Tom from leaving Britain. William Penfold and John Baroncelli were playing rough. They had brought the writ *ex parte* – without representation of or notification to Tom – catching him by surprise and causing him to spend the previous three days in a debtors' prison. *The Examiner* reported that Tom claimed he had been badly wronged – and by his own brother, a clergyman for God's sake!

> The learned counsel said that the real facts of the case, which had been concealed from the knowledge of the Court when the writ was obtained *ex parte*, now disclosed one of the most cruel and wicked cases that had been presented to the Court for some time. The facts which the Rev. Mr Penfold and Dr Baroncelli represented to the Court were simply that Mr J. Penfold, the father, had died intestate ... leaving his widow and ten children entitled to his personal property as next of kin; that administration had been granted to Mr Thomas Brooks Penfold, who had collected the debts due to the estate; and had possessed himself of sufficient assets, after payment of all the liabilities of the deceased, to leave a large residue, to which the plaintiffs and the other children would become entitled ...[3]

In obtaining the writ to have Tom imprisoned, his brother and brother-in-law swore that 'Mr T. B. Penfold had a large sum of money in his hands belonging to the estate (having admitted a balance of 175 pounds), and that he threatened and intended to leave the kingdom, and reside in Australia'.

Tom's barrister said the real facts of the case were that, in 1834, on his return from Calcutta, where he had been based with the East India Company, Tom found his father 'in most embarrassed circumstances', and made him such considerable advances of money 'to extricate him from his difficulties' that when Reverend Penfold died, he owed Tom £1000.[4]

Richard Bethell showed the court that on a full statement of the accounts of Reverend John Penfold, there was still £800 owed to creditors. Tom had not only paid to his brothers and sisters all that was due to them, Bethell said, but had in fact left the estate very largely indebted to him. Bethell looked around the imposing courtroom as William Penfold and John Baroncelli averted their eyes and shifted in their seats.

'Could the Court believe it possible,' the theatrical barrister asked, pausing for effect:

> that the plaintiffs, who only were entitled to two-elevenths of the residue, in any event, and which on their own representation, unfair as it was, only amounted to the miserable sum of 32 pounds, could come to the Court, concealing the whole of these circumstances which the answer disclosed, and obtain an order to restrain a brother who had acted towards his family as the defendant had done, and on that order to throw him into prison?[5]

Bethell paused once more and looked slowly about the court, letting his words sink in. 'Could the Court believe,' he continued, 'that one of the parties was a clergyman of the Church of England?'

Now murmurs broke the silence. Bethell skewered the plaintiffs some more and suggested that perhaps they were the ones who should be facing the judges for sanction. Tom Penfold might not be the most pleasant brother one could have, but was this really a fair way to treat him?

The court agreed, deciding that it had been 'very improperly dealt with' by William Penfold and John Baroncelli, who had withheld crucial evidence. The three judges scolded their conduct and ordered them to pay costs.[6]

Five days after that victory, Tom finally boarded the 400-ton barque *Augustus* at Torquay, in Devon, with Emma, Emma Mary and a servant, and set off for another court battle in Adelaide.

Mary and Christopher did not see him coming.

CHRIS PENFOLD WAS HAVING considerable success with his patients in Adelaide, using imported ports and brandies as tonics, and he eagerly awaited the first batch that he and Mary could make.

Another Adelaide vintner, Dr Alexander Charles Kelly,[7] was also a firm believer in the medicinal power of wine. Kelly had graduated from the University of Edinburgh in 1832, and after practising briefly in Scotland became a surgeon aboard the East India Company ship *Kellie Castle*. After the doctor's brother, Thomas, migrated to South Australia in 1839, Alexander followed him, arriving on the *Baboo* in 1840.

He became the resident dispenser at Adelaide Hospital two years later,[8] and bought 32 hectares of land near Morphett Vale, south of Adelaide. Like the Penfolds, he planted a vineyard so that he would have a steady supply of red wine as medicine for his patients. He called his house 'Trinity', after three hatmakers who worked as labourers on the construction, and he started planting the vineyard on around five hectares of land in 1845.

Mary and Chris were encouraged by a report of his methods published in *The South Australian*:

> We are glad to hear that there is a great demand this year for rooted vines and fruit trees, and that a number of gentlemen intend to plant vineyards. It has been proved by Dr Kelly, of Morphett Vale (whose vines are described to us as having made amazing progress), that in the calcareous soils of that district, trench planting for vines is perfectly sufficient; so that the important object of planting a vineyard may, in all such soils, be very easily accomplished.[9]

The vines, though, didn't make the progress Kelly expected, and he later blamed bad advice that he'd drawn from a book by William Macarthur, who by this time was one of Australia's most influential viticulturists. Macarthur had published his small but popular volume on wine, *Letters on the Culture of the Vine, Fermentation, and the Management of the Cellar*, under his pen-name, 'Maro'.[10] It would be some years before Kelly's vines produced good wine, but he would eventually be a pioneer of the Hardys and Tintara brands.

The publication of several other important books and manuals on Australian winemaking at that time encouraged vintners across the continent to plant grapes. George McEwin had published *The South Australian Vigneron and Gardeners' Manual* in 1843,[11] the same year George Suttor produced *The Culture of the Grape-vine and the Orange in Australia and New Zealand*.[12] In Perth, the prominent lawyer Richard West Nash wrote *A Manual for the Cultivation of the Vine and Olive in Western Australia*. Twenty years after the Scottish physician Dr Alexander Henderson had written *The History of Ancient and Modern Wines*, he released an Australian edition, *An Essay on the Making of Wine*.

Winemaking was expanding throughout all the Australian colonies. Jacob Stein, a vine dresser from Nassau, on the Rhine, was working along with other German winemakers for William Macarthur and his family at Camden Park; there were now 225 hectares under vines in New South Wales.[13] Within a few years that would double.

Encouraged by the success of the Macarthurs, Thomas Mitchell,[14] the New South Wales surveyor-general who had explored much of that colony, had planted a vineyard on his 2.5-hectare estate, 'Craigend', situated in modern-day Kings Cross, and on his country property, 'Parkhall', now the St Marys Towers Catholic retreat in Douglas Park, about eighty kilometres south-west of Sydney. Mitchell bought 7000 cuttings from the Macarthurs, including madeira vines, and in 1844 handed over management to Frenchman Jean d'Auvergne, who produced the first vintage in 1845.[15] Mitchell was taking a trip to southern Spain to inspect vineyards, and while there had an idea for another book on wine based on his travels and observations.[16]

At the same time, Swiss and German settlers were improving the viticulture in what would eventually become the colony of Victoria. Charles La Trobe, a London-born mountaineer and travel writer who became superintendent of the Port Phillip District, had spent several years in Neuchâtel Canton, in Switzerland, and encouraged the emigration of Swiss families to his new home. They planted vineyards at Geelong and Lilydale, and in the Barrabool Hills.[17]

ANGRY, RELENTLESS Tom Penfold, together with his family and servant, sailed into Port Adelaide on 15 October 1845, three and a half months after leaving England.[18] He had ambitious plans to make money in the new colony – starting with his debt recovery operation against his baby brother at Makgill.

And Christopher and Mary were becoming more prosperous. The embarrassment of their debts in Brighton seemed like a distant memory. Mary was now managing the farm more and more as Chris tended to the sick, the injured and the dying from his surgery at The Grange. Mary and Ellen Timbrell also worked in Christopher's office, keeping his accounts and managing patients.

With the help of John and Elizabeth Horsnell, their hired man Elijah Lovelock and other farm workers, Mary was turning Makgill into a money-making venture. Although she was inexperienced in farm management, Mary began to supervise the ploughing, sowing, vine planting and harvesting. Entries in her day book showed that she kept the accounts for both the farm and the medical practice, purchased farming supplies and paid the farm workers.

John and Elizabeth Horsnell were tireless workers for the Penfolds.
State Library of South Australia B 40898, 40899

The vine cuttings Mary and Chris had brought with them on the *Taglioni* had now been in South Australian soil for eighteen months. And there was a couple of hundred acres of flourishing wheat. Mary was too busy to pay much attention to the threats of Tom Penfold that reached Adelaide. Her mother had been so ill and her father so concerned with the deteriorating condition of his wife that the news of Tom's departure for Adelaide had not reached Mary when the *Augustus* arrived at Port Adelaide.

According to Penfold family legend, Mary was hard at work in October 1845 when she caught sight of a familiar, ominous figure walking along the path from Penfold Road to The Grange. She shrieked 'Oh! It's old Tom!'

And promptly fainted.

Chapter 17

THE APPEARANCE OF Tom Penfold cast a shadow over The Grange at a time when the sun had been shining brightly on the new lives that Mary and Christopher were creating for themselves on Adelaide's outskirts. Tom told Chris directly that he wanted his money. The two argued over the terms of the arrangement, Chris standing firm in his very different view of the deal. Tom threatened to take him to court in Adelaide; Chris said he'd see him there.

Despite Tom's demands, the South Australian summer of 1845 was shaping as a heady time for Mary. It would be months before she learnt the heartbreaking news that her father, Dr Tom Holt, had buried his beloved wife, Elizabeth, at the All Souls Church in London's Kensal Green, a few miles from their Edmonton house, which no longer felt like a home.[1]

The wheat in the vast fields around Mary's stone cottage had thrived, although as ever she received no credit for her contribution in newspaper reports that 'Dr. Penfold's wheat' was being shipped to Liverpool, England, on the transport vessel *Bleng*.

On 29 November 1845, Tom Penfold must have ground his teeth in anger when he read in the *Register* that Chris, who constantly refused to settle his loan, was sending 1800 bushels – about fifty tonnes – of high-quality wheat to be made into English flour, and that he had received eight shillings a bushel (a bushel was about 27 kilograms). Five precious shillings per bushel were profit.² Tom calculated that Chris was making £450 on the deal. He wanted his cut.

The newspaper reported that the land at Makgill was especially fertile, with 'spontaneous production' – or very little tilling – needed.³ Tom liked the sound of that and decided to buy into the neighbourhood as well.

He was already starting to throw his weight around in Adelaide as a retired officer with the East India Company, and he grabbed a spot on the special jury list at the Quarterly Meeting of Magistrates, after taking the 'necessary oath of qualification'.⁴

The meeting was chaired by a key government official, Thomas Gilbert,⁵ who was South Australia's first postmaster and its first colonial storekeeper, responsible for all government stores. Gilbert had been on the First Fleet to South Australia, attended the proclamation and proposed a toast to 'Mrs Hindmarsh and the Ladies'.

Chris managed to fob off Tom's demands for money for a time, but there were other dark moments in Mary and Chris's second summer at Makgill.

On the broiling hot Saturday evening two days after Christmas 1845, Mary Langmead,⁶ a 48-year-old mother of three and the wife of a local bootmaker, was milking her cows with her eleven-year-old daughter, Emma, on their farm near The Second Creek.⁷ After the milking, Mrs Langmead walked out through her garden and then headed towards a neighbouring cottage for a cup of tea with some friends. The walk took her through thick grass next to her property, and Mrs Langmead felt a sharp sting in her leg. She cried out with intense pain that something had bitten her on the heel.⁸

She stumbled back to her home and collapsed. The noise woke her husband, and he sent another of the couple's children rushing on horseback, hurtling through the dark brush by moonlight, to summon the nearest doctor – Christopher Penfold from The Grange. Mary rushed about their stone cottage to get Chris's medical bag together, and he leapt upon his horse and spurred it to go as fast as it could to the Langmead's farmhouse, five kilometres away.

Mrs Langmead's agony and panic had only intensified while Chris was racing to her. He arrived on his breathless horse to find Mrs Langmead wheezing and gasping too. Her skin was flushed, her swollen tongue lolled heavy in her red-raw throat, and her pulse was weak and rapid. Sadly, he had arrived just in time to see Mrs Langmead die.

Her death was reported as the first fatality among the South Australian colonists from a snakebite, but Chris said it appeared that she had died not from snake venom, but from 'the rupture of a blood vessel from excessive fright'.[9] South Australia's colonial surgeon, James George Nash,[10] concurred.

Nash, who had been at St Bartholomew's medical school a few years before Chris, examined Mrs Langmead's body and recorded that 'from the evidence it appeared that the deceased being a person of excitable temperament was so much alarmed that she died in consequence'. He believed Mrs Langmead had been bitten by a centipede, not a snake, but that in her anguish at 'thinking it was a snake that had struck her, she died from the shock'.[11]

EVERY WINEMAKER IN South Australia was thrilled at the news, in February 1846, that not only had Queen Victoria received her twelve bottles of hock made at Echunga by Walter Duffield and Jacob Hagen, but she was well pleased to accept them.

The Queen was impressed by the wine, and by the prospects for winemaking in South Australia. She told Edward Stanley, Secretary of State for the Colonies, that she felt 'much interested in the success of this new branch of commerce in the colony'.[12] The Queen's husband, Prince Albert, bestowed a medal on the importer of this fine South Australian white at the Society of Arts, Manufactures and Commerce.[13]

At Adelaide's 1846 Agricultural and Horticultural Exhibition, held a few days after the Queen's thoughts were made public in Adelaide, Duffield's wine took out the first prize of ten guineas 'for the best cask of not less than five gallons [about 22.5 litres]'.[14] There were three wine exhibitors at the 1846 exhibition – Duffield, George Stevenson and George Anstey – and they were all lauded for

Walter Duffield, who became Treasurer of South Australia, was a leading winemaker when Mary arrived in the colony. *State Library of South Australia B 10776*

the way they were helping to furnish what was seen as potentially a huge export commodity. The wine was all from the 1845 growth.

Mary and Chris read the analysis of each entry in *The South Australian Register*, 'whose judgment in such matters [was] considered an authority' by even rival publications.[15]

The first wine sampled was listed as 'No 6, red, (Mr Stevenson's)'. The *Register* described it as 'Sort of Hermitage, or more like red Hock'.

> We may add that this was a truly good wine, but ... it had not time to show its quality unless to a very practised palate. The judges, who really are good judges of wine, saw its goodness, and evidently regretted that its condition prevented their doing more than giving a complimentary notice.[16]

The paper's assessment of the other offerings was:

> No. 4, white, (Mr Duffield's). Out of condition, (almost sour), otherwise a pleasant wine, and promising. We

think an unfortunate bottle was opened, but the bulk was evidently somewhat unsound. The quantity made was small, but the vines from which it was produced will do better. We can see a prospect of something very like Rhenish.

No. 5. White (Mr Anstey). Frontignac, a good wine but too new. (By this we mean that its newness was too evident to the palate. The wines, as we have already said, were of equal age). This is really a good sample but it will require much more time to show itself. The flavour of the Frontignac is strong, and requires mellowing.

No 1. White (Mr Duffield). Hock, good condition, Rhenish flavour, wants age. This was a very nice glass of wine, and in tolerable order for the table. A man ought to be very rich indeed, who, a few years hence, shall go to the expense of importing a dinner wine. No one who was at the Horticultural Show can doubt that we can well supply ourselves.

No. 2. White (Mr Duffield). A strong-bodied wine, but much out of condition – the grape not ripe – earthy flavour.

No. 3. White (Mr Duffield). Harsh and rough: a strong peculiar flavour.[17]

Duffield's No. 1 white was the clear winner. Mary and Chris took encouragement from the fact that South Australia was already producing quality wines worthy of being served to royalty.

TOM PENFOLD BOUGHT a site of almost two hectares along Makgill Road, just a little north of The Grange. It was not only prime land, but from there he could keep an eye on what his brother was doing, and gauge how much he was earning and spending.

Tom moved his wife and daughter into a cosy home he called 'Evington Cottage'. A few months later, a half-acre block was set aside for a one-room building that became the local school,[18] which little Georgina Penfold would soon attend.

Tom started work on a bakehouse and general store. While Mary and Chris had their future rooted in wheat and wine, he had designs to develop his much smaller patch into a lucrative mid-19th-century shopping mall.

Within six months of arriving in Adelaide, Emma Penfold was pregnant again, but the angst between the brothers took away much of the joy of her pregnancy and the prospect of a thriving new life in their new home.

Tom announced his court action for repayment of his loan in the South Australian Supreme Court in October 1846, and the case would be heard at a date to be determined.[19] Despite their personal animosity, the brothers were able to join forces in doing what they saw as the work of the Lord – work that took precedence over any court action or personal argument. They both joined the building committee[20] for the erection of the Anglican Church of St George, the first to be consecrated in the colony of South Australia. This was a dear project to Mary, as in their last combined letter her parents had encouraged her to stay close to God, and always to rest from her labours to worship on the Sabbath.[21]

Tom Penfold was one of the trustees tasked with raising £280 by private subscription to build the church on a plot of about 6000 square metres[22] of land at Woodforde, about a mile north of The Grange – the land donated by John Finlay Duff.

On 18 January 1847, although Emma was about to give birth, the two Penfold families took their carriages to the site for the new church, where Mrs Elizabeth Bayne laid the foundation stone. She was the wife of Fred Bayne,[23] a former sheriff of South Australia[24] and the owner of the grand home 'Stradbroke' at Woodforde. He was an attorney at Messrs Solomon, a renowned Adelaide law firm, and the treasurer of the church building committee. But he was not a man to be trusted.

In the blistering dry heat coming off South Australia's arid interior, Mary, overheating in her long frock underneath her wide hat, joined the assembled throng as they listened while blessings were offered for the new church. The newly arrived Irish-born minister, Arthur Forbes Lloyd,[25] gave a rousing dedication:

May this sacred edifice, which is to be raised by the voluntary exertions of the inhabitants of [Woodforde] and its vicinity serve as a memorial of their anxiety to secure for themselves and their posterity the ordinances of religion; as also of their attachment to the Church of their Fathers. Never may it, through the malice of Satan, or the machinations of evil men and seducers, be perverted from the use to which it is now solemnly dedicated, nor wrested from the South Australian branch of the Established Church of England and Ireland. May it be hallowed as the dwelling place of the Divine Jehovah; and be filled from generation to generation with humble and devout Worshipers.[26]

Six days after the ceremony,[27] Emma Penfold gave birth to a daughter she named Laura, a sister for Emma Mary and a cousin for Georgina. But the new baby came into the world at a time of strife among the Penfolds.

ABOUT SIXTY KILOMETRES north-east of the church site, a new wave of Silesian Lutherans from Germany were establishing farms and vineyards in the Barossa Valley.

South Australia's surveyor-general, William Light, had named the valley after Spain's Barrosa Ridge in Andalusia, where he had fought in March 1811 during the Peninsular War, but a clerical error resulted in the spelling 'Barossa' being adopted.[28] The region had been home to the Peramangk, Ngadjuri and Kaurna people, but while South Australia's government acknowledged Aboriginal land rights from the beginning of colonisation, the First Peoples were quickly pushed off the land in the Barossa to make way for German farmers.

The first German settlement there was called Bethanien, or sometimes New Silesia; it is now known as Bethany.[29] It was established in 1842, two years before Mary and Chris arrived at Makgill. In 1847, Johann Gramp moved from his farm at Yatala, on Adelaide's northern outskirts, and planted a vineyard in the

Johann Gramp from a farm at Jacobs Creek was among the more prominent German winemakers in the Barossa Valley.

Barossa at Jacobs Creek, a short waterway named for William Light's assistant surveyor, William Jacob.[30] Gramp eagerly awaited the appearance of grapes on his vines so that he too could make a style of hock, which would later earn him a degree of fame when marketed as his 'Carte Blanche'.[31]

At the same time, in the neighbouring Eden Valley, Englishman Joseph Gilbert[32] established the Pewsey Vale winery, named after his birthplace in Wiltshire. He planned to produce hock, claret and burgundy.

Samuel Hoffman, a skilled potter, was another German from Silesia who came to the Barossa at that time. He planted vines along the North Para River and made his home at Tanunda.

A brewer from Dorset, England named Samuel Smith[33] arrived in Adelaide in 1847, bringing his wife and five children with him. He settled at Klemzig, before becoming George Fife Angas's gardener at Angaston, on the eastern side of the Barossa. He eventually founded a winery that he called Yalumba, using an Indigenous word that meant 'all the land around'.

MARY COULD ONLY THROW her hands up at the financial difficulties in which Chris managed to find himself. He had Tom chasing him for money, but now a local builder was also taking him to court,[34] claiming the doctor wouldn't pay him for work done at The Grange. Two of Chris's best horses had also gone missing.[35]

Then, on 24 February, a very distracted Tom Penfold – who suddenly had much weightier matters on his mind than money – brought his case against his brother before a judge in the Adelaide Supreme Court. The case was listed as *Penfold v. Penfold*.[36]

Tom's barrister said Chris had signed a contract for a loan of £200, drafted in Sussex by Brighton solicitor George Dempster, and that Chris's friend Ann Guillod, now living at Makgill, had also signed the document. Chris's barrister disputed the legality of the agreement and questioned the authenticity of the loan document.

Now Tom showed his trump card. The cousin of solicitor George Dempster lived in Adelaide and verified the attorney's signature on the contract. Then Tom produced correspondence that proved Chris knew what he was signing, whether he now disputed the terms or not. The judge ruled in Tom's favour, awarding him £217 4s.[37]

It was a slap in the face for Mary's husband, but it was a hollow victory for Tom, who left the court not in triumph but in despair. The previous night, his daughter Laura, not quite one month old, had died at Evington Cottage.[38]

Mary held Georgina tighter than ever. She tried to comfort Laura's mother, young Emma Penfold, and their little girl. Both had endured so much turmoil since Tom decided to try his luck in the new colony. But for a long time Mary's heartbroken sister-in-law was inconsolable.

Chapter 18

AFTER THREE YEARS in the nurturing soil of Makgill, the vine cuttings Chris and Mary had brought from London were growing and twisting into pregnant maturity under the warm South Australian sun.

The Penfolds had left their grapes on the vine to sweeten and develop full flavours through the last dry, hot summer, and the eager rookie winemakers were delighted with the way the bunches of grapes were forming. In particular, the grenache grapes – well suited to warmer climates, and now dark and fat and so full of promise – would be ideal for crushing.

All over South Australia, skilled vintners were displaying their talents and offering advice, and the literature about the process of turning ripe grapes into precious, delicious, soul-stirring wine was copious. Mary and Chris went over everything they had gleaned about wine in their three years in Adelaide as they looked forward to the first harvest of their prized plantings.

Emma Penfold, although devasted by the loss of her little baby Laura, had fallen pregnant again within a few weeks of the tragedy. There was now the prospect of new life to erase the sorrow of the little one lost thousands of miles from the bosom of her extended family in England.

Mary would ride one of her horses the mile or so to Evington Cottage at every opportunity to see Emma and little Emma Mary, whom everyone now simply called 'Mary' in honour of her

Bishop Augustus Short suffered great tragedy after consecrating Mary's local church.
State Library of South Australia B-7939

aunt.[1] She would encourage them to read their scriptures and look on the bright side.

Mary Penfold found, though, that 'Old Tom' could still be as prickly as ever. He was now using the impressive title of Captain Thomas Brooks Penfold[2] as he pursued business opportunities in his new home and courted influential friends.

Despite his difficult personality, Tom had done an outstanding job raising money for the new St George's church, just across the track from Evington Cottage, and both Mary and Emma eagerly awaited its consecration, set down for January 1848. The new Bishop of Adelaide, Augustus Short,[3] who had only arrived with his family from London a month earlier, would perform the ceremony.

The church bell had already been cast in bronze and inscribed with the name of the manufacturer, William Pybus of Hindley Street, and the words 'Adelaide, February 9th 1847'. It was the earliest recorded casting of a bronze bell in South Australia; it would still be used for Sunday services at the church almost 180 years later.[4]

If all went well with the crushing of the grapes at The Grange, Mary and Chris figured they could drink a toast to Emma's new child and the new church in the new year, with some of their very own home-grown Penfolds wine.

MARY HAD MADE UP HER mind that Chris was not going to embarrass her over money matters again. Her parents had always been unimpressed by his often careless approach to the family finances, and Mary began to take a much more active role in managing the budget and the business at The Grange, even if her husband received the public acclaim for the continued success of their farm and their flourishing wheat and corn crops. That was the lot of a young colonial farm wife and mother in the 1840s.

Having come off second best in his court battle with Captain Tom, Chris had one more court action to defend: over the building work at The Grange. A couple of days after the Supreme Court in Adelaide ordered Chris to pay his brother more than £200, a local builder and stonemason named James Alder took Chris to court for unpaid work at The Grange.

Chris's barrister said his client had been overcharged, and dismissed the testimony over the terms of the contract from the mason's star witness, a builder named Bill Somerville. Chris had previously sacked Somerville 'through getting a glass of grog too much',[5] and the court heard that the disgruntled worker held a grudge.

There was no proof of a written contract with the stonemason, Chris's barrister told the judge, and 'the testimony was a loose one, being that of a discharged servant for drunkenness'. 'Mr James Alder, the plaintiff,' the barrister continued, 'was as fond of his glass as he was of trowel or hod, or any other implement of his trade'.[6] Chris produced his family friend, Ann Guillod, who told the court that she was present when Chris and the stonemason had agreed to a price, and it was a lot less than what Mr Alder was now saying. In any case, she said, the walls Alder had built at The Grange were not straight.

Alder was seeking £108, 15s from Chris but the jury instead awarded him just £33 16s 6d.

Although Chris had to pay the lesser amount, the court case was still a public embarrassment for him following his loss in *Penfold v Penfold* a few days earlier. Still, he was a popular figure in his community: a public meeting of citizens in the area, while noting the aggression of Captain Penfold, recorded that the doctor was 'a very honourable man'.[7]

From their first harvest, Mary, Chris and Ellen Timbrell gathered about seventy kilograms of grapes. They crushed them with a small press and produced about fifty litres of grape juice. Then the process of fermentation began. Mary and Chris used small French oak casks for storage that had previously been used to store water in ships sailing from England.[8]

The wild yeast within the grapes began to turn the fruit sugar into alcohol and carbon dioxide. Relying on what she'd read and learnt from other winemakers, Mary added brandy to fortify her creation, and in a few days turned the juice into a port-style wine, richer, sweeter and heavier than unfortified table wines.[9] In the end, Mary made about forty-five litres in her first batch of wine.[10]

When it was finally ready for tasting, Mary and Chris sipped the product of the soil and the sun that they had travelled around the world to enjoy, and the declared it a fine vintage. Chris was sure the iron-rich port would be an ideal pick-me-up for his patients, especially those suffering from anaemia.[11] Given the growing enthusiasm around winegrowing in South Australia, Mary knew that this new line of farm produce for the Penfolds would be good for them too.

As it turned out, those first experiments with fortified wine at the Makgill vineyard would be the foundation for almost 180 years of Penfolds wines to follow.

The vineyard next to The Grange was extended, with Mary supervising the planting of the cultivars palomino, frontignac and muscat.[12] Before long, the Penfolds would try their hand at making sherry and brandy as well.

While Chris Penfold recommended his port to help his patients, Mary became more and more concerned with the practical and scientific aspects of winemaking. She took an even keener interest in the farm's account books and the family's business affairs, seeing the production of medicinal wine as an important investment in the family's future. With Chris's increasing medical demands, soon she became solely responsible for the management and early winemaking on their estate.[13]

As the demand for Penfolds ports, sherries and brandies grew, Mary and Chris expanded the vineyard and winery even further.[14] As more grape plantings were ripening and the far more extensive fields of cereal crops fed the Penfold bank balance, Chris began seeing patients at a medical practice and office at Gawler Place, in central Adelaide. He and Mary sold off parcels of their farm to pay down their mortgage to Edmund Trimmer, and they found cheap ways to clear more land for crops. They also took out newspaper advertisements:

> To be Let, at Makgill,
> A TEAM OF SIX BULLOCKS and Dray complete, with permission to cut wood, and from ten to fifty acres of land, with a small dairy now making from 25 to 30 pounds of butter a-week, together with daily utensils and cottage.
>
> Apply to Mr Penfold, Surgeon, Gawler-place, or at Makgill, on Tuesday or Friday, between the hours of 12 and 4.[15]

The Penfolds were also looking for 'a Man and his Wife without family, to occupy a portion of the premises in Gawler-place ... They must be thorough respectable people.' Another advertisement was for a nurse of good character, 'who well understands her business'.[16]

TOM PENFOLD WAS EAGERLY awaiting another addition to his family after the tragic loss of his baby at the start of 1847.

With an eye to building his family fortune, he immersed himself in the life of the Makgill settlement, working on the development of his land and his shops. Despite their differences, he now coexisted with Mary and Chris with a degree of cordiality, and he managed to become a leading light in public and religious life in their little community, which, although it numbered just thirty-two houses, had big ambitions.[17]

Tom had become a church warden, supervising the construction of the St George's church, which had what was termed a 'Kentish' design.[18] Thanks partly to Tom's fundraising, the project had been paid for well within a year of the foundation stone being laid. Now the construction was nearly finished. Cobblestones were taken from the creeks around Makgill to build the decorative walls, and the beams and timbers for the roof were sawn from local blue gum.[19] The church's consecration by Bishop Augustus Short was set to take place in January 1848.[20]

St George's had a seating capacity of 250 and in time was recognised as one of the 'prettiest of the old-time churches' in South Australia.[21] Mary and the heavily pregnant Emma Penfold were eagerly awaiting the chance to worship there.

At the end of 1847, ten months after she lost her little daughter Laura, Emma Penfold spent Christmas day in rapt expectation of the new child she was about to deliver. It was a time of joyous anticipation among the Penfold families. Young Georgina was excited at the prospect of another young cousin as a neighbour. The Grange was full of hiding places for Georgina and Emma Mary to explore and play hide-and-seek in with their parents and Ellen, although the children were always warned to stay away from woodpiles or fallen logs and not to run through long vegetation in case there were snakes.

Other dangers abounded.

On 29 December 1847 *The South Australian Register* reported on the birth of the Penfolds' baby. It was a small notice, brutal in its finality:

BIRTHS. At Evington Cottage, Makgill, on the 26th inst., Mrs Thomas B. Penfold, of a daughter, still born.[22]

The pain for Mary's sister-in-law, who had now lost two babies within a year, was immense – but life did not stand still for anyone in the village of Makgill, even in a summer of stifling heat.

WITHIN THREE WEEKS of the second tragedy for his family in 1847, Tom Penfold joined Fred Bayne in their capacity as church wardens to advertise that St George's would be opened for divine service on Sunday, 30 January 1848, at eleven o'clock, when the Lord Bishop of Adelaide would consecrate it. 'All persons interested therein, are invited to attend,' the announcement read.[23]

Mary and Chris Penfold joined a large crowd in the sweltering South Australian heat, as they prepared to listen to Bishop Short make St George's the first consecrated Anglican church in South Australia, solemnly dedicating it for Christian worship. Despite the tragedies that Tom and Emma had experienced, it was a joyous occasion for the faithful. Mary was delighted that such a heavenly place of worship had arrived near her home.

Tom Penfold helped the bishop with his arrangements. The overflowing congregation were seated and standing while others peered in from open doors and windows. Almost everyone fanned themselves constantly against the heat as they awaited the service. Sweaty brows needed constant wiping.

Bishop Short, newly arrived in South Australia from England, had encountered blast-furnace winds from the moment he set foot in Adelaide, unlike anything he had ever experienced. His family suffered immensely in the conditions, despite the hospitality of the new South Australian governor, Frederick Robe.[24] The bishop later described the 'intense heat at the period of our landing, [with] the thermometer in our bed-rooms at Government house at night being 95' – about 35 degrees Celsius.[25] Even so, the bishop found the countryside around the South Australian capital both harsh and glorious:

> The approach to Adelaide is not prepossessing at this time of the year [December]. The face of the ground is like a brickfield; the sun and the locusts have destroyed the grass. The view of the Mount Lofty range, about five miles off, is magnificent from North Adelaide. The park lands up the Torrens are beautiful; magnificent olives and gum-trees, some stems four or five feet in diameter, with foliage in colour something between the ash and the willow, but pendent like the latter. The climate is very delightful, or disagreeable, according as the north or south wind blows. The former brings a blast as from a furnace red hot ... Then comes the sea-breeze, raising a tornado of dust, which hides the town and everything else from view, filling every crevice. This subsides, the thermometer sinks to 72F° [21 degrees Celsius], and the air is fresh as by the sea-side ...[26]

He expressed 'gratified surprise', about the refreshing warmth of the people in such blistering conditions.

Short wrote that after his family's arrival into Adelaide on the *Derwent* on 28 December 1847, '[n]othing could exceed the friendliness of my reception by his Excellency the Governor, Col. Robe, who pressed me to take up my abode, with all my family and servants, at his house'.

> In the evening there was a large assembly in honour of the day [the anniversary of the Colony], which afforded me the opportunity of being introduced to many of the principal persons of the Colony, and seeing a large portion of the society of Adelaide. It was like a dream. The tone and appearance of the party assembled, the music, lights, uniforms, and dresses, were so thoroughly that of an English country town on occasion of some local festival, that I could hardly realize the fact that I was at the antipodes of England.

The bishop knew of Tom and Emma Penfold's tragedies, and that all the settlers in the area, including Mary and Chris, were enduring tough times, thousands of miles distant from their support networks in Britain. He had prepared a sermon designed to encourage the congregation to persevere through their ordeals. He had based his address on Paul's letter to the Hebrews, focusing on the importance of faith, the 'substance of things hoped for, the evidence of things not seen'.[27]

He was visibly distracted as he approached the pulpit, however, as his youngest child, twelve-month-old Caroline, had been 'very ill' because of the heat.[28] On the advice of Thomas Taylor, the ship's surgeon from their voyage, Bishop Short had driven little Caroline and her nursemaid to Glenelg the day before travelling to Makgill, hoping the sea breeze might give the baby some relief. But he and his wife, Millicent, were clearly distressed as he stood to speak to the congregation an hour before noon.

He reminded those gathered – and himself – that it was by faith that Noah, 'being warned by God of things not seen as yet', built an ark to save his household in a world condemned, and that it was by faith that Abraham went to a foreign land 'not knowing whither he went'.[29] 'By faith he sojourned in the land of promise, as in a strange country ... For he looked for a city which hath foundations, whose builder and maker is God.'

The congregation, many of them also newly arrived in a 'strange country' – and a very hot one – were suitably impressed. The parishioners placed £24 8s 8d in the collection plate, and Fred and Elizabeth Bayne hosted Bishop Short's family for lunch at their grand residence, 'Stradbroke House'. It was 'a sweet spot', the bishop remarked, and they served him 'beautiful fruit'.

After lunch, Bishop Short presided over another ceremony at St George's, with his chaplain, Reverend Theodore Percival Wilson, giving the sermon as a fierce, hot wind raged outside. The bishop consecrated St George's churchyard, noting in his diary that it was at that stage 'unenclosed' but there were 'graves there'.[30]

Bishop Short's sermon on faith seemed providential. That night, he scratched into his diary: 'Baby thank God better.'[31] His faith would soon be tested again.

THE PENFOLDS WERE NOT the only settlers finding success with their harvest. Many other vintners in the area increased their vine plantings, hoping to make their wines into valuable commodities. At Richard Hamilton's 'Ewell Farm', at Glenelg, his son Henry began increasing the area under grapes from two hectares to thirty-two, mostly shiraz, grenache, Pedro Ximénez, muscatel and Doradilla.[32]

Elsewhere in South Australia, vines were thriving. A writer for *The South Australian* reported on his visit to the Barossa and Eden valleys:

> We passed through Langmeil, a village in a cultivated grove ... Angaston, a pretty highland township, with a good Inn, Angas Park, Flaxman Valley, and the Barossa Ranges, all of which present scenes of much beauty and interest. Everywhere we saw fields waving with yellow corn, fruit trees yielding fruit, and vines giving splendid promise of abundance of grapes and wine. At one gentleman's place was the finest sight we have yet witnessed in the province. In a little experimental orchard he had planted vines, figs, apricots, nectarines, peaches, apples, gooseberries, plums, raspberries, currants, loquats, and cherries; and everything was growing with such excessive luxuriance, that it was extremely difficult to determine which deserved the palm ... To show the capabilities of the vines (which cannot be more than six years old), four of them last year yielded sufficient grapes to produce 15 gallons [almost seventy litres] of wine. Everything we saw and heard tended more and more to convince us that this is rapidly becoming one of the most delightful countries in the world, a country which shall be second to none in producing everything that can give gladness to the heart of man.[33]

But that summer was brutal.

The health of Bishop Short's daughter Caroline wavered in the hot winds. She improved in the first week of February, but by the eighth of that month Bishop Short noted in his diary at Government House: 'Baby still very poorly.' The following day: 'Baby very ill but rallied a little.' On 10 February it was 'Baby something better'; then it was 'baby very ill', followed by 'Baby rallied', then 'Baby very ill' and 'Baby weaker, rallied during day'.

On 13 February, he grimly wrote: 'Baby's expected death determined me to stay at home.' The following day: 'Baby not very well.' And then on 15 February: 'Baby very weak.' Finally, the same day, with a wavering hand, he scrawled: '¼ before 12 Baby fell asleep in Jesus ... all children very sad.'[34]

Bishop Short lamented that the heat of South Australia, which was unlike anything Caroline had ever experienced, seemed 'to have overpowered her'.

> [S]he gradually grew worse and worse till it pleased God to take her from us, I humbly trust, to Himself. This is indeed the only consolation I and my dear wife have. She has fallen a martyr to the cause in which we are embarked; – nothing could be stronger or healthier when she landed; – in seven short weeks she is in her grave.[35]

Only a fortnight after he had consecrated St George's in Makgill, Bishop Short buried his daughter in its churchyard.

Three days later, the church hosted its first wedding. Finally the heat of summer began to give way to milder days and cool nights. South Australia was occasionally a sunburnt country, but not always. Even the broken-hearted bishop could write positively of his new home at the end of a traumatic month:

> I can hardly imagine myself out of England, – everything is so English. Even the country wears a less foreign air than France. We have enjoyed a very cool February hitherto, the wind from the hills or the sea having tempered the heat of the sun, which is great as that of Naples, or the south of France. The garden productions are the same;

luscious grapes, figs, pomegranates, olives, peaches, and the finest nectarines and melons. In short, it is a highly favoured country.

Mary Penfold thought so too.

Chapter 19

THE AUTUMN OF 1848 was spectacular for Mary and everyone else in Adelaide. The brutal summer had gone, and as she experimented with another harvest of grapes at Magill – the 'k' had gradually been dropped from the spelling – she did so in idyllic conditions that made her love the Adelaide climate more than ever.

Since the beginning of March, the weather had been perfect: 'a mild, soft, dry, warm, clear, blue sky, with fresh evenings and mornings'.[1] For four months, there had hardly been a day when brilliant sunshine had not greeted Mary's eyes on waking. After four years in the colony, she found herself agreeing with Bishop Short that the year could definitely be broken into four distinct seasons – 'three months very hot; three temperate; three very wet, and three deliciously mild'.[2]

Despite the tragedy of his daughter's passing, Bishop Short predicted that in 'a few years' time, with abundance of labour, this plain of Adelaide, about thirty-five miles long by ten broad [fifty-six by sixteen kilometres], will be filled with beautiful farms, and corn-fields, and vineyards, spreading up the sides of the hills, mixed with olive-yards and pomegranates'.[3]

Chris Penfold found that the fortified wine tonics he made with Mary were of great benefit in helping some patients restore their health. But some of those he saw needed a lot more than wine.

Early in March 1848, Chris returned to The Grange ghostly white after a horrible day at work. A man named Shield had fallen off his dray near the Fifth Creek, and before he could get back to his feet, the bullocks had leapt forward and the wheels of the heavy vehicle rolled over both his legs. One leg was so badly crushed, with bone jutting through flesh, that it would have to be amputated immediately to save Shield's life.[4]

Shield's rescuers immediately sent riders to find Dr Penfold, while another charged into the city to find Dr Friedrich Bayer,[5] a brilliant young German who had become Adelaide's best-known surgeon. Only a few months earlier, Bayer had performed the first operation in Adelaide using the new anaesthetic ether, removing a tumour from the breast of a cancer patient after she was rendered unconscious by the numbing vapour.[6]

Bayer arrived at the scene of the accident and asked Chris to assist him in performing an immediate amputation. There was no time or opportunity to prepare ether. Bayer took out a knife and bone saw, and in his thick German accent told the injured man to be brave. He sterilised his instruments with alcohol and fire, while Chris tied a belt tightly around Shield's thigh to reduce his blood flow and the pain as much as possible. He gave him another belt to bite on. A good helping of wine couldn't hurt the distressed patient. Other farm workers gathered around to hold Shield down. Then Dr Bayer, working as fast as he could, sliced and sawed, skilfully amputating the mangled limb just below the knee.

Chris told Mary about the whole awful business – including that Shield 'bore the pain of amputation with fortitude, and was now doing as well as could be expected under the circumstances'.[7] He recommended more wine. It might not aid his recovery, but at least it might help his mental state.

A few weeks later, Dr Bayer married the daughter of Dr Benjamin Archer Kent,[8] the man who had mixed the ether for the first Adelaide amputation. Their union would produce ten children.

Bayer had arrived in Adelaide only a year before the amputation of Shield's leg.[9] He had been barred from practising medicine in his native Bavaria after refusing to divulge the names of participants in a fatal duel, despite having rendered aid to the

Dr Friedrich Bayer used Chris Penfold as his assistant to perform an amputation in the field not far from Mary's home at The Grange. *State Library of South Australia B 929*

victim.[10] After migrating to South Australia, he would build the largest medical practice in Adelaide, as well as a grand home on North Terrace.[11]

MARY WAS HORRIFIED by the story of the grisly amputation, which came so soon after the tragedies endured by Emma Penfold and Bishop Short. She and the other parishioners of St George's were also appalled by the downfall of solicitor Fred Bayne, Tom Penfold's fellow church warden and the wealthy treasurer of their church building committee.

It had gradually emerged that Bayne's wealth, displayed most ostentatiously in his lavish home, Stradbroke House, had been funded by his embezzlement of his clients' accounts.

The local press reported a stunning 'instance of professional delinquency and flight which the colonial term "bolting" is utterly insufficient to characterise':

> Mr Frederic Bayne, Solicitor, of Stephens-place had disappeared, some alleging that he had taken a passage by the Constance, to China … others that he was merely playing at hide-and-seek; others again pictured him cantering along the overland route … [T]he disappearance of Mr Bayne was an event that occasioned no surprise, for pecuniary difficulties superinduced by extravagance, were known to have been succeeded by transaction of a fraudulent character, and suspected to have been followed up by acts of forgery, of which the absolute proofs have since come to light.'[12]

Dr Bayer had given Bayne £300 to buy an acre (4000 square metres) of land on North Terrace, but Bayne put the money in his own pocket rather than the vendor's. He had robbed the accounts of several other clients too, and had racked up large bills with tradesmen across the city.

Bayne's wife, Elizabeth, who was about to give birth for the fourth time,[13] told the press she had no idea of her husband's dishonest dealings, and that he had left her a note to say she would never see him again.[14] The Baynes were in fact reunited a few months later in Van Diemen's Land, which would soon be known officially as Tasmania. They moved to Victoria and had eight more children. Bayne went bankrupt building the Theatre Royal in Melbourne.[15] Having escaped prison for his shady dealings in Adelaide, he died in 1875 while working as a country solicitor in Kyneton, about eighty kilometres north-west of Melbourne.[16]

In 1848, about the same time Bayne was dodging his creditors in Adelaide, Mary read in the press about the death of her relative John Jacob Astor in New York. At the time of his passing, Astor was the richest man in the United States and one of the wealthiest men who had ever lived. 'His life is a lesson of successful perseverance under difficulties,' *The South Australian* reported, noting that when Astor arrived in America from London sixty years before, 'the main portion of Mr Astor's property ... consisted of seven flutes from his brother's manufactory'.

As Mary looked out at her crops and grapevines ripening in the spring sunshine, she felt some pride in the achievements of her great-uncle.[17] Astor had made a fortune in the fur trade and then, accurately predicting the rapid growth of New York City, had invested in large tracts of Manhattan real estate. His legacy is evident in the New York Public Library, which he helped to finance; in the neighbourhood of Astoria, in Queens, New York City; in Manhattan's celebrated Waldorf Astoria Hotel; and in the Astorhaus museum in his hometown of Walldorf, Germany. The Astor family also bankrolled the discoveries of scientist Nikola Tesla.

FIVE-YEAR-OLD GEORGINA'S education was beginning in 1848: she learnt reading, writing and arithmetic. To these Mary added further studies in the blending and fermenting of the grape juices coming from the vineyard beside The Grange.

Making wine was far more pleasant work than what Chris had to confront. December 1848 arrived with another heatwave, which killed William Curnew, a fifty-year-old who had arrived from England just days earlier and who was working at Magill, loading hay. Workmates heard Curnew groan before he collapsed. They had doused him with water and fanned him with a hat, but he died before Chris could treat him. The coroner's verdict was that he had succumbed to '[l]e coup de soleil, better known as sun stroke'.[18] Mary ensured everyone at The Grange wore a wide-brimmed hat.

Her knowledge about winemaking was constantly improving, with advice from other vintners around Adelaide and from experts who shared their findings in print. On 1 November 1848, sixty years after Arthur Phillip had planted the first vines in Australian soil, Earl Grey,[19] Britain's Secretary of State for War and the

Colonies, wrote to the new governor of New South Wales, Sir Charles Augustus FitzRoy, from his office at Downing Street, London, with the latest advice on winemaking.

There was still no export market of note for the produce of Australian vineyards. Grey wanted that to change, sending FitzRoy the thoughts of British economist T.C. Banfield,[20] who had studied winemaking in Germany and southern Europe for many years as tutor to the sons of King Ludwig I of Bavaria. Banfield wrote:

> It appears that a great variety of soils can yield superior Wines, and we are by this circumstance confirmed in notion that success depends more upon the treatment of the Juice after it is obtained than upon the soil on which the grape is raised.
>
> The Vine is a plant which very much exhausts the soil. It has a tap root throwing out feeders at the side, which admit of its being nourished from manure buried at some distance from the plant ... The rows of Vines are easily kept far enough apart to allow a bullock to draw several furrows between them, without injuring the Vines. The furrows should be 8 or 10 inches deep, and one in the centre might be made still deeper into which the Manure should be thrown. The best manure is Bullocks dung, especially in a warm climate, and Vines are the better for being manured every three years.
>
> Woollen rags, which are also used for hops, are an excellent manure for Vines and are improved by soaking in the dung pit. But it has been satisfactorily proved that frequently turning over the Earth, so as to bring down the surface to the roots is even of more use than Animal Manure, the best nourishment being afforded by the salts evolved in the decomposition of the soil by the Atmosphere. The Vine ought not to be allowed to form too much Wood, but should be cut annually, so as to leave but a few shoots to each.[21]

Banfield told Australian readers that new winemakers needed to experiment with grape varieties to determine what was best for their soil:

> The highest priced wines upon the Rhine are made from a small white grape called 'Riesling' which is an abundant bearer and has a fine flavour. The Aroma of the Muscatel grape is more powerful in the fruit, but is not so powerful in the press, nor is it so durable in the Wine as the simple delicate flavour of the 'Riesling.' The small Black cluster grape of Burgundy is much in use on the Rhine, in Hungary, and in Southern Europe generally.
>
> It is to be feared, however, that the French red wines are to a great extent artificially flavoured, for which purpose peach Kernels are much resorted to.

Banfield reported that a 'large black grape, and also a white variety of the same kind, was much spread in Europe by the Emperor Probus, who exerted himself to improve the production of wine in the Roman Empire, with great success. This grape is found at Tokay, Malaga, Bronte, Lisbon, and Madeira.'[22]

But, Banfield asserted, by far the most important subject for winemakers to consider was 'the proper fermentation of the Juice, obtained from the ripe grape'. Fermentation, he wrote 'has several stages, as both the Brewer and the scientific wine grower well know. According to the stage at which the process is arrested, the liquor obtained differs in nature, the two extremes being wine and Vinegar.' A slow process was essential, therefore, to a perfect vinous fermentation.

Mary took in Banfield's advice on 'the choice of a cool cellar':

> The choice of the cellar in which [the] wine presses stand is the first object to be considered. It should, if possible, be underground excavations in hills, whether Natural or artificial ... because the Water filtering through the Earth keeps up a cool temperature. If there is much water it should

be collected into a little stream to flow along the floor under the doorway.

The water absorbs, and carries with it the Carbonic Acid Gas, which escapes from the casks, in which the Fermentation goes on and keeps the air in the Cellar sweet and wholesome.

The entrance should if possible be turned towards the North, or should be defended from the Sun's rays by Trees; it should only be opened early in the morning or at night.

The temperature should not rise above 50° Fahrenheit [10 degrees Celsius] in the Cellar; but, if it can be kept lower, it is so much the better.[23]

In time, due in part to her careful study of the ideas of Banfield and other experts, Mary would be regarded as one of the most astute winemakers in Australia. In the meantime she and Chris kept paying down their mortgage. By July 1849 they had sold off enough small pieces of their farm to give Edmund Trimmer £600 of the £1000 they owed him. They then negotiated an extension of payment for the remainder until 1852.[24]

HENRY LINDEMAN, Chris Penfold's old classmate at St Bartholomew's Hospital in London, was having mixed success with his grapes. He had experimented with a wide variety, but most were not well suited to the conditions in the Hunter Valley of New South Wales. He did have some early success with his white wines, made from verdelho and aucerot, and with what he called 'Hermitage' (most likely shiraz) and cabernet sauvignon for red wines.[25]

In his report to the Hunter River Vineyard Association in 1850, Lindeman explained that the two samples of wines he brought with him were made from French grapes – 'ciras' (syrah) for red wines and 'rousette' (roussanne, from the Rhône Valley) for the whites. Lindeman agreed with the principles of George Suttor, who had described the advantages of the French wine for medicinal purposes, declaring:

The light wines of France are for a warm climate a very healthy beverage; they constitute the chief support of the people of the country. A bottle of wine and decanter of pure water, with some *été*, are grateful accompaniments to a *déjeuner*; the same at dinner and supper. So that in France they do not use much tea or coffee, their wines superseding the use of all foreign beverages. Thus in time they may become in Australia and New Zealand, if due attention be paid to the cultivation of the vine; wine will give the best support to health, and contribute much to the wealth of the colony.[26]

At the midpoint of the 19th century, while winemakers such as Lindeman experimented with their varieties, members of the Macarthur family remained the most important figures in the small Australian industry. Their vine cuttings sent from Camden Park had taken root throughout South Australia, and they were leading the push to find export markets for Australian wine.

John Macarthur had seen the export potential for winegrowers a quarter of a century earlier, when he wrote to his son John Junior in 1824 suggesting that the first vintage of Camden wine produced by 24-year-old William, including a German-style hock, might find a market in India.[27] Macarthur Senior had sent bottles of this wine to England but was suffering mental health problems that eventually saw him declared a lunatic, bringing an end to the career of one of Australia's most important early entrepreneurs.

William Macarthur planted a new nine-hectare vineyard at Camden Park in 1830,[28] and began to import German vinedressers to tend it. Bringing in teams of non-British migrants was controversial at the time. The Macarthurs argued not only that the colonists of Australia would benefit from the specialised knowledge the Germans offered, but also that there were definite social benefits to more wine being produced from Australian soil.

In his 1837 appeal to the British government to allow German migration, John Macarthur's oldest son, Edward,[29] wrote:

[T]here can be no doubt, [that wine] may in a very short time by the application of Capital and practical skill be produced in such quantity as to supply a cheap and wholesome beverage for the labouring Classes; and this will probably afford the best check to the consumption of ardent spirits, which now takes place to a lamentable extent, and is a principal cause of the disorder and crime so prevalent in the Colony.[30]

A dozen years later, as 1850 approached, James Macarthur, the member for the county of Camden in the New South Wales Legislative Council, campaigned for a reduction in tariffs on Australian wines so they could be sold more readily into British markets.[31] He told the upper house that there were around 400 hectares of vineyards in New South Wales, yielding about 470,000 litres of wine, and about 5700 litres of brandy. If sent to a British market, Australian wine attracted an import duty of five shillings and sixpence per gallon, whereas wine from the Cape of Good Hope was admitted at a duty of half that. 'This high rate of duty,' Macarthur declared, 'in a great measure, precludes the shipment of Australian Wine to England, and operates as a discouragement to the Australian winegrower.'[32]

Mary, reading this report in her local newspaper, was anything but discouraged. She was not yet ready to export any of her wine from the Magill estate, but she and Chris were well pleased with what they were making for local consumption in their little cottage industry. They imagined that one day their small winery might grow into something that little Georgina would benefit from.

Just as these hopes began to take root, however, South Australian vineyards were devastated by a series of events that would dramatically change colonial Australian society.

Chapter 20

IN 1850 IN THE SMALL, cosy kitchen of The Grange, Mary and Ellen prepared meals on a woodfired stove and drew water from the only pump in the house. Georgina, now seven, watched on with fascination as Mary and Ellen experimented with mixtures for wines that in time would become synonymous with the Penfold name.

Georgina was a pretty girl, with her mother's round face and her father's wide, expressive eyes and thick, wavy hair. Mary gave her a gold crucifix to wear around her neck, and she had a daguerreotype photograph taken of the little girl, which she sent to her widowed father, Dr Tom Holt, back in London.

While Mary and Chris were building a strong reputation for their wine-based medicinal tonics, the Australian industry was bolstered in 1850 when Thomas Hardy,[1] a native of Devon, arrived in Adelaide and began working at John Reynell's farm. He absorbed everything he could about the science of winemaking from the area's German immigrants. In future years he became one of the leading figures in the Australian wine industry.

In 1851, William Macarthur sent a selection of the best eight wines from his family's vineyard at Camden to the 'Great Exhibition of the Works of Industry of All Nations', which was being held inside a huge glass hall called Crystal Palace in London. It was the first in a series of world's fairs and drew exhibitors from around the globe. At the time, the Macarthurs had 106,000 litres of wine in cellarage and were producing up to 68,000 litres of wine and brandy a year.[2]

In a booklet published for the Great Exhibition, Macarthur explained that his 'Wines have a certain dryness and bitterness peculiar to the Wines of New South Wales, to which the palate becomes accustomed: but with age this bitterness passes off, as in the specimens now in England'.[3] The wines were grown in soil that, he said, was 'porous, brown, fine grained silicious loam of great depth, containing much decomposed vegetable matter, peroxide of iron, and probably a considerable quantity of potash'.[4]

The eight Macarthur wines he described were:

No. 1. A hogshead [about 240 litres] from the first Camden vineyard planted in 1820 and made from a grape imported from France called 'La Folk', mixed to the extent of about one-third with another sort from Madeira, called the 'Verdelho,' the former being very productive and the latter remarkable for its richness in the saccharine principle. Three years old in March 1851.

No. 2. A hogshead from the same Vineyard, and made in the same manner as the last, but entirely from the Verdelho grape. Three years old in March 1851.

No. 3. A quarter cask [about 125 litres], the produce of the last described Vineyard on the hill, from the White Muscat of Lunelle. To this Wine, during the tumultuous fermentation, was added at different times very pure Brandy of home manufacture, previously filtered through charcoal to render it quite flavourless, in the proportion of two pints of pure alcohol to the hundred pints of Wine.

No. 4. A quarter cask from part of the same Vineyard, made from the 'Red and Black Muscat of Frontignac' in the same manner as the last, and with the addition of the same quantity of spirit. Three years old, April 1851.

No. 5. A quarter cask from the same Vineyard, produced from the 'Riesling Grape,' a variety imported from the Rhine, where it is the sort chiefly cultivated in the best

Vineyards, made in the same manner as the preceding. Two years old, March 1851.

No. 6. A quarter cask from the same Vineyard, made in the same manner as the last, from 'La Folle Grape,' mixed with the 'Muscat Noir de Frontignac,' in the proportion of four to one. Six years old in March 1851.

No. 7. A quarter cask of Red Wine, made from a variety called the 'Seyras' [Shiraz], cultivated at the hill of the Hermitage (Tain). Two years old, March 1851.

No. 8. A case containing, in bottle, samples of a Wine made in April 1844, from the same Vineyard and the same kind of Grapes as No. 4, but in a still more desiccated state, fermented in the same manner but without the addition of any ardent spirits.[5]

Macarthur declared that Australian wine could be an agricultural product that would benefit the British Empire in the same way as the 'Golden Fleece', the symbol of the Australian industry his father had nurtured with the importation of merino sheep, and which by 1851 was producing more than 16 million kilograms of wool a year, worth £2 million.[6]

The Macarthurs predicted a time when Australian wines were so popular that Britain's 'tired artizan [sic], in his hours of relaxation from toil', would call for a quart of Australian wine as his preferred beverage.[7]

Their hopes of huge demand for Australian wine had been lifted by the heavy duties on wine shipped direct from Oporto to Great Britain. The impost added £132,000 to Britain's bar tab each year, compared to what it would be paying if it preferred wine from other countries. There was a mere nominal duty being charged on the same wines being shipped from Oporto to American ports. Some English wine merchants had decided to save money by buying Portuguese wines from traders in Canada, but there were calls among British politicians to find cheaper alternatives. Australian winemakers, including Mary and Chris Penfold, were excited as a result.[8]

Patrons visiting the 1851 Great Exhibition included extraordinary figures such as Charles Darwin, Karl Marx, Charlotte Brontë, Charles Dickens, Lewis Carroll, Alfred Tennyson and William Makepeace Thackeray. The esteemed chemist and physicist Michael Faraday assisted with the planning and judging of exhibits, while the American gun-maker Samuel Colt displayed his latest killing machine, a prototype of his 'Revolving Belt' Navy Pistol.

The Macarthurs hoped for their eight Australian wines to become the talk of the Great Exhibition, but their offerings failed to attract the interest they expected. The most talked about object was not Australian shiraz, verdelho or riesling but the Koh-i-Noor, the world's largest known diamond at the time. Another hit for the crowds at Crystal Palace were the first modern public flush toilets: more than 800,000 visitors paid the penny fee to use them.

MARY'S SISTER-IN-LAW Emma Penfold was struggling with the loss of two babies in a year, but her husband, Tom, worked hard to make the most of their new home. His property development transformed the infant Magill village, as he built a bakehouse, a general store, a butcher's shop and five cottages along Magill Road. The area surrounding his shopping precinct in Magill featured large estates set amid vineyards and orchards.[9]

Tom became a director of the South Australian Mining Association, headquartered in Rundle Street, Adelaide,[10] and both he and Chris campaigned, unsuccessfully, for pastoralist Charles Campbell to represent the East Torrens electorate in South Australia's Legislative Council.[11] The Penfold brothers sat on a committee to improve Magill's roads,[12] and while Mary might have wished to sit on the committee too, such positions were unavailable to women.

Tom took over the 4000-square-metre site on the north-east corner of Magill and St Bernards roads, where the Woodforde Arms hotel had been built in 1840. The Woodforde Arms had been a five-room weatherboard public house that also contained a blacksmith's shop and a skittle ground – the era's version of tenpin bowling. The inn had ceased trading in 1844, and the World's End Inn had been built a hundred metres away the following year, to take over the trade.

Tom's workmen started constructing a two-storey, ten-room brick building on the old Woodforde Arms site, with a plan to make it a rival hotel. In fact, Tom was lucky to get any workmen at all, as the biggest social upheaval in Australia since the arrival of the First Fleet had upended the local workforce.

ON 17 MAY 1851, a New South Wales newspaper reported breathlessly that the countryside around the Blue Mountains 'to an indefinite extent into the interior is one immense gold field'. The news had produced tremendous excitement in the town of Bathurst and the surrounding districts. Business in that town was now utterly paralysed, as *The Bathurst Free Press* reported:

> A complete mental madness appears to have seized almost every member of the community, and as a natural consequence there has been a universal rush to the 'diggings'. Any attempt to describe the numberless scenes – grave, gay and ludicrous, – which have arisen out of this state of things, would require the graphic power of a Dickens, and would exceed any limit which could be assigned to it in a newspaper ... People of all trades, callings and pursuits, were quickly transformed into miners, and many a hand which had been trained to kid gloves, or accustomed to wield nothing heavier than the grey goose-quill became nervous to clutch the pick and crow-bar or 'rock the [gold] cradle' at our infant mines. The blacksmiths of the town could not turn off the picks fast enough ... the roads to Summer Hill Creek became literally alive with new made miners from every quarter, some armed with picks, others shouldering crowbars, or shovels and not a few strung round with wash-hand basins, tin-pots and [colanders]. Garden and agricultural implements of every

variety either hung from the saddle bow or dangled about the persons of the pilgrims to Ophir ... Such is the intensity of the excitement that people appear almost regardless of their present comfort, and think of nothing but gold.[13]

A few weeks later, as Mary and Chris experienced the wettest winter since the foundation of South Australia,[14] they read the grim prediction in their local publications about the danger to the colony posed by a gold rush in New South Wales, just three years after the Californian gold rush.

The South Australian Register claimed that the 'gold-seeking mania which has seized on our fellow-colonists in New South Wales will unquestionably affect us here, not only by increasing the price of provisions, but still more injuriously in furnishing inducements to the working men to quit our shores for the dangerous and maddening pursuit of gold-digging'.

The *Register* claimed that, in South Australia, 'many a respectable and thriving' workman had sold his small property 'at a ruinous depreciation' during the rush to California, and 'many a prosperous servant threw up his employment in the feverish haste to get rich suddenly out of the sands of the Sacramento [River] ... Of those who left us many have returned dejected in spirit, and broken in health, and few richer than when they left our shores.'[15]

Before long, the remarkable gold discoveries around Ophir, west of the Blue Mountains, were being overshadowed by discoveries in Victoria, at Warrandyte, Clunes and Buninyong, Ballarat, Castlemaine and Bendigo. The rush to those goldfields accelerated.

Reports of golden nuggets in Australia appeared in newspapers throughout England, Europe and the Americas, and over the next decade the population almost tripled, increasing from around 430,000 to almost 1.2 million.[16] Victoria became the most populous of the Australian colonies, and Melbourne its biggest and wealthiest city.

The Victorian gold rush soon caused a major labour shortage and economic turmoil in South Australia.[17] Within a few

Dr Henry Lindeman, a former classmate of Chris Penfold's, became a major winemaker in Australia.

months of the discoveries in Ballarat, 16,000 South Australians – half the male population – had migrated east.[18] The dearth of skilled workers – and especially of geologists – caused the suspension of copper mining operations at Kapunda, Burra and other South Australian mines. The artist S.T. Gill, having long sold his photography equipment as it was not profitable, packed up his sketchbook and headed for the diggings too. He would become one of Australia's most celebrated illustrators during that turbulent period.

After fire ravaged the Hunter Valley property of Henry Lindeman, consuming his stores, cellars and equipment, and the 18,000 litres of wine he had stored,[19] he headed for the goldfields to rebuild his finances. When not panning for gold, Lindeman worked as a doctor. Cashed up, he returned to Cawarra and rebuilt the winery, though he found it a struggle to make any wine for some years. His 1853 crop, for instance, was blighted by the arrival of 'a small green grasshopper which appeared around the time of the grapes blossoming, and by a small grey beetle'.[20]

John Reynell was one leading South Australian winemaker who believed there was more money in gold than grapes, and he headed for Victoria as well. Unlike most prospectors, Reynell had some success, finding sixty-four ounces of gold, worth more than $300,000 in 2025.

Samuel Smith left his home at the Yalumba vineyard, in Angaston, with his son Sidney. After sinking sixteen mineshafts in a four-month frenzy, they returned to South Australia £300 richer. Smith bought more land to let out, as well as two horses with harness and a plough. With the money he had left, he built a new house and cellars at Yalumba.

Thomas Hardy also headed for the goldfields – but not with pick and shovel. He took mobs of fat cattle from South Australia's Fleurieu Peninsula. Leaving John Reynell's German vintners behind, Hardy found work with a butcher, cashing in on the hunger of the miners by providing meat on the diggings. He would soon pour the wages he saved into wine.

Likewise, two brothers, Joseph[21] and Henry Best,[22] from Richmond in Surrey, made a tidy sum providing hungry diggers near Ararat and Stawell with food and stores, and used their profits to establish vineyards at Great Western, in Victoria's Grampians region, 230 kilometres from Melbourne.

Mary and Chris and other farmers and winemakers struggled to find staff to harvest crops and grapes as the South Australia workforce dwindled. Most of the hopefuls who left the colony made little money. And many endured extreme misery in their quest for riches. A wine and spirit merchant named Richard Clode[23] had only bad luck on his quest, and was fortunate to live to tell the tale.

Clode had arrived in South Australia on 2 June 1849[24] with his wife and seven children. On 20 October 1851, the intrepid husband and father left Adelaide on foot for the Victorian goldfields, with a blanket on his back and his faithful dog, Tiger, by his side. He tramped through countryside that was a mass of mud after heavy rains, and into areas where there were no roads. After 160 kilometres, he and Tiger came to a swamp that took them two hours to cross.[25]

Knee-deep in mud and slime, Clode crawled onto a bank, only to find not a track in sight. 'It appeared that the heavy growth after winter rains had obliterated them,' Clode wrote.

> Fortunately, I fell in with a few friendly natives who put me on the right scent. Next morning I trudged on admiring the luxuriant shrubs which grew in profusion around many salt water lakes. I finally came to a most formidable swamp about four miles across and in places chin deep ... Tiger could have swum the distance but would not go ahead and kept swimming back to me, for I could not keep up with him. It took me six hours to get out of that infernal swamp, but, alas, I found myself quite alone. My poor dog had drowned.[26]

On and on Clode went, through swamp after swamp. He waded for miles, meeting occasionally a shepherd or stockman.

> The natives I encountered were very civil and of great assistance, supplying me with fish they caught in the Coorong ... One tribe I fell in with was very warlike. They understood no English and I did not comprehend their dialect. From what I could gather they were on a war expedition against another tribe. They were painted in red, white, blue and yellow, each male with three of four spears, war clubs and boomerangs. I felt much more at ease where I was out of their reach.[27]

Travelling barefoot for another 160 kilometres, he finally reached the Glenelg River. Finding it necessary to replenish his pockets – so that he could complete his journey and have the means to buy a miner's licence and tools – Clode found work at a sheep station during the shearing season, earning thirty shillings a week, plus keep.

> One night as I lay asleep I was bitten on my left hand by a snake. Involuntarily, I put out my right hand to find out what was wrong and I was bitten again on the second finger of that hand on the top joint. I held on to my enemy until a light was procured by which time the snake had entwined my right arm and taken a coil around my neck with its tail.

There were 14 men in the hut with me but none of them would lay a hold of the snake which still had hold of my right finger, so I placed my hand on a table and cut its head off with a knife; it gradually uncoiled itself and was found to measure between four and five feet. It was a diamond snake concerning which no one knew anything further other than dogs had been bitten by them and died. This, you will agree, was not the most agreeable intelligence, especially as on enquiry I learned the nearest doctor was about 200 miles [320 kilometres] away. I sucked the poison out of the wounds as best I could, cauterised them and applied warm olive oil and poultices. Medical assistance appeared essential and so I headed off for Geelong. The station manager lent me a horse to take me as far as Black Swamp, thirty miles [fifty kilometres] away, and a letter to the overseer there to lend me another.

The overseer was not there. Clode left the horse and set out to walk the remaining 270 kilometres. His left arm was swelling rapidly and the pain was excruciating, so much so that he barely slept a minute for the next eight days on his trek.

A doctor at Geelong dosed me with laudanum. He soon reduced the inflammation, but my hand broke out into a wound of the worst description which defied for four months all attempts to heal ... my left hand is almost useless, two fingers are grown together, Siamese fashion, as far as the middle joint and I will never be able to close my hand. The only wonder is that I have a hand left, for the doctors I consulted at Geelong, Melbourne and Adelaide were almost unanimous in their wish for amputation, but I stuck out against it, and am glad now that I was so obstinate. A great wonder is that I survived to tell the adventure of my overland trip. Nevertheless I am taking a few weeks off to try my luck at the Echunga goldfield, the accounts of which are very good. I mean to obtain at least half a hundredweight before next winter and you may be assured that I shall keep a close look out for snakes.[28]

WITH THIS SNAKEBITE survivor's extraordinary tale making news around Adelaide, Chris Penfold gave up any ideas of finding his own El Dorado on the goldfields: he would stay at The Grange to mend patients and make wine with Mary. Still, he and Mary managed to pay off their mortgage to Edmund Trimmer in December in 1851, after selling off more of their farm for £400 to James George Nash, the colonial surgeon.[29]

Production from South Australian vineyards slowed to a trickle over the next few years because of the absence of farm workers. But Mary needed every available hand when fire erupted in the hills behind The Grange in January 1853 and 'ran with surprising rapidity'.[30] The fire was said to have originated 'from some persons shooting ... with paper wadding – a most dangerous practice in the summer'. About thirty farm workers were soon on the spot of the blaze, beating out the flames.

But the fire had a life of its own, racing on in the direction of Magill. Mary, Chris and Georgina watched on in horror as a wall of flames raced towards them. To their relief, the local dirt roads acted as a firebreak and the Penfold corn and vines were spared.[31]

ALTHOUGH THE AGRICULTURAL workforce had been dramatically reduced by the rush to the goldfields, Mary was well pleased that the accompanying boom in the Australian settler population was causing a rise in the demand for local wines.

She and Chris were still making fortified tonics for medicinal use, but already Mary could see the potential for the garden vineyard beside The Grange to be greatly expanded. With their mortgage paid off, the Penfolds now owned outright a huge parcel of fertile land close to the city of Adelaide, including their well-established vineyard.

Mary believed their vines had limitless potential.

Chapter 21

MARY AND CHRIS WATCHED on with astonishment as the Australian population was rapidly trebling, creating greater demand for the produce of the continent's vineyards. But the vast volume of wine being created to cope with that sudden expansion still struggled to find export markets because of high duties on intercolonial trade and high transport costs in exporting to Europe.[1]

The first significant export of Australian wine to Britain came in 1854, but it was only in small amounts, totalling 6291 litres[2] in the first year. Over the first decade, Australia exported only 32,000 litres, on average, to Britain annually.[3] Wine remained a niche industry by comparison with meat and wool, mining and cereal crops. The number of sheep rose from 100,000 in 1820 to 1 million in 1830, 4 million in 1840 and 13 million in 1850. Australia supplied one-tenth of British wool imports in 1830, and half by 1850.

While gold was the flavour of the decade for the thousands flocking to Victoria from around the world, other immigrants searched for treasures among their grapevines. Included in their number were the de Castella brothers, descendants of Swiss nobility.

In 1850, Paul de Castella,[4] just off the boat from London,[5] bought 'Yering Station', in Victoria's Yarra Valley, from the Scottish-born Ryrie brothers. The Ryries had built a small wine cellar and planted a four-hectare vineyard with two grape varieties: black cluster (pinot noir) and sweetwater. When de Castella arrived at Yering to negotiate the purchase of 12,000 hectares, Donald Ryrie welcomed him with his own wine, which was 'labelled with ironic overstatement as "Chateau Yering"'.[6]

De Castella hired Samuel de Pury, one of a large group of immigrants originating from around De Castella's hometown, to expand the vineyard, gradually increasing it to 20.5 hectares and extending the property's cellar. He was later joined in developing the station by Samuel de Pury's brother, Baron Guillame de Pury, who founded the Yeringberg vineyard.[7]

Paul de Castella lived in Donald Ryrie's house until 1854, when his own mansion was completed, built with bricks made on site and with costly fittings such as marble fire surrounds and cedar timbers sent by ship from New South Wales and then carried by bullock cart from Melbourne. The grand house quickly became the social centre of the Yarra Valley, and the setting for lavish parties that drew socialites from Melbourne and beyond for luxury weekend escapes.

In that same year that the mansion was finished, de Castella's older brother, Hubert,[8] arrived to pursue business interests in Victoria as well. He was a naturalised Frenchman, having studied architecture in Paris after a Jesuit education in his Swiss homeland. In April 1855, he paid Donald Ryrie £7868 for the 6070-hectare station 'Dalry', adjoining his brothers' Yering. He ran cattle but had his mind set on making wine in the French style.[9]

Hubert de Castella was not a doctor, but he believed passionately in wine's medicinal qualities, writing many years after arriving in Victoria that it was 'the most nourishing, the most invigorating, the most restorative beverage that God has given to mankind'. Further, wines 'increase the appetite, they exhilarate the spirits, they tend to fill the veins with pure healthy blood, and at the same time favour the action of the excretory organs; they are good in anaemia and chlorosis'.[10]

Hubert recommended wine for children, with the addition of two parts water, stating that it would predispose them for habits of temperance in later life. He claimed the prevalence of wine in the southern districts of Europe allowed 'a balanced alimentary diet and limited drunkenness', and he awaited the day when, 'in Victoria, every farmer will have his one or two acres of vineyard for the supply of wine for his family'.[11]

MARY AND CHRIS PENFOLD faced all kinds of obstacles with their crops during the gold rush era. In the summer of 1854, Chris lamented that his wheat and corn were 'inferior in quality and quantity' compared with that of previous years; the yield from his property would 'most decidedly' be down on previous harvests.[12]

The Penfolds' long-term mainstays, Elijah Lovelock and John Horsnell, had by now moved on, with Lovelock settling in the Inman Valley and Horsnell concentrating on growing his family and cultivating his own farm, 'Woodvale', along the Third Creek.

Chris told a newspaper reporter that while he might be able to find sufficient workers for his next harvest, labour in Adelaide was 'not abundant'.[13] He was looking for a working overseer, 'capable of managing 300 acres [121 hectares] of arable land'.[14]

The Penfolds had sold off a large part of their original farm, and their rate assessment from the District Council of East Torrens now described the Penfold property as having a stone cottage of five rooms and two and a half acres (one hectare) of garden.[15] The Penfolds refused a plea from their local council to allow a road to run through their property, even though £1000 of government money had been made available to build it, using fifty men 'from among the newly-arrived immigrants for six weeks'.[16]

John Reynell had returned to South Australia enriched by his gold prospecting in Victoria, and was ready to cash in further by selling grapes and land. In February 1854, in response to 'numerous applications for land',[17] Reynell drew up a notice of sale for about sixteen hectares of his Reynella Farm for the establishment of the township of Reynella. He described it as '13 miles [22 kilometres] from Adelaide, on the Great South-road, commanding running Water all the year'. The sale of ninety-four allotments netted him almost £3000.

His vineyard continued to make up to 2250 litres of wine annually in the 1850s, depending on the season. The varieties

Thomas Hardy started working at John Reynell's vineyard and after a short time as a cattleman became a leading figure in the Australian wine industry.
National Library of Australia obj-32986578

he was growing included malbec, gouais, verdelho, Constantia, roussillon, Pedro Ximénez and cabernet.[18] In the 1850s, he began exporting wines to Victoria, England and New Zealand.

Reynell's former employee Thomas Hardy returned from the diggings to work on a cattle station for a time, before buying 18.6 hectares of land on the River Torrens, in Adelaide's west, in 1853. He called his new property 'Bankside' and planted 3000 square metres of vines, mostly shiraz, and 8000 square metres of fruit trees. The land now centres on the suburb of Underdale.

In the Clare Valley, about 100 kilometres north of Adelaide, vines were abundant. The founder of the town of Clare, Paddy Gleeson,[19] was growing grapes on his sheep run 'Inchiquin', and John Horrocks had planted them at his 'Hope Farm' at Penwortham.

German Jesuits had started making sacramental wine for Catholic worship. In a similar fashion to the migration of the Silesian Lutherans who had settled in the Barossa Valley, Jesuit priests Aloysius Kranewitter and Maximillian Klinkowstrom came to South Australia in 1848 as chaplains to a group of 130 German Catholics. They were hoping to establish a monastic community in this new land where they could enjoy religious freedom.

The Jesuits were soon joined by Catholic Prussians from the Barossa, and in 1851 bought forty hectares of land for their community near the town of Clare. They named their village Sevenhill, after the seven hills of Rome. Soon Irish and Polish Catholics settled in the area as well. The Jesuits bought vine rootlings – young grapevines produced by taking cuttings and allowing them to develop roots – from the Hawker brothers' nearby sheep station, 'Bungaree'.[20]

Closer to Adelaide, another prominent Catholic was the Gloucestershire-born winemaker Edward Peake.[21] He had arrived in Adelaide in 1852, built a career as a land agent and auctioneer, and become prominent in Adelaide politics before winning the seat of The Burra and Clare in the South Australian House of Assembly. Peake eventually managed the Clarendon vineyard for absent landlord William Leigh, having been steward on Leigh's estate at Woodchester, in Gloucestershire. Later Peake purchased the estate for £4407, greatly improving the production at the vineyard. He made many notable sketches around Adelaide, and his knowledge of the English Gothic Revival architectural style influenced the design of Adelaide's Cathedral of St Francis Xavier.[22]

Tom Penfold's land development was going at a fair clip too. The ten-room, two-storey building he had built on Magill Road was named the East Torrens Hotel, though it would later become known as the Tower Hotel. It still serves thirsty and hungry patrons today, more than 170 years later.

AUSTRALIAN WINES RECEIVED perhaps their most valuable exposure yet in 1855, when the indefatigable William Macarthur took his samples to the Paris Exposition Universelle on the Champs-Élysées. Macarthur was appointed the commissioner representing New South Wales and tasked with preparing products from the colony for display.

He resigned his seat in parliament and went to Paris at his own expense with the exhibits. These included wool, wine and native wood, of which he had 130 different kinds from the Illawarra region alone. Macarthur began asserting himself as soon as he arrived in Paris. He complained that the allocated space for his display was too small, and he instead secured what he called '300 superficial feet in one of the very best situations in the *Palais d'Industrie*'.[23]

He watched the jury of experts sample 156 wines from around the world in a single sitting on 25 August, and when the tasting of the New South Wales wines started at 8 a.m. the next day, he recalled that there was a long pause at the tasting of the first wine – a red of 1853 produced by James King at his vineyard at Irrawang, near Port Stephens, east of the Hunter Valley. Macarthur described a look of surprise, and then of approval as the judge remarked, *'Jolie vin, tres bon'* – nice wine, very good.[24] The judges called out their mark: ten out of twenty.

After the judging was complete, Macarthur calculated that 'the averages of the six samples from James King was 10-and-a-half'. The offerings from the Macarthurs' own Camden Park was '11-and-two-thirds'.[25] Macarthur had brought white riesling of 1849 and 1851, two vintages of muscats 'that had been around the world in wood', and an aucerot of 1848.

The Paris Exposition Universelle proved a wonderful showcase of Australian wines with William Macarthur earning the favour of Queen Victoria.

One of the judges told Macarthur that 'we were all perfectly astonished at the quality of the Australian wines – we had tasted the slightest ... of it, & it is evident that in addition to soil and climate favourable to their growth first care must have been taken in their manufacture. They do your colony infinite credit.'[26]

Macarthur asked what European or other wines were comparable. The judge told him that 'we were unanimous in giving them a place in strength & flavour between the wines of Madeira and those of the Cotes du Rhone – they have some resemblance to both'. William wrote to his brother James: 'I cannot describe the number of applications as have since had to be showed to taste.'[27]

Queen Victoria and Prince Albert spent ten days visiting Paris during the Exposition, on the invitation of Napoleon III in a historic state visit intended to celebrate the military alliance between Britain and France during the Crimean War. The two nations had been mortal enemies forty years earlier, but now all seemed forgiven. It was the first time in 400 years that a British monarch visited France.

Victoria and Albert, accompanied by Napoleon, visited Macarthur's exhibit. Victoria asked to taste the New South Wales wines, and Macarthur told James that – after a 'certainly your majesty' – he had finally conquered not only Paris but London as well.[28]

Macarthur later said that 'at the express request of the Emperor, some of the best [wines] were sent to the Tuileries during her Majesty's visit to Paris ... Sample bottles were applied for, to be sent to the Emperor of Austria, as well as to several agricultural societies in Germany. Innumerable were the applications to taste the wine, and both the French and the English press speak of it in terms of marked praise.'[29]

The Times reported that during the royal visit to the Exposition, 'Mr McArthur [sic] was too modest to tell the Prince a "fact" which is creating a great sensation here, viz. – that Australia exhibits wine of extraordinary excellence, Tokay [or Camden muscat, as Macarthur called his offering] especially being fairer than the best produced in Hungary'.[30]

Macarthur became a chevalier of the *Légion d'honneur* by imperial decree a month after the Exposition, the first such award for an Australian. Queen Victoria knighted him the following March.

These honours were welcome news for Mary and Chris Penfold and other vintners around Australia, because the whole of the Australian wine industry, small as it was, benefited. There was increasing interest in wine and its health benefits, and a considerable increase in sales, albeit temporarily, because of the Exposition. In 1855 Great Britain imported close to 112,000 litres of Australian wine from New South Wales, Victoria and South Australia.[31]

WINE EXPORTS WERE still not a high priority for the Penfolds, though, as they were making only small amounts of fortified wine for Christopher's patients. They were more worried about protecting their family, friends and lucrative crops from the harsh realities of farm life. Fire was a constant threat to lives and livelihoods around Adelaide, and sparked terror for Mary and the rest of the rural population.

On a fiercely hot summer's evening two days before Christmas 1855, fire broke out near the Third Creek. The strong wind pushed the flames through Patrick Auld's section, approaching 'very nearly to his house'. Soon they reached Mary and Christopher's adjoining land and threatened the lives of everyone at The Grange[32] – and not just the humans. There were the four dairy cows, Nelly, Duchess, Lilly and Daisy, and all the horses, Dolly and Gypsey, Captain and Farmer, and half a dozen others that had panic in their wild eyes.[33]

The Penfolds had twenty-eight hectares of standing corn, as well as a quantity of stacked hay. They and all their neighbours rushed into action with wet blankets and whatever else they could find to drive back the blazes that were breaking out all around the Penfold cottage.

Before long, there were about 150 volunteer firefighters from the neighbourhood extinguishing the flames as best they could.

A firebreak was created to prevent any resurrection of the blaze from spreading.

A considerable quantity of feed had been destroyed, but Mary breathed a sigh of relief that there were no lives lost, and that the corn was safe.

The cause of the fire was not ascertained, though many suspected that 'some persons' were shooting in the afternoon and the wadding from their muzzle-loading firearms might have ignited the tinder-dry grass.[34]

After a spate of fires over the next few days, Chris was appointed the foreman of a jury at an official enquiry, held at his brother's East Torrens Hotel. But despite Chris's suspicions over who had been out shooting, the fires were blamed on 'the wilful act of some person unknown'.[35] Chris's request to increase the powers of the judiciary to interrogate suspects was denied.

The lives of the Penfolds had changed beyond recognition since their days living beside the sea in Brighton a dozen years earlier, when they'd been supported by a large family network. Chris and Mary had both grown older and rounder in the years since they stepped off the *Taglioni* and into life as South Australian farmers and vintners.

Chris remained ever busy with his medical practice, even though he had still not completed his local registration as a doctor, and Mary continued to make wines for him in small batches. Georgina had grown into a bright, pretty and energetic teenager who was keen to explore the rest of Australia.

Ellen Timbrell, though, had grown old before her time and was not in good health. Although there was a vibrant community in Magill and at the St George's church in particular, Ellen remained a solitary figure, living in a small bedroom at The Grange. Mary despaired over the future of her friend, who had followed the Penfold family to this far corner of the world.

Chapter 22

MARY AND EMMA PENFOLD had long been the best of friends, and Mary had supported her sister-in-law through her often difficult life with Tom and the tragedies of her lost babies. They had navigated the sorrows and the joys of life and death together in their new land.

Now Mary faced the imminent prospect of losing Emma.

Tom, Emma and Emma Mary, who had grown into a kindly child, had been in Adelaide for more than a decade but were now heading home, richer financially but poorer emotionally after the death of the family's two baby girls.

Tom advertised 'to be let or sold' his nine-room residence opposite his East Torrens Hotel. It was situated on almost two hectares, which included a garden, and it came with a cellar, storeroom and stabling.[1] He assured buyers that 'a large portion of the purchase money may remain for several years, if required'.[2] Before long, Tom was auctioning off all his household furniture and goods: chairs, tables, sofas, piano, feather beds, carpets, bookcases, garden tools – the lot.[3] He would, though, keep some of his property and lease it out.

Mary was crestfallen. Tom had a reputation as an ogre, but she had seen how hard he had worked for the Magill community; every time she went to Sunday worship, she thought of his efforts to raise money for St George's. God had not always blessed Tom's family, but she knew He moved in mysterious ways, and she gave thanks for their lives and for the sunshine and the rain. Emma remained Mary's dear friend, and her daughter a dear niece. She would always think of them fondly.

Tom and his family finally left Adelaide for London on 5 January 1857[4] aboard the three-masted barque *Irene*. They arrived at Gravesend four and a half months later.[5] They settled at Mount Radford, a prestigious estate on the east side of Exeter, in Devon. Emma soon became pregnant again on British soil, and she finally gave birth to another little girl, whom she and Tom named Georgina Frances Penfold in honour of her Adelaide cousin.[6]

But Emma Penfold died from an infection six days after the birth. She was just forty-one.

MARY SUPPORTED CHRIS in all his ventures. By 1856, those now included political ambitions, even though she, as a woman, had no voting rights, and no say on how her community was run. She had proved herself an astute businesswoman and homemaker, but – like so many women of her time – she existed in the shadow of her husband's profile.

After Tom's departure, Chris had emerged to become a leader in his community. When Burnside, the area encompassing Magill, had been proclaimed a district worthy of its own council, Chris was elected as its first chairman at a meeting held on 19 August 1856[7] at the Green Gate Inn.[8] He would remain in the position only six months, but he went to work immediately, applying to the South Australian government for funds and advertising for an accountant to keep the council's books and to record the minutes of future meetings.[9]

Chris was preoccupied with the business of running the council and meeting with the heads of other Adelaide districts to consider new roads and bridges. He was also intrigued by a new fertiliser being produced from the blood of slaughtered sheep – which in the past had been a health nuisance for the city and was typically buried. Adelaide's Inspector of Slaughterhouses told him there were twenty-seven tonnes of blood and animal waste presently rotting that could be used.

Chris also continued work as a rural doctor, which meant he inevitably had to deal with the accidents that occurred on farms. A few months after he started his role as the chairman of the Burnside Council, Chris was riding home to The Grange when he was summoned by the friends of a local farm worker who had been knocked unconscious by a horse.

The wounded man, a fellow resident of Magill, had tried to climb upon a horse that had 'a disinclination to be mounted'.[10] The rider, tired of the horse's obstinance, had punched the animal in the head – only to be thrown off, kicked in the head and then trampled on. Rendered insensible, the man was carried to a friend's house, and Chris was called in to provide emergency care. He brought the man around, diagnosed a broken rib and warned him against punching horses again.[11]

Mary, meanwhile, could not have any public input into the establishment of a local library reading room, known as the Magill Institute, but she did give Chris her views on what needed to be done to improve life for the Magill community. Chris echoed her thoughts at a public meeting held at the Magill school.

The Penfolds' neighbour and fellow vintner Patrick Auld also gave his whole-hearted support to that cause, and a list was opened for subscribers. More than thirty Magill locals entered their names, promising a subscription of £1 1s, and several of the subscribers promised to donate books.[12] The library soon opened at the Magill school, offering education and entertainment for adults.

THE REPUTATION OF Australian wines continued to grow in Europe. The royal favour William Macarthur had enjoyed at the Paris Exposition made him even more determined to produce wines to rival the very best from France.

The exposition had celebrated the Bordeaux *grands crus* – wines from the finest producers in that region of France. These were wines that were regarded by the French as among the best in the world: Château Lafite Rothschild, Château Latour, Château Margaux, Château Mouton Rothschild and Château Haut-Brion.

Along with meeting the British Royal Family, Emperor Napoleon III and many of France's leading vintners in Paris, Macarthur had visited the Loire Valley, Poitiers, Bordeaux and Burgundy, before heading to England, Belgium, Germany, Switzerland and Italy. All along his journey he studied the latest methods and technologies of winemaking and looked for skilled workers he could entice to the vineyards of Australia.[13]

Over time, he ordered cases of fine wines from Burgundy, Médoc, Sauternes and Hermitage, so he could compare them with the wines he and his brother James were making.[14] He also bought winemaking equipment: several glass and iron plugs, a copper filter, a tap for bottles and some tasting and cooperage tools, as well as pruning tools, secateurs and serpettes.[15]

The continued promotion of Australian wine in Europe by the Macarthur brothers enhanced its reputation, even if international sales remained insignificant. But *The Times* predicted that great things lay ahead. 'In a few years,' it reported, 'we hope to see the names of Camden Park, Irrawang, Tomago, Lochinvar, Cawarra, Tuteela, &c. rank as high in the wine-market as Lafitte, Latour, Chateau-Margaux.'[16] The paper imagined that one day wine might eventually equal 'wool, tallow, gold and coal' as export commodities from the eastern Australian colonies.[17]

At the same time, Thomas Hardy made his first wine at his 'Bankside' vineyard on the Torrens, about thirteen kilometres from The Grange. Soon he would ship two hogsheads – about 600 litres in total – of his finest vintage to England.

ELLEN TIMBRELL HAD BEEN Mary's friend for almost twenty years. While she had infuriated Mary when they first arrived in Adelaide with her reluctance for toil, the bond between them was always strong. For Mary, she represented a link to her old life in England. She eventually became an eager assistant for Mary and Chris, and her involvement in producing wine became greater as Chris's work as a doctor and councillor devoured most of his time.

But Ellen had long struggled with her health. In August 1857 she became gravely ill. Ellen came down with a sudden fever and severe headaches. Within days she was covered with a rash.

Mary watched in forlorn hopelessness as she saw her friend racked with typhus fever.[18] Chris did all he could to make Ellen more comfortable, but nothing could turn back the inevitable tide of the disease.

Ellen became so sensitive to light that she had to be kept in a blackened room, and soon the darkness gave way to delirium and panic.

Typhus fever, caused by the bite of fleas or lice, was in epidemic proportions at different times during Mary's lifetime, starting with the famine during the Year Without a Summer in 1816, when Mary was born.

The fact that the disease was so common did not make the pain any more bearable for those watching loved ones melt away to nothing in a pool of sweat.

MARY'S HEART WAS BROKEN when Ellen died at The Grange in September 1857, despite all that Chris could do for her. *The South Australian* register reported her passing:

> "On the 3rd instant, at the residence of Mr. C.R. Penfold, Magill, Ellen, youngest daughter of the late Captain James Timbrell, of the H.E.I.C.S. [Honourable East India Company Service].[19]

Ellen was just forty. After she was buried, Mary cut the notice from the newspaper and enclosed it in a black-bordered envelope. Many years later, she attached a handwritten note that eulogised her dear friend. Mary took the words from an epic poem she had read, *The Light of Asia*, about the life of Buddha:[20] 'A life of perfect service ended – duties done – in Charity – soft speech –and stainless days.'[21]

The loss of both Ellen and Emma was a painful blow for Mary, but life went on, even though Chris had lost much of his youthful vigour. The bright-eyed young medical student she had met two decades earlier was now heavier, his eyes becoming wearier and his face covered with thick whiskers. His hair was quickly disappearing.

Without Ellen to assist, Mary took on even more of the winemaking and farm management responsibilities, directing her workers and keeping the accounts. From her narrow office under a sloping roof at the rear of The Grange – the room that had once been Chris's surgery – she looked out on the vines and made entries in her daybook, sitting at a small wooden desk.[22]

Among those entries were such observations as:

Made out Bank Account – Paid Hacket, – Bought Mangol Wurzel 1 [shilling] – Pat finished ploughing Alberta, Gathering Almonds, – Ann went into town, – Bought plough shares, – W. Eagle came with child (sick) cash 5 [shillings]. – Pat ploughing, all things well – Emily bought sugar for brewing from Hales 5 [shillings a pound] – Gathering Almonds – Sent Pat into town in the dray to buy oysters for supper.[23]

She also made an entry that said, '[B]egan making wine.'[24]

BY 1858, SOUTH AUSTRALIA'S population was estimated at 118,665,[25] and the Penfolds saw business opportunities aplenty. While wine remained only a small part of their farm business, they were always looking to expand their horizons. They had acquired a rental property in the Adelaide seaside suburb of Brighton, a place that conjured up happy memories of their time as newlyweds by the Sussex coast, when they'd walked past the Royal Pavilion and strolled on the Steine. This Brighton property consisted of an 'Acre of Land, fenced; Two Cottages, Well of good Water, and Sheds'; it was also 'close to the sea'.[26]

The Penfolds had also opened quarries and started supplying road metal for the major infrastructure projects taking place in Adelaide. On 30 August 1858, Chris wrote to the Adelaide Town Clerk and Council:

> Having almost completed my 1,000 yards of metal for the city, and the original contract being for 2,000, I hope I may be allowed to deliver the remainder. I much regret that some delay has occurred in the quickness of its delivery, but the weather rendered the cross roads impassable. Having opened a new quarry and found excellent metal on a better road, no delay shall occur. I have also a quantity of small metal … to offer for bottom metal or filling up holes, at [6 shillings three pence] per yard for the stone and 1 shilling nine pence for cracking, or will pitch it anywhere in the city under your surveyor's orders for 10 shillings sixpence per dray load (two horses.)[27]

There was still plenty of building work happening around Adelaide despite the ongoing labour shortages, but by the end of the 1850s it was Melbourne that had become the richest city in the world.[28] The gold rush had poured unprecedented wealth into Victoria, sparking an extraordinary population boom that saw the colony grow from 70,000 people in 1850 to almost 500,000 a decade later.[29]

But migration on such a scale also brought the threat of a smallpox pandemic, and the colony was severely lacking in doctors. Chris was offered an important medical position in Victoria by the government there. He had already been thinking about retiring from farm life, and on speculation had started to advertise The Grange and its surrounding farmland:

> TO be LET or SOLD, with long Credit if required, either in one lot of say 300 Acres [121 hectares], or subdivided into three, the FARM of Mr. C.R. PENFOLD, MAGILL; and at a future date the whole of the FARMING STOCK, alive and dead.[30]

In October 1858, Chris travelled alone to Melbourne on the *Havilah*[31] to secure his government position.

At the new Magill library, readers were buzzing with news of the arrival of a shipment of books at John Howell's store on

Hindley Street. The bookshop would now have all the latest bestsellers, including David Livingstone's *Missionary Travels and Researches in Africa* and Charles Dickens's *Little Dorrit*.[32] But the big news among the farmers and winemakers of the town was that the Penfolds were leaving.

On 11 January 1859, under the wide verandahs of The Grange, Chris and Mary Penfold auctioned off all their animals and farm equipment, including all their 'superior horse stock, drays, wagons, farming implements, hay &c.'.[33] Among the auction items were a variety of strong, reliable mares, namely 'Dolly (aged), foal at foot, Nancy 6 years, Jenny 4, and Gypsey (aged), foal at foot'. There were many well-bred and valuable carthorses too: 'Farmer (aged), Captain, 6, Punch 5, Duncan, 5, (out of Dolly by Warwick), Colonel 3, Jock, 2, Comet, 2, and Violet, 2, (out of Nancy by Briton)'.

Also going under the hammer were:

> 1 wagon, 3 drays (quite new), a 15-foot wooden roller, 3 ploughs (iron), 2 pair of harrows, a crushing mill and sack holder, a mowing machine, 2 water tanks of 300 gallons [1360 litres] each, a winnowing machine, a chaff cutter, cultivator and water cart, a horse rake and gig, a cart, a stack of 'wheaton hay' – about 60 tons and half an acre of reaped wheat.[34]

Chris had no plans to come back soon.

The Grange and the Penfold farm did not sell, but most of the stock and animals went. On 16 February, Mary auctioned off all the family's furniture, including her grandfather George Astor's square piano, a rosewood piano made by Broadwood, tables, chairs, sofas and bedding, along with three young heifers and four dairy cows – Nelly, Duchess, Lilly and Daisy – who were a few weeks off calving.[35]

With farm workers looking after the property, Mary, Chris and Georgina, now fifteen, set sail for Melbourne a few days later aboard the *Admella*.[36] Two weeks earlier, Chris had been publicly approved to practise medicine in the colony of Victoria.[37]

It was a difficult departure for Mary. She was now forty-two and had grown to love The Grange, her home for the last fifteen years. She adored the grapevines beside it. But Mary was a dutiful wife. Despite her protests and those of her parents, whom she would never see again, she had followed Chris from England to Adelaide. Going another 800 kilometres east to Melbourne was not such a stretch.

But something about the warm, Mediterranean climate of the Adelaide Hills, with its rich, loamy soil, and the slope of her land, which faced the sun so perfectly, told Mary that she would one day come home to make a lot of marvellous wine.

Chapter 23

AFTER ARRIVING IN MELBOURNE, Mary and Chris took a comfortable home on Nicholson Street,[1] by the sumptuous Carlton Gardens,[2] and prepared for a fast-paced life in a city that was growing at phenomenal speed.

The vast wealth generated by gold meant that timber buildings such as the Town Hall and the General Post Office were being replaced by substantial and beautifully decorated stone buildings.[3] New suburbs fanned out from them to house the growing population. But overcrowding led to slum areas close to the city, with the urban poor living in dilapidated, ramshackle buildings with poor sanitation. The result was a range of social problems and the threat of rapidly spreading disease.

On 17 June 1859, 'Christopher R. Penfold Esq, surgeon' was appointed as the Government Vaccinator for the district of Carlton, Melbourne.[4]

Smallpox was in plague proportions around the world and had killed millions of people. It did not discriminate between rich, poor, young, or old. One in three people infected died in agony, with raging fevers, vomiting, mouth sores and pus-filled lesions all over their bodies.[5] Survivors often suffered lasting effects such as blindness or infertility.

Dr Edward Jenner had developed a vaccine at the end of the 18th century, which involved introducing some pus from a less virulent cowpox sore into a cut. The vaccine had proved highly effective, despite widespread alarm about government conspiracies against civil liberties and rumours from anti-vaxxers that the treatment could turn humans into cows.[6] In 1854, with the gold rush at its height, Victoria followed Britain and the United States in making vaccinations compulsory, using fines and other threats to ensure public compliance.[7]

As Mary longed to return to The Grange, and Georgina finished her formal education in Melbourne, Chris was kept busy performing hundreds of inoculations in the Carlton area. But he also had other important medical duties to perform.

Two days before Christmas in 1859, he was called to examine the body of 33-year-old Patrick Kildea, who had died 'from an act of violence' a week earlier while watching a wrestling match at the Barkly Hotel, in Barkly Street, Carlton.[8] Chris made a post-mortem examination and found that ruptures in the gall bladder and small intestine had resulted in acute peritonitis, which, in his opinion, was the cause of death. Because of Chris's testimony, a man named James Hart was convicted of manslaughter.[9]

Mary and Chris found someone to rent out their farm, but they were still considering their options as Chris stayed busy vaccinating multitudes in Carlton and making emergency calls in his neighbourhood. The Penfolds wrote to a young neighbour in Magill named David Packham,[10] later the local member for their area in the South Australian parliament, and asked him to plant a few more hectares of grapes on their property ahead of an expected return.[11]

The Penfolds had been in Melbourne for a year and a half when a man watching a dog fight in Brunswick Street found out what it was like to be mauled after a horse kicked him in the chest and broke his breastbone. Chris and two other doctors were called to provide immediate aid, but the dog-fighting fan died within five minutes of the horse's mighty blow. A verdict of accidental death was recorded.[12]

Towards the end of 1861, Melbourne was buzzing with talk of a new horse race at Flemington, to be called the Melbourne Cup. In Adelaide, meanwhile, the big news was that the *Municipal Corporations Act* would allow South Australian women who were landholders to vote in local government elections – an Australian first. This idea thrilled Mary and Chris, who were starting to hanker for life back in Magill.

They thought about moving to a smaller property, and tried to find a buyer for the farm at Magill, grapevines and all. While still living in Melbourne, they advertised in the Adelaide newspapers:

> Valuable suburban farm consisting of 296 1/2 ACRES of fine LAND suitable for GARDENS, VINEYARDS, or DAIRY, situated at Magill. There is also a Substantial RESIDENCE on the Property, which is fenced, and well-known as Dr. Penfold's. The above is let for a short term as a grass rental.[13]

But Chris and Mary could not attract the price they wanted, so they continued to rent out the land, mostly for sheep grazing. Occasionally they would come back to check on the property's upkeep. More than ever Mary wanted to return and make wine. She was especially excited at the prospect after the Adelaide press began to describe Australia as 'the France of the southern hemisphere' because of its winemaking potential.[14]

STORIES ABOUT THE growing sophistication of Australian wines were building momentum.

In 1859, William Acland Anderson, Paul de Castella's brother-in-law, brought back some cuttings to the Yarra Valley from the celebrated Château Lafite, in the hope that they might produce high-quality wine in Victoria as well.[15] Hubert de Castella's son François[16] heard stories about a wine degustation at Uncle Paul's Yering Station. After the exquisite Pommard wines from Burgundy were exhausted at the event, Paul produced some wine made from the grapes the Ryrie brothers had planted, and which had been bottled by a Swiss vigneron from Burgundy. This Yarra Valley wine was received with an enthusiastic chorus of 'Better than Pommard!'[17]

While South Australian wine had developed a good reputation among wealthier colonists, the rapid population expansion in

Victoria had led to mass demand for South Australian wheat. By 1860, South Australia had more arable land than any other colony, and much of that 145,000 hectares was being used to grow cereal crops, an export whose value now outstripped that of copper.[18]

Others saw the vast potential in South Australia's expanding vineyards, and the value of grapes over grain. At his Trinity vineyard near Morphett Vale, Dr Alexander Charles Kelly soaked up the writings of French and other European vintners, which he translated and expanded upon for his first bestseller, *The Vine in Australia*.[19] It introduced the latest scientific ideas on wine chemistry to Australian winegrowers and was the precursor to another book, *Wine-Growing in Australia*.[20]

Kelly would soon form a partnership with five leading Adelaide businessmen[21] to form the Tintara Vineyard Co., and would become its manager. He sold Trinity to concentrate on clearing the eighty-six hectares of forest near McLaren Vale to plant grapes for the production of mostly table wine.

BY 1862, THREE YEARS after moving to Melbourne, Mary and Chris were living in the seaside suburb of St Kilda, which had become popular with wealthier families, with mansions and impressive terrace houses being built along its waterfront, hills and wide streets. They watched with pride as Georgina grew into a beautiful young woman. For Mary, though, seeing her daughter blossom was bittersweet, as she knew she would soon lose her.

Georgina was eighteen when she fell in love with a rising Victorian bureaucrat named Thomas Francis Hyland,[22] a handsome thirty-year-old Irishman who had just been appointed as the governor of Portland Gaol, in the oldest European settlement in the colony, 360 kilometres west of Melbourne.

Portland Gaol was a significant engineering feat for its time, with a large underground tunnel to drain its wastewater to the foreshore.[23] A young teacher, Mary MacKillop, had arrived in Portland at about the same time as Hyland, but while his work involved the confinement of sinners, she took a job teaching local schoolchildren before establishing a seminary for 'young ladies';

Irish-born Tom Hyland had a colourful, brutal past but he became Mary's son-in-law and eventually the hard-driving boss of her wine empire.

it is now known as Bayview College. Nearly a century and a half later, Mary MacKillop became Australia's first Catholic saint.

Hyland was a strapping and gallant character, with a neatly trimmed beard and thick wavy hair that looked like a breeze was always moving it about. His demeanour spoke of a rugged man who could get a job done and overcome anyone or anything in his way.

He thrilled, and often shocked, his new love and her parents with stories of his life. The youngest of seven children, Tom had been born just outside Tipperary,[24] and he was busy working his way up the public service in his new home. Like the hundreds of thousands of migrants in Victoria, Tom came to Australia during the gold rush, but he found there was better money to be made in the penal department in Melbourne. He became a prison warder in 1853, guarding convicts at the Pentridge Stockade, which at the time consisted of a few wooden huts surrounded by a wall of slabs, with the warders living in tents.[25] Later that year he was chosen as one of the guards to oversee convicts breaking rocks at Melbourne's Williamstown quarry.

It was dangerous work, as some of the prisoners were regarded as the worst offenders in Australia, brought from the notoriously cruel settlements of Norfolk Island and Port Arthur. They were housed in penal hulks anchored in Hobsons Bay, while Tom and other guards slept on their own police ship.[26] Conditions for the prisoners were horrific and they made frequent escape attempts, some of which ended in brutal deaths. There were also many vicious assaults committed as acts of revenge on warders. Most of the prisoners were forced to work in irons to prevent violence, but many smashed away their rivets with hammers when the guards were out of sight.

In 1856, Hyland was the chief warder on the prison hulk *Success* when convicts from that rancid vessel were being taken by boat across to Gellibrand Point to work. Ten of them tried to make their escape, in the process beating the boatman to death with a hammer and boathook. Hyland ordered the other warders to open fire, and one of the convicts was shot dead. The guards gave chase in boats under sail, but the leader of the convict band, a bushranger known as Captain Melville,[27] blew a kiss as he was making his escape.[28] He despised Hyland for what he said was his rough treatment of prisoners, and he cried out to him as he sailed away, 'Good-bye Hyland, do your worst.'[29]

It had been a windy day, and the prisoners had trouble manoeuvring the boat that they had commandeered. As gunshots rang out from their pursuers, the flesh of some of the convicts exploded with wounds, splattering the others with blood. They were all quickly recaptured and dealt with roughly for the murder of the boatman.[30]

Melville was an intelligent man who had been captured at a brothel in Corio Street, Geelong, after committing a spate of hold-ups in Victoria. He was four years into a thirty-two-year sentence for armed robberies. For his previous good conduct, he had been given a job translating the Bible into Indigenous languages, which he claimed to speak fluently.

At his trial for the murder of the prison boatman, Melville acted as his own lawyer and gave an impassioned defence, protesting against the brutality and humiliations convicts were forced to endure on the prison hulks. No wonder, he said, men went mad. One reporter at the trial said it was 'monstrous indeed, that within sight of Melbourne such floating hells should have been suffered to exist, and that men who are of the same flesh and blood with ourselves, and who will have to stand with us before the same Almighty Judge, should be treated as if they were already consigned to final torment'.[31] All the accused escaped the noose, but Melville, disinclined to still spend decades behind bars, committed suicide in his cell.[32]

Mary and Georgina Penfold were aghast at Tom Hyland's horror stories; Chris, who had performed many post-mortems, not so much.

Only a few weeks after that attempted escape by the convicts, all the men on Hyland's hulk *Success* went on strike, alleging that, on the night after Christmas, he had beaten a prisoner insensible in revenge for having a toilet seat thrown at him. *The Age*, campaigning against the cruel treatment of prisoners, reported:

> An offence undoubtedly had been committed, and, as undoubtedly, would have met the utmost punishment in the mode provided by law. But Mr Chief Warder Hyland could by no means wait! Oh, dear no! He had his own particular little private account to square first with the prisoner, and the Government and the law might afterwards do as they pleased.[33]

According to the newspaper, the prisoners hooted and jeered during the attack, and their anger towards the chief warder and the prison system festered. Insubordination grew.

Hyland seemed like a polite young man who treated the Penfolds with great respect, but Mary must have had serious doubts that Georgina should be involved with this man.

Soon after that incident, Hyland and several other guards from the *Success* were on a tour of prison labourers at Williamstown with John Giles Price, the inspector-general of penal establishments in Victoria. Price was the haughty, monocle-wearing son of an English baronet and was infamous for his unwavering belief that flogging was the key to convict order.

Price asked some workers if they had any grievances about the way they were being treated. They all did – but the inspector-general dismissed each one.

Some of the men grew angry and one shook his fist at Price, shouting, 'You old tyrant, your race will soon be run!' Price ordered that the convict be taken away for discipline. When Tom Hyland moved in to stop the jeers from the convicts, one of the men shouted to him, 'That's the bloody bastard ... that's the bloody tyrant!'[34]

The men began to throw large clumps of earth at their gaolers; Hyland later gave evidence that 'forty or fifty prisoners marched up in regular order from the quarry ... and complained tyranny' and said they would work no more. He continued:

> Four of them rushed forward and laid hold of Mr. Price by the shoulders and head. Mulloney struck him with a stone on the head. [Price] wrested himself from the grasp of the four men, and ran in the direction where I was. I had ran backwards about ten yards, when I heard Mulloney shout out, 'Lay hold of bloody Hyland.' At this time a number of stones were thrown at me and Mr Price. I saw one of them strike Mr Price above the small of the back, and he fell against the back of the tramway to his left. He rose and staggered about three yards, when he fell into a gutter. I saw prisoner Thomas Williams rush after him and strike him with a shovel on the back of the head. Williams raised the shovel above his right shoulder, and struck him, as it appeared to me, with the edge of it with all his force. It prostrated him. I did not see him move afterwards.[35]

Hyland was chased by several convicts, but jumped a stone wall and took refuge there.

As he and other guards were pelted with stones, a number of convicts kept battering John Price with iron bars, hammers and shovels until they were brought under control by a heavy police presence. Price died the next day.

The Penfolds had heard all about this murder – it had been one of the most publicised crimes of the decade. They were glad that South Australia had been a free settlement without convict transportation and the desperate, tormented men it produced.

Despite the punishment doled out to him, there was not a lot of sympathy in the community for John Giles Price. His three sons led the funeral procession from the Prince's Bridge to the Melbourne General Cemetery; other mourners included the governor of Victoria, the warders of the several prisons and many of Price's friends, who went in carriages, on horseback and on foot.[36] *The Age*, which had long campaigned against police brutality, reported that the funeral was 'eminently formal and official – not eliciting a scintilla of popular sympathy'.[37] Meanwhile, Justice Robert Molesworth had offered to adjourn the Supreme Court in order to let the legal fraternity attend the funeral if they pleased, 'but not a single gentleman rose from his seat'.[38]

Tom Hyland had escaped with his life, and he was made chief warder at the Collingwood Stockade as a reward for his service. In 1861 he was selected to govern the Portland Gaol.[39]

The kind of violence Tom Hyland had experienced was unlike anything Mary had imagined – not while she was living in the home of her genteel parents all those years ago in London, not while she was strolling with Chris along the shore at Brighton, and certainly not while enjoying the life of a well-off farming family on a large estate with her own vineyard outside the lovely city of Adelaide.

Tom told the Penfolds that he was just doing his job, and that no one outside the prison system knew how tough the job was. He had to deal with dangerous criminals every day. But he was a different man away from all that chaos, he said. And they would see that. Tom had fallen in love with Georgina and he asked for her hand in marriage. After much discussion, her parents agreed.

Mary prayed that Georgina was making the right decision.

Chapter 24

MARY HAD BEEN invisible in the announcement of Georgina's birth nineteen years earlier in Sussex, and so it was with her daughter's marriage in 1862, half a world away in Melbourne. The public notice of the wedding in the morning newspapers of the Victorian capital reported without adornment:

> HYLAND—PENFOLD.— On the 24th inst., at St. Peter's, Melbourne, by the Rev. H.P. Handfield, Thomas Francis, youngest son of the late John Hyland, of Ballinilard [sic], Ireland, to Mary Georgina Anne, only child of Christopher Rawson Penfold, surgeon, of the Grange, Magill, South Australia.[1]

Still, the wedding was a joyous affair at the cavernous Anglican church at Melbourne's Eastern Hill, on the outskirts of the city centre. Just as Mary had needed her parents' permission as a minor to marry Chris back in 1835, so Georgina, who was still well under the age of twenty-one, needed her parents' permission to marry Tom Hyland. In this, at least, Mary had some say in proceedings. Reverend Henry Handfield,[2] who performed the wedding, wrote on the marriage registration form: 'The above named Mary Georgina Anne Penfold was married with the written consent of her mother Mary Penfold dated 23 September 1862 delivered to me previous to the solemnization of the marriage – H.H.P. Handfield.'[3]

Georgina was described on the marriage certificate as a spinster from St Kilda, and Tom as a government officer from Portland.[4] That town would be their new home.

It was not insignificant that Mary and Chris gave their address as The Grange, Magill. Chris had resigned as the official Carlton vaccinator two months before Georgina's wedding, and he and Mary had travelled home to restart their life there. Mary's dream of returning to her whitewashed cottage and her grapevines had come true. This time, wine would play a bigger role for them at The Grange, as winemaking began to grow in popularity across the Australian colonies.

On her return to Magill, Mary found the economic conditions in South Australia improved. The Victorian gold rush had faded and many prospectors had returned home, some with savings that allowed them to invest in farming or mining ventures.

South Australia was now one of most egalitarian places in the world, offering voting rights to all male British subjects twenty-one years or older, including Indigenous men, and to all women who owned property.[5] It was not fully democratic, but it was a start.

All around Mary, grapevines were springing into life. At a vineyard just south of The Grange, Henry Clark had just planted eight hectares of black Portugal vines, as well as muscat, Mataro, sercial and Doradilla plantings. The erection of his stone cellars was well underway inside a two-storey building about thirteen metres by thirteen. His grapes would be crushed by foot in the evening and the wine would be stored in casks holding 1350 litres each, some of which were made from local red gum.[6] Clark's fiancée, Annie Martin, had named his vineyard 'Stonyfell' after the slopes of the Adelaide Hills, which resembled barren English fells.[7] Sadly, Annie died before the marriage could take place.

In 1862, at the Tintara vineyard in McLaren Vale, Dr Alex Kelly planted thirty-six hectares with shiraz, cabernet, Mataro, grenache and sauvignon blanc vines. Cellars were made in 1863 by digging into the hillside next to the house. The fermentation tanks for the cellars were lined with slate quarried by Cornish miners in the Willunga hills, about forty kilometres south of Adelaide. Within a few years the grapes would be crushed to make a full-bodied, burgundy-type wine, which Dr Kelly would use as a medicine.[8]

Thomas Hardy's Bankside vineyard on the Torrens now covered fourteen hectares with shiraz, roussillon, grenache and zante currant. The grape varieties were separated by rows of olive trees. Hardy had produced 6750 litres of wine in 1862, but that would soon rise to a yearly output of some 66,000 litres.[9]

George Anstey had sold his Adelaide Hills vineyard, 'Highercombe', to George Waterhouse,[10] who became premier of South Australia and later premier of New Zealand. Waterhouse planted nine more hectares of vines between 1858 and 1863.[11]

Mary's neighbour, Patrick Auld, had founded the South Australian Vineyard Association and sent a shipment of its members' wines to the 1862 London Exhibition at South Kensington,[12] where they were well received.

At the 'Home Park' property on Penfold Road, Magill, the architect Edmund W. Wright had planted more than eight hectares of vineyards, mostly muscatel grapes that would be dried, but also some grenache and Doradilla for making wine.[13]

Mary could only have been inspired after the politician and journalist Ebenezer Ward visited the Clarendon property and gave a detailed report. He wrote that Edward Peake's vineyard 'towers high above the surrounding objects, and appears, as it truly is, a gigantic pyramid of verdure. Its slopes and summits are clothed with luxuriant vines, and their dense and verdant foliage is unbroken by one barren spot, and unvaried by one foreign plant.'[14]

MARY AND CHRIS HAD a lot of catching up to do if they were to match the size, output and quality of these neighbouring vineyards. Almost as soon as they returned to Magill to restock their farm, they were given permission by their local council to 'burn grass and burr' over a portion of their land, promising to use every precaution against injury to their neighbours. They would then begin adding to their already sizable vineyard[15] so that it stretched to sixteen hectares.[16]

They also immediately reconnected with the Magill community and Chris was reappointed as a church warden at St George's.[17]

The telegraph had come to South Australia, and there now was a wire connecting Adelaide with Portland. In August 1863 Georgina sent an urgent message to her mother, saying it was time she visited. Georgina was about to celebrate her twentieth birthday with the birth of her first child. Mary quickly sailed from Adelaide[18] to be with Georgina, who delivered a pretty but sickly baby the couple named Inez.[19]

Like her mother, Georgina was kept anonymous in the birth announcement, Portland's newspaper reporting simply: 'On the 16th [August] at Portland, the wife of Thomas Francis Hyland, Esq., of a daughter.'[20]

Mary was besotted with her first grandchild and would form a strong bond with Inez as she grew into a kind and sensitive child who loved poetry. She would watch over Inez for the rest of her life.

MARY AND CHRIS HAD decided to expand their winemaking interests, and with Mary supervising a growing workforce they began planting more and more acres of vines. By 1864, however, they were still making wine only in small quantities as tonics.

Mary kept notes about the produce from their limited number of productive vines. The volumes they were producing were more than she and Chris and their circle of friends could drink in a year, but not enough to be commercial.[21] In 1864, they made wine of different varieties in volumes from 22.5 litres to 135 litres, and sold the wine in bulk in stone jars. They made wine from sweetwater, which was known as 'palomino' in Spain and was used to make sherry, and from frontignac, muscatel and some red varieties. Still, their production was minuscule compared with that of some other vineyards in Adelaide.

To reduce their workload, Chris and Mary continually tried to downsize, advertising large parcels of their land to let, including one parcel of about fifty-five hectares and another of twenty-eight hectares, with a house and 'a good well of water'.[22] He and Mary wanted to plant grapes on a large part of the remaining forty or so hectares of their property.

Chris was often unwell, struggling with what he suspected was diabetes. He had once had the gentle features of a romantic poet, but at fifty-three he was a haggard figure, balding, fatigued and with a long, straggly beard. He and Mary must have started to wonder about their own mortality.

MARY'S FATHER, DR TOM HOLT, died in the Surrey town of Chertsey in 1864, at the age of seventy-six. But many members of Chris's large family lived abbreviated lives. His siblings Catherine Baroncelli and George Rawson Penfold had died while he was in Adelaide. And, despite their differences, Chris was saddened to learn that Thomas Brooks Penfold had passed away at Croydon, Surrey, in 1864.

A few months later, Tom's daughter, Emma Mary, had become Mrs Whitling through her marriage to a London doctor.[23] She inherited Tom's landholdings at Magill, and many years later she would donate some of it to build a Magill Institute in honour of her father.[24] Tom made many enemies, but Emma Mary was always convinced her father was a great man.

THE PLANS MARY AND CHRIS made to plant more vines were delayed again in the mid-1860s, when Georgina fell pregnant with her second child. Mary had become a round, cheery-faced grandmother, and she was constantly travelling between Magill and the governor's residence at the Portland Gaol, where Georgina had made her home with Tom and two-year-old Inez.

On 25 April 1865,[25] Georgina gave birth to another little girl, whom she named Imogene Olivia Ethel Hyland. Mary was over the moon at the arrival of her second grandchild, and she resolved to spend many weeks helping Georgina back to full health and growing ever closer to the cheerful, astonishing child that was Inez. Mary could tell Inez about the great boat ride she had made from England with Georgina and Inez's grandpa, and about the cosy little home among the grapevines and wheatfields they had at The Grange. It was much nicer there than living in a prison, although Mary would not tell Inez that until she was older.

Every time Mary took the steamer to Portland, the bond between her and the little girl grew ever stronger. Mary hoped that she would share the same sort of bond with the equally lovely Imogene, now a few days old.

In June 1865, Mary was staying with the Hylands, helping Georgina and Tom with the two children. Inez had a bad cough – she was often poorly – but Imogene was always quite well, except that her parents worried that she seemed to sleep a little too much.[26]

Imogene slept in a cot beside her parents' bed. About daybreak on 11 June, Mary heard the new baby crying, but was not alarmed. Then the crying stopped; Tom had got up to pacify the baby with a little milk formula. Tom put Imogene back in the cot beside the bed at about a quarter past six, and Mary thought the baby was 'perfectly quiet' for the next hour and a half.

At a quarter to eight, Mary came into the Hylands' bedroom to give Imogene her bath.[27] As she bent down to pick up the little girl, though, her eyes widened with shock. Imogene wasn't breathing. Oh, dear God!

The baby was lying on her side with her hands crossed across her chest; she looked peaceful. Mary thought for a moment that she had imagined it – surely this serene, peaceful little child was just sleeping? But when Mary picked Imogene up, she stifled a scream of terror. The baby was not breathing. She was still, and ghostly pale.

Tom and Georgina leapt out of bed as Mary put Imogene into a warm bath, trying desperately to revive her. Georgina looked on, mute with shock. Tom yelled out for someone to get his medical attendant. Mary wrapped Imogene in a blanket. Tom, his hard exterior cracking with fear, tried to inflate Imogene's little lungs with short, sharp puffs of air, but Imogene didn't stir.[28]

The gaol's medical supervisor arrived, but it was soon clear there was no hope. Imogene was beyond recovery. The morning passed into a day and night of tears, regret and stupor over a precious life lost.

The following day, at an inquest held before a twelve-man jury at Portland Gaol, Mary gave a stark, joyless deposition that bluntly described Imogene's sad demise. 'I have seen the body of the child on the premises,' her statement began. 'It is that of my granddaughter.'

Tom's deposition began: 'I have seen the body lying in the gaol, it is that of my daughter. She was six weeks, five days old and she was always in good health up to [yesterday].'[29]

The coroner, Henry Edward Brewer, ruled that Imogene died 'from accidental suffocation in her cot'.

Mary could not stop thinking of the tragedy and the little baby's lifeless face all the way home on the return voyage to Adelaide. The image would haunt her for long after.

Chapter 25

IT TOOK MARY A LONG time to recover from the grief of her visit to Portland in June 1865. But she knew she would be back soon to see Inez, and that Georgina would likely want more children to help her heal from the cruel loss.

In 1866, Chris was appointed as his local district medical officer, supplying care to the 'destitute poor' in an area covering Magill and its surrounds.[1] Mary was proud, but by now she was pouring almost all her energies into the vineyard.

The science of winemaking was constantly evolving. The famed French biologist Louis Pasteur was a great believer in its therapeutic value and wrote extensively about it. Pasteur made discoveries that were of immense importance to Mary and other winemakers of the 1860s. He showed how fermentation was due to the action of yeasts reproducing, and why, when wine was exposed to air, its resident bacteria took over and turned the wine to vinegar. Pasteur's solution was to heat the wine in its bottle for long enough to kill the bacteria, and then rapidly cool it.

This process, which came to be known as 'pasteurisation', destroyed harmful microorganisms without significantly altering the product's taste. It eventually made milk much safer to drink, and also prevented wine from spoiling. Pasteurisation prevented further fermentation and stabilised the wine. At a time when water was still unsafe in many parts of the world, Pasteur described wine as possibly 'the most healthful and hygienic of all beverages'.[2]

More and more Australians thought wine was delightful. By 1866, John Reynell was producing 11,250 litres of wine with each vintage. He had found that shipping his wine to England in hogsheads was risky, as it often arrived spoiled. Instead he sold his product to two Adelaide wine merchants: his former employee Thomas Hardy, and Patrick Auld's son William.[3] Hardy himself was producing 63,000 litres of wine from Bankside annually in the mid-1860s, but over the next decade that would grow to 240,000 litres – both from his own vines and about forty smaller growers.[4]

In the Yarra Valley, Hubert de Castella and Guillaume de Pury had planted the St Hubert's and Yeringberg vineyards near Paul de Castella's grapes at Yering Station, and other new areas were opened in Victoria. Lindsey Brown had planted the first vines in the Rutherglen district of northern Victoria at 'Gooramadda', and George Morris[5] planted the 'Fairfield' vineyard near Chiltern. 'Gehrigs', 'Chambers Rosewood' and 'St Leonards' were all planted around the same time.

Henry Lindeman was impressed by the Rutherglen wines and eventually bought the 'Haffner' vineyard across the Murray in Corowa, New South Wales.[6] Lindeman was tireless in his promotion of wine as a therapeutic agent, writing to *The Sydney Morning Herald* in 1867 to declare:

> How soon our refreshing, exhilarating and restorative wine will take the place of poisonous spirits. We shall then rapidly become a sober instead of a drunken community. The soil through nearly all the extent of the country is admirably adapted for the growth of the vine, and it merely requires tapping with a cutting to overflow with nectar … and when the law will allow wine to become our national beverage, thousands of acres now encumbered with the 'dreary eucalyptus', will smile with the vine, and another civilising industry will spring up in our midst to employ thousands of families in the light and pleasing labour it requires, and to attract a desirable class of immigrant to our shore.[7]

Wine as a 'national beverage' – Mary, Chris and every winemaker on the continent liked the sound of that.

By the mid-1860s, the Murray Valley Vineyard at Albury, New South Wales, had sixty hectares under vines, and Adam Roth's 'Craigmoor', on the banks of Pipeclay Creek at Mudgee, on the western side of the Blue Mountains, was flourishing.[8] In the Hunter Valley, Edward Tyrrell had started his vineyards, and in Queensland Samuel Bassett had grapes growing beside Roma's Bungil Creek, having planted them in 1863.

In the Barossa, Joseph Seppelt,[9] who hailed from an area of Prussia that is now part of Poland, had started making wine in 1867 in his wife's small dairy on a property he called 'Seppeltsfield'. Closer to The Grange, German-born Friedrich Lindrum had planted vines at his Norwood property, though much of his time was taken up running hotels and billiard halls, which did a roaring trade – especially after 1865, when he beat the touring British player John Roberts,[10] who claimed to be the world billiards champion.[11] Friedrich's descendants included generations of billiards champions, among them Walter and Horace Lindrum; Friedrich himself would become a gold medal winemaker on the world stage.

MARY AND CHRIS WERE stunned by the sudden death of their friend Friedrich Bayer, Adelaide's leading doctor, in 1867, and they supported a public fund to honour him.[12] Bayer had succumbed to a stroke at the age of fifty-two, and *The South Australian Register* said his sudden demise while in the prime of life had 'awakened feelings of sorrow in many a South Australian home':

> We question if the death of any man amongst us would excite emotions of more universal regret than that of the able and kind-hearted physician who has been cut down in the flower of his days, and whose loss so many persons are now lamenting. The Doctor was acknowledged to be at the head of the medical profession in this colony, and this

favourable position was conceded to him by his colleagues rather than claimed by himself.[13]

Time moved on, though, and the grief that gripped Adelaide after Bayer's death was soon alleviated by the excitement over the great representation of South Australian winemakers at the Intercolonial Exhibition of Australasia – a mini world's fair that took place in two specially built halls behind Melbourne's Public Library for four months from 24 October 1866.[14]

There were exhibits from Victoria, New South Wales, Queensland, South Australia, Tasmania, Western Australia and New Zealand, as well as from New Caledonia, Mauritius and what was then called Netherlands–India – the settlements and trading posts of the Dutch East India Company.

South Australia sent twenty-three exhibitors for the 'Wines and Spirits' display, including samples from Yalumba, Pewsey Vale, Bankside, Auldana, Clarendon, and the Reynell and Seppeltsfield properties.[15] Mary longed for a time when wines from the Penfolds' vineyard would appear alongside them.

Another exhibitor was the 45-year-old Joseph Gillard Senior,[16] who had been in Adelaide for almost twenty years since arriving in 1849 from Devonshire. He had enjoyed some success on the Victorian goldfields and planted his vineyard, 'Sylvania', at Norwood, about five kilometres from The Grange. He had taught his son, Joseph Junior, all he knew about winemaking.[17]

SOUTH AUSTRALIA'S winemakers were thrilled to have the chance to impress with their produce in Melbourne, but nothing gripped Adelaide as much as the arrival into the colony of Prince Alfred, the 23-year-old Duke of Edinburgh and son of Queen Victoria. It was the first time a member of Britain's royal family had visited Australia. Huge crowds turned out to see the young prince wherever he went.

Alfred's ship, HMS *Galatea*, docked at Glenelg on the afternoon of 31 October 1867. Massive crowds lined the roads to cheer him,[18] and a crowd of 40,000 gathered in the gaslit streets of

Prince Alfred concludes his visit to Adelaide after a gala event which Chris Penfold attended. *National Library of Australia obj-140401734*

the city to celebrate that night.[19] The prince spent three weeks in South Australia and was lauded wherever he went.

As a prominent citizen of Adelaide, Dr Christopher Penfold was invited to the Grand Civic Banquet held at the Town Hall on 9 November 1867. As a woman, Mary Penfold was not. The feast was unlike anything seen in Adelaide's thirty years of European history, and Chris told Mary all about it.

After singing 'God Save the Queen', and offering many prayers and toasts with local red wine, the diners sat down to an array of food fit for a prince. There was mock turtle soup, oyster soup, kangaroo-tail soup, Murray cod, whiting *à la crème au gratin*, oyster patties, supreme of fowl, *foie gras à la gelle*, epigrammes of lamb, fricandeau of veal, stewed rump of beef flamande, compote of pigeons, saddles of mutton, roast turkey, turkey braised *à la Toulouse*, Westphalia ham, spring chicken *à la regence*, roast duckling, haunch of kangaroo, guinea fowl, pea fowl, roast chicken and fresh lobster.

If anyone was still hungry after all that, there were sixteen different desserts.[20]

Huge crowds welcomed Prince Alfred when he travelled on to Melbourne, but many Irish Catholics gathered outside the Protestant community hall there to protest. The Catholics sang republican songs and threw stones. The Protestants stuck guns out of the hall windows and started shooting. A thirteen-year-old Catholic boy was killed.[21]

A week later, on 27 November, a free public benefit at Yarra Park, Melbourne, turned into a disastrous farce.[22] The organising committee had catered for the expected crowd of 10,000 people, but 50,000 arrived, all demanding the free food and wine that was being dispensed from two fountains.[23] Three vignerons had contributed 2700 litres of wine and there was a similar amount of free ale. But a riot ensued as the crowds surged to help themselves before it all ran out, and Prince Alfred cancelled his appearance.

There was a similar incident in Geelong, while at Bendigo three boys were trapped inside the public display of a model of the prince's ship and burnt to death when some fireworks ignited.[24] The town's newly built Alfred Hall burnt to the ground shortly before it was due to host a gala ball honouring the royal visitor. A sailor had his hand blown off at a military display in Flemington.

Already an unmitigated disaster, Australia's first royal tour ended in March 1868, when a mentally unstable Irish Catholic shot the prince in the back at a picnic at Clontarf, in Sydney. Alfred recovered, but the assailant[25] was hanged at Darlinghurst Gaol, despite the prince's pleas for mercy.

So, as it turned out, Prince Alfred's time in Adelaide was the happiest of his tour.

While Chris had been hobnobbing with the regal and the royal, Mary was back at The Grange, minding the farm and the grapes. But she was not as interested in dinner with the prince as she was in another dinner that was soon to be hosted in Adelaide, one that would honour wine royalty. She wanted to learn as much from this world-renowned expert as she could.

WINE WAS TAKING a leading position at the Intercolonial Exhibition in Melbourne, and was being promoted as one of the most hopeful sources for the future prosperity of the Australian colonies.[26]

According to the official report on the exhibition, none of the colonies showed nearly such large and varied exhibits in wine as South Australia, which the organisers said 'had to be regarded as one of the wine-producing countries of the world'.[27]

> It is the industry to which, after grain crops and mining, the largest amount of capital and labour is devoted. Here the vineyards will average, for forty miles [sixty-five kilometres] around Adelaide, at least thirty acres [twelve hectares] each; some exceeding a hundred acres [forty hectares], and many attaining to fifty [twenty hectares]. The whole of the country about the capital seems formed to be the home of those vines which nature has destined to produce strong, generous, full-bodied wines.[28]

All that was needed, according to the report, was a little experience from expert Portuguese or Spanish winemakers and South Australia would be producing port and sherry to rival the best from Europe.

Mary studied the report closely. 'In South Australia nature herself is opposed to the production of thin, high-bouquet wines,' it claimed.

> Here she demands consideration for body, sweetness, spirit, and the other high qualities of generous wines. The Riesling and Verdelho, when not tortured, yield wines second only to the Bucellas of Lisbon and the sweeter kinds of Madeira; while the Donzellinha, the Black Portugal, the [syrahs, aka shiraz], Mataro, and Grenache yield wines of the character of good Port, such as it is known in Portugal, and the strongest of Hermitage, and that peculiar produce known as Roussillon.[29]

At the time there were 2682 hectares of South Australia under vines. There were some 7,361,863 vines planted, which in 1866 had produced 3.8 million litres of wine. Mary wanted to add significantly to that number. South Australia had also produced 1574 tonnes of grapes for local table use and export. Its success as a wine-producing colony had pushed leading New South Wales industry figures, such as the Macarthurs, into the background.[30]

The reputation of South Australian wine had never been better, and with the perfect aspect of the farm at Magill and that gently sloping land heading up to the Adelaide Hills, the time was right to devote The Grange to making wine on a commercial scale.

The Special Commissioner for Jurors awarding prizes at the Intercolonial Exhibition was a well-travelled Catholic clergyman named Reverend Dr John Bleasdale,[31] who had a great interest in viticulture. Bleasdale taught science at St Patrick's College in Melbourne. Part of his training as a priest had taken place in Portugal, where he became an expert in winemaking. Like Chris Penfold, he was a great proponent of wine for medicinal purposes; he was an honorary member of the Victoria Medical Association and president of the Royal Society of Victoria.

When Bleasdale arrived in Australia in 1851, his first posting was to Geelong. He visited the vineyards of Swiss immigrants in the Barrabool Hills, giving them advice on their 'agreeable hock' and 'quite unsatisfactory' reds. Sixteen years later, he could say that their improved methods had yielded 'really good wine'.[32]

The South Australian Institute hoped Bleasdale would help them improve their already well-regarded wines, and invited him to Adelaide for a series of meetings with winegrowers in December 1867.

Mary was all ears. She wanted to make wine that people would be talking about for generations.

Chapter 26

MARY COULD NOT have been prouder when Dr Bleasdale arrived at The Grange to tour the still-modest winemaking operation known as Penfolds.

Bleasdale had limited time in South Australia and wanted to see as many wineries as he could. He cast a critical eye over all of them and was pleased by what he saw. Mary showed him through The Grange and gave him a tour of the few acres they had already planted and the many more they were planning.

Bleasdale and Chris compared notes on the medicinal benefits of the fruit of the vine, though Chris was no longer such a good advertisement for its benefits. His diabetes was making him frailer, and with his long, grey beard and bald dome he looked much older than his fifty-six years.

The potential of the vineyards excited Bleasdale. He also was a guest at Clarendon, Stonyfell, Tintara, Yalumba, Highercombe, Pewsey Vale and several other operations.[1] Clarendon was producing 68,000 litres of wine a year and the winery had been expanded to four floors. Edward Peake had won several bronze medals at the Intercolonial Exhibition, as well as a bronze medal for verdelho at the Paris Exhibition.

At Tintara, Dr Kelly told Bleasdale that when he'd arrived in the colony twenty-eight years earlier, he was an invalid 'not expected to live more than a very few years'. He said he had always 'been sanguine for the success of the winegrowing industry' in South Australia: he well remembered the difficulty medical men in Scotland had 'getting good wholesome wine for patients'. In cases of typhus fever, in particular, Dr Kelly had known a time when 'nothing but whisky or porter or coarse port or sherry were to be procured'. How thankful the doctors in his home country would have been for anything like South Australian wine, he said.[2]

On 12 December 1867, Bleasdale read a paper on winemaking to the South Australian Institute before a large crowd that included Chris and Mary Penfold. He told the audience that in his report as chairman of the jurors for wines at the Intercolonial Exhibition, he had noted how difficult it was to imagine anything but success for 'well-managed vineyards in well-selected sites and soils in such a glorious climate'.[3] The last few years were 'an epoch in winemaking in South Australia', given the improvements in the product; Bleasdale believed that consumers in Victoria were anxious to have South Australian wines and would soon move to have the heavy intercolonial tariffs removed. The tariffs were the bane of South Australian winemakers.

Edward Peake proposed a toast to '[i]ntercolonial free trade, and fair play to our wine growers with New South Wales'. The gathered winemakers had been protesting that New South Wales, which now produced only a small quantity of wine compared with South Australia, was allowed to send their produce across

Edward Peake at his Clarendon vineyard. *State Library of South Australia B 34318*

the border into Victoria without paying any duty, while heavy tariffs were imposed on the South Australian product.

Chris rose to say that he was full of praise for the improvement in Clarendon wines in recent years and hoped he could produce something to match it.[4]

Bleasdale quoted evidence suggesting that the Melbourne Hospital and the Melbourne Benevolent Asylum had already substituted colonial wines for the imported products they had formerly used. As a result of his visit to South Australia, the Adelaide Hospital decided to adopt his suggestion to substitute colonial for foreign wines to use in the treatment of their patients.[5]

GEORGINA WAS ABOUT to give birth for the third time. After the tragedy of little Imogene's passing, Mary was back in Portland to help in any way she could. She left Chris to navigate the new developments in the winemaking industry while she took care of their precious family.

John Bleasdale's ringing endorsement for the wines of South Australia and their potential filled the Penfolds and many others in the colony with enthusiasm and expectation. A report from the South Australian commissioners at the Paris Universal Exhibition in 1867 had asserted that 'some of the best Judges of Wine in France have pronounced most unequivocal opinions as to the quality of the South Australian Wines, and look on the prospects of the Wine Industry in these latitudes as alarming to the Winegrowers of France'.[6]

More wineries continued to emerge in South Australia. Another Silesian immigrant, Johann Christian Henschke, had planted a small vineyard in the Barossa's Eden Valley in the early 1860s; the first recorded sale of Henschke wine came in 1868.

Mary and Chris had determined to base the future of their life at The Grange around their grapes, and as a result the name C.R. Penfold was added to the male-only list of promoters[7] at the founding of the South Australian Wine Company in July 1868. The company was designed to help those winemakers with smaller vineyards grow their businesses by pooling knowledge and resources. It planned a capital raise of £50,000, made up of 10,000 five-pound shares. On 22 July, the association's bold prospectus announced:

> That the climate of South Australia is congenial to the culture of the vine and the manufacture of wine is placed beyond the shadow of a doubt. During the last 25 years private enterprise has been testing, over a large and scattered area, the varieties of the grape best suited to the soil and climatic influences of the colony and the experience so gained has now become the common property of the community. Much time and money have been expended by individual growers, and in many instances with the most marked and satisfactory results.
>
> Indeed, in almost every instance in which wine has been properly stored and matured it has obtained a ready market and a good reputation; but unfortunately, from the want of knowledge, proper storage, or from other causes, the produce of our smaller vineyards is forced upon the market before it is fit for use, to the loss of the growers; and the detriment of the character of our wines. This Company is therefore established for the following objects:
>
> 1st. To establish a Factory for the manufacture and treatment of Australian Wines.
>
> 2nd. To purchase Grapes, Must [the freshly crushed fruit] and young Wines, for the purpose of maturing them and producing samples of a uniform character.
>
> 3rd. The importation of such skilled labour from Europe as may be deemed necessary to attain these objects.
>
> 4th. The carrying on of a Distillery in connection with the Factory.
>
> 5th. The opening up and establishment of Markets for the products with which it is proposed to deal.
>
> It requires only the accommodation which this Association will afford to render the cultivation of the Vine generally profitable, and to make it one of the leading industries of the Province.[8]

The prospectus went on to declare:

> It has been observed by a competent and unprejudiced authority (Dr Bleasdale) that 'The whole of the country about the capital seems formed to be the home of those Vines which nature has destined to produce strong, generous, and full-bodied Wines.' With regard to the quality of the South Australian Wines, there is corroborative evidence on all sides as to the high standard they are capable of obtaining under practical and judicious treatment. With skilled labour such as the Company will be in a position to command, there is no reason to doubt but that the Association will be able, year after year, to produce exactly the same character of Wines and [be] quite capable of competing with the European wines in the markets which legitimately belong to these colonies, viz., Australasia, Tasmania, New Zealand, Mauritius, Ceylon, India, Straits Settlements, Java, China, and Japan.

The association promised to avail itself of all the latest improvements and scientific advances in winemaking, 'particularly those gained in France by the experiments conducted by M. Pasteur ... under the auspices of the French Government, and which have been pronounced by the most competent Wine judges in France as eminently successful'.[9]

Chris promoted this new venture while continuing to work as a doctor, even though his own health was in serious decline. In April 1868, he was re-appointed as the government medical officer to attend to the destitute poor in the area around Magill,[10] and he was frequently called upon to examine the bodies of suicide victims, with his late brother's old hotel, the East Torrens on Magill Road, a favoured venue for coroner's inquests.[11]

But then there was also the prospect of new life, too. On 20 August 1868 in Portland, Georgina gave birth to her third daughter, Estelle Ianthe Hyland.[12] Mary prayed that mother and little girl would survive. They both did.

Two months later, Mary and Chris exported about 500 litres of wine to Melbourne as their production increased. They began to imagine a future as major wine producers.[13] Their son-in-law, Tom Hyland, was helping to market the wine to Victorian buyers.[14] More exports would soon follow.[15]

Two days after the birth of the Penfolds' new granddaughter, Mary, Georgina, five-year-old Inez and baby Estelle arrived in Adelaide to visit the children's ageing grandpa and see all the vines he and Mary had planted.[16]

BY 1869, MARY AND CHRIS knew they needed expert help to build up their vineyard and establish a commercial winery. They had always liked the Gillard family at the nearby Sylvania vineyard, and they hired 23-year-old Joe Gillard Junior[17] as their vineyard manager and winemaker. He was an industrious and enterprising lad with a wife[18] and young son,[19] and he had been schooled in the wine business from infancy.

Joe Gillard had arrived in South Australia from Devon in 1849 with his father, Joseph Senior, and mother, Jane. Sadly, she died soon after the arrival, and the Gillards' infant daughter, Jane Junior, followed soon after, aged only twelve days. Joseph remarried and eventually had three more children. After chancing his luck on the Victorian goldfields, he settled down to life as a vigneron at Sylvania, not far from the Penfolds.

When Joe Junior was fifteen, his father won all the prizes at the show staged by the Vinegrowers Association in Adelaide.[20] Joseph Senior taught his son all he knew about growing grapes and making wines, and Joe Junior was a fast learner. Many years later, a reporter would observe that Joe Junior could do any task on a vineyard, from planting and pruning vines to building cellars, making the wine, making the casks to put it in, watching it mature and sending it to show to take a prize – 'or to the consumer to praise its quality'.[21]

Now Joe Gillard was working around the clock under the direction of Mary and Chris, clearing more land, planting more vines and overseeing the construction of a crushing room, cellars and warehouses for the rapid expansion of the vineyard at The Grange.

Meanwhile, in Portland, Tom Hyland was increasing his work representing his in-laws' business interests in Victoria, and obtaining shelf space for some of the Penfolds' wine. He was doing an impressive job as a prison boss, and in 1869 he was promoted to take over the Castlemaine Gaol.[22] He took his harsh discipline with him, making many of his new prisoners wonder if they were in Central Victoria or hell.[23]

Tom was a tough, uncompromising man, and Mary would have hated to be his enemy. But she believed she had his measure, and in any case retailers liked him. What's more, they were starting to love the small samples of fortified wines coming from the Penfolds of Magill.

ON THE FIRST DAY OF 1870, Richard Clarke, a wine merchant at 46 Moorabool Street, Geelong, began a long-term advertising campaign for 'New Muscatels, New Sultanas, New Currants and New samples of Dr Penfold's South Australian Wines just to hand'.[24] Other retailers started following his lead, and soon Penfolds wines were being promoted throughout the Australian colonies. Mary received no credit in the advertising campaign.

The Australian wine industry was still hindered by the lack of a sizable domestic market on a continent where the population was still small. Additionally, the six colonies continued to use high tariffs to protect their local growers. Hubert de Castella argued forcefully that the intercolonial customs duties were the greatest obstacle to the industry.[25] Other beverages such as beer and spirits were still popular, and the heavy tariffs on wine left a sour taste for both the eager growers and their potential customers.

Among the small number of wine connoisseurs in Australia there was also some wine snobbery, with a preference for European offerings over the local product. Some vignerons complained that many publicans refused point blank to sell Australian wine. In 1860, Dr Alexander Kelly had complained that 'popular prejudice' generally opposed the consumption of local wine in Adelaide, and that while colonial wine was consumed in clubs and at private dinner parties, it could not be bought in any of the 420 public houses in Sydney.[26]

There were, of course, other threats to the Australian wine industry. At the end of January 1870, the Penfold vines escaped another fast-moving fire that wreaked havoc on the property of their old friend John Horsnell.

After their crisis was averted, Mary and Chris visited Tom, Georgina and the girls in Victoria, taking the steamer to Melbourne and then the train to Castlemaine.[27] Chris was looking increasingly ill. He was often pale and cold, and frequently lethargic and weak. Sometimes his heartbeat was worryingly fast. Although he had advocated red wine for anaemia since his days as a medical student at St Barts, it could no longer cure his ills. Mary began to suspect that Chris had sailed to Melbourne for one last goodbye with Georgina and the children.

A few weeks later, at the first general meeting of the all-male Adelaide Vignerons' Club, with John Reynell and Thomas Hardy presiding, Chris was admitted as a founding member.[28] He left the meeting at the Prince Alfred Hotel on King William Street knowing that the Penfolds' winery was now firmly part of the South Australian wine industry.

Chris and Mary had now been married for thirty-five years. Having crossed the seas to Adelaide, they were now embarking on an adventure just as thrilling, with a shared dream of producing high-quality wines as one of Australia's leading producers.

That was still Chris's dream when he took ill at The Grange a few weeks later, surrounded by his precious vines and the wife who had been by his side since he was a young and carefree medical student. He grew weaker and whiter and more wizened in his four-poster bed, and died on 26 March 1870. Chris was fifty-eight.[29]

Mary was now without the life partner she had loved since she was a teenage bride all those decades ago.

Chapter 27

MARY STAYED WITH CHRIS's emaciated body at The Grange until the undertakers came to prepare her beloved husband for burial. Two days later, on 28 March 1870, his funeral cortege left the cottage and travelled through Magill – past the houses where he had treated sick patients, where he had given wine to those who needed it, and past his brother's shops and the East Torrens Hotel. Flags throughout the area flew at half-mast, and shop-owners closed their stores, a sign of the esteem in which Chris was held by his local community.[1]

His funeral service took place at St George's, where he and Mary had first sat as a young couple with little Georgina, listening to Bishop Short's consecration service. Chris's coffin was then carried to the churchyard and lowered into the dark, loamy earth, farewelled by a large number of friends, neighbours and patients who desired to pay their respects.

Newspapers said Chris 'was much respected for the kindness of his disposition'.[2] His cause of death was listed as 'diabetes insipidus' – a rare condition characterised by the body's inability to regulate fluid balance, leading to excessive urination and thirst. Despite his endorsement of red wine, he had also been suffering anaemia.[3]

Adelaide's *Evening Journal* reported that 'of late years Dr. Penfold had been most energetic in the wine trade, having planted a vineyard and opened a good trade with Victoria; but for some time failing health had prevented him from paying so much attention to the interest'.[4]

Mary was not mentioned for the work she had been doing while Chris struggled with his health. Nor was her name even mentioned in the list of his mourners. 'He leaves a widow,' the journal noted, 'and one daughter, who is married to Mr. Hyland, a gentleman in the Victorian Civil Service.' Such was the invisible life of women at that time. Even in her grief, Mary had a plan to smash through that stilted thinking.

Tom Hyland wrote Mary a heartfelt letter of sympathy, addressing it to 'Dear Mother', as he called her. He offered her moral support but also suggested that running the Penfolds' wine business was not a job for a woman. He was also worried about where Chris's death left him. Tom had been growing sales in Victoria, and was concerned his efforts would go to waste. He advised Mary to sell the farm and retire, though he noted it might take a while to offload. The land and wine business were valuable, he said, and the proceeds of a sale would allow her to live in comfort for the rest of her days:

> I fear it will be some time before you can sell the place. I can advise you to [do] nothing definite until I hear from you, but you should direct the man to prepare it for cropping as the season must not be allowed to pass. If you thought you could manage things for, say six months, it would give us more time to sell the property well, as if things brighten in Melbourne and the Border Duty gets settled, we could then sell it well in Melbourne.[5]

After her husband's funeral, and after she read Tom's letter, Mary stood outside The Grange, gazing at the Adelaide Hills awash in the soft glow of sunset. Her rows of vines seemed almost to invite her to taste their fruit. Mary had no intention of selling The Grange or the grapes she and Chris had tended so lovingly.

She had always been in the background of her husband's public life, an asterisk to his achievements, precluded from the male-dominated societies and associations linked with colonial business. Now she found herself on her own, with a business to run, at a time when women remained unnoticed in the corporate world.

Mary was more determined than ever to make a success of her winery. Chris was dead, but she promised herself that she would keep their business alive.

MARY SET OUT TO MAKE the best wine possible and sell it to as many customers as she could, trading as 'M. Penfold & Company, The Grange Vineyards, Magill'.[6]

Two days after Chris's funeral, Mary made the first of her regular mortgage payments of £103 9s 8d to fund the extraordinary building work that was taking place on the property, in preparation for what she anticipated would be huge demand for the wines from The Grange.[7]

Mary sent copies of recent accounts to Tom Hyland in Castlemaine to demonstrate the viability of her business, and show that she could run it herself. A few weeks later, another considerate letter arrived from Tom. Although affectionate, he was writing to suggest a business partnership. Tom was growing tired of dealing with some of the toughest criminals in Victoria and wanted a change. He found selling wine in his spare time much more enjoyable than his day job.

> [I have] your letter enclosing statement of accounts to hand. I am quite pleased at the practical way in which you are taking the business in hand and your resolutions, and determination and instructions could not be better – in fact if you go at it determinedly and keep nothing but what is useful you will be alright.[8]

Tom told Mary he was glad she had sold her domestic animals, as they took up a 'good deal of valuable time' and prevented a person doing 'more important business'. Tom was not a sentimentalist. He now proposed a business partnership: he would loan Mary a little over £2000 at 8 per cent interest as an advance on wine sales, which he would oversee. She would manage the vineyard and winemaking operation and he would deal with the retailers.

'Now as regards my commission on the sale of the wine,' he continued, 'I wish to be more literal as I am equally interested in the estate with yourselves and I will therefore only demand my expenses which I estimate would amount to about fifty pounds per annum.'[9] He would make two trips yearly, he said, to Melbourne, Geelong and Ballarat, which would cost £30, as well as visits to other towns such as Daylesford and Kyneton. He estimated he'd take sixteen days each year to visit hotels and wine merchants, spending about a pound a day, as well as railway fares and coach tickets. Postage had gone up recently too, he noted.

> Should you approve of this arrangement we will also let it take effect from the 1st of May just as we will start with the accounts as they appear on the statement now forwarded. Let me have your reply to these two proposals as soon as possible and I will then forward the bills for your acceptance.[10]

Two weeks after he wrote to Mary, and while she was still mulling over his offer, Tom was standing on the gallows at Castlemaine Gaol overseeing the execution of a Chinese man, Ah Pew, who had been convicted of murdering a nine-year-old girl. All through the previous week, Ah Pew had been lying chained in his cell as he awaited his fate. On the gallows, the condemned prisoner was still protesting his innocence.

As part of the medieval ritual of judicial executions, at 10 a.m. on 21 May, Tom, as the prison governor, formally handed over the condemned man to a sheriff. The colony's official hangman and flogger, a one-eyed ogre named William Bamford, led the prisoner onto the scaffold, shook his limp hand as a farewell, trussed up his arms and legs and placed a hood over his head. Then he put a rope around his neck and released the gallows platform, sending the prisoner to a sudden, gruesome death.[11]

Seeing Ah Pew's body swinging lifeless in the prison corridor below, Tom Hyland thought the wine trade was much more pleasant than this line of work.

MARY PENFOLD ACCEPTED Tom's deal and a partnership was struck.

She ran a tight ship as the commander in chief of The Grange vineyard, supervising the workmen building the large stone and tin warehouses and bottling rooms high above her home. But she also believed in cutting out the middleman, and so she paid for economical advertisements in her local Adelaide newspapers to attract customers to the Penfolds cellar door:

GOOD HARVEST WINES,
at the GRANGE, MAGILL.
—MARY PENFOLD.[12]

Australian wine remained an acquired taste, though the push was on from around the continent to promote the health benefits of fermented grape juice. Chris would have approved when his old classmate Henry Lindeman wrote to the editors of the *New South Wales Medical Gazette* in 1872, asking for their help in promoting his message about wine as an elixir:

> More than thirty years ago, when I first arrived in the colony, I was induced to plant the vine, and to impress upon my fellow-colonists the desirability of doing so likewise, seeing the great necessity there existed for supplying a pure exhilarating wine to take the place of ardent spirits and of adulterated wines and beers then and now the popular beverage of our community, the use of which frequently induces the diseases I have found mostly to be guarded against in our climate – namely, those arising from derangement of the liver; to suffer from which too often robs life of enjoyment by enveloping it in a perpetual fog of mental depression, and for which depression relief is

generally sought in the deleterious stimulants above-named, which invariably add fuel to fire, thereby crowding our community with the inebriate and insane.[13]

It was natural, Lindeman wrote, to hope that a wise government would see the value of encouraging health and enjoyment, and to advance sobriety among its people. He advocated for Australian wine to be sold without any restrictions, other than a small fee in the form of a vendor's licence, 'sufficient to pay for the surveillance necessitated' on the dishonest trader, who might try to profit by watering it down or substituting an inferior wine.

> Sir, the advocacy of this cause I cannot but think should be taken up by the members of the medical profession, who are for the most part aware of the value of a pure wine as a therapeutic agent, and how materially we should benefit both in health and morals if it became our national beverage.
>
> I have spent many years of my life trying to bring this about by doing everything within my limited orbit to inculcate a taste for a pure, dry, and thoroughly fermented wine, free from excess of undecomposed sugar and light in alcohol, resembling as much as possible the pure growths of Bordeaux and the Rheingau, and for the production of which our climate and soil are pre-eminently adapted.
>
> To change a national taste in a life-time I never had the vanity to propose to myself, but to advance it somewhat is something to be proud of and it will be a grand step gained to get the members of our profession to enlist themselves in this good cause, which, by bringing it prominently before them (with your permission) in the leaves of the Medical Gazette, I hope to do, knowing how great is the influence of the profession when stepping forward to advance mankind.[14]

GEORGINA GAVE BIRTH to Mary's first grandson in Castlemaine on 20 June 1871,[15] but tragically had to bury him just five weeks later. She had now lost two children within the first weeks of their lives, but would try again before too long. The newspapers were no comfort to her, reporting the death of little Harold Francis Hyland merely as the 'infant son of Thomas Francis Hyland, Esq'.[16]

It was a heartbreaking time for the whole family – but Mary was used to heartbreak. The best way she knew to deal with sadness was to press on. She had decided to divest herself of all the encumbrances against her future as the premier female vintner in Australia, perhaps the world. There were few Australian women in any business field matching her enterprise.

The ageing Ann Bickford,[17] another Adelaide widow, was running A.M. Bickford & Sons and was about to build the South Australian Cordial Factory, with Bickford's lime juice as her signature product. But there were precious few other women running corporations in Australia with the daring and reach of Mary Penfold.

Mary decided to sell off all her farmland that had been under wheat and corn, and concentrate purely on her vines, which now covered sixteen hectares on perfectly sloping land stretching back towards the Adelaide Hills. She began advertising:

> 'THE GRANGE' ESTATE, Comprising about 250 Acres of fine Land at the foot of the hills. It is substantially fenced and subdivided. It will be sold in one or more lots. This fine property commands a most beautiful view, and affords admirable sites for residences or vineyards. It is known as Mrs Penfold's.[18]

With young Joe Gillard proving a brilliant and indefatigable assistant – hiring staff, supervising the planting and harvesting of the vines, and overseeing construction work – Mary upped the production from The Grange every year. Her shipments to Melbourne for Tom Hyland to sell were steadily rising: by October 1872, her inventory for each delivery included eight quarter-casks (400 litres) and four hogsheads (1000 litres) of wine.[19]

Mary had taken to riding about her property on a spectacular white mare. Using her spyglass, she could see the rapidly changing skyline of Adelaide, a city that had mushroomed from humble beginnings when she and Chris had arrived almost thirty years earlier. Adelaide Oval was now hosting international cricket matches. A university was about to open on North Terrace, while the Town Hall and General Post Office were ornaments of colonial architecture.

The sailing ships that brought Mary and Chris to Port Adelaide had been replaced by sleeker, faster clippers. With the Suez Canal having opened in 1869, steamships were now replacing those vessels. The completion of the Overland telegraph line made Adelaide the first Australian capital linked by wire to London. The time it took to communicate with Europe had dropped from months to hours. That could only help the local wine trade as it looked to sell into Britain and Europe.

Despite all the busyness around her, Mary felt the great loss of Chris and a gnawing sense of loneliness. She was no fan of cats but liked dogs, especially her little pug, Toby.[20] But as much as the dog's face was adorable, she still felt the absence of family keenly. For the first time in almost forty years, and even with Joe Gillard and other vineyard workers coming by The Grange every day, she felt alone.

Georgina and Tom decided to let their daughter Inez, now eight years old, come and live with her grandmother for a good part of each year.[21] Inez did not enjoy good health, and everyone involved thought Adelaide's hot summers and drier climate might help invigorate her.

Mary also wanted to teach the little girl some life lessons. In a society in which women were so anonymous, and in which men received the credit for just about everything – even for the birth of children! – Mary wanted to be an example of enterprise for other women.

This plump and ageing grandmother was about to become known as one of her colony's great business leaders.

Chapter 28

LITTLE INEZ PROVED a wonderful companion and helper for Mary. The young girl watched her grandmother's every move with adoration as Mary commanded her winemaking business from the small back room of The Grange. Looking out on her vines, Mary made entries in her day book, which was perched on a small wooden desk. Then the pair would go out into the vineyards, supervising the care and pruning of the vines, and at other times the crushing and storing of the grapes.

Tom Hyland was doing well selling Penfolds wines not just into Victoria but into other large markets he was tapping such as Tasmania. With her guidance, he had also sent some samples on to New Zealand, and there was great promise for exports to Great Britain as well.[1]

Patrick Auld had set up the Australian Wine Company (later the Emu Wine Co. Ltd) as a vehicle to promote South Australian wines in Britain, and, with the support of Dr Kelly at Tintara, young London merchant P.B. Burgoyne[2] began importing and bottling Australian wines, which at the time were still curiosities for British consumers.

Australian wines were also winning fans at the many international exhibitions being held around the world. Mary was thrilled when, at the 1873 London International Exhibition at South Kensington, many South Australian vineyards, including those of Thomas Hardy, Patrick Auld and Edward Peake, were praised for their vintages, while the Norwood billiards whiz

Friedrich Lindrum claimed the first International Gold Medal for South Australian shiraz.[3]

WHEN NOT GLAD-HANDING wine merchants and retailers around Victoria and beyond as Mary's sales manager, Tom Hyland was cracking his whip – literally – bringing rigid order at Castlemaine Gaol. His motto was that if a man did not want to work, he didn't deserve to eat. Prisoners who refused to join prison work gangs were put on limited rations, while those who wanted to eat were made to work hard for their fare.

According to *The Age*, Tom's harsh discipline had completely transformed Castlemaine into a model prison:

> This officer, who has had a long penal experience, has transformed the place from a desert to a miniature garden of delight, and done his work at no cost to the State. He has utilised the brains and the sinews of the men at his command ... it is not merely in the gaol itself that Mr. Hyland has utilised the labour at his command. He has done much more. He has made in a goldfields town some of the best streets in the colony. To the extent of five miles he has made the ways of cabmen and of draymen easy and gentle. Mr. Hyland's principle is that every man who is relegated to his establishment must work for his living.[4]

Despite his grim workplace and the horrors he saw, Tom remained chipper – even cheeky – in his dealings with his wife's mother. He sent Mary a birthday letter in 1873. 'Dear old Mother,' he started, in stirring mode.

> Although the years are getting long and time keeps flying past, I must still wish you very many happy returns of your birthday and may you see many a happy one as yet old lady. I feel your 57th will still find you in harness but like a good old civil servant you will be pensioned off before your 60th and I then do most sincerely hope that you will have

many happy years before you to praise and cheer up your old boy Toby [the dog]. Be of good heart old gal and work on cheerfully and I am sure we will meet with our just reward, as I am now quite satisfied that our wines are good and we must ourselves set value on and be confident of their goodness. I wish you to buy any little thing in the shape of a bonnet, dress or other article, as a present from me and receive it with my best love and sincere affection. You are a noble, good old woman, Mother, and God bless you![5]

It was patronising, perhaps, but Mary sensed that Tom's heart was in the right place.

Tom was not always of such good cheer, of course, as his day job was no laughing matter. By early 1873 he had presided over two more hangings at Castlemaine Gaol[6] and was eager to escape.

In March that year Tom and Georgina were finally blessed with a boy who survived beyond his first weeks. They named him Frank Astor Hyland,[7] with his middle name honouring Mary's mother.

BY 1874, TOM WAS FINDING so many customers for Penfolds wine that Mary's own vineyard wasn't producing enough grapes to meet the demand. She started advertising for other vineyards to supply her: 'Grapes red or white. Purchased by Mrs Penfold.'[8]

Her reputation as the commander in chief of what was emerging as a major vineyard in South Australia encouraged a newspaper reporter to visit her impressive operation at Magill in June 1874 and take her story to the rest of the continent. A hard-driving businesswoman, a widow and a grandmother, she was such a rarity for the times that the story sparked national attention. *The South Australian Register*'s article, which was reprinted around Australia, told readers:

It has often been urged that it would be desirable to form a large Company for the purpose of purchasing grapes from various Vineyards and producing a limited number of varieties, which should be of uniform character and quality, from season to season. The advice thus given has not been carried out, but the object has within the last year or two been met to a very large extent by private persons of enterprise, who have made large purchases of their neighbours' fruit, and succeeded in blending the juice obtained from it so as to produce three or four distinct classes of wine of even quality. On previous occasions we have alluded to the praiseworthy efforts made by prominent growers, and we have now had the pleasure of inspecting the winehouses and vineyard belonging to Mrs. Penfold, of Magill, who has done much in the same direction.[9]

Mary and Joe Gillard gave the reporter an eye-opening tour of the vineyard and all the buildings connected with the winemaking. Mary explained that she had about sixteen hectares under vines and that she'd bought more grapes from neighbouring properties.

Mrs. Penfold's vineyard, which is situated a mile or so to the south of Magill, is on one of the hills which with their red loamy soil have proved so congenial to viniculture. The crowding of vines closely together has often been proved to be a fruitful source of disease, and health has been here ensured by planting the vines eight feet apart. Free circulation of air is thus allowed, and the gathering of the grapes is facilitated, as a cart can be taken between the rows when the vintage comes on. During the winter it is intended to plant another 15 acres [six hectares], and the proprietress intends placing the vines eight feet apart from each other one way and six the other. The advantages of the other arrangement will be thus preserved, and the vines will shade each other to a considerable extent. The vineyard yielded last season about three tons of grapes to the acre, and in addition Mrs. Penfold purchased from 250 to 280 tons, making a total of nearly 400 tons crushed. The yield from this has been a very fine one, amounting to 38,000 gallons

[173,000 litres] of wine, which is now undergoing the natural process of fermentation.¹⁰

Mary explained that she made only four varieties of wine – 'namely, sweet and dry red and sweet and dry white'. Grapes of all kinds were used, she said, and the uniformity, which was so important, was secured by the blending of the wines when they were two or three years old.

This is done under Mrs. Penfold's personal direction, not in conformity with any fixed and definite rule, but according to her judgment and taste. Very little spirit is used – not more than 1½ per cent, and this year even less than this small average will probably be required. The season has proved a remarkably good one for fermentation, which has proceeded quietly and not in such a violent manner as is sometimes the case in very hot weather, and from this cause, and owing to the good quality of the fruit, this year's produce promises to be of excellent character. Mrs. Penfold is aiming to get such a stock that she need not sell any which is under four years of age. There are now in the cellars about 20,000 gallons [91,000 litres] of wine of that age, which is ready for market, but the total stock is close upon 90,000 gallons [409,000 litres].¹¹

Mary complained that one of the great stumbling blocks to growing her export business was the Victorian duty of three shillings per gallon, which, she said, 'severely handicaps our wines in the sister colony'.

She and Joe Gillard showed the reporter the property's three large warehouses in which the wine was made and stored. They were built of stone and roofed with galvanised iron, and looked strong and substantial.

The total area of these stores is 103 foot [thirty-one metres] by 67 feet [twenty metres], and the largest room is 67 feet square [about 400 square metres]. The grape-press employed is an improvement on the ordinary machine, made by the foreman, Mr. Gillard, a son of the well-known winemaker at Norwood. The grapes are put through a network of cane, upon the top of which the stalks are left, and the fruit then descends to be crushed by two spiked rollers, which work in spiked concaves. The spikes are closer together than is ordinarily the case, and it is found that nearly every grape is crushed, while very few, if any, seeds are broken. This machine has hitherto been worked by hand, and during last season it crushed 20 tons of fruit per day, but if steam-power were applied it would be capable of dealing with 40 tons per diem. From the crusher the broken fruit passes into a cage, or a cask with the staves about half an inch apart. The cage stands in a large tub into which the juice passes, and from which it is allowed to flow into a small open keg, whence it can be pumped into any part of the buildings. The fruit from the cage is afterwards pressed in an ordinary screw-press, which gives a pressure of about 90 tons. The juice passes into a small tub, and is conveyed to the various fermenting vats in tubs. The dry husks are put in a tank with water and are again fermented for spirit.[12]

Mary waved her hand towards the immense storage facilities, and said they would only get bigger with rising demand for the Penfolds product.

The storage in casks amounted to about 409,000 litres, and some of the vats were of huge dimensions. The largest held about 22,000 litres, was almost four metres high and about three metres in diameter. There were seven casks of 3600 litres, which Mary explained were the first casks of this size made in South Australia:

'We did not know whether such large casks would answer the purpose, but they have proved a great acquisition, and the experiment has been a thoroughly successful one. The materials used for the casks and vats are South Australian redgum and English oak. The gum has been found to answer admirably, and timber is now being obtained at Lobethal [in the Adelaide Hills] for next year's supply of storing vessels.'[13]

There were two square slate vats, holding 3600 litres each, on the vineyard, but Mary was not happy with them, as they occupied as much room as would three oval vats 'containing altogether about 4000 gallons [18,000 litres]'. New casks and vats were needed every year; last season she had paid the coopers about £800.

The prices paid for grapes during the past vintage were very favourable to the growers who disposed of the produce of their vines to the manufacturers. Tokays and Madeiras we are informed fetched about £4 per ton, and Frontignacs, Verdelhos, and Muscats from £4 10s. to £5. As many vineyards will yield three tons of grapes to the acre it can readily be seen that vinegrowing is a really profitable investment. A good many people who have been foolish enough to root up their vines are now sorry that they took so ill-advised a step, and others who have small patches, which they have perhaps hitherto considered more bother than they are worth, will do well to avoid following their example. If they have not got sufficiently valuable or useful varieties they can obtain better kinds by grafting, and without much trouble they will be able to make considerable additions to their incomes.[14]

Not long after that article appeared, bringing the extraordinary story of this far-sighted businesswoman to the Australian public, Mary sent some of her wines to the 1874 London Exhibition.[15]

A year later, Mary had twenty-four hectares under vines. With the grapes she had purchased, Penfolds had turned out 112,000 litres for the year. She told reporters that sixteen of the twenty-four hectares were fourteen-year-old vines she had planted with her late husband. Her grape varieties included tokay, madeira, riesling, muscatel, Doradilla, shiraz, grenache and Mataro.[16]

Mary told *The Adelaide Observer* that while she had a large staff, 'she personally superintended' the business and personally bought any of the grapes she used from other growers. 'I take care,' she said, 'that only the best sorts are admitted to the press, and they are all delivered in boxes, so that it may be seen that they are in proper condition.'[17]

By 1875 Mary was making six kinds of wine and – thanks to Tom Hyland – was doing what she called a 'considerable' trade with Victoria. She complained that she could grow her business even more if it were not for the heavy duty being placed on imported wine into Victoria, which in the last year had risen from three shillings a gallon to four.[18]

There was a far more serious threat to Mary's vineyard, though, than the burdensome intercolonial tariffs. This was a menace that would batter the Australian wine industry like nothing since Arthur Phillip's first cuttings in Australia had withered on the vine a hundred years earlier. Winegrowers could see it coming but were powerless to do anything when it bit them hard.

Chapter 29

MARY'S FAMILY KEPT growing despite the tragedies of childbirth Georgina suffered. By 1877, her latest energetic grandson, Leslie,[1] was two years old and showing such athleticism for a toddler as to suggest that he would one day be a champion sportsman. Sadly, though, the seventh and last child Georgina bore, Vivien Hyland,[2] survived for only four months,[3] passing away in December that year. She was the third baby that the Hylands had to bury.

It was little consolation for Georgina's grief that she finally received some public acknowledgement for the part she played in her fourth daughter's short life: 'HYLAND.—On the 12th inst., Vivien Dolores, the infant daughter of T.F. and G. Hyland.'[4]

In 1876 Tom Hyland took a leave of absence as governor of the Castlemaine Gaol.[5] He was now forty-four years old and a father of four. He was praised in his farewell as 'an old and valued officer who had worked his way up to the position he occupied through the force of merit'.[6] His decision to leave meant he could now devote himself full-time to expanding Mary's business, both in the Australian colonies and overseas.

But his decision was also influenced by the horrors of his work in the prison service. Only two weeks before his departure, Mary's strapping Irish son-in-law had supervised his sixth and final execution at Castlemaine Gaol, the hanging of the condemned child rapist John Duffus.[7]

A deranged former convict named Michael Gately had replaced William Bamford as the colony's hangman, and he took 'a grim pleasure in his hideous calling'.[8] Another prison governor described Gately as a 'great brute who would boil babies if ordered to do so'.[9] One of Gately's favourite entertainments was to place a number of live rats in a room and, 'getting in among them, catch them in his teeth like a terrier dog and shake them to death. Afterwards he would put them on a spit, roast them, and eat them with every expression of relish.'[10] Gately was certainly not the sort of man with whom Tom did business over a tasting of Penfolds wine.

With Tom supervising, Gately performed the execution of Duffus at the Castlemaine Gaol just after 10 a.m. on 22 May 1876. The hanging was botched, perhaps deliberately: it was suspected that Gately sometimes positioned the noose in such a way that the hanged prisoner would not die quickly from a broken neck, but slowly from strangulation instead.[11]

To his last moment, the condemned man maintained his innocence. One sickened reporter wrote of the execution that, while Tom Hyland watched on in his official capacity, Gately stepped forward briskly at the prisoner's cell:

> [W]ith the air of a professional dancing master, [he] led the man to the gallows, pinioned his arms, and tied his legs ... the signal was given, the bolt shot, the platform fell, and the wretched man was launched into eternity ... Gately's bungling became only too apparent; the man had been placed at least six inches too far forward ... his head struck the front edge of the opening, inflicting an extensive wound, from which the blood flowed; then again the knot slipped from under the ear to the back of the neck, nearly severing the ear from the head, and prolonging the unhappy man's suffering.
>
> The fact is he was strangled, but not hung, the nervous twitching of the legs and body continuing for about eight minutes, and pulsation at the wrist for two or three minutes beyond that.[12]

It was a ghastly scene and one Tom never wanted to see again. From now on his work would focus on selling a drink steeped in sophistication and culture, something that made the heart glad and the soul rejoice.

IN THE SECOND HALF of the 1870s, South Australian vineyards were threatened on several fronts – first by a fungal disease and then by what became the scourge of Australian winemakers.

The ravages of *Oidium tuckeri*, a fungus that covers grapes in a powdery, greyish-white mildew, were for the most part confined to rich alluvial flats near water, mostly in the Torrens Valley, and mostly to the verdelho and black Hamburg grapes. The only remedy at the time was sulphur applied with a bellows early in the season, something Joseph Gillard Senior did constantly at his Sylvania vineyard in Norwood.

Joe Gillard Junior brought the defensive measure to The Grange as well, and Mary's grapes and those of her neighbours along the foot of the hills largely escaped the early attack of the fungus. In January 1876, Mary reported that the grapes 'were looking splendidly', and all that was required to ensure an excellent vintage was some warm weather, at least towards harvest time.[13] But not everyone was so fortunate, and wine production in South Australia that year fell off to such an extent that the colony produced only a third of its normal output.[14]

The setback could not stop the steady progress of Mary and other winegrowers, though, as wine became a major driver of the South Australian economy. *The South Australian Advertiser* listed Mary as one of the Adelaide district's few first-class manufacturers of wine, along with Thomas Hardy, the Gillards and 'one or two others' who purchased the bulk of the produce of smaller vineyards for their wine.[15]

> This arrangement suits the small growers much better than attempting to make wine themselves. It is also calculated to be beneficial in every way, as a superior wine can be

made by the large manufacturers, who are able to provide the best appliances, and to employ the best available talent for the manufacture and treatment of the wines. The trade with England is not yet established on a good footing but gradually new markets are opening up, and in the course of a few years South Australian wines will be known and appreciated in every quarter of the world. They are gradually but surely taking the place of imported wines among our own population.[16]

While Mary was winning the battle against the white fungus that attacked so many vines in South Australia, a more dangerous menace was devastating the vineyards in Victoria. Grape phylloxera, or 'vine louse' – tiny, almost microscopic insects – created huge headaches for winemakers in many places around the world.

Native to North America, these yellow sap-suckers destroyed whole vineyards in Britain, and then from 1863 began chewing their way through the roots of the vineyards in the southern Rhône region of France. French wine production eventually fell by more than two-thirds; some estimates claim that 90 per cent of European vineyards were ruined.[17]

Australian winemakers monitored the unrelenting march of these aphid-like monsters with trepidation.

In 1877, after some European vines supplied by an English firm were introduced into Victoria, phylloxera was identified in the vineyards of the steep hills around Fyansford, rolling down to the banks of the Moorabool, near Geelong,[18] where planting had begun thirty-five years earlier. By June 1878, phylloxera had been found in thirteen of the 116 vineyards around that city. A scorched-earth policy was necessary: the infested vineyards were completely uprooted, as were another six the following year.[19] But phylloxera continued moving northwards through Victoria to the Murray, which it would reach by the end of the 19th century. Thousands of acres were affected, leading to the destruction of the wine industry around Geelong and Bendigo.

Mary's home The Grange (left) with her wine-making operation in the distance.
State Library of South Australia PRG 631/2/327

Many winemakers were unfazed, though. Irish-born Samuel McWilliam[20] planted vines on the outskirts of Corowa in New South Wales in 1877, and in time McWilliam's Wines would become one the biggest names in the Australian industry.

Mary was eternally grateful that South Australia's strict quarantine regulations – introduced in 1875 and subsequently strengthened – protected her and the rest of the colony's grape growers and winemakers from these imported menaces.[21]

WITH INEZ – NOW A QUIET, pretty teenager – by her side, Mary rode about her vineyard on her white mare, spyglass in hand, watching her workers and looking out at Adelaide's blooming splendour in the distance below the hills.

Inez had made friends all around Adelaide and was proving to be an extremely clever young writer and amateur actress in local productions. She was much loved for what one observer described as her 'amiability and charitable disposition',[22] but she was not interested in romance. She preferred to find beauty in her poetry, jotting down lines of verse on any scrap of paper she could find. She was a marvellous companion for her grandmother.

Mary made the most of the ideal conditions and burgeoning opportunities. The havoc wreaked by phylloxera across Europe created a demand for Australian wines, and with Tom selling into every market he could, M. Penfold and Co. was flourishing. By the end of 1877 the ship *Aristides* carried twenty-one cases of Penfolds wine to London.[23]

Mary was still renting out 134 acres at Magill for pasture or crops,[24] but her focus was on her vineyard, now so bountiful that for the harvest of 1878 she was advertising that horse-drawn 'busses' would ferry her 'Grape Gatherers' from Adelaide's Globe Hotel to Magill, ready for work.[25]

While the Victorian tariffs continued to stifle imports from South Australian vineyards, markets in New Zealand and Queensland were growing.[26] Mary's Mataro, grenache, Pedro Ximénez, tokay, frontignac and muscadine were all selling well from their distributor in Brisbane.[27] She had produced 95,000 litres at Magill that year.[28] To cap off her success, Penfolds had won a bronze medal at the Paris Exhibition of 1878,[29] the *Exposition Universelle* held on the northern bank of the River Seine, in the Trocadéro Palace, built for the occasion.

In Blyth Street, Adelaide, the 'Brewers and Bottlers' Strutton & Trapman were acting as local agents for Mary's 'Celebrated Wines, from the Grange Vineyard, Magill'. They ran display ads for her wares: 20 shillings for a dozen quart bottles (about a litre) of her reds, grenache and Mataro, and 22 shillings for a dozen of the frontignac dessert wine. The whites made from Pedro Ximénez and tokay were also 20 shillings a dozen, and 22 shillings for the white muscadine dessert wine. All the wines were 12 shillings a dozen for pint bottles (600 millilitres). Strutton & Trapman would deliver cases of Mary's finest by horse and cart to Port Adelaide, Glenelg, Adelaide and suburbs.[30]

BY THE LATE 1870s the population of Australia had surpassed 2 million, and although only 250,000 of them were South Australians, the city of Adelaide was spreading in all directions.[31]

The Express and Telegraph speculated in 1879 on how long large vineyards such as Mary's could hold off the city's appetite for residential land:

> Situated immediately below [the vineyard] Auldana, and easily approached from the township, The Grange is a property that from the increasing value of suburban lands, and its admirable position, must in the course of a few years be required for other purposes than grape-growing.[32]
>
> From the higher slopes of the ground some capital views are obtained of the city and surrounding country, and the visitor cannot help being struck with the pleasing appearance of the vineyard itself with its well-cleared rows of healthy vines laden with luscious fruit.

Five years after she had first hosted the press at The Grange, Mary gave a team from *The Express and Telegraph* a tour of her extensive 'wine manufactory' in 1879. The journalists rode down the now-metalled Penfolds Road to her whitewashed cottage, to be met by a stout woman of sixty-three years with her hair tied back and bearing a huge smile. After decades in Chris's shadow, Mary was at last being acknowledged for her work as a winemaker, and one whose produce was gaining international attention.

She told the reporters how she and Chris had paid a little more than £2 an acre for the property in 1844, and the real estate value had increased significantly since then. Given the land prices so close to Adelaide, Mary had ceased planting at The Grange and was looking to sell off the rest of her old wheat and cornfields. She was happy with what her vineyard was supplying, and that produce was combined with grapes purchased from other growers, which she estimated was 'something like 250 tons a year'.[33]

Her medal from the Paris Exhibition had given M. Penfold and Co. excellent publicity. Output from Mary's vineyard had doubled within the last few years, proof that her wines were sound and well appreciated by the public.[34] The biggest demand, she said, was for grenache and tokay. The grenache, she explained, was 'a sound rich wine, like a port in colour and flavour, full of life and free of acid'. The Mataro was a red wine, lighter and drier than the grenache, and the tokay a rich white, somewhat resembling sherry. The Pedro Ximénez was similar to the tokay, only slightly drier, and the frontignac and muscadine were dessert wines with a rich character.

Mary was a self-taught vintner, but she had learnt her lessons well. She told the press team that her twenty-four hectares of grapes now included four hectares of young vines in their third year. They had not yet produced a crop, but she was chuffed that they looked healthy and promising.

Mary pointed out the different grapes growing all about her home. The Mataro was 'a dark-coloured hardy grape that stands all kinds of weather, and may be planted almost in any soil', she explained. The grenache required more care and attention, because if it were allowed to bunch together, the fruit would rot. In winemaking, she said, those two varieties blended well, and with the black Portugal.

There were some verdelho grapes, but they had proved to be more troublesome and more liable to disease than any other kind. On hot days they would often shrivel, and on wet days they were susceptible to the *Oidium* fungus. Although Joe Gillard, her vineyard manager, had used sulphur when the fungus had first appeared a couple of years earlier, now he simply opened up the vine by taking off some foliage. He and Mary found that sunshine and fresh air – a chemical-free, organic remedy – was the best treatment. Even so, Joe was careful not to expose the fruit, but to create a current of air through the centre of the plant.

Some of Mary's vines were planted four feet (1.2 metres) apart, but she and Joe realised that this was much too close. The plants did not have the necessary room to thrive, and the cost of the labour they needed for extra care absorbed most of the profit the grapes should have been producing. Mary said the most successful configuration was to have the vines eight feet (2.4 metres) apart, so that horses and a dray could pass between the rows in every direction. To the inexperienced vine-grower, she noted, her layout might seem like a waste of valuable space, but practical vignerons like her and Joe Gillard had 'fully ascertained the advantages of this system'.

'It may be accepted as an axiom,' she stated, 'that the vine in the colonies must have free scope to develop itself, and that the uses of horses must be encouraged where manual labour is so expensive and difficult to obtain.'[35]

One of the reporters mentioned that even though 1879 had been an exceptionally dry season, all the vineyards in the hills looked healthy. The newspapermen listened attentively as Mary pointed to the soil all about. She was glad that there was a good surface soil at The Grange, and the limestone bottom was reached at about three feet. Lime, she explained, was an essential constituent of the soil for successful grape-growing.

'The next thing required is water,' Mary said, 'and for this the roots will go down to an enormous depth, from a hundred feet [thirty metres] to a hundred yards [ninety metres].'[36] While sinking wells, Joe Gillard had traced vine roots down to twenty metres, but Mary said that there were many instances recorded where the vine roots had gone even deeper in search of moisture.

Mary drove her cart to a rise between The Grange and the Adelaide Hills to show the press her cellars, which were all on the surface, rather than underground as they were at some vineyards. The reporters noted that the structures were 'spacious and well-built'. Mary said that no wine came into the larger storage cellar until it had spent twelve months in the vintage casks. One of the storage vats held 24,000 litres, and another 22,000 litres; she speculated that they were perhaps the largest wine vats in the colonies.

Joe Gillard had just finished the construction of a massive new wine press to meet the growing demand for Mary's offerings, the bulk of which were exported out of South Australia in fifty-litre quarter-casks, while others were sent bottled in cases.[37]

Mary had spent decades in her husband's shadow, anonymous most of the time, and until recently had rarely been accorded any recognition for her role in what was now an internationally successful business and one of the leading wine companies in South Australia. She was keen to sell more wine into Victoria, in particular, and she was forthright in her views. She would be silent no longer, and was ready to tackle the highest echelons of government.

She would become a spokesperson for the whole industry.

Chapter 30

MARY WAS ANGRY. She sat at her desk in her cottage at Magill, picked up her steel-nibbed pen and dipped it into the inkwell. She then fired a rocket at the lawmakers in Melbourne.

Her twenty-four hectares of vines and the hundreds across South Australia that were producing fine wine were being stunted in their growth by bureaucratic wrangling. Even before Mary and Chris had arrived in South Australia, there had been calls for the colonies of the continent to become one federated Australian nation.[1] But as far as Mary was concerned, in the thirty-five years since, bureaucracy had worked towards chaos rather than cohesion.

The colonies had enormous trouble agreeing on anything that might be mutually advantageous. Even the development of railway lines across the continent had been problematic, with the colonies failing to agree to a standard track gauge. Each had opted for its own preference, despite the obvious inconvenience to passengers. Anyone travelling by train between the Australian capitals usually had to climb off their train at the border and climb onto another locomotive on the other side.

The protectionist policies in Victoria saw tariffs rise to 450 per cent on South Australian wine. Only the wealthiest of Melbourne's wine drinkers could afford to imbibe anything but their own colony's produce.

Removing tariffs was a matter of vital importance to every primary producer and manufacturer in South Australia, and Mary wanted to do her bit in the war against what she saw as financial stupidity. On 9 August 1879 she wrote to the premier of Victoria, a former grocer named Graham Berry, to complain about the folly of tariffs and how they were stymying the growth of economies across the continent. As a former small-business owner, he should have known all about that, though at the time he was preoccupied with the hunt for the bushranger Ned Kelly.

A month later, John Chatfield Tyler, the assistant commissioner at Victoria's Department of Trade and Customs, wrote back to Mary at The Grange:

> I am desired by the Honourable the Commissioner of Trade and Customs to acknowledge the receipt of your letter of the 9th ultimo, addressed to the Hon. Graham Berry, which has been forwarded by that gentleman to this department, and I am to inform you in reply that the Victorian Government would gladly consider any propositions for intercolonial reciprocity in the production referred to by you, and that some time since proposition for the mutual interchange of commodities across the border between South Australia and Victoria was made to the Hon. The Chief Secretary at Adelaide, but that no reply has been received.[2]

Mary was emboldened, writing to the Victorian government again on 3 October on 'the question of differential duties on wines from other colonies'. Tyler replied that '[t]he Victorian Government would gladly enter into an agreement in connection with the wine-duties' and had already made 'certain proposals to the South Australian Government'.[3]

Mary forwarded her correspondence to the former South Australian treasurer, Robert Dalrymple Ross,[4] who was president of South Australia's Vignerons' Club and now owned the Highercombe vineyard in the Adelaide Hills. Mary told him:

> I have the honour to forward, for the information of your club, copies of two letters received from the Hon. the Commissioner of Trade and Customs, Melbourne, from

which you will see that the Victorian Government are anxious to enter into an agreement with our own Ministers on the question of wine duties. No doubt this bold proposal on the part of Victoria will surprise our South Australian winegrowers, as we have hitherto been led to believe that the Victorian Government would not agree to anything of the kind. However, now that we have a most unmistakable proposal from Victoria let us take action with our own Government, and endeavour to bring about a satisfactory settlement of this question as between the two colonies.[5]

The Adelaide Observer reported soon after that 'Mrs. Penfold, of The Grange, and the Government of Victoria' had engaged in important correspondence 'on the subject of intercolonial reciprocity':[6]

We do not at all know the particulars of the proposition referred to. But, looking merely at the interests of vignerons in the matter, it would be very satisfactory if free trade in wines – a measure which has been warmly advocated in past times – could be established between this colony and Victoria. At present the wines in South Australia are shut out from the sister colony by a prohibitive duty of six shillings per gallon, the tax on Victorian wines imported into this colony being, we believe, only 4 shillings.

The Victorian wines are comparatively light, while those of this colony are for the most part full-bodied, and it would be greatly [helpful] to the interests of vignerons in the two colonies if facilities were afforded for blending the vines for export. This, however, can only be accomplished under a system of mutual free trade.

We fear that the Victorian Government are too firmly wedded to protectionist principles to acquiesce in any arrangement of this kind.[7]

The Vignerons' Club thanked Mary for her attention to this matter and decided to form a deputation to lobby the South

Australian parliament to act on this promising olive branch offered by Victoria. Although she'd done all the leg work, Mary wasn't invited to be part of the deputation – she was a woman, after all. The architect Edmund Wright, Mary's neighbour at the Home Park vineyard, and Thomas Hardy did most of the talking when they met the South Australian treasurer, Charles Mann.

Wright showed the treasurer Mary's correspondence with the Victorian government. These letters, he said, showed an inclination by the Victorians to enter into an arrangement for free trade in colonial wine. 'I need hardly remind you,' Wright told Mann, 'that this matter has frequently been brought before the Government, but it was doubly necessary now that if this boon could be procured for the wine growers of South Australia, it should be procured.'[8]

Wright and Hardy pointed out that, in France, the phylloxera scourge had cut their last vintage by two-thirds; if the pest kept spreading, the French wine industry would be a thing of the past. They pushed Mann to pursue an end to the trade barriers with both Victoria and New South Wales, because the wines of these colonies blended well with the produce of South Australian vineyards. 'Our wines resemble those of Spain and Portugal,' Wright said, 'theirs resemble France and Germany. If these vintages were blended they might produce a wine which could be advantageously sent to England.'[9]

Charles Mann thought this an idea worthy of merit.

Wright then made clear that there was a general feeling among South Australian winemakers that more could be done to facilitate intercolonial trade in wine.

Mann said he recognised the importance of the matter not only to vine-growers, but to the public of South Australia generally. Personally, he thought it would be an 'exceedingly good thing' to have free trade. He promised to bring the matter before cabinet, with a view to meeting their wishes, which he had little doubt he would be able to achieve.[10]

In this he was wrong: trade barriers between the colonies would exist for more than two decades. Still, Mary had been the voice of South Australia's winemakers, something that had previously seemed unthinkable for a woman.

THE VINES OUTSIDE The Grange had never looked better or been more productive. Joe Gillard did a sterling job keeping the *Oidium* fungus off Mary's grapes and none of the crop for 1880 was badly affected.

Penfolds was getting ready for its biggest year yet, producing 135,000 litres of wine, made both from the grapes of Mary's twenty-four hectares and from others she purchased.[11] Mary was at the peak of her powers as a winemaker. Having started as a hobbyist in her cottage kitchen, she was now one of the premier wine producers in the Australian colonies, internationally recognised. She was hugely respected by everyone in the industry, even if, as a woman, she rarely received public accolades.

In 1879 she sent four of her finest vintages to a colonial event of unprecedented scale: the Sydney International Exhibition. She had a good feeling about them.

THE GARDEN PALACE was unlike anything Sydney had seen. It was a magnificent wooden edifice, 250 metres long, built within Sydney's Botanic Gardens along Macquarie Street. Its 65-metre-high dome,[12] complete with the first hydraulic elevator in Sydney, dominated the skyline.

The builders imported electric lighting from England, allowing work to be carried out around the clock. In an astonishing feat of engineering, it took 3000 men, including 650 carpenters, just eight months to erect the awe-inspiring structure at a cost of just under £200,000, which had the buying power of about $A300 million in 2025.[13]

The Garden Palace became the centrepiece of a seven-month event that drew over 1.1 million visitors across 1879–1880. Thirty-four countries and colonies participated in what was the largest international exhibition yet staged in the Australian colonies. A steam tramway was installed to transport visitors around the Harbour City.

The magnificent Garden Palace in Sydney where Mary's wines were a huge hit for the Sydney International Exhibition in 1879. *State Library of Victoria Accession No. H26426*

There was a huge display of both local and European wines, and all the prominent Australian winemakers were represented, including Wyndham's, Lindeman's, Thomas Hardy, and Seppelt – as well as M. Penfold and Co. Mary's wines were star performers: her tokay, grenache and frontignac all won first-place prizes, and she took home a fourth place for her Mataro.[14]

The Garden Palace burnt down in September 1882, not long after the exhibition closed – but Mary's wines would still be going strong more than 140 years later. At home beside the fireplace at The Grange, Mary missed Chris very much, but Inez was great company. The elderly lady and her teenage granddaughter delighted in each other's conversation.

Inez was showing real promise as a poet. She had a wild imagination and a spontaneous nature, and would scribble verses as she thought of them on anything that came to hand – the backs of envelopes, sheets of music, the margins of books – sometimes in a handwriting that was almost illegible. Her writing was influenced by the Americans Mark Twain and Bret Harte, but she had her own acerbic tone as well, railing against pretence and hypocrisy.[15]

Mary encouraged her poetic gift and told her she should one day put all her poems in a book.

MARY WAS WELL SATISFIED with how she had transformed her farm into one of Australia's most respected wineries. She had become an astute vintner and an admired businesswoman, and had even been brave enough to take on government leaders. She reckoned to have almost half a million litres of wine in her cellars at Magill – said to be just over a third of the total wine stock in South Australia at that time.[16] But Mary was now sixty-five years of age, and not getting any younger.

Tom Hyland, meanwhile, having created so many sales channels for Mary's wines, had gone back to his former career as a prison governor at Castlemaine. In 1881 he took a year's absence, saying he wanted to visit 'the old country', Ireland, though in reality he had a more thrilling business journey planned.[17] The mayor of Castlemaine described Tom as a 'thorough disciplinarian' who had rendered important assistance to the town and had largely aided in beautifying the surroundings of the gaol, transforming rocky places into gardens and turning the streets of the town into well-made roads.[18]

Tom and Georgina and their children left Castlemaine for Melbourne on the train.[19] They were moving into a grand bluestone mansion in Were Street, in the beachside suburb of Brighton. Being a gaol governor for many years had paid well, as had Tom's investments.

The huge home was called 'Moorabbin House' and had been built way back in 1842 by the politician and investor Jonathan Binns Were.[20] It was later the residence of Melbourne's first Catholic archbishop, James Alipius Goold. The walls were almost a metre thick, and the property's lush grounds and colourful garden were enclosed by huge iron gates. Some of the rooms were ten metres long. There was an immense crystal chandelier hanging in the drawing room, while a fine avenue of trees led from the house to the beach.[21] The interior walls were ornately stencilled by hand, and the ceiling was hand-painted in delicate colours. Georgina planned to fill the house with fine pieces and curios that she would gather from overseas travels,[22] and they intended to add a fine ballroom to the house.[23]

Tom had proved himself a business dynamo. Although he had not been brought up in the wine trade, he had learnt quickly, finding new markets and new opportunities to grow the business from its humble beginnings. Even though he had been working remotely – 800 kilometres away from Magill – Mary felt no one could have done a better job promoting her interests.

When Mary heard her daughter's family was moving to Brighton, she was pleased. She cast her mind back to the wonderful years she and Chris had spent at the original Brighton, in Sussex, where Georgina was born. She longed for the chance to visit her daughter and grandchildren more often. Mary loved The Grange, though, and wanted to stay enveloped by the vines that had been her life.

Ever since Mary's husband had died, Tom and Georgina had been trying to convince her to retire from winemaking. Tom had seemed to doubt Mary's ability to run the growing concern that was the Penfolds vineyard back then, but she had shown him, and every other male winemaker in the business, just what she could do. She figured now that she'd done just about enough. But she wasn't ready to pack it in just yet.

Instead, with Tom financing a new business structure and contemplating rapid expansion, Mary entered into a partnership agreement with him and Joe Gillard, forming a new business called Penfolds and Co.[24] She was handing the assets she and her husband had built to the next generation, but she had an eye on the generations still to come.

With a flourish of her pen, 'Mary Penfold of Magill near Adelaide South Australia, widow', signed a legal agreement on 14 September 1881 with 'Thomas Francis Hyland of Melbourne, in the colony of Victoria, Esquire', agreeing that she would continue in the 'trade or business of a winemaker and wine-seller now carried on by him in conjunction with Mr. Joseph Gillard at the Grange Vineyard Magill for the term of seven years'.[25]

Mary agreed that, 'during such time', she would 'keep the books of account of the said trade or business, make out all necessary invoices, attend to all necessary correspondence attached to the receiving and paying of all necessary accounts, wages and outgoings of the business, and attend to the banking of all necessary monies to the banking account of the business of Penfold and Co.' She was to 'generally give her whole time and attention to the promotion and advancement of the interest and profits of the said trade or business in conjunction with the said Joseph Gillard during the said term'.[26]

In consideration of her agreed duties, Tom agreed to a partnership in which she could stay at The Grange rent-free, with as much firewood and water from the estate as she needed for her 'domestic use and consumption', as well as one-tenth of the profits of the new company.

Joe Gillard also signed a deal giving him one-tenth of the profits and a subsequent agreement to sell all the grapes from his father's Norwood vineyard, after Joseph Senior bought the Clarendon estate.

Lest there be any doubt as to who was now running Penfolds Wines, Tom Hyland added a clause to the contract:

> [I]t is hereby further agreed and declared that all the freehold property known as the Grange Vineyard and Estate and the buildings and business plant and stock of wine thereon are and are to remain the sole property of the said Thomas Francis Hyland ... and it has been agreed by and between the parties hereto that the quantity of wine in stock on the first day of January 1881 amounted to 107,000 gallons [486,000 litres].

Mary had built the business into an extraordinary investment vehicle, and now it was time to pass the reins to another driver.

Chapter 31

MARY FINALLY RETIRED from an active role in the family wine business in 1884, forty years after she and Chris had planted the first vines in a gully behind The Grange cottage.

She had decided she'd done enough bookkeeping for one lifetime, and Tom Hyland appointed Giffard Bannister,[1] a thirty-year-old Englishman, as the new Penfolds accountant. In time, unfortunately, he would develop a reputation for dishonesty — but that was something for Tom, the former prison governor, to sort out. Mary was now sixty-eight and had earned a carefree retirement.

After formally resigning from the Victorian civil service at the end of 1882, Tom began building on the already enormous achievements Mary had made. He travelled frequently to Adelaide to visit Inez and to talk business with Mary and Joe Gillard. He was always up for a fight, as well, and unsuccessfully battled the Commissioner for Railways in New South Wales all the way to the Supreme Court in Sydney over what he said were excessive charges to carry his wine from Adelaide.[2] He also continued Mary's struggle on behalf of all South Australian vintners protesting the intercolonial tariffs.[3]

Tom had much more success when he took samples of Penfolds wine to London for the Colonial and Indian Exhibition of 1886. Queen Victoria opened the festival at South Kensington in May, and over the next six months 5.5 million visitors toured the displays. As a result, Tom eventually sold 300 hogsheads — about

90,000 litres – of his product to the London wine merchant P.B. Burgoyne.[4]

Tom also acted as the spokesman for the South Australian vintners at the exhibition, shaking hands and providing all the information about the kind of wines each vineyard produced.[5] Manning the information desk at this world's fair in London was a lot more enjoyable for him than supervising the final breaths of condemned prisoners at Castlemaine Gaol.

An Australian correspondent noted that *Harper's Weekly Gazette* – 'a journal devoted specially to the interests of the wine and spirit trade, and considered one of the best authorities in the matter of wine' – had heaped enormous praise on the Penfolds offerings in London:

> Penfold and Co. may be congratulated upon the excellent condition of their exhibits, each one showing care and attention ... In white wines their Tokay showed very well, and met with much approval, and the Muscadine, a thin, clean wine, was good of the kind, but hardly suitable to the market here. Of red wines, by far the best showed by this firm was the Grenache, a good wine with fine bouquet, which was picked out by several experts as the best sample of wine exhibited.[6]

ALTHOUGH MARY NO longer had an active role in the wine business, the veteran colonists of Adelaide were well aware of her place in building Penfolds.

While Tom and Georgina toured Ireland and Europe after the London exhibition, the governor of South Australia, Sir William Robinson, led a delegation of more than a dozen cabinet ministers, politicians and newspaper reporters to The Grange for a tour of what was becoming an iconic Adelaide business. In the governor's party were the former premier Henry Ayers,[7] the pastoralist and politician Thomas Elder,[8] South Australia's Minister of Education, the Commissioner of Crown Lands, and E.T. Smith,[9] the mayor of Adelaide.

Officially, they were received at Magill by Giffard Bannister and Joe Gillard, but it was Mary, now seventy and portly, who held their attention.

The governor and the ministers were escorted into the small, neat cottage that had been Mary's home for more than forty years. Henry Ayers said he was amazed by the way the vineyard had grown in recent years; he remembered the much smaller operation when Mary's husband was alive.[10] Mayor Smith had known Chris thirty years earlier, and said he was glad to know that his widow was still healthy and fit, and still living among the vines that Chris loved so much.

Mary told the august group how she and her beloved husband had arrived in Adelaide in 1844 after a four-and-a-half-month journey from England. Future generations would use the slogan 'From 1844 to Evermore' in their Penfolds advertising campaigns.[11] 'We brought vine cuttings with us from England,' Mary explained, 'simply wrapped in canvas and their ends sealed up, and though those cuttings were kept out of the earth all that time they were alive.'[12]

She described how she and Chris had planted the vines in a gully behind the room in which they were all now standing.[13] The visitors were suitably impressed. She and Chris had transplanted the vines two years later, and some of them were still flourishing. In 1847, Mary went on, she had made the first small vintage of Penfolds wine, ten gallons [forty-five litres], that formed the nucleus of the huge business it had become. By 1869, the cellars at The Grange held 45,000 litres. She was proud to say that there were now 900,000 litres in the cellars on the rise behind the cottage.

The governor nodded approvingly. When Mary finished speaking, he said she was an example of what patience and perseverance could achieve in developing an industry.[14]

The fight over tariffs with the other colonies was continuing. Mary had given Bannister the information for his welcome speech, and in the politest way he could, the polished accountant told the vice-regal deputation that the government seemed to have lost sight of the fact that the wine industry was sure to be one of the mainstays of the colony in the future. He told the delegation that South Australian wines were being slugged four to six shillings a gallon on border duties, making their cost prohibitive for many.

'Australia resembled some other winemaking countries,' Bannister said, 'in that each district produced its own particular wine, according to the quality of the soil and the nature of the climate. We hope that the government will fully recognise the very great importance of such a colonial industry as that of winemaking.'

Mary was no longer sprightly, so Joe Gillard and Giffard Bannister left her inside the cottage as they took the delegation around the property. The governor and other members of the party made careful enquiries into the history and development of the business.[15]

The Magill vineyard now had forty-two hectares under vines.[16] 'The land is sloping up to the foot of the hills, and commands a beautiful view of the city and its surroundings,' *The Express and Telegraph* newspaper reported.

> The soil seems to be a strong chocolate loam, and is evidently well suited for the purposes of the vigneron. In addition to their own crop the firm purchase largely from other growers – taking the grapes, but declining the 'must' – crushed grapes – as Mr. Gillard, the manager, is averse to using 'must' made by other people. Mr. Gillard has such faith in the wine industry that he has purchased on his own account land in Rosslyn Park, just below the vineyard, where he is planting vines, and he is afraid that in few years grapes will not be obtainable in the colony in quantities sufficient to fulfil the orders that will be sent in from the home and foreign markets.

At harvest time, Joe explained, about fifty hands were employed at The Grange in picking and other operations. After the grapes were picked, they were taken to the mill in brandy cases; a stock of more than a thousand cases was kept on hand for this purpose. The mill was driven by a four-horsepower Tangye vertical steam engine. There were now nine cellars, all impressive stone buildings with iron roofs.[17] The visitors were astounded by the huge storage vats; there were now six, each holding between 22,000 and 27,000 litres.

Joe told the visitors that the red wines made there were cabernet, grenache, frontignac and port, and the whites riesling, tokay, muscadine and sherry. The grapes grown in the vineyard were Mataro, grenache and frontignac for the reds, and riesling, Pedro Ximénez, tokay and muscat for the whites.

After toasts were given in the sampling room, Sir William expressed his surprise and pleasure at seeing such a huge establishment, far grander than he had imagined. He had seen Penfolds wines many times when travelling to other colonies, he said, but not so much in Adelaide, and he assumed that the business was more concerned with export than local consumption, despite the tariffs. He hoped the wine connoisseurs of South Australia would come to celebrate one of their local success stories and their superb products.

After a good sampling of the wines, and assorted promises from the dignitaries to do all that they could to remove the tariffs and to promote South Australian winemakers, the regal party bade farewell to their hosts. On their way out to Penfolds Road, they visited the cottage of Mary Penfold and 'paid their adieus' to the elderly grandmother who had started it all.[18]

Four months later, Mayor Smith came back for seconds, having enjoyed the free wine tasting so much. He brought several members of the City Council with him, along with the town clerk and other notable Adelaide figures to meet Mary. Then the eager visitors headed up the hill to the sampling room and a 'light repast'.[19] The mayor said he did not know of any industry more likely to prove the salvation of South Australia than the wine industry. The tour ended with a toast to the health of Mary Penfold.[20]

With the international reputation of South Australian wines growing, Tom sent Giffard Bannister on a sales expedition to

Britain in 1888, and he based himself at the Covent Garden Hotel in London.[21] Bannister had a great time, but his tenure with Penfolds would not last. After leaving the company, he served two prison sentences for passing bad cheques.[22]

MARY'S GRANDCHILDREN were growing fast. Inez was twenty-five in 1888, and while she was a marvellous help to Mary, she had become painfully shy and reclusive. Her poetry brought her out of her shell a little, though, and Mary kept telling Inez that she should collect her verses in a book.

Tom sent some of his daughter's poems to the American consul in Melbourne, asking him to forward them to the great short-story writer Bret Harte, one of Inez's literary heroes, and the subject of some of her verses.

Meanwhile, the Hylands' second daughter, Estelle, was planning to marry a wealthy young Englishman, Charles Knight.[23] Mary would soon become a great-grandmother,[24] although the young Knight family would eventually make their home in England.

The *Intercolonial Express* had started running between Adelaide and Melbourne, using the same railway gauge so that passengers could make the whole journey on one train. But it was still a slow ride of more than twenty-four hours. Despite this, Mary was enthusiastic about the new rail service, and was always delighted to visit Georgina and her two lively teenage boys, Frank and Leslie, at Moorabbin House in Brighton.

On one occasion Mary wrote to Leslie to say she was coming soon. At the time, The Grange was being plagued by stray cats and wild dogs, and she joked with her grandson that she and Inez 'could manage an air gun'.[25]

> I will be over to see you very soon now the rail is opened, it will be so much nicer than the sea voyage …
>
> We have got a pug puppy and Mrs. Longbottom gave me back the pug I gave her, so we now have two … we gave away the mother to a kind woman in Adelaide who feeds

her on hot mutton chops. The weather here is very hot and uncomfortable. The poor pugs feel it so much ... Beppo, the old one, quite cries if anything affronts him ... he sat himself against the wall of the verandah and the tears ran down his face because I took more notice of the puppy than him and [despite] all we could do he would not move ...

We went for such a nice drive when your Father was over: up into the hills and we had tea at such a nice clean place and a lovely drive by moonlight.

We saw some men washing gold and I wanted to get out and see what they had got but directly they caught sight of our waggonette they took us for a wedding party and yelled at us in a very Colonial fashion.

The reason they took us for a wedding party was that Lottie Murray was all in white, bonnet and all ... So we teased her about it.

Now I must say goodbye as it is getting very late, so best love from Inez and ever your affectionate Grannie,

Mary Penfold[26]

Mary and Inez made frequent use of the *Intercolonial Express*,[27] and Mary was always keen to share the latest news about what was happening at The Grange. She knew the day was not far off when Frank and Leslie would become directly involved in the wine trade, as it was their inheritance. And the news around the business was better and better.

WHILE MARY AND INEZ were staying with the Hylands in Melbourne in March 1889, a French engineer named Gustave Eiffel was leading a group of government officials and newspaper reporters[28] to the top of his 300-metre-high tower, the tallest structure in the world. The lifts were not working yet, so only the fittest of the group made it up the stairs to the top of the engineering marvel that was to be the centrepiece of the 1889 *Exposition Universelle* in Paris, which celebrated the centenary of the French Revolution.

The Eiffel Tower was the star attraction of the Paris Exposition in 1889 but Mary Penfold's port was a standout as well, taking a gold medal.

Eiffel's tower was not opened to the public until nine days after the start of the exposition on 6 May, but it was the great drawcard of this world's fair, which ran for six months and attracted more than 32 million visitors to Paris at a time when France was trying to trade its way out of an economic recession.[29]

The exposition drew 61,722 official exhibitors, with 25,000 of them coming from outside France. While the Eiffel Tower was the undoubted star of the show, Australian wines were a big hit too. On 4 July 1889, the wine jurors examined the Australian offerings and spent an hour and a half tasting the wines from South Australia. When the French experts had finished sniffing, swirling and sipping, the Penfolds tokay, muscadine and port were 'specially commended'.[30]

According to a reporter in Paris:

> Penfold's Port was considered most excellent, and was tasted twice by the jurors. It obtained 15 marks, which is close to the maximum. The Portuguese juror – who, with his Spanish colleague, has throughout shown hostility to the Australian wines – asked what business South Australians had to sell a local wine as Port.[31]

There was considerable friction over the matter – friction that continues over the naming of wines to this day. The South Australian contingent told the pugnacious Portuguese judge that the Penfolds port was made from the port grape.

'Besides, no confusion between our wines and yours is possible,' a spokesman offered, 'because, in accordance with the law, all South Australian wines are labelled as such, and the further mention "Bottled in South Australia," is on every label.'[32]

The Portuguese winegrowers wanted to follow the French Champagne Growers' Syndicate at the exposition and claim an exclusive right to use the word 'Port'. 'This is obviously absurd,' the South Australian spokesman told the press in Paris, 'as "Port" is a purely English word, the Anglicisation of the Portuguese "Oporto".'[33] In what the Australian press called 'a manifestation of international jealousy', the jury 'refused to look at some samples of Australian wines shown by a private firm of bottlers as "Pommard,"' the name of the French wine region.[34]

Despite the squabbles over names, the jurors knew their wine. Mary could not have been prouder when she read in the Adelaide newspapers the following month that the Penfolds port had been awarded a gold medal by the Paris jury.[35]

From those little things planted behind The Grange in 1844, great things had grown.

DEMAND FOR WINE with the Penfolds label was now so great that the company vineyards covered fifty-six hectares, and there were 'very nearly 300,000 gallons [1.35 million litres] in the cellars'.³⁶ The new, giant Adelaide-made wine vat known as the 'Brobdignagian Falstaff' could hold almost 50,000 litres of Penfolds' finest inside its Russian oak.

More and more winemakers were planting vines in South Australia. Like Chris Penfold and Dr Alexander Kelly at Tintara, Dr William Thomas Angove,³⁷ a graduate of St Bartholomew's in London, was a great believer in the power of wine as a restorative tonic. Like Chris, he was also a government medical officer and a public vaccinator. In 1889, Dr Angove bought thirteen hectares of farmland next to his house at Tea Tree Gully, about thirteen kilometres north-west of The Grange, and leased another sixty-four hectares nearby to grow grapes.³⁸

Two years later, the pastoralist John Riddoch³⁹ planted the first vineyard at Coonawarra, 330 kilometres south-east of Adelaide, on the limestone coast, an area that would become synonymous with the cabernet sauvignon wines produced on its red soil.

It was a happy time at The Grange. Inez was sending some of her poems to the local press anonymously, just for the thrill that she and Mary received at seeing her words in print.

In 1891, the old lady and her granddaughter had paid six shillings each for tickets to hear the University of Adelaide's vice-chancellor, Roby Fletcher, give a presentation on ancient Egypt at the Young Men's Christian Association's Victoria Hall in Gawler Place.⁴⁰ Inez was fascinated by the lecture, and a picture of an Egyptian mummy propelled her to dash off some verses in response. She sent her poem 'Pharoah Lives for Ever', bearing the signature Inez K. Hyland, to *The Adelaide Observer* and it appeared in print with her name.⁴¹ Mary and Inez were overjoyed.

Another poem by 'Inez Hyland of The Grange Vineyards, Magill', entitled 'Dot Confides to a Friend', appeared in the weekly Adelaide publication *Quiz and the Lantern* a few weeks later.⁴²

Mary was so happy. Her life was beautiful here in this little whitewashed house among the grapevines and the rich dark soil in the shadow of the Adelaide Hills.

But life was full of surprises; it could knock you flat when you least expected it.

Chapter 32

AS THE SUMMER approached in late 1891, Inez started to feel unusually hot. Mary suspected it wasn't just another ferocious Adelaide summer of the type that had claimed Bishop Short's daughter forty-five years before. Inez felt weak and lethargic, and began to suffer blinding headaches. She quickly became nauseous. When Mary summoned medical help, the doctors diagnosed enteric fever, a collective term that included typhoid.[1]

Inez had likely ingested salmonella bacteria, through contaminated food or water. As Mary prayed for her grandchild's deliverance, Inez only became weaker. And for the next six weeks[2] the shy, delicate young woman was gripped with fever and pain, sweats and chills, shakes and panic. Georgina and Tom rushed to their daughter's bedside from Melbourne,[3] but Inez died in her bedroom at The Grange on 11 January 1892.

That morning, Tom had received a letter, via the American consul, from Bret Harte himself, congratulating Tom on the beauty of Inez's works and predicting 'a very brilliant future' for her as a writer.[4]

Mary was devastated. The light of her life had been snuffed out just as it started to burn brightly.

The Adelaide newspapers announced Inez's passing:

HYLAND.—On the 11th January, at the Grange Vineyards, Magill, Inez K., the eldest daughter of Mr. T.F. Hyland, of Brighton, Victoria, and grand-daughter of the late Dr. Penfold, of Magill, South Australia.[5]

There was no mention of Inez's grieving mother, or of the broken-hearted grandmother she had lived with for the last twenty years.[6]

The Adelaide undertaker John Knabe prepared Inez's body for burial.[7] The day after her death, she was taken from The Grange at 3 p.m. for the solemn funeral procession to the churchyard at St George's. Mary rode in one of the mourning carriages behind the coffin for the one-mile journey north to the little cemetery where Chris Penfold had rested for more than twenty years now. Inez was buried across the path from the grandfather she had barely known.

Her family paid for a two-metre stone cross to be placed above her, and Mary ordered the inscription of similar words to those she had written in remembrance of Ellen Timbrell all those years ago: 'A life of perfect service ended. Duties done. In charity. Kind words and stainless days.'[8]

Mary gave Adelaide's *Evening Journal* the details of a young life cut short:

THE LATE MISS HYLAND.—The death of Miss Inez Kathleen Hyland, which it has been our sad duty to record, has removed one who, in the opinion of those who had an opportunity of judging, gave every promise of literary distinction.

Born only twenty-eight years ago in Victoria, where her parents (Mr. and Mrs. T.F. Hyland, of Brighton, in that colony) still reside, she lived since she was eight years old with her grandmother at the Grange Vineyards, Magill. From her childhood she exhibited great intelligence, and as she grew to womanhood it became apparent that she was richly endowed with mental powers. Of a retiring disposition she lived the life almost of a recluse, but her days and nights were spent in patient study, unfortunately perhaps to the injury of her health.

Brilliant in conversation, well read, fluent, and quick at repartee, she was equally facile with her pen. She occasionally contributed verses and letters to our columns, but seldom with her own name appended to them. Most of her literary productions are still unpublished, but those given to the public exhibit so much freshness, vigour, and originality that it is hoped her relatives may be induced to collect and publish her works. In the neighbourhood of Magill her name will be long remembered as well for her habit of charity among the poor and suffering as for her remarkable personality.[9]

It was a lovely tribute, but Mary wanted something more lasting for the sweet girl whose absence from The Grange left her feeling utterly broken. Mary knew what it was like to go through life unrecognised for one's achievements.

She gathered all of Inez's completed verses, jottings and scribblings and did a deal with the Melbourne publisher Charles Robertson, who had taken over his father's business, George Robertson & Co. Mary agreed to fund the cost of publication. The result was *In Sunshine and in Shadow*, a 354-page volume of poems and short stories that Inez had written while living with her grandmother. It was published a year after Inez's death. The dedication read:

All Who Hold Her Memory Dear
At the request of many friends I publish this little volume of poems and short stories, written by my beloved granddaughter. Much has necessarily been omitted, as they were for the most part written down on anything available at the moment – backs of envelopes, pieces of music, margins of books – in pencil, and in many instances almost illegible.

> Thus I have had great difficulty in collecting them; but I rest satisfied that, whatever their faults, they will meet with no harsh criticism, for her dear sake.
> MARY PENFOLD.

There were some unkind reviews from around Australia, but an Adelaide newspaper gave credit where it was due:

> The author was the daughter of a gentleman now resident in Victoria, but well known in Adelaide, and she was the granddaughter of Mrs. Penfold, a pioneer colonist, who has by her many virtues won the esteem of all who know her. Miss Hyland wrote for pleasure, not for fame, and it is only through the appreciation of friends and the thoughtfulness of Mrs. Penfold that this volume has been given to the world. It contains some crude creations, which, however, are so obviously earnest of purpose that they disarm criticism and invite sympathy, and it also has within its covers numerous sweet and tender sentiments gracefully conveyed in melodious rhythm.[10]

Among them was 'A Lily's Shadow':

> Tis a bird's voice which is singing
> In a sweet, regretful tone,
> Of the shadows night is bringing,
> And a day for ever flown.[11]

As she gathered Inez's effects in the days after her passing, Mary also began packing a few of her own belongings. She had lived at The Grange for forty-eight years, but now, at seventy-five, it was time to say goodbye. Georgina and Tom insisted that Mary, who was inconsolable and lonely, leave the little cottage and move into their expansive home by the beach in Melbourne.

Inez had only been in her grave a few days when a series of advertisements from the Adelaide auctioneers C.G. Gurr & Co. began appearing in the Adelaide press each day:

> On MONDAY, February 1, at 11 o'clock ... At The Grange Vineyard, Magill, Mrs. Penfold's Very Superior Household Furniture And Effects. Superb Piano In Ebony Frame, By Rönisch – Cost 80 Guineas. Rare Biscuit-ware. Dresden, Sèvres, And Wedgwood Ware, Bronzes, Bric-A-Brac, Bevel Plate Plush-Framed Mirrors, And Costly Hangings. Under instructions from Mrs. Penfold, who has left the colony.[12]

Virtually everything Mary had accumulated in her seventy-five years was to go: an oak hall stand, linoleum, oil paintings and choice hall decorations, occasional chairs, settees and a Chippendale cabinet by Mayfield. There were Brussels carpets, oilcloths, Queen Anne tables, and 'a splendidly upholstered armchair and couches'. There was an oval dining table, lamps, an expensive breakfast and tea service with a willow pattern, sterling silverware, 'first quality Electro-plated ware'. There was a superior double half-poster bedstead and a single bed, nickel-plated and brass-mounted spring mattresses, wardrobes, bedroom suites, washstands, linen, a kitchen table, a large copper for washing clothes, laundry utensils, choice pot-plants, a garden hose, and twelve slate tanks each of 4500 litres.[13]

No reserve price was set on anything. Mary didn't care how much the auction made because she no longer had need of money. The items went for bargain basement prices and for some time the Grange remained empty.

MARY TRAVELLED WITH Tom and Georgina back to Melbourne and was made to feel at home in the much bigger house at Brighton. She was glad that in the same year she arrived at the Hylands' mansion, her nineteen-year-old grandson, Frank

Astor Hyland, started as a sales representative with Penfolds. Leslie joined him soon after.

As Mary listened for the sounds of the sea at Brighton Beach and thought of the years that had passed since she and Chris and Georgina left Brighton in Sussex for life in South Australia, she could justly feel satisfied at a job well done.

But night brought the shadows of the days and they flew by for Mary, one after another, so fast. Three years later, in the winter of 1895, Mary began to suffer chest pains, shortness of breath and a persistent cough. In September that year she was diagnosed with carcinoma of the pleural lining, a cancer of the thin tissue over the lungs and chest cavity.[14]

For three months Mary said her prayers, asking that the agony she was experiencing would stop. She patiently waited to be reunited with her beloved husband. Then, on the last day of 1895, at Moorabbin House, in Were Street, Brighton, Mary Penfold, the mother of the Australian wine industry, passed away at the age of seventy-nine.

The obituaries were brief. They all credited 'Dr Penfold' with starting the family wine business, but some acknowledged that, after his death, Mary had 'assisted in carrying on the business, which is known as Penfold & Co, until about three years ago', when she went to live with her daughter in Melbourne and died there 'after a short and painful illness'.[15]

Mary had lived in the shadow of men all her life, and so it was in death.

Mary's last wish was that she be buried with Inez. Georgina and her family accompanied Mary's body on the overnight *Intercolonial Express* to Adelaide, and left the Adelaide Railway Station bound for the St George's churchyard on the morning of 3 January 1896.[16] There, she was laid to rest in the same thick, loamy soil in which her granddaughter had been interred four years earlier.

Mary's funeral was a small affair. Although she had built one of the great South Australian companies from her kitchen table, there were no civic accolades for her, no lavish public praise, no vice-regal mourners. Her epitaph was a simple inscription carved into the base of Inez's elaborate monument, as though it were an afterthought:

> Mary Penfold
> Wife of the late Dr C.R. Penfold
> On the 31st of Dec, 1895,
> In the 79th year of her age
> Found a fairer region, and a happier life forever with our Lord

Mary's grave was placed a little behind her husband's. But she would not remain in his shadow forever.

Epilogue

MARY HAD GIVEN HER MONEY and property to her descendants long before she died, and she bequeathed all that remained – £259 7s worth of BHP shares – to Georgina and Tom.[1] But her example of tenacity and her pursuit of excellence comprised a legacy that offered so much more.

Just a month after Mary was buried, her go-getting grandson Frank Hyland was in Perth, selling his family product to as many retailers as he could. He told reporters that it was his third trip to Western Australia, where there was now 'a very large demand for dry, red, full bodied wines'. Penfolds was looking to increase its sales in the west despite the border duties, which now amounted to six shillings and sixpence a gallon, a tariff of more than 100 per cent.[2] Frank had already toured England and the Continent at the age of twenty-three, buying machinery and equipment and studying winemaking techniques wherever he went.[3]

Tom Hyland was now sixty-five years old, and although he was always looking for ways to expand Penfolds' market share, he eventually left the running of the company to Frank and Leslie. As a nod to their maternal grandparents, and to emphasise that theirs was a family business, the brothers changed their surnames to 'Penfold Hyland'.[4]

The intercolonial border duties were finally removed in 1901, when the separate Australian colonies formed a federated nation, as toasts of wine were offered to its future across the vast land. That same year, Leslie was runner-up in the Victorian Amateur Golf

Championship.[5] After he moved to South Australia, Leslie won the amateur championship there, but he and Frank would have much greater success in the wine industry than on the golf links.

Frank opened a Penfolds office in Pitt Street, Sydney, in 1901, while Leslie ran the South Australian arm. The brothers were voracious in their acquisitions, bringing a number of other vineyards under the company umbrella. In 1904, Frank bought Dalwood, the original Wyndham Estate, in the Hunter Valley of New South Wales.

Leslie organised the building of cellars at McLaren Vale in 1910, the year before his mother, Georgina, Mary Penfold's only child, passed away in Brighton.

In 1911, Leslie began work on developing a new winery at Nuriootpa, in the Barossa Valley, and the following year Frank bought the Minchinbury winery and vineyard at Rooty Hill, west of Sydney. With Leo Buring,[6] a graduate of Adelaide's Prince Alfred College, managing the property, it grew and grew as a producer of fine champagne.

Tom Hyland, Mary Penfold's son-in-law, died at Brighton in 1920. His mansion, Moorabbin House, was knocked down soon after and redeveloped.[7] But Frank and Leslie kept building up the value of their grandmother's business, establishing in 1921 a winery at Griffith, in New South Wales, taking advantage of land and an eager post-war workforce in the Murrumbidgee Irrigation Area.

The Penfolds logo, which today is one of Australia's most recognisable trademarks, first adorned the company's wine bottles in 1923.

By the time Leslie died in 1940, Penfolds controlled vineyards and wineries at Magill, Nuriootpa, Eden Valley and McLaren Vale in South Australia, and Minchinbury, Griffith, Dalwood, Allandale and other areas of the Hunter Valley in New South Wales.[8]

And they kept growing, acquiring the Auldana winery next door to their grandmother's property at Magill, the Modbury vineyard a few miles north, and the Kalimna vineyards, winery and distillery in the Barossa Valley.[9] Auldana's flagship was the award-winning St Henri claret, developed by Edmond Mazure,[10] a French-trained winemaker. In the 1950s, John Davoren, Auldana's winemaker, created a much-admired unwooded light claret for Penfolds using the St Henri name.

Mary's family members ran Penfolds until the 1970s. Frank's widow, Gladys,[11] was chairman of the company from 1949 to 1961. She was a great-granddaughter of Governor Philip Gidley King, who had sailed with the First Fleet and offered wine to the Eora people he met at Botany Bay as a peace offering in 1788 before the ships reached Sydney Cove.

Frank and Gladys's glamourous socialite daughter Rada[12] became the company's director of publicity. Her daughter, Rebel Penfold-Russell, like her ancestor Mary Penfold, defied convention and became the executive producer of the multi-award-winning film *The Adventures of Priscilla, Queen of the Desert*. Jeffrey Penfold Hyland,[13] Leslie's son, was the last family member to run Penfolds. Jeffrey, Mary's two grandsons, as well as Inez and many other members of the Penfold family, are buried near Mary and Chris in the St George's churchyard.

In 1976, New South Wales brewer Tooth and Co. gained control of Penfolds, and six years later it became part of the multi-layered conglomerate that was the Adelaide Steamship Company. In 1990, South Australian Brewing bought Adelaide Steamship's wineries and renamed its wine assets as Southcorp Wines, which became a part of the Foster's Group in 2005. Penfolds is now under the umbrella of Treasury Wine Estates.

Despite the changing corporate structures, the company traditions started by Mary and Christopher Penfold persist today. Much of the land they planted with vines so long ago has been cut into suburban housing blocks, but five hectares of the Magill vineyard remain surrounding Mary's restored whitewashed cottage. Since 1983, the eighty-year-old vines there have been used to make Penfolds Magill Estate Shiraz, famous for its velvety texture and fine tannins, with hints of lavender and violet from the flowers growing around Mary's old garden.

Mary's home and legacy were neglected for many years after her death, before a concerted revival to acknowledge her

Mary's great-grandson Jeffrey Penfold Hyland OBE was the last member of the family to run her company before it was sold to Tooths Brewing in 1976.

extraordinary life and contribution to one of Australia's flourishing industries. In 2019, Penfolds released The Commander in Chief Shiraz Cabernet in tribute to their 'original leading lady'.[14]

Perhaps the greatest tribute had been made much earlier, though. In 1931, Max Schubert,[15] born to Lutheran parents in the Barossa Valley, started work as a messenger boy for Penfolds and then became the assistant to the company's chemist, learning about yeast and bacteria. Because of his enthusiasm for winemaking, Leslie Penfold Hyland invited him to come and work at Magill. Schubert enrolled to study chemistry at the Adelaide School of Mines and in 1948 became Penfolds' first chief winemaker, a position he held for twenty-seven years. For a time, Schubert worked alongside a Penfolds veteran, a long-time cellar foreman named Jim Warner, who started work at Magill in 1893, a few months after Mary left The Grange for Melbourne. Warner was still working there sixty-five years later. When Warner retired, he was saluted at a ceremony at the Penfolds Magill winery by ninety-year-old Septimus Pitman, who had first been employed by Mary at The Grange in 1888.[16]

Both men lived to see Max Schubert develop the most famous wine to carry the Penfolds brand.

On a fact-finding mission to France in 1949–50 to study fortified wines, Schubert visited the vineyards of Burgundy and had long discussions with Christian Cruz, one of France's foremost winemakers.[17] He sampled the aged wines of Château Lafite Rothschild, Château Latour and Château Margaux, and was inspired to create a Penfolds wine from the shiraz grapes at Magill. He wanted to make a wine that could age for many years like the best of the wines he had sampled in France.

After returning to Adelaide, Schubert made a new experimental Penfolds wine in 1951, and after much refinement and ageing it began to win major wine prizes.

In 1971, it won first prize for shiraz at the Wine Olympics in Paris, continuing a trend for Penfolds wines that started with a gold medal for port there in 1889. The 1990 vintage of Max Schubert's creation was named 'Wine of the Year' in 1995 by *Wine Spectator* magazine.

Over several decades, Schubert's masterpiece gained a reputation as one of the world's great wines. Appropriately, Penfolds call it 'Grange'.

For almost half a century, the waving green vines, the dark loamy soil and the sun-kissed flowers surrounding The Grange had been the heart, soul and home of Mary Penfold.

Acknowledgements

JUST LIKE THE GRAPES growing in the fertile soil of Mary Penfold's Magill Estate, this book was nurtured by great care and advice from many helping hands.

It would not have been possible without the backing of my wonderful publishers HarperCollins and ABC Books, especially Roberta Ivers, Lachlan McLaine, Brigitta Doyle, Helen Littleton, Hannah Lynch, Jim Demetriou and Nicolette Houben.

I owe a great debt of gratitude to Louisa Maggio who designed the wonderful cover for this book, so tenderly capturing Mary Penfold's devotion to her grapes and to her wine.

Many thanks to my tireless and diligent editors Julian Welch and Kevin McDonald, and to the writings of Geoffrey Bishop, Philip Norrie, Julie McIntyre and Andrew Caillard.

Ivan Pachnik and the tremendously helpful team at Mary's first vineyard at the Magill Estate gave me a great insight into her life and passion, while John Apter at the Old Government House in Parramatta was a shining light in an area where some of the first vines were grown in Australia.

I'm very much indebted to Linda Guthrie, the Local History Officer at South Australia's Campbelltown City Council, and to Hannah Shaw, the Historical Cultural Officer for the City of Burnside.

Thanks also to Des Houghton from *The Courier-Mail* newspaper for his advice, and to David Brereton and the staff of the State Library of South Australia, the Burnside Library, and to the staff of the National Library of Australia, the State Library of Queensland, the State Library of Victoria, and the State Library of New South Wales.

And, as always, special thanks to my wonderful wife Colleen for her advice and support.

Appendix

Mary Penfold's Family
Grandfather: George Peter Astor (1752–1813) German-born manufacturer of musical instruments in London
Grandmother: Elizabeth Dorothea Wright (Astor) (1757–1842)
Great Uncle: John Jacob Astor (1763–1848), America's first multi-millionaire
Father: Dr Thomas Glover Holt Jr (1788–1864), London medical practitioner, and son of an esteemed doctor
Mother: Elizabeth Astor (Holt) (1788–1845)
Brother: George William Astor Holt (1811–1890) photographer and artist who lived most of his life in New York
Brother: Alfred Astor Holt (1813–1900), tailor and amateur fisherman who lived most of his life in New York

Christopher Rawson Penfold's Background
Father: Rev John Penfold (1764–1840), vicar of Steyning, Sussex
Mother: Charlotte Jane Brooks (1770–1843) daughter of a well-to-do London landowner
Brother: John Sandys Penfold (1793–1872), solicitor
Brother: Richard Penfold (1795–1795), died a baby
Brother: Thomas Brooks Penfold (1796–1864) Known in the family as 'bad tempered old Tom'.[1] Officer with the East India Company and later a businessman in Adelaide and London
Brother: Richard Penfold II (1796–1829), surgeon

Sister: Catherine Jane Penfold (1799–1860), married Giovanni (John) Baroncelli of Florence, and lived most of her life there

Brother: Rev William Brooks Penfold (1800–1881) Chaplain to the Duke of Beaufort

Brother James Vowler Penfold (1802–1882), solicitor

Sister: Francis Esther Penfold (1803–1838), Raised by the Rawson family in Halifax. Married twice and died young. Inherited a fortune after her first husband died on their honeymoon

Brother: Robert Perkins Penfold (1805–1813) Died as a child after a fall from a swing

Sister: Charlotte Charity Penfold (1806–1888) Married William Whitling 1836

Brother: George Saxby Rawson Penfold (1808–1872) Officer with the East India Company, spent most of his life in Ontario, Canada

Sister: Mary Ann Sarah Penfold (1809–1877) Married Rev. Henry Boys in 1837

Bibliography

Books & Magazines

Arthur Allen, *A Silent Profession: Asylums, Prisons and Architects*, Friesen Press, 2020.

Kym Anderson, *Growth and Cycles in Australia's Wine Industry, A Statistical Compendium, 1843 to 2013*, The University of Adelaide, 2015.

Edwin Arnold, *The Light of Asia, or The Great Renunciation (Mahâbhinishkramana)*, A.L. Burt, 1879.

Australian Dictionary of Biography, Australian National University, 1967.

Joseph Banks, *The Endeavour Journal of Sir Joseph Banks 1768–1761*, State Library of New South Wales (SLNSW).

Geoffrey C. Bishop, *The Vineyards of Adelaide*, Lynton Publications, 1977.

F. M. Bladen (ed.), *Historical Records of New South Wales*, Vol. 1, Part 2 (1783–1792), Charles Potter, Government Printer, 1892.

J.I. Bleasdale. 'On colonial wines', *Transactions and Proceedings of the Royal Society of Victoria* 1867, Vol. VIII.

Lt. W. Bligh, *The Log of the H.M.S. Bounty 1787–1789*, Genesis Publications, 1975.

Wally Boehm, *The Phylloxera Fight: Protecting South Australia from the Phylloxera Threat*, Winetitles, 1996.

Arthur Bowes Smyth, Surgeon, *A Journal of a Voyage from Portsmouth to New South Wales and China, in the Lady Penrhyn*, National Library of Australia, MS 4568.

The British Journal, Aylott & Jones, 1853.

James Busby, *A Manual of Plain Directions for Planting and Cultivating a Vineyard and for Making Wine in New South Wales*, R. Mansfield, for the executors of R. Howe, 1830.

James Busby, *A Treatise on the Culture of the Vine and the Art of Making Wine, Compiled from the Works of Chaptal, and other French Writers, and from the Notes of the Compiler, during a Residence In Some Of The Wine Provinces Of France*, R. Howe Government Printer, 1825.

Timothy Carder, *The Encyclopaedia of Brighton*, East Sussex County Libraries, 1990.

David Collins, *An Account of the English Colony in New South Wales*, T. Cadell Jr. And W. Davies, 1798.

François de Castella, 'Early Victorian Winegrowing,' *The Victorian Historical Magazine*, no. 4, 1942.

Hubert de Castella, *Extracts from an English Book on Wine*, Still and Knight, 1877.

Hubert de Castella, *John Bull's Vineyard*, Sands & McDougall, 1886.

Susanna de Vries, *The Complete Book of Heroic Australian Women*, HarperCollins, 2010.

J. F. Denovan, *Transactions of the Society, Instituted at London, for the Encouragement of Arts, Manufactures, and Commerce*, Vol. 41, 1823.

The Empire Achievement, 1844 to 1934, State Library of South Australia, 663.200994.

K. T. H. Farrer, 'The Rev Dr J. I. Bleasdale and the Medical Society of Victoria', *Journal of the Royal Society of Medicine*, Volume 86, March 1993.

Mark Finnane, ed., *The Difficulties Of My Position: The Diaries of Prison Governor John Buckley Castieau 1855–1884*, National Library of Australia, 2004.

John Gould, *Handbook to the Birds of Australia*, Vol. 1, John Gould, 1865.

Knut Haeger, *The Illustrated History of Surgery*, Harold Starke Publishers, 2000.

John Healey, *S.A.'s Greats – The Men and Women of the North Terrace Plaques*, Historical Society of South Australia Incorporated, 2001.

Ian Hernon, *Riot!: Civil Insurrection from Peterloo to the Present Day*, Pluto Press, 2006.

Nathaniel Hodges, *Loimologia: Or an Historical Account of the Plague in London in 1665*, E. Bell, 1720.

Holograph journal of Captain James Cook on HMS *Resolution* (605 ff.), 10 February 1776–6 January 1779 (File Egerton MS 2177A).

Inez K. Hyland, *In Sunshine and in Shadow*, George Robertson and Company, 1893.

Randle Jackson, 'Considerations On The Increase Of Crime', *The Pamphleteer*, Vol. 29, 1828.

Eve Jolly, *The Penfold Cottage Magill*, State Library of South Australia, 663.20092 P397.

Journal of the Royal Australian Historical Society.

Eve Keane, *The Penfold Story*, Oswald L Ziegler, 1951.

Journals of the House of Commons, Vol. 37, 1803.

Eve Keane, *The Penfold Story*, Oswald L Ziegler, 1951.

A. C. Kelly, *The Vine in Australia*, Sands and Kenny, 1861.

Alex C. Kelly, *Wine-growing in Australia: And the Teachings of Modern Writers on Vine-culture and Wine-making*, E.S. Wigg, 1867.

Philip Gidley King, *Private journal, in two volumes, 1786–1792*, SLNSW, Safe 1/16.

H. E. Laffer, *The Wine Industry of Australia*, Australian Wine Board, 1949.

Geoffrey Lancaster, *The First Fleet Piano*, Vol. 1, ANU Press, 2015.

Lloyd's List (London).

James Macarthur, *Journal of a tour in France and Switzerland, March 1815-April 1816,* p. 12, A 2929/Item 1, Mitchell Library, SLNSW.

Sibella Macarthur Onslow (ed), *Some Early Records of the Macarthurs Of Camden*, Angus & Robertson, 1914.

George McEwin, *South Australian Vigneron and Gardeners' Manual*, James Allen, 1843.

Julie McIntyre, 'A "Civilized" Drink and a "Civilizing" Industry: Wine Growing and Cultural Imagining in Colonial New South Wales', Doctoral Thesis, University of Sydney, 2008.

Julie McIntyre, *First Vintage: Wine in Colonial New South Wales*, UNSW Press, 2012.

Stuart Macintyre, *A Concise History of Australia*, Cambridge University Press, 2020.

Axel Madsen, *John Jacob Astor: America's First Multimillionaire*, Wiley, 2002.

The Magazine of Natural History, Vol. 3, 1839.

Maro [William Macarthur] *Letters on the Culture of the Vine, Fermentation, and the Management of the Cellar*, Statham & Forster, 1844.

Lieut. Colonel Sir T. L. Mitchell, *Notes On The Cultivation Of The Vine And The Olive: Methods Of Making Wine And Oil, In The Southern Parts Of Spain*, D. L. Welch, 1849.

Jacob Nagle, *The Nagle Journal: A Diary of the Life of Jacob Nagle, Sailor, from the year 1775 to 1841*, ed. J.C. Dann, Weidenfeld and Nicolson, 1988

New South Wales Medical Gazette, July 1872.

New World Translation of the Holy Scriptures, Revised 2013, Watchtower Bible and Tract Society of Pennsylvania.

The New York Times Guide to Essential Knowledge, St. Martin's Publishing Group, 2011.

Philip Norrie, *Lindeman: Australia's Classic Wine Maker*, Apollo Books, 1993.

Dr Philip Norrie, 'Wine and Health Through the Ages with Special Reference to Australia', Doctoral Thesis, University of Western Sydney, 2005.

Louis Pasteur, *Études Sur Le Vin [Wine Studies]*, A L'imprimerie Impériale, 1866.

'The Penal Hulks of Williamstown', *Williamstown Historical Society Newsletter*, No.5, 6 October 1971.

The Piano: An Encyclopedia, Routledge, 2003.

Arthur Phillip, *The Voyage of Governor Phillip to Botany Bay*, John Stockdale, 1789.

Lenore Reynell and Margaret Hopton, *John Reynell of Reynella: A South Australian Pioneer*, Investigator Press, 1988.

George Scharf, Peter Jackson, *Drawings of Westminster*, London Topographical Society, 1994.

Arthur M. Silverstein, *A History of Immunology* (2nd ed.), Academic Press, 2009.

Some Account of the Vineyards at Camden on the Nepean River, Forty Miles South West of Sydney, the Property of James and William Macarthur, John Nichols, 1851.

Charles Sturt, *Narrative of an Expedition into Central Australia*, T and W Boone, Vol. 1, 1849.

Charles Sturt, *Two expeditions into the interior of southern Australia: during the years 1828, 1829, 1830, and 1831, vol. 2, Smith*, Elder & Co., 1833.

Southwood Smith, *A Treatise On Fever*, Longman, Rees, Orme, Brown, and Green, 1830.

George Suttor, *The Culture of the Grape-Vine and the Orange in Australia and New Zealand*, Smith, Elder, 1843.

Watkin Tench, *A Complete Account of the Settlement at Port Jackson, in New South Wales*, G. Nicol and J. Sewell, 1793.

Watkin Tench, *A Narrative of the Expedition to Botany Bay*, J. Debrett, 1789.

Transactions of the Society, Instituted at London, for the Encouragement of Arts, Manufactures, and Commerce, Vol. 41, 1823.

Keir Waddington, *Medical Education at St Bartholomew's Hospital: 1123–1995*, St Edmundsbury Press Ltd, 2003.

Mackenzie E.C. Walcott, *The Memorials of Westminster*, Francis & John Rivington, 1851.

Frederick Watson (ed.), *Historical Records of Australia, Series I: Governors' Despatches to and from England, Volume I: 1788–1796*, Library Committee of the Commonwealth Parliament, 1914.

John White, *Journal of a Voyage to New South Wales*, J. Debrett, 1790.

George B. Worgan, *Journal of a First Fleet Surgeon* (1788), Letter Journal, SLNSW, Safe 1/114.

Oswald Ziegler, *The Penfold Story*, Penfolds Wines Australia, 1975.

Internet

adelaidenow.com.au,

adelaideaz.com.

Susan Glen Amos, 'James Monroe's White House: The Genius of Politics and Place – A Dissertation Submitted to the Faculty of the School of History in Candidacy for the Degree of Doctor of Philosophy', Department of History, Liberty University, December 2022, digitalcommons.liberty.edu.

'A Short History of the House', chateauyering.com.au.

'Astor & Company', School Of Music, Australian National University College of Arts & Social Sciences, music.cass.anu.edu.au.

'Astor & Horwood Square Piano', musictreasures.vassarspaces.net.

'Astor, George Peter', earlypianos.org.

The Barrel Building', schloss-heidelberg.de.

J.G. Bartholomew, *The Pocket Atlas and Guide to London*, 1899, victorianlondon.org

'Body Snatchers And Abnormalities In Jars: A History Of Barts Pathology Museum', londonist.com.

burnsidehistory.org.au.

Andrew Caillard, 'The Australian Ark: The storied history of Australia's pre-phylloxera grapevines', worldoffinewine.com

Ellie Cawthorne, 'Extravagance, crowds and blunders: the coronation of Queen Victoria', historyextra.com, 2 May 2023.

D. U. Bloor, 'The rise of the general practitioner in the nineteenth century', British Journal of General Practice, bjgp.org

'Bartholomew Broughton, Tasmania's First Viniculturist', daverbroughton.wordpress.com.

'Child mortality rate (under five years old) in the United Kingdom from 1800 to 2020', statista.com.

theclergydatabase.org.uk.

collections.museumsvictoria.com.au.

Geoffrey Crawford, 'Wine & Medicine', guildsomm.com, 8 May 2020.

Daniel Crown, 'How A Thirst For Portuguese Wine Fuelled The American Revolution', atlasobscura.com, 13 December 2017.

Diane Cummings, 'Taglioni 1844', bound-for-south-australia. collections.slsa.sa.gov.au.

Jonathon Dadds, 'Horsnell, John – Pioneer', Campbelltown City Council, South Australia, campbelltown.sa.gov.au.

'Daguerreotype and Early Photography', David Coome History, coombe.id.au.

'Dufour Jean Jacques', glossary.wein.plus.

Ferguson Conservation Park Management Plan, Adelaide, South Australia, cdn.environment.sa.gov.au.

Kevin Gogler and Barry Philp, 'Pioneer Vignerons', Government of South Australia Department of Primary Industries and Regions, pir.sa.gov.au

'Hardy's Reynella Winery Complex', onkaparingacity.com.

Jaap Harskamp, 'The Astor Dynasty: Rag Street to Broadway, A Waldorf Tale of New York', Roosevelt Island Historical Society, rihs.us, 24 October 2021

'Historical Timeline: Wine and Grape History in the Sydney Region', hawkesbury.net.au.

'History', barossa.com.

'History', Brighton & Hove Museums, brightonmuseums.org.uk.

'History: Discovering Faith, Sharing our Story', stgeorgesmagill.org.

'The History of German Riesling', wineenthusiast.com.

'History of John Broadwood & Sons Ltd', broadwood.co.uk.

'The History of The Vineyard and Subiaco Estate – Rydalmere', historyandheritage.cityofparramatta.nsw.gov.au.

'Magill Village, An historical overview', campbelltown.sa.gov.au.

Caroline Maillard, 'Frances Penfold Walker Clarke (1803–1838) A Consequential Life', insearchofannwalker.com.

National Museum of Australia, nma.gov.au.

Rev. William Norris, M.A., *Annals of the Diocese of Adelaide, Society for Promoting Christian Knowledge*, 1852, Chapter III, anglicanhistory.org.

Old Ship Hotel, Brighton, oldshipbrighton.co.uk

Mikaël Pierre, 'France of the southern hemisphere: transferring a European wine model to colonial Australia', History,

Université Michel de Montaigne–Bordeaux III; University of Newcastle (Newcastle, Australia), 2020, theses.hal.science.
Office of National Statistics, demographia.com.
'Our Building', steyningparishchurch.org.
'Our history', benean.com.au.
Penfolds.com
'Penfolds Wines', wineaustralia.com.
'Pioneer Vignerons', adelaidia.sa.gov.au.
Catherine Price, 'The Age of Scurvy', sciencehistory.org, 14 August 2017.
State Library of Victoria, Research Guides, guides.slv.vic.gov.au
Stuart Read, 'Early vineyards and viticulture in the Sydney basin', gardenhistorysociety.org.au.
Dave Roos, 'How the East India Company Became the World's Most Powerful Monopoly', history.com, 29 June 2023.
'South Australia in Crisis', sbs.com.au.
'Square Piano: George Astor', The Metropolitan Museum of Art, New York, metmuseum.org.
'Statistics of the Colony of Victoria, 1850 and 1860', Australian Bureau of Statistics, abs.gov.au.
'Steyning Parish Church of St Andrew and St Cuthman, UK', darcawards.com.
'The Stonyfell Story', stonyfellwines.com.au.
thequeenvictoriafiles.wordpress.com.
Cheryl Timbury, 'First Fleet Surgeons', firstfleetfellowship.org.au, 26 October 2017.
'Victorian gold rush and South Australia', State Library of South Australia, digital.collections.slsa.sa.gov.au.
Gerald Walsh, 'The Wine Industry of Australia 1788–1979', Third wine symposium, August 3–4 1979, University House, Australian National University, from artserve.anu.edu.au.
'Weather In History 1800 To 1849 AD', premium.weatherweb.net.
'West Parklands', sahistoryhub.history.sa.gov.au.
'Wine Competition History', Royal Agricultural Society of NSW, rasnsw.com.au.

World Health Organization, who.int.
youngqueenvictoria.co.uk.

Newspapers
The Adelaide Chronicle and South Australian Literary Record.
The Adelaide Observer.
The Adelaide Times.
The Advertiser (Adelaide).
The Age (Melbourne).
The Ararat and Mount Pleasant Creek Advertiser and Chronicle for the District of the Wimmera (Victoria).
The Argus (Melbourne).
Aris's Birmingham Gazette.
The Australasian (Melbourne).
The Australian Advertiser (Albany, W.A.).
The Ballarat Star.
The Bathurst Free Press.
The Bendigo Advertiser.
The Brisbane Courier.
The Brooklyn Eagle (Brooklyn, New York, U.S.A.).
The Burnside News-Review (Adelaide).
Colonial Times and Tasmanian Advertiser (Hobart).
The Courier (Hobart)
The Daily Advertiser; Political, Historical, and Commercial (New York).
The Derby Mercury (Derbyshire, U.K.).
The Empire (Sydney).
English Chronicle and Whitehall Evening Post (London).
The Evening Chronicle (London, U.K.).
The Evening Journal (Adelaide).
The Examiner (London, U.K.).
The Express and Telegraph (Adelaide).
The Geelong Advertiser.
The Glasgow Herald.
The Hampshire Chronicle (Winchester, Hampshire, U.K.).
The Herald (Melbourne).
Hobart Town Gazette and Van Diemen's Land Advertiser.

Illustrated Sydney News.
The Kyneton Guardian (Victoria).
The Kyneton Observer (Victoria).
The London Chronicle.
The London Gazette.
The Maitland Mercury and Hunter River General Advertiser.
Melbourne Punch.
The Morning Chronicle (London, U.K.).
The Morning Herald (London).
Mount Alexander Mail (Victoria).
The New York Packet and the American Advertiser.
The Northampton Mercury (Northamptonshire, U.K.).
The Observer (London, U.K.).
The Perth Gazette and Independent Journal of Politics and News.
The Perth Gazette and Western Australian Journal.
The Port Phillip Gazette and Settler's Journal (Melbourne).
The Portland Guardian and Normanby General Advertiser (Victoria).
Quiz and the Lantern (Adelaide).
The Register (Adelaide).
The South Australian (Adelaide).
The South Australian Advertiser (Adelaide).
The South Australian Chronicle and Weekly Mail (Adelaide).
The South Australian Colonist and Settlers' Weekly Record of British, Foreign and Colonial Intelligence (London, U.K.).
The South Australian Gazette and Colonial Register (Adelaide).
The South Australian Police Gazette (Adelaide).
The South Australian Register (Adelaide).
The South Australian Weekly Chronicle (Adelaide).
The Southern Australian (Adelaide).
The Sun (London*)*.
The Sussex Advertiser (Brighton, U.K.).
The Sydney Gazette and New South Wales Advertiser.
The Sydney Herald.
The Sydney Monitor.
The Sydney Morning Herald.

The Tarrangower Times and Maldon, Newstead, Baringhup, Laancoorie and Muckleford Advertiser (Victoria).
The Telegraph (London, U.K.).
The Times (London, U.K.).
The Victorian Farmers Journal and Gardeners Chronicle (Melbourne).
The Western Mail (Perth, W.A.).
The Worcestershire Chronicle (Worcester, U.K.).
The Yorkshire Gazette, (York, U.K.).

Endnotes

Abbreviations
HRA – Historical Records of Australia
HRNSW – Historical Records of New South Wales
NLA – National Library of Australia
SLNSW – State Library of New South Wales
SLSA – State Library of South Australia

Prologue
1. Mary Penfold (nee Holt), b. 6 November 1816 (Southwark, London), d. 31 December 1895 (Brighton, Melbourne).
2. 'The Commander In Chief: Mary Penfold', penfolds.com
3. *Ibid.*
4. 'Mrs. Penfold's Wine Manufactory Magill', *The South Australian Register* (Adelaide), 4 June 1874, p. 3.
5. Ellen Timbrell, b. 11 November 1816 (Hampstead, London, U.K.), d. 3 September 1857 (Magill, South Australia).
6. Dr Christopher Rawson Penfold, b. 2 August 1811 (Steyning, Sussex, England.), d. 26 March 1870 (Magill, South Australia).
7. Mary Georgina Anne Hyland (nee Penfold), b. 13 August 1843 (Brighton, Sussex, England), d. 27 August 1911 (Moorabbin House, Were St, Brighton, Melbourne).
8. 'Mrs. Penfold's Wine Manufactory Magill', *The South Australian Register* (Adelaide), 4 June 1874, p. 3.
9. 'The All-England Cricket Match, Adelaide', *The South Australian Advertiser* (Adelaide), 28 March 1874, p. 5.
10. 'Local Intelligence', *The Adelaide Observer*, 3 August 1844, p. 5.
11. 'Our Grenache Story', penfolds.com
12. 'The Commander In Chief: Mary Penfold', penfolds.com

13 'Mrs. Penfold's Wine Manufactory Magill', *The South Australian Register* (Adelaide), 4 June 1874, p. 3.
14 Louis Pasteur, *Études Sur Le Vin [Wine Studies]*, A L'imprimerie Impériale, 1866.
15 'Mrs. Penfold's Wine Manufactory Magill', *The South Australian Register* (Adelaide), 4 June 1874, p. 3.
16 *Ibid.*
17 'Penfolds History', penfolds.com

Chapter 1

1 Georg Peter Astor, b. 1752, (Walldorf, Electoral Palatinate, Holy Roman Empire, now in the Rhein-Neckar-Kreis region, Baden-Wuerttemberg, Germany), d. 9 November 1813 (Tottenham St, Cornhill, London).
2 'Astor & Company', School Of Music, Australian National University College of Arts & Social Sciences, music.cass.anu.edu.au.
3 His father was Johann Jacob Astor, b. 7 July 1724, d. 18 April 1816.
4 Office of National Statistics, demographia.com.
5 From 1756–1763.
6 'The History of German Riesling', wineenthusiast.com.
7 'The Barrel Building', schloss-heidelberg.de.
8 'History of John Broadwood & Sons Ltd', broadwood.co.uk.
9 *Ibid.*
10 Gerard de Visme to Banks, 4 November 1767, Banks Correspondence, Library of the Royal Botanic Gardens at Kew, 1:13.
11 Catherine Price, 'The Age of Scurvy', sciencehistory.org, 14 August 2017.
12 Oswald Ziegler, *The Penfold Story*, Penfolds Wines Australia, 1975, p. 19.
13 Geoffrey Crawford, 'Wine & Medicine', guildsomm.com, 8 May 2020.
14 Randle Jackson, 'Considerations On The Increase Of Crime', *The Pamphleteer*, Vol. 29, 1828, p. 326.
15 *The New York Times Guide to Essential Knowledge*, St. Martin's Publishing Group, 2011, p. 1027.
16 1 Timothy 5:23, Judges 9:13, *New World Translation of the Holy Scriptures*, Revised 2013, Watchtower Bible and Tract Society of Pennsylvania.
17 1 Timothy 5:23, *ibid.*
18 William Shakespeare, *Othello*, Act II, Scene III.
19 Julie McIntyre, *First Vintage: Wine in Colonial New South Wales*, UNSW Press, 2012, p. 12.
20 Joseph Banks, *The Endeavour Journal of Sir Joseph Banks 1768–1761*, State Library of New South Wales (SLNSW), Series 03: Volumes 1 & 2, 13 September 1768.

21 Daniel Crown, 'How A Thirst For Portuguese Wine Fuelled The American Revolution', atlasobscura.com, 13 December 2017.
22 *Journals of the House of Commons*, Vol. 37, 1803, pp. 311.
23 On 9 November 1779; London, England, Church of England Marriages and Banns, 1754–1938.
24 Elizabeth Dorothea Wright, b. 3 July 1757 (London, U.K.), d. 28 January 1842 (London, U.K.).
25 John Jacob Astor (originally Johann Jakob Astor), b. July 17, 1763 (Walldorf, Electoral Palatinate, Holy Roman Empire, now in the Rhein-Neckar-Kreis region, Baden-Wuerttemberg, Germany) d. 29 March 1848 (New York City, U.S.A.).
26 'Astor, George Peter', earlypianos.org.
27 'Astor & Horwood Square Piano', musictreasures.vassarspaces.net.
28 On 2 August 1776, at the Pennsylvania State House, later renamed Independence Hall, in Philadelphia.
29 George Washington Papers, Series 5, Financial Papers: George Washington's Revolutionary War Expense Account, 1775–1783, MSS 44693: Reel 116, Library of Congress.
30 Arthur Allen, *A Silent Profession: Asylums, Prisons and Architects*, Friesen Press, 2020, p. 94.
31 From Benjamin Franklin to the Abbé Morellet, [after 5 July 1779], *The Papers of Benjamin Franklin*, vol. 30, July 1 through October 31, 1779, ed. Barbara B. Oberg, New Haven and London: Yale University Press, 1993, pp. 50–53. Reprinted from M. Lémontey, ed., *Mémoires de l'abbé Morellet* (2 vols., Paris, 1821), Vol 1, 294–7; copy: American Philosophical Society.
32 'Astor & Horwood Square Piano', musictreasures.vassarspaces.net. George made pianos at the time but also sold instruments labelled with his name which were made by John Geib and possibly Thomas Culliford.
33 John Astor to Washington Irving, 25 November 1836, John Jacob Astor Papers, Historical Society of Pennsylvania, Philadelphia.
34 Jaap Harskamp, 'The Astor Dynasty: Rag Street to Broadway, A Waldorf Tale of New York', Roosevelt Island Historical Society, rihs.us, 24 October 2021.
35 *New York Packet and the American Advertiser*, 23 September 1784.
36 *Daily Advertiser; Political, Historical, and Commercial (New York)*, 19 November 1785.
37 Axel Madsen, *John Jacob Astor: America's First Multimillionaire*, Wiley, 2002.

Chapter 2
1. James Maria [Mario] Matra, 'A proposal for establishing a settlement in NSW', in F. M. Bladen (ed.), *Historical Records of New South Wales*, Vol. 1, Part 2 (1783–1792), Charles Potter, Government Printer, 1892, pp. 1–6.
2. Thomas Townshend, 1st Viscount Sydney (24 February 1733 – 30 June 1800).
3. Sir Evan Nepean (9 July 1752 – 2 October 1822).
4. Lord Sydney to The Lords Commissioners of the Treasury, Whitehall, 18 August, 1786, HRNSW, Vol. 1, Part 2, p. 14.
5. Instead, Matra was appointed the Consul at Tangiers in Morocco.
6. Arthur Phillip, b. 11 October 1738 (Bread Street, London), d. 31 August 1814 (19 Bennett Street, Bath, England).
7. Arthur Phillip, *The Voyage of Governor Phillip to Botany Bay*, John Stockdale, 1789, p. 80.
8. John White, b. c.1756, d. 20 February 1832 (Worthing, Sussex, England).
9. Cheryl Timbury, 'First Fleet Surgeons', firstfleetfellowship.org.au, 26 October 2017.
10. John White, Journal of a Voyage to New South Wales, J. Debrett, 1790, p. 8.
11. William Balmain, b. 2 February 1762 (Balhepburn, Rhynd, Perthshire, Scotland), d. 17 November 1803 (London).
12. Balmain to Shortland, Shortland to Navy Board, 17 February 1787, T 1/643, no. 409; Navy Board, Minutes, 19 and 22 February 1787, ADM [Admiralty] 106/2623, Public Record Office (PRO), The National Archives (Kew, London).
13. Petition, 7 May 1787, Colonial Office 201/2, fos 327, 340, 342, 344, (PRO), The National Archives (Kew, London).
14. Navy Board, Minute, 4 April 1787, ADM 106/2623.
15. Nepean to Steele, 14 November 1786, T 1/639, no. 2643; Steele to Nepean, 18 December 1786, HO 35/7; Nepean to Phillip, 21 December 1786, HO 43/2, pp. 186–7.
16. Sir Toby Belch in *Twelfth Night* and Doll Tearsheet in *Henry IV, Part II*.
17. Banks, 'Scheme of plants for Botany Bay', and List, Ic. 28 November 1786], Sutro Library, California State Library, Banks SS 1/48, 49.
18. *The Northampton Mercury* (Northamptonshire, U.K.), 19 May 1787, p. 1.
19. The piano was most likely built by Frederick Beck and donated to the Edith Cowan University in Perth in 2016.
20. Geoffrey Lancaster, *The First Fleet Piano*, Vol. 1, ANU Press, 2015, p. 29, press.anu.edu.au.
21. Watkin Tench, *A Narrative of the Expedition to Botany Bay*, J. Debrett, 1789, p. 15.

22 Phillip, *The Voyage of Governor Phillip to Botany Bay*, p. 18
23 Arthur Bowes Smyth, Surgeon, *A Journal of a Voyage from Portsmouth to New South Wales and China, in the Lady Penrhyn*, National Library of Australia, MS 4568, 7, 20 August 1787.
24 Arthur Phillip to Joseph Banks, 22 August 1790, Banks Papers, Series 37:13, SLNSW.
25 David Collins, *An Account of the English Colony in New South Wales*, T. Cadell Jr. And W. Davies, 1798, p. xxviii.
26 Arthur Phillip to Evan Nepean, 2 September 1787, HRNSW, Vol. 1, p 112.
27 Arthur Bowes Smyth, b. 23 August, 1750 (Tolleshunt D'Arcy, Essex, England), d. 31 March, 1790 (England).
28 Arthur Bowes Smyth, Surgeon, *A Journal of a Voyage from Portsmouth to New South Wales and China, in the Lady Penrhyn*, National Library of Australia, MS 4568, 17 August 1787.
29 Jacob Nagle, *The Nagle Journal: A Diary of the Life of Jacob Nagle, Sailor, from the year 1775 to 1841*, ed. J.C. Dann, Weidenfeld and Nicolson, 1988, p. 106.
30 Phillip, *The Voyage of Governor Phillip to Botany Bay*, p. 39.
31 David Collins, b. 3 March 1756 (London), d. 24 March 1810 (Hobart, Van Diemen's Land).
32 George Suttor to Joseph Banks, 18 December 1800, Banks Letters, Series 19.41, SLNSW.
33 Collins, *An Account of the English Colony in New South Wales*, p. xxxii.
34 *Ibid.*, p. xxviii.
35 *Ibid.*, p. xxvii.
36 John White, *Journal of a Voyage to New South Wales*, p. 104–5.
37 Arthur Bowes Smyth, Surgeon, *A Journal of a Voyage from Portsmouth to New South Wales and China, in the Lady Penrhyn*, National Library of Australia, MS 4568, 7 January 1788.
38 *Ibid.*, 9 January 1788.
39 Governor Phillip's Instructions, from Frederick Watson (ed.), *Historical Records of Australia, Series I: Governors' Despatches to and from England, Volume I: 1788–1796*, Library Committee of the Commonwealth Parliament, 1914, p. 23.
40 Philip Gidley King, *Private journal, in two volumes, 1786–1792*. Vol. 1 titled: 'Remarks & Journal kept on the Expedition to form a Colony in His Majestys Territory of New South Wales in His Majesty's Ship Sirius ...', 24 October 1786–12 January 1789, SLNSW, Safe 1 / 16 vol. 1, p. 79.
41 Philip Gidley King, *Private journal, in two volumes*, pp. 80–81.
42 White, *Journal of a Voyage to New South Wales*, p. 120.
43 Phillip, *The Voyage of Governor Phillip to Botany Bay*, p. 58.

44 Collins, *An Account of the English Colony in New South Wales*, p. 7.
45 Elizabeth Holt, nee Astor, b. 1788 (London), d. 20 October 1845 (Church St, Edmonton, Middlesex, U.K.).

Chapter 3

1 Julie McIntyre, 'A "Civilized" Drink and a "Civilizing" Industry: Wine Growing and Cultural Imagining in Colonial New South Wales', Doctoral Thesis, University of Sydney, 2008, p. 21.
2 Phillip, *The Voyage of Governor Phillip*, p. 129.
3 *Ibid.*
4 William Bradley, b. 14 November 1758 (Portsmouth, Hampshire, England), d. 13 March 1833 (France).
5 George B. Worgan, *Journal of a First Fleet Surgeon* (1788), Letter Journal, SLNSW, Safe 1/114, 14 May 1788.
6 *Ibid.*, 16 May 1788.
7 Lt. W. Bligh, *The Log of the H.M.S. Bounty 1787–1789*, Genesis Publications, 1975, August 30, 1788.
8 Watkin Tench, *A Complete Account of the Settlement at Port Jackson, in New South Wales*, G. Nicol and J. Sewell, 1793, p. 11.
9 *Ibid.*, p. 14.
10 *Ibid.*, p. 35.
11 *Ibid.*, pp. 57–8.
12 William Balmain (1762–1803).
13 Arthur Phillip to Joseph Banks, 24 March 1791, SLNSW, SAFE/Banks Papers/Series 37.14.
14 Ralph Clark, Letterbook, 3 April 1787 – 30 September 1791, SLNSW, C 221.
15 Major Robert Ross (c.1740 – 9 June 1794).
16 Remarks and Observations on Norfolk Island by Major Ross, c. December 1790, HRNSW, Vol. 1, Part 2 (1783–1792), p. 419.
17 Arthur Phillip to Joseph Banks, 22 August 1790, SLNSW, Series 37.13,
18 Tench, *A Complete Account*, p. 75.
19 Rev. Richard Johnson to Henry Fricker, 21 August. 1790, Letters from Rev. Richard Johnson to Henry Fricker, 30 May 1787010 Aug. 1797, SLNSW, Safe 1/121.
20 Dr Philip Norrie, 'Wine and Health Through the Ages with Special Reference to Australia', Doctoral Thesis, University of Western Sydney, 2005, p. 153.
21 Arthur Phillip to Joseph Banks, 22 August 1790, Banks papers, SLNSW, Series 37.13,
22 On 4 June 1791. The Darug word sounded like 'Baramada' or 'Burramatta'.

23 The Right Hon. W.W. Grenville to Governor Phillip, 24 August 1789, from F. M. Bladen (ed.), *Historical Records of New South Wales, Vol. 1, Part 2 (1783–1792)*, Charles Potter, Government Printer, 1892, pp. 260–1.
24 *Ibid.*
25 Thomas Tegg, 'Melancholy Disaster of His Majesty's Ship the Guardian', 1808, SLNSW, MLMSS 5711/6 (Safe 1/233b).
26 'The History of The Vineyard and Subiaco Estate – Rydalmere', historyandheritage.cityofparramatta.nsw.gov.au
27 The building was destroyed in 1961 when the company Rheem redeveloped The Vineyard as an industrial site.
28 Tench, *A Complete Account*, p. 165.
29 *Ibid.*, pp. 153–4.
30 *Ibid.*
31 Andrew Caillard, 'The Australian Ark: The storied history of Australia's pre-phylloxera grapevines', worldoffinewine.com.
32 *Ibid.*
33 Collins, *An Account of the English Colony of NSW*, p. 189.
34 Watkin Tench, *A Complete Account*, pp. 142–3.
35 Arthur Phillip to Joseph Banks, 17 November 1791, Banks Papers, SLNSW, Series 37:18, .
36 *Ibid.*, 3 December 1791, Series 37:20.
37 On 24 January 1791, Tench, *A Complete Account*, p. 106.
38 Elizabeth Macarthur, b. 14 August 1766 (Devon, U.K.), d. 9 February 1850 (Clovelly, Sydney).
39 John Macarthur, b. 1767 (Stoke, Plymouth, U.K.), d. 11 April 1834 (Camden, New South Wales).
40 Letter to Bridget Kingdon, from Elizabeth Macarthur, Sydney, 7 March 1791, page 9; Macarthur family papers, 1789–1936 [First Collection] SAFE/A 2897-A 2908, Series 02:Vol. 10, SLNSW.
41 Elizabeth Macarthur to her mother, 18 March 1791, *ibid.*
42 *Ibid.*
43 Geoffrey Lancaster, The First Fleet Piano, Vol. 1, ANU Press, 2015, Appendix E, press.anu.edu.au.
44 *The Times* (London, U.K.), 30 October 1787, p. 3.
45 'Square Piano: George Astor', The Metropolitan Museum of Art, New York, metmuseum.org.
46 Marc Nobel, 'Notes on the Restoration of the Astor Barrel Organ', (A paper delivered as part of the Organ Historical Trust of Australia 25th Annual Conference, on 20 September 2002 at the Queen Victoria Museum & Art Gallery, Launceston, and published in OHTA News January 2003), ohta.org.au.

47 Mary Louise Boehm, Darcy Kuronen 'Astor & Company', in Robert Palmieri, *The Piano: An Encyclopedia*, Routledge, 2003, pp. 26–27.
48 Timo Jouko Herrmann, *Eine Studie zur Geschichte des kommunalen Konzertlebens in Walldorf*, Stadt Walldorf, 2022, p. 12.

Chapter 4

1 *The Morning Chronicle* (London, U.K.), 8 July 1795.
2 *The Telegraph* (London, U.K.), 25 October 1796.
3 In an advertisement in *The Observer* on 25 June 1797, George was selling a collection of 'Twenty-two Songs and Glees, upon different subjects, written by Mr. [William] Wennington, and adapted to music by various modern Composers'.
4 *The Telegraph* (London), 20 December 1796.
5 Elizabeth Macarthur to Relatives and Friends in England, 21 December 1793, HRNSW Vol. 2 (1793–1795), 1893, p. 508.
6 John Macarthur to his brother James, quoted by Elizabeth in a letter to her mother, 23 August 1794, *Macarthur Family Papers*, A2908, SLNSW.
7 Collins, *An Account of the English Colony*, p. 240–1.
8 *Ibid.*
9 J.F. Blumenbach to Banks, 28 December 1794, National Library of Australia, Mfm M 1192-Papers of Sir Joseph Banks, 1st Baronet (as filmed by the AJCP) [microform] : [M1192], 1768–1820./Fonds MS Add 8094-8100/ Series MS 8098/File ff.221–22/J.F.
10 William Paterson, b. 1755 (Scotland), d. 21 June 1810 (at sea, off Cape Town).
11 William Paterson to Joseph Banks, 17 March 1795, SLNSW, Banks Papers, Series 27.09.
12 Thomas Fyshe Palmer, letter to un-named recipient, 16 September 1795, Mfm M 391-Letters of Reverend Thomas Fyshe Palmer (as filmed by the AJCP) [microform] : [M391], NLA.
13 *Ibid.*
14 Governor John Hunter to the Duke of Portland, 19 August 1797, HRNSW, Vol. 1, Part 3 (1796–1799), p. 297.
15 David Collins, *An Account of the English Colony* in New South Wales, Vol. 2, T. Cadell and W. Davies, 1802, gutenberg.net.au.
16 Acting-Governor King to The Duke of Portland, 10 March 1801, HRA Series 1, vol. 3 (1801–1802), p. 6.
17 George Suttor, b. 11 June 1774 (Chelsea, London, U.K.) d. 5 May 1858 (Bathurst, NSW).
18 *Ibid.*, 4 August 1801, Series 19.43.

19 George Suttor to Joseph Banks, 18 December 1800, Banks Papers, SLNSW, Series 19.41.
20 George Suttor, *The Culture of the Grape-Vine and the Orange in Australia and New Zealand*, Smith, Elder, 1843, p. 18.
21 On 20 November 1800.
22 Also known as Landrien.
23 The Duke of Portland to The Governor of New South Wales, 22 April, 1800, HRNSW Vol. 4 (1800, 1801, 1802), p. 76.
24 Ibid., HRA Series 1, Vol. 2. (1797–1800), p. 497.
25 William Henry Cavendish Cavendish-Bentinck, 3rd Duke of Portland (14 April 1738 – 30 October 1809).
26 The Duke of Portland to The Admiralty, 24 April 1800, HRNSW Vol. 4 (1800, 1801, 1802), p. 78.
27 *Ibid.*
28 The Duke of Portland to The Governor of New South Wales, 22 April, 1800, HRNSW Vol. 4 (1800, 1801, 1802), p. 76.
29 Acting-Governor King to The Duke of Portland, 10 March 1801, HRA Series 1, vol. 3 (1801–1802), p. 6.
30 Governor King to Lord Hobart, 30 October 1802, HRNSW, Vol. 4 (1800, 1801, 1802), p. 870.
31 Acting-Governor King to The Duke of Portland, 10 March 1801, HRA Series 1, vol. 3 (1801–1802), p. 6.
32 'Method Of Preparing A Piece Of Land For The Purpose Of Forming A Vineyard', *The Sydney Gazette and New South Wales Advertiser*, 5 March 1803, p. 4.
33 Governor King to Lord Hobart, 30 October 1802, HRNSW, Vol. 4 (1800, 1801, 1802), p. 870.
34 'Method Of Preparing A Piece Of Land For The Purpose Of Forming A Vineyard', *The Sydney Gazette and New South Wales Advertiser*, 5 March 1803, p. 4.
35 Governor King to Lord Hobart, 3 November 1804, HRA Series 1, Vol. 4 (1803-June 1804), p. 460.
36 L'Andre survived an agonising centipede bite in 1809 and died two years later aged 40.
37 Gerald Walsh, 'The Wine Industry of Australia 1788–1979', Third wine symposium, August 3–4 1979, University House, Australian National University, from artserve.anu.edu.au.
38 Susan Glen Amos, 'James Monroe's White House: The Genius of Politics and Place – A Dissertation Submitted to the Faculty of the School of History in

Candidacy for the Degree of Doctor of Philosophy', Department of History, Liberty University, December 2022, digitalcommons.liberty.edu.
39 In 1817. James Monroe Museum and Memorial Library, Fredericksburg, Virginia, jamesmonroemuseum.umw.edu.
40 Thomas Glover Holt Jr, b. 1788 (London, U.K.), d. 6 Dec 1864 (Hardwick Lane, Chertsey, Surrey, U.K.).
41 On 12 February 1809.
42 *Aris's Birmingham Gazette*, 2 June 1817, p. 4.
43 Thomas Glover Holt Sr, b. 1763 (Tottenham, London, U.K.), d. 25 February 1837 (Spring Terrace, Wandsworth, London, U.K.)
44 'List of Churchwardens', Mackenzie E.C. Walcott, *The Memorials of Westminster*, Francis & John Rivington, 1851, p. 317.
45 George William Astor Holt, b. 8 September 1811 (London, U.K.), d. 5 August 1890 (New York City, U.S.A).
46 Alfred Astor Holt, b. 2 June 1813 (Southwark, London, U.K.), d. 4 February 1900 (330A Kosciusko Street, New York City, U.S.A.
47 'Astor & Horwood Square Piano', musictreasures.vassarspaces.net.

Chapter 5

1 Birth certificate, Mary Holt, England & Wales, Non-Conformist and Non-Parochial Registers, 1567–1936 for Thos [Glover] Holt, No. 2062, Dr Williams' Library Registry, Birth Certificates, 1817–1820.
2 'Weather In History 1800 To 1849 AD', premium.weatherweb.net.
3 'Child mortality rate (under five years old) in the United Kingdom from 1800 to 2020', statista.com.
4 *The Morning Chronicle*, (London), 6 November 1816, p. 1.
5 'British Parliament', *The London Chronicle* (London), 6 November 1816, p. 1.
6 Ian Hernon, *Riot!: Civil Insurrection from Peterloo to the Present Day*, Pluto Press, 2006, p. 22.
7 'Sales by Auction', *The Morning Chronicle*, (London), 6 November 1816, p. 4.
8 Gregory Blaxland to Governor Macquarie, October 1818, reprinted in J. F. Denovan, *Transactions of the Society, Instituted at London, for the Encouragement of Arts, Manufactures, and Commerce*, Vol. 41, 1823, p. 287.
9 Gregory Blaxland, b. 17 June 1778 (Fordwich, Kent, U.K.,), d. 1 January 1853 (Sydney, N.S.W).
10 Dr Philip Norrie, 'Wine and Health Through the Ages with Special Reference to Australia', Doctoral Thesis, University of Western Sydney, 2005, p. 168.
11 Born Jean-Jacques Dufour (1763–1827).
12 'Dufour Jean Jacques', glossary.wein.plus.

13 Gregory Blaxland to John Thomas Bigge, 28 November 1819, SLNSW, Bigge Appendix, Bonwick Transcripts, Box 15, p. 1473.
14 Petra Koci, 'The first commercial winery in the United States – established by a Swiss immigrant!', blog.nationalmuseum.ch.
15 Dr Philip Norrie, 'Wine and Health Through the Ages with Special Reference to Australia', Doctoral Thesis, University of Western Sydney, 2005, p. 169.
16 John Blaxland, b. 4 January 1769, (Fordwich, Kent, U.K.,), d. 5 August 1845 (Newington House, Silverwater, Sydney).
17 *The Sydney Gazette and New South Wales Advertiser*, 4 March 1815, p. 2.
18 Gerald Walsh, 'The Wine Industry of Australia 1788–1979', Third wine symposium, August 3–4 1979, University House, Australian National University, from artserve.anu.edu.au.
19 Gregory Blaxland to Governor Macquarie, October 1818, reprinted in J. F. Denovan, *Transactions of the Society, Instituted at London, for the Encouragement of Arts, Manufactures, and Commerce, Vol. 41*, 1823, p. 287.
20 Stuart Read, 'Early vineyards and viticulture in the Sydney basin', Paper presented at AGHS seminar – Adelaide, 15 October 2015, gardenhistorysociety.org.au.
21 Gregory Blaxland to Earl Bathurst, August 1816, SLNSW, Bigge Appendix, Bonwick Transcripts, Box 15, p. 1473.
22 Stuart Read, 'Early vineyards and viticulture in the Sydney basin', Paper presented at AGHS seminar – Adelaide, 15 October 2015, gardenhistorysociety.org.au.
23 Macquarie, Journals, 5 August 1793, Vol. Z A768-2, Item 2, SLNSW.
24 *Ibid.*, 7 March 1803, Vol. Z A770, Item 1, *ibid.*
25 Also called the *Surry*.
26 Governor Macquarie to the Commissioners of the Transport Board, 1 October 1814, HRA, Series 1, vol. 8 (July 1813–December 1815), p. 274.
27 *Ibid.*, pp. 286–7.
28 Redfern Cottage is now a childcare centre at 20 Lind St, Minto, New South Wales.
29 Dr Philip Norrie, 'Wine and Health Through the Ages with Special Reference to Australia', Doctoral Thesis, University of Western Sydney, 2005, p. 114
30 Elizabeth Holt to Mary Penfold, 4 June 1844, Personal papers of Christopher Rawson Penfold and Mary Penfold and family, State Library of South Australia, BRG 330/1, Reel 3.
31 'Holt is an old hermit', *The Brooklyn Eagle*, 20 January 1895, p. 19
32 *Ibid.*

33 Ibid.
34 J.G. Bartholomew, The Pocket Atlas and Guide to London, 1899, victorianlondon.org.
35 Acting-Governor King to Under Secretary John King, 8 November 1801, HRA, Series 1, Vol. III, p. 322.
36 John Macarthur to his wife Elizabeth, 29 April 1815, Macarthur family papers 1789–1930 [First collection], Volume 02: Letters written by John Macarthur to his wife, 1808–1832, A 2898 (Safe 1/394) p. 265, SLNSW.
37 James Macarthur, Journal of a tour in France and Switzerland, March 1815-April 1816, p. 12, A 2929/Item 1, Mitchell Library, SLNSW.
38 'Dufour Jean Jacques', glossary.wein.plus.
39 Sibella Macarthur Onslow (ed), Some Early Records of the Macarthurs Of Camden, Angus & Robertson, 1914.
40 John Macarthur to his wife Elizabeth, 29 April 1815, Macarthur family papers 1789–1930 [First collection], Volume 02: Letters written by John Macarthur to his wife, 1808–1832, A 2898 (Safe 1/394) p. 265, SLNSW.
41 James Macarthur, journal of a tour in France and Switzerland, March 1815-April 1816, SLNSW, A2929, Item 1, pp. 94–5.
42 Sibella Macarthur Onslow (ed), *Some Early Records Of The Macarthurs Of Camden*, p. 253.
43 Ibid.
44 James Macarthur, Unpublished journal 12 March 1815 to 28 April 1816, Macarthur Family Papers, SLNSW A2929.
45 Macarthur to Elizabeth, 24 March 1817, Macarthur family papers 1789–1930, A 2898 (Safe 1/394) p. 352, SLNSW.
46 Andrew Caillard, 'The Australian Ark: The storied history of Australia's pre-phylloxera grapevines', worldoffinewine.com.
47 Ibid.
48 James Busby, *A Manual of Plain Directions for Planting and Cultivating a Vineyard and for Making Wine in New South Wales*, R. Mansfield, for the executors of R. Howe, 1830, p. 39.
49 Charles Gordon, *may* have planted vines at Rangihoua and Waitangi in 1817.
50 Papers (Ethel Gaunt Collection) of Reverend Samuel Marsden (as filmed by the AJCP) [microform] : [M1619] 1819–1966./File 1/, 24 September 1819, p. 64, NLA.
51 Ibid.
52 Ambrose Serle (1742–1812).
53 Ambrose Serle to Samuel Marsden, 15 April 1805, Marsden Papers, vol. 1, MLMSS, A 1992, p. 27.
54 Ibid.

Chapter 6

1. Gregory Blaxland to John Thomas Bigge, 28 November 1819, SLNSW, Bigge Appendix, Bonwick Transcripts, Box 15, p. 1473.
2. J. F. Denovan, *Transactions of the Society, Instituted at London, for the Encouragement of Arts, Manufactures, and Commerce*, Vol. 41, 1823, p. 285.
3. *Ibid.*, pp. 285–6.
4. 'Wine from New South Wales', *Transactions of the Society*, Vol. 46, pp. 133–135.
5. *Ibid.*
6. James Busby, b 7 February 1801 (Edinburgh, U.K.), d. 15 July, 1871 (London, U.K.).
7. James Busby, *A Treatise on the Culture of the Vine and the Art of Making Wine, Compiled from the Works of Chaptal, and other French Writers, and from the Notes of the Compiler, during a Residence In Some Of The Wine Provinces Of France*, R. Howe Government Printer, 1825.
8. James Busby, *A Manual of Plain Directions for Planting and Cultivating Vineyards and for Making Wine in New South Wales*, Executors of R. Howe, 1830.
9. Gerald Walsh, 'The Wine Industry of Australia 1788–1979', Third wine symposium, August 3–4 1979, University House, Australian National University, from artserve.anu.edu.au.
10. By then the vineyard was under the management of Richard Sadlier.
11. 'To Alexander Berry, Esq', *The Sydney Morning Herald*, 4 August 1870, p. 6.
12. 'Growers And Grapes', *The Herald* (Melbourne), 1 October 1932, p. 6.
13. Australian Agricultural Company, Court of Directors, Minutes, 160189, vol. A, 26 November 1824, p. 58. N.G. Butlin Archives, Australian National University.
14. Robert Townson (c.1762–1827).
15. V. W. E. Goodin, 'Townson, Robert (1762–1827)', *Australian Dictionary of Biography*, Australian National University, 1967.
16. Bartholomew Broughton, b. 1792 (London, U.K.) d. 21 July 1828 (Prospect Farm, New Town, Van Diemen's Land).
17. 'Bartholomew Broughton, Tasmania's First Viniculturist', daverbroughton. wordpress.com.
18. 'Magistrate Court Hearings', The Times, (London), 13 March 1819.
19. NSW Settlers and Convict Lists, National Archives, (Canberra: 1787–1834). HO 10/18.
20. Don Martin, 'Early Tasmanian Horticulture,' (Address to a meeting of the Royal Society of Tasmania, Hobart, 7 December 1976), p. 3.
21. *Hobart Town Gazette and Van Diemen's Land Advertiser*, 23 March, 1822. A similar advertisement appeared in the *Gazette* on 29 December 1821.

22 Convicts Conduct Book, Tasmanian Archive Office, (Hobart: 1824). CON31-1-1 00155.
23 *Hobart Town Gazette and Van Diemen's Land Advertiser*, 13 December 1823, p. 1.
24 *Ibid*. 23 January, 1824, p. 2.
25 *Ibid*. 2 July, 1824, p. 7.
26 Lieut.-Governor Arthur to Earl Bathurst, 27 October, 1824. *Historical Records of Australia*, Series III, Vol. 4, p. 206.
27 *Hobart Town Gazette and Van Diemen's Land Advertiser*, 21 October, 1826, p.4.
28 B. Broughton to Earl Bathurst, 20 March 1827, HRA, Series 3, Vol. 5, p. 614.
29 *Colonial Times and Tasmanian Advertiser*, (Hobart). 16 February, 1827, p.4.
30 *Ibid*,. 9 February, 1827, p.3
31 *Colonial Times and Tasmanian Advertiser*, 23 February, 1827, p 2.
32 'Ship News', *Ibid*., 23 March 1827, p. 2.
33 *Hobart Town Gazette and Van Diemen's Land Advertiser*, 23 July, 1828, p.2
34 Dr. Philip Norrie, 'Wine and Health Through the Ages with Special Reference to Australia, A Thesis submitted in fulfilment of the requirements for the degree of Doctor of Philosophy, School of Social Ecology and Lifelong Learning, University of Western Sydney, 2005, p. 102.
35 Knut Haeger, *The Illustrated History of Surgery*, Harold Starke Publishers, 2000, p. 139.
36 Nathaniel Hodges, *Loimologia: Or an Historical Account of the Plague in London in 1665*, E. Bell, 1720, p. 225.
37 Emanuel (Serrao) Serong, b c.1793 (Funchal, Madeira), d. 29 September 1880 (Wangoom, Victoria).
38 Antonia De Jesus (De Freitas) Serong, b. 1803 (São Martinho, Funchal, Madeira), d. 31 March 1890 (Wangoom, Victoria).
39 Established in 1822.
40 'Wine Competition History', Royal Agricultural Society of NSW, rasnsw.com.au.
41 'The Grape', *The Sydney Herald*, 30 May 1833, p. 1.
42 *Ibid*.
43 *Ibid*.
44 'The Grape', *The Sydney Monitor*, 23 February 1833, p. 2.

Chapter 7

1 Tom and Elizabeth Holt to Mary Penfold, 4 June 1844 and 21 March 1845, Personal Papers of Christopher Rawson Penfold and Mary Penfold and family, State Library of South Australia (SLSA), BRG 330/1.
2 Southwood Smith, *A Treatise On Fever*, Longman, Rees, Orme, Brown, and Green, 1830.

Mary Penfold

3   Dr Philip Norrie, 'Wine and Health Through the Ages', p. 137.
4   Tom and Elizabeth Holt to Mary Penfold, 4 June 1844, Personal Papers of Christopher Rawson Penfold and Mary Penfold and family, SLSA, BRG 330/1.
5   Richard Penfold, b. 1 January 1798 (Steyning, Sussex, U.K.), d. 1829 (Steyning, Sussex, U.K.).
6   Philip Norrie, *Lindeman: Australia's Classic Wine Maker*, Apollo Books, 1993, pp. 13–4.
7   'Apothecaries Hall', *English Chronicle and Whitehall Evening Post*, 28 December 1833, p. 3.
8   D. U. Bloor, 'The rise of the general practitioner in the nineteenth century', British Journal of General Practice, bjgp.org.
9   *Ibid.*
10 *Ibid.*
11 Mary Anne Boys, nee Penfold, b. 29 December 1809 (Steyning, Sussex, U.K.), d. 31 December 1877 (Sandgate Road, Folkestone, U.K.).
12 Tom and Elizabeth Holt to Mary Penfold, 4 June 1844, SLSA, BRG 330/1.
13 *The Hampshire Chronicle* (Winchester, Hampshire, U.K.), 3 December 1792, p. 3.
14 Rev. John Penfold, b. 1 July 1764 (Steyning, Sussex, U.K.), d. 30 April 1840 (Wisborough Green, Sussex, U.K.).
15 Charlotte Jane Rawson, nee Brooks, b. 1770 (Battersea, Surrey, U.K.), d. 29 October 1843 (Steyning, Sussex, U.K.).
16 theclergydatabase.org.uk.
17 *The Derby Mercury* (Derbyshire, U.K.), 15 May 1752, p. 1.
18 Arthur M. Silverstein, *A History of Immunology* (2nd ed.), Academic Press, 2009, p. 293.
19 'A Brief History of Vaccination', World Health Organization, who.int.
20 *The Sussex Advertiser* (Brighton, U.K.), 12 April 1813, p. 3.
21 Family Notes, Personal papers of Christopher Rawson Penfold and Mary Penfold and family, SLSA, BRG 330/1.
22 Now the Steyning Parish Church of St Andrew and St Cuthman.
23 'Steyning Parish Church of St Andrew and St Cuthman, UK', darcawards.com.
24 *The Sussex Advertiser* (Brighton, U.K.), 27 September 1819, p. 3.
25 George Scharf, Peter Jackson, *Drawings of Westminster*, London Topographical Society, 1994, p. 34.
26 Inventory book of Charlotte Jane Penfold (nee Brooks), Personal papers of Christopher Rawson Penfold and Mary Penfold and family, SLSA, BRG 330/1.

27 *Ibid.*
28 *Ibid.*
29 *Ibid.*
30 Christopher Rawson Diary: West Yorkshire Archive Service, Calderdale 1525/2/5/2.
31 Christopher Rawson, b. 17 December 1777 (Stoney Royd, Halifax, Yorkshire, U.K.), d. 6 May 1849 (Hope House, Halifax, Yorkshire, U.K.).
32 Caroline Maillard, 'Frances Penfold Walker Clarke (1803–1838) A Consequential Life', insearchofannwalker.com.
33 On 25 January 1807, at Westminster (St Margaret, Parliament Square), London, U.K.
34 Mary Ann Rawson, nee Brooks, b. 1783 (Southwark, London, U.K.), d. 29 July 1836 (Halifax, West Yorkshire, U.K.).
35 George Rawson Saxby Penfold, b. 28 August 1808 (Broadwater, Worthing Borough, West Sussex, U.K.), d. December 1846 (London, U.K.).
36 'Our Building', steyningparishchurch.org.
37 Thomas Brooks Penfold, b. 15 August 1796 (Steyning, Sussex, U.K.), d. 19 February 1864 (Croydon, Surrey, U.K.).
38 Dave Roos, 'How the East India Company Became the World's Most Powerful Monopoly', history.com, 29 June 2023.
39 *The Worcestershire Chronicle* (Worcester, U.K.), 2 July 1845, p. 2.
40 *The Sussex Advertiser*, 3 May 1819, p. 2.
41 *Ibid.*, 21 January 1828, pp. 2–3.
42 *Ibid.*
43 *The Sydney Gazette and New South Wales Advertiser*, 6 February 1834, p. 2.
44 *Journal of the Royal Australian Historical Society*, Vol. 65, 1978, p. 6.
45 The NSW Government Gazette of 12 March 1834, reported there were '543 varieties in the whole and only 334 are at present alive'.
46 'Wine Competition History', Royal Agricultural Society of NSW, rasnsw.com.au.
47 Journal of a Tour Through Some of the Vineyards of Spain and France (1833); and Report on the Vines Introduced into the Colony of New South Wales in the Year 1832 (1834).
48 George Wyndham, b. 20 June 1801 (Dinton, Wiltshire, U.K.), d. 24 December 1870 (Sydney, N.S.W.).
49 In 1830.

Chapter 8
1 Frances (Fanny) Esther Penfold, b 26 August 1803 (Steyning, West Sussex, U.K.), d. 7 August 1838 (Penzance, Cornwall, U.K.).

2   Letter from Mary Anne to Christopher Penfold, Christopher Rawson (C. Rawson) Diary: West Yorkshire Archive Service, Calderdale 1525/2/5/2.
3   Caroline Maillard, 'Frances Penfold Walker Clarke (1803–1838) A Consequential Life', insearchofannwalker.com, 23 June 2022.
4   Inventory book of Charlotte Jane Penfold (nee Brooks), Personal papers of Christopher Rawson Penfold and Mary Penfold and family, SLSA, BRG 330/1.
5   Caroline Maillard, 'Frances Penfold Walker Clarke (1803–1838) A Consequential Life', insearchofannwalker.com, 23 June 2022.
6   C. Rawson Diary: West Yorkshire Archive Service, Calderdale 1525/2/5/2.
7   On 28 July 1829.
8   Catherine Jane Penfold, b. 22 April 1799 (Steyning, Sussex, U.K.), d. 14 November 1860 (Florence, Italy).
9   Charlotte Charity Penfold, b. 7 Oct 1806 (Steyning, Sussex, U.K.), d. April 1888 (Kensington, London, U.K.).
10 'John Walker Jr and Frances Esther Penfold's Honeymoon Storymap', insearchofannwalker.com.
11 Inventory book of Charlotte Jane Penfold (nee Brooks), Personal papers of Christopher Rawson Penfold and Mary Penfold and family, SLSA, BRG 330/1.
12 C. Rawson Diary: West Yorkshire Archive Service, Calderdale 1525/2/5/2.
13 James Vowler Penfold, b, 17 January 1802 (Steyning, Sussex, U.K.), d. 21 March 1882 (Hastings, Sussex, U.K.).
14 Giovanni 'John' Baroncelli, b. 1783 Florence, Italy.
15 'Family Notice', *The Yorkshire Gazette*, (York, U.K.), 16 October 1830, p. 3.
16 *The English Chronicle and Whitehall Evening Post*, (London, U.K.), 2 October 1830, p. 3.
17 Henry John Lindeman, b. 21 September 1811 (Egham, Surrey, U.K.), d. 23 May 1881, (Gresford, New South Wales).
18 Keir Waddington, *Medical Education at St Bartholomew's Hospital: 1123–1995*, St Edmundsbury Press Ltd, 2003, pp. 6, 64.
19 'Body Snatchers And Abnormalities In Jars: A History Of Barts Pathology Museum', londonist.com, 14 December 2020.
20 Henry Lewer Sanders, b. 2 April 1799 (London, U.K.). d. 9 March 1864 (Jersey City, New Jersey, U.S.A).
21 *The London Gazette*, 1 February 825, p. 196.
22 Caroline Maillard, 'Frances Penfold Walker Clarke (1803–1838) A Consequential Life', insearchofannwalker.com, 23 June 2022.
23 C. Rawson Diary: West Yorkshire Archive Service, Calderdale 1525/2/5/2.
24 *Ibid.*

25 Caroline Maillard, 'Frances Penfold Walker Clarke (1803–1838) A Consequential Life', insearchofannwalker.com, 23 June 2022.
26 In 1838.
27 Tom and Elizabeth Holt to Mary Penfold, 4 June 1844 and 21 March 1845, Personal Papers of Christopher Rawson Penfold and Mary Penfold and family, SLSA, BRG 330/1.
28 Inventory book of Charlotte Jane Penfold (nee Brooks), Personal papers of Christopher Rawson Penfold and Mary Penfold and family, SLSA, BRG 330/1.
29 *Ibid.*
30 *Ibid.*
31 *Ibid.*
32 *Ibid.*
33 Harriett Timbrell, nee Armstrong, b. c.1786 (St Pancras, London, U.K.), d. 18 September 1884 (5 Castelnau Cottage, Barnes, London, U.K.).
34 Elizabeth Winterton Micklethwait, nee Timbrell, b. 5 October 1811 (London, U.K.), d. 30 April 1891 (Lewisham, London, U.K.).
35 *The Evening Chronicle* (London, U.K.), 10 October 1835, p. 1.
36 Inventory book of Charlotte Jane Penfold (nee Brooks), Personal papers of Christopher Rawson Penfold and Mary Penfold and family, SLSA, BRG 330/1.
37 *Ibid.*
38 Gilbert Beresford, b. c.1774 (Hungry Bentley, Derbyshire, U.K.), d. 2 June 1843 (Blaby, Leicestershire, U.K.).
39 Church of England Marriages and Banns, 1754–1940, St Andrew Holborn: Holborn Circus, 1832–1837, London Archives, cityoflondon.gov.uk/lma.

Chapter 9

1 Inventory book of Charlotte Jane Penfold (nee Brooks), Personal papers of Christopher Rawson Penfold and Mary Penfold and family, SLSA, BRG 330/1.
2 Timothy Carder, *The Encyclopaedia of Brighton*, East Sussex County Libraries, 1990, p. 17.
3 'History', Brighton & Hove Museums, brightonmuseums.org.uk.
4 '28th June 1838 – Diary Entry – The Coronation Of Queen Victoria', thequeenvictoriafiles.wordpress.com.
5 Ellie Cawthorne, 'Extravagance, crowds and blunders: the coronation of Queen Victoria', historyextra.com, 2 May 2023.

6   Inventory book of Charlotte Jane Penfold (nee Brooks), Personal papers of Christopher Rawson Penfold and Mary Penfold and family, SLSA, BRG 330/1.
7   'Brighton and Hove timeline', brightonhistory.org.uk.
8   Queen Victoria, Lithograph by Day and Haghe, 1838, Brighton & Hove Museums.
9   'The 1830s in Fashionable Gowns: A Visual Guide to the Decade', mimimatthews.com.
10 *The Brighton Gazette*, 25 July 1839, p. 2.
11 Dr Philip Norrie, 'Wine and Health Through the Ages with Special Reference to Australia', Doctoral Thesis, University of Western Sydney, 2005, p. 141.
12 Queen Victoria's Journal, 4 October 1837, 'Queen Victoria and Brighton's Royal Pavilion – Royal Splendour and Stately homes', youngqueenvictoria.co.uk.
13 'History Of The Old Ship', oldshipbrighton.co.uk.
14 *The Brighton Gazette*, 24 May 1849, p. 4.
15 Andrew Caillard, 'The Australian Ark: The storied history of Australia's pre-phylloxera grapevines', worldoffinewine.com.
16 Register of Heritage Places 1, Olive Farm Cellars, South Guildford, 1 April 2014, inherit.dplh.wa.gov.au.
17 'The Fruit Growing Industry', *The Western Mail* (Perth, W.A.) 21 December 1917, p. 33.
18 'Government Notice', *The Perth Gazette and Western Australian Journal*, 6 September 1834, p. 349.
19 John Batman, Journal, 8 June 1835, manuscript, State Library of Victoria, MS 13181.
20 Andrew Caillard, *The Australian Ark: The storied history of Australia's pre-phylloxera grapevines*, worldoffinewine.com.
21 Oswald Ziegler, *The Penfold Story*, Penfolds Wine, Australia Ltd, 1975, p. 19.
22 Edward Gibbon Wakefield (20 March 1796 – 16 May 1862).
23 Charles Sturt, Two expeditions into the interior of southern Australia: during the years 1828, 1829, 1830, and 1831, vol. 2, Smith, Elder & Co., 1833, p. 246.
24 Tom and Elizabeth Holt to Mary Penfold, Personal Papers of Christopher Rawson Penfold and Mary Penfold and family, SLSA, BRG 330/1.
25 South Australian Association, issuing body, New colony of South Australia, obj-3461873066, National Library of Australia.
26 Letters Patent under the Great Seal of the United Kingdom erecting and establishing the Province of South Australia and fixing the boundaries thereof, State Records of South Australia, SRSA: GRG 2/64.

27 George Stevenson, b. 13 April 1799 (Berwick upon Tweed, Northumberland, U.K.), d. 19 October 1856 (Lytton Lodge, Finniss Street, North Adelaide).
28 *South Australian Gazette and Colonial Register* (Adelaide, S.A.), 18 June 1836, p. 1.
29 Also known as 'The Proclamation Tree'.
30 'Proclamation by his Excellency John Hindmarsh', State Records of South Australia, GRG 24/90/401.
31 'Kaurna Place Names', kaurnaplacenames.com.
32 Frank Potts, b. 11 July 1815 (Hounslow, London), d. 15 December 1890 (Langhorne Creek, South Australia).
33 Robert Cock, b. 25 May 1801 (Fife, Scotland), d. 23 March 1871 (Mount Gambier, South Australia).
34 William Ferguson, b. c.1809 (Hawick, Scotland), d. 3 December 1892 (Glen Osmond, South Australia).
35 burnsidehistory.org.au.
36 'Magill Village, An historical overview', campbelltown.sa.gov.au.

Chapter 10
1 *The Sussex Advertiser*, 7 January 1839, p. 3.
2 *Ibid.*
3 *Ibid.*
4 *Ibid.*
5 'Magill Village, An historical overview', campbelltown.sa.gov.au.
6 *Ibid.*
7 'Advertising', *The South Australian Gazette and Colonial Register* (Adelaide), 20 October 1838, p. 4.
8 'Holt is an old Hermit', *The Brooklyn Eagle* (Brooklyn, New York, U.S.A.), 20 January 1895, p. 19.
9 *Ibid.*
10 'Alfred Astor Holt', *ibid.*,6 February 1900, p. 3.
11 *Ibid.*
12 In 1841.
13 In 1847.
14 'Holt is an old Hermit', *The Brooklyn Eagle* (Brooklyn, New York, U.S.A.), 20 January 1895, p. 19.
15 'Coroners Inquests', *The Brighton Gazette*, 25 July 1839, p. 2.
16 *Ibid.*
17 *Ibid.*
18 Inventory book of Charlotte Jane Penfold (nee Brooks), Personal papers of Christopher Rawson Penfold and Mary Penfold and family, SLSA, BRG 330/1.

19 *Ibid*.
20 *Ibid*.
21 John Gould, *Handbook to the Birds of Australia*, Vol. 1, John Gould, 1865, p. 484.
22 *Ibid*.
23 'West Parklands', sahistoryhub.history.sa.gov.au.
24 John Gould to Edwin Prince, 30 June 1839, from *The Magazine of Natural History*, Vol. 3, 1839, p. 568.
25 John Barton Hack, b. 2 July 1805 (Chichester, U.K.) d. 4 October 1884 (Semaphore, Adelaide).
26 'Horticulture in South Australia', *The South Australian Colonist and Settlers' Weekly Record of British, Foreign and Colonial Intelligence* (London, U.K.), 23 June 1840, p. 241.
27 Published in 1843.
28 Richard Hamilton (18 February 1792 – 13 August 1852).
29 Anthony Hopkins Davis (c. August 1796 – 4 June 1866).
30 'Importation of Vines', *The Southern Australian* (Adelaide), 23 October 1840, p. 4.
31 'Early S.A Vines', *The Register* (Adelaide), 27 May 1921, p. 5.
32 'Vine Association', *The Southern Australian* (Adelaide) 28 May 1841, p. 3.
33 'Importation Of Vines From The Cape', *The South Australian Register* (Adelaide), 23 October 1841, p. 2.
34 Geoffrey C. Bishop, *The Vineyards of Adelaide*, Lynton Publications, 1977, p.17. Other varieties were Lachryma Christi, 4000; Early Blue Muscatel, 5000; Pontac, 5000; Hanneporte (Muscat of Alexandria), 6000; Frontignac, 3000; Red Constantia, 2500; White Constantia, 2500; Corinth, 300; Stein (Chenin Blanc), 600.
35 'Early S.A Vines', *The Register* (Adelaide), 27 May 1921, p. 5.

Chapter 11
1 'Partnerships Dissolved', *The Sun* (London), 3 February 1844, p. 4.
2 From the will of Harriet's son William Timbrell, 1844, ancestry.com.
3 *The Brighton Gazette*, 11 December 1834, p. 1.
4 *Ibid*.
5 Dr Geoffrey Bishop, 'Mary Penfold and Joseph Gillard Jr: A different view of the Penfolds Wines', Burnside Library, South Australia, 374 T.
6 *The Brighton Gazette*, 17 August 1843, p. 3.
7 Holograph journal of Captain James Cook on HMS *Resolution* (605 ff.), 10 February 1776–6 January 1779 (File Egerton MS 2177A), Image 24, 6 November 1776.

8 *The Hampshire Chronicle*, 22 October 1781, p. 2.
9 Elizabeth Winterton Timbrell, b. 5 October 1811 (Derbyshire, England), d. 22 February 1899 (St Pancras, London).
10 John Micklethwait (1798–1857).
11 Tom and Elizabeth Holt to Mary Penfold, 14 May 1845, Personal papers of Christopher Rawson Penfold and Mary Penfold and family, SLSA, BRG 330/1.
12 Angela Skujins, 'Spinning South Australia: how colonial "marketing" was undermined by reality', indaily.com.au, 28 June 2019.
13 'McLaren Wharf', sahistoryhub.history.sa.gov.au.
14 'Extracts From Settlers' Letters', *The South Australian Colonist and Settlers' Weekly Record of British, Foreign and Colonial Intelligence* (London, U.K.) 5 May 1840, p. 131.
15 Ibid.
16 'Six Months in South Australia', *The South Australian Register* (Adelaide), 29 June 1839. p. 5.
17 Ibid.
18 Ibid.
19 Mary Thomas, b. 30 August 1787 (Southampton, Hampshire, U.K.), d. 10 February 1875 (Adelaide, S.A.).
20 Mary Thomas to her brother George Harris, 1 March 1840, Collections held by the Royal Commonwealth Society relating to Australia, New Zealand and the Pacific (as filmed by the AJCP), 1810–1973, [M1690-M1703], National Library of Australia.
21 'Letter Writing Home', *South Australian Register* (Adelaide, S.A.), 29 June 1839, p. 4.
22 'Financial Crisis Of The Colony', *The Adelaide Chronicle and South Australian Literary Record*, 28 April 1841, p. 2.
23 'Colony bankrupt by 1840s; land speculation crash dashes Dissenters' settlement ideal', adelaideaz.com.
24 Philip Norrie, *Lindeman: Australia's Classic Wine Maker*, Apollo Books, 1993, pp. 13–4.
25 'Our history', benean.com.au.
26 Norrie, *Lindeman: Australia's Classic Wine Maker*, pp. 13–4.
27 In 1990, Penfolds acquired the Lindemans brand from Philip Morris, a US tobacco company.
28 1841 England Census, Class: HO107; Piece: 675; Book: 3; Civil Parish: St Marylebone; County: Middlesex; Enumeration District: 4; Folio: 14; Page: 20; Line: 23; GSU roll: 438791.

29 New York, Passenger and Crew Lists 1820–1957, Year: 1842; Arrival: New York, New York, USA; Microfilm Serial: M237, 1820–1897; Line: 1; List Number: 891.
30 Episcopal Diocese of New York Church Records, 1767–1970, Manhattan, All Saints Church 1881 – 1892, p. 466.

Chapter 12
1   Elizabeth Holt to Mary Penfold, 4 June 1844, Personal papers of Christopher Rawson Penfold and Mary Penfold and family, SLSA, BRG 330/1.
2   *Ibid.*
3   Elizabeth Holt to Mary Penfold, 4 June 1844, Personal papers of Christopher Rawson Penfold and Mary Penfold and family, SLSA, BRG 330/1.
4   Personal papers of Christopher Rawson Penfold and Mary Penfold and family, SLSA, BRG 330/1, Reel 3.
5   'Law and Police Courts.', *The South Australian Register* (Adelaide), 27 February 1847, p. 1. Also recorded as Ann Guillod.
6   'Penfold v. Penfold and Another', *The South Australian* (Adelaide), 26 February 1847, p. 3.
7   'Partnerships Dissolved', *The Sun* (London), 3 February 1844, p. 4.
8   'Taglioni', shippingandshipbuilding.uk.
9   Elizabeth Holt to Mary Penfold, 4 June 1844, SLSA, BRG 330/1.
10 *Ibid.*
11 Susanna de Vries, *The Complete Book of Heroic Australian Women*, HarperCollins, 2010, p. 336.
12 *The Empire Achievement, 1844 to 1934*, State Library of South Australia, 663.200994.
13 *Ibid.*
14 Geoffrey C. Bishop, *The Vineyards of Adelaide*, Lynton Publications, 1977, p. 45. Other varieties that the Penfolds grew during Mary's lifetime were Pedro Ximénez, Verdelho, Mataro, Frontignac, Tokay, Black Portugal, Muscatel and Shiraz.
15 Diane Cummings, 'Taglioni 1844', bound-for-south-australia.collections.slsa.sa.gov.au.
16 *Ibid.*
17 Church of England Births and Baptisms, 1813–1924, St Botolph Bishopsgate 1843–1850, p. 31, London Archives.
18 Personal papers of Christopher Rawson Penfold and Mary Penfold and family, SLSA, BRG 330/1, Reel 3.

19 *The South Australian Register* (Adelaide), 19 June 1844, p. 2.
20 *The Morning Herald* (London), 15 February 1844, p. 7.
21 'Shipping Intelligence. Arrived', *The South Australian Register* (Adelaide), 19 June 1844, p. 2.
22 *Ibid.*
23 Elizabeth Holt to Mary Penfold, 4 June 1844, SLSA, BRG 330/1.
24 *The South Australian Register* (Adelaide), 19 June 1844, p. 2.
25 'Captain Hall's Salting Machine', *The South Australian Register* (Adelaide), 17 July 1844. p. 4.
26 'Daguerreotype and Early Photography', David Coome History, coombe.id.au.
27 'English News Per "Taglioni"', *The South Australian Register* (Adelaide), 22 June 1844, p. 4.
28 Now called Tynte Street.
29 *The South Australian Register* (Adelaide), 22 June 1844, p. 2.
30 'Local News', *The Southern Australian* (Adelaide), 25 June 1844, p. 3.
31 'The "*Taglioni*" From London', *The Adelaide Observer*, 22 June 1844, p. 4.
32 *Ibid.*
33 *Ibid.*
34 Elizabeth Holt to Mary Penfold, 4 June 1844, SLSA, BRG 330/1.
35 *Ibid.*
36 *Ibid.*
37 *Ibid.*
38 'The "Taglioni" From London', *The Adelaide Observer*, 22 June 1844, p. 4.
39 *Ibid.*

Chapter 13

1 *Lloyd's List* (London), 16 February 1844, p. 1.
2 'The "Taglioni" From London', *The Adelaide Observer*, 22 June 1844, p. 4.
3 Diane Cummings, 'Taglioni 1844', bound-for-south-australia.collections.slsa.sa.gov.au.
4 *Ibid.*
5 'Opening Of The New Port', *The Adelaide Chronicle and South Australian Literary Record*, 14 October 1840, p. 2.
6 *Ibid.*
7 'McLaren Wharf', sahistoryhub.history.sa.gov.au.
8 'Opening Of The New Port', *The Adelaide Chronicle and South Australian Literary Record*, 14 October 1840, p. 2.
9 Johann Gramp, b. 28 August 1819 (Kulmbach, Kingdom of Bavaria), d. 9 August 1903 (Barossa Valley, South Australia).

10 De Vries, *The Complete Book of Heroic Australian Women*, p. 336.
11 Margaret Anderson, History Trust of South Australia, 'West Parklands', SA History Hub, History Trust of South Australia, sahistoryhub.history.sa.gov.au.
12 'The "Taglioni" From London', *The Adelaide Observer*, 22 June 1844, p. 4.
13 'Major O'Halloran's Instructions and Execution of two Natives at Encounter Bay', *The Southern Australian* (Adelaide), 15 September 1840, p. 3.
14 'Culture of Adelaide tribe, the Kaurna, nearly wiped out by lost land, disease and a broken tribal order', adelaideaz.com.
15 'German Missionaries in Australia: Piltawodli Native Location (1838–1845)', Griffith University, missionaries.griffith.edu.au.
16 'Aborigines Evidence Act No 8 of 7 and 8 Vic, 1844', legislation.sa.gov.au.
17 Sir John William Jeffcott (1796 – 12 December 1837).
18 *The South Australian Gazette and Colonial Register* (Adelaide), 3 June 1837, p. 4.
19 *Ibid*.
20 Samuel Thomas Gill, b. 21 May 1818 (Perriton, Somerset, U.K.), d. 27 October 1880 (Melbourne, Victoria).
21 'Advertising', *The South Australian Gazette and Colonial Register* (Adelaide), 7 March 1840, p. 1.
22 Feby [i.e. February] [picture] / S.T.G, Gill, Samuel Thomas, 1818–1880, PIC Solander Box A49 #R3294, National Library of Australia, nla.obj-134354667-1.
23 Ferguson Conservation Park Management Plan, Adelaide, South Australia, cdn.environment.sa.gov.au.
24 'Local Intelligence', *The Adelaide Observer*, 3 August 1844, p. 5.
25 'Meteorological Tables', *The South Australian Register* (Adelaide), 24 August 1844, p. 2.
26 *The Southern Australian* (Adelaide), 13 August 1844, p. 2.
27 'Local Intelligence', *The Adelaide Observer*, 3 August 1844, p. 5
28 *Ibid*.
29 'Ferguson Conservation Park Management Plan: Adelaide – South Australia', cdn.environment.sa.gov.au.
30 Edmund Isaac Stephen Trimmer, b. 23 April 23 1803 (London, U.K.), d. 1882 (London, U.K.).
31 Dr Geoffrey Bishop, 'Mary Penfold and Joseph Gillard Jr: A different view of the Penfolds Wines', Recorded 18 August 2014, Burnside Library, South Australia, 374 T.
32 Philip Norrie, 'Wine And Health Through the Ages with Special Reference to Australia', A Thesis submitted in fulfilment of the requirements for the

degree of Doctor of Philosophy, School of Social Ecology and Lifelong Learning, University of Western Sydney, 2005, p. 142.
33 'Memories of Magill', *The Register* (Adelaide), 29 January 1921, p. 4.
34 S.T. Gill, Sturt's Overland Expedition leaving Adelaide, 10th August 1844, watercolour on paper, South Australian Government Grant 1939, Art Gallery of South Australia, Adelaide.
35 'Public Breakfast To Capt. Sturt', *The Southern Australian* (Adelaide), 13 August 1844, p. 2.
36 Charles Sturt, *Narrative of an Expedition into Central Australia*, T and W Boone, 1849, Vol. 1, p. 39.
37 Elizabeth Holt to Mary Penfold, 4 June 1844, Personal papers of Christopher Rawson Penfold and Mary Penfold and family, SLSA, BRG 330/1.
38 *Ibid.*
39 *Ibid.*
40 *Ibid.*
41 *Ibid.*
42 *Ibid.*
43 *The Morning Herald* (London), 21 November 1844, p. 6.
44 Elizabeth Holt to Mary Penfold, 4 June 1844, SLSA, BRG 330/1.
45 *Ibid.*

Chapter 14
1 'Orchard & Vineyard', *The Adelaide Observer*, 11 December 1886, p. 11.
2 Geoffrey C. Bishop, *The Vineyards of Adelaide*, p. 45.
3 On 18 September 1844.
4 'Births, Deaths, Marriages and Obituaries', *The Glasgow Herald*, 16 December 1844, p. 2.
5 John Horsnell, b. 16 September 1812 (Brentwood, Essex, U.K.) d. 24 November 1895 (Woodforde, South Australia).
6 Jonathon Dadds, 'Horsnell, John – Pioneer', Campbelltown City Council, South Australia, campbelltown.sa.gov.au.
7 Julie McIntyre, *First Vintage: Wine in Colonial New South Wales*, UNSW Press, 2012, p. 12.
8 *Ibid.*
9 Elizabeth Smythe, b. 31 August 1824 (St Mawgan-in Pyder, Cornwall, U.K.), d. 17 April 1900 (Woodvale, South Australia).
10 On 14 November 1848 at St John's Church, Halifax Street, Adelaide.
11 Jonathon Dadds, 'Horsnell, John – Pioneer', Campbelltown City Council, South Australia, campbelltown.sa.gov.au.

12 Elijah Richard Euphiema Lovelock, b. 7 March 1829 (Wiltshire, U.K.), d. 17 September 1907 (Salisbury, South Australia).
13 burnsidehistory.org.au.
14 'Advertising', *The Adelaide Observer*, 17 August 1844, p. 1.
15 Patrick Auld, b. 1811 (Scotland), d. 21 January 1886 (Onehunga, Waitakere, Auckland, New Zealand).
16 William Patrick Auld, b. 27 May 1840 (Manchester U.K.), d. September 1912 (Adelaide, South Australia).
17 Andrew Caillard, 'The Australian Ark: The storied history of Australia's pre-phylloxera grapevines', worldoffinewine.com.
18 William Leigh to John Morphett, 26 October 1839, Morphett Family Papers, SLSA, PRG 239/2-15.
19 William Oliver, b. 1812 (Roxburgh, Scottish Borders, Scotland, U.K.), d. 17 May 1888 (McLaren Vale, Onkaparinga City, South Australia).
20 John Reynell, b. 9 February 1809 (Ilfracombe, Devon, England, U.K.), d. 15 June 1873 (York Hotel, Adelaide, South Australia).
21 Also known as the *Surry*.
22 'John Reynell expresses his confidence in South Australia vine potential with the first plantings on his farm in 1841', adelaideaz.com.
23 'Hardy's Reynella Winery Complex', onkaparingacity.com.
24 John Reynell to his distant Irish cousin Sir Thomas Reynell, 21 July 1843, from Lenore Reynell and Margaret Hopton, *John Reynell of Reynella: A South Australian Pioneer*, Investigator Press, 1988, p. 59.
25 Kevin Gogler and Barry Philp, 'Pioneer Vignerons', Government of South Australia Department of Primary Industries and Regions, pir.sa.gov.au
26 George Alexander Anstey, b. 1814 (Kentish Town, London, U.K.), d. 18 February 1895 (London, U.K.).
27 'Hardy's Reynella Winery Complex', onkaparingacity.com.
28 Emma Penfold, nee Bouch, b. 26 April 1818 (London, U.K.), d. 20 July 1859 (Bouverie Place, Mt Radford, Exeter, Devon, U.K.).
29 Emma Mary Whitling, nee Penfold, b. 18 November 1844 (Notting Hill, London, U.K.), d. 10 December 1895 (Bognor, Sussex, U.K.).
30 *The Morning Herald* (London), 21 November 1844, p. 6.
31 'Law And Police Courts', *The Adelaide Observer*, 14 March 1846, p. 6.

Chapter 15
1 'The Exhibition Of Colonial Produce And Manufactures', *The South Australian* (Adelaide), 18 February 1845, p. 2.
2 *Ibid.*

3   S. T. Gill, Agricultural and Horticultural Show, Adelaide 1845, watercolour on paper, Art Gallery of South Australia.
4   'The Exhibition Of Colonial Produce And Manufactures', *The South Australian* (Adelaide), 18 February 1845, p. 2.
5   'Fruits', *The Adelaide Observer*, 22 February 1845, p. 7.
6   They were: 1. Royal Muscadine, introduced 1839, by Mr Bailey, Hackney Nursery, 2. Black Hamburg 3. White Hamburg, 4. Black Damascus, 5. White Muscat of Alexandria, 6. Black St. Peter's, 7. Grey Pineau, 8. Grizzly Frontignac, 9. Golden Chasselas.
7   The complete list was: 1. Douro Grape, 2. Pedro Ximenes, 3. Panse, 4. Olivette Noire, 5. Gros Ribico, 6. Pineau dore, 7. Pineau blamc, 8. Pineau rouge, 9. Pineau noir, 10. Verdelho, 11. Malaga, 12. Red Constantia, 13. White Constantia, 14. Cognac Brandy Grape, 15. White Frontignac, 16. Red Frontignac, 17. Black Frontignac, 18. Chasselas Jura, 19. Chasselas de Fontainebleau, 20. Moulane de Bernardy, 21. Ugne noir, 22. Raisin de Daville, 23. Augiber blanc, 24. Aucarot, 25. Espar noir, 26. Alicant de l' Herault, 27. Terret Moireau noir, 28. Chasselas Bernardy, 29. Meslier blanc.
8   'Fruits', *The Adelaide Observer*, 22 February 1845, p. 7.
9   *Ibid.*
10 'Wines And Ale', *ibid.* p. 6
11 'Agricultural and Horticultural Exhibition', *The South Australian Register* (Adelaide), 15 February 1845, p. 3.
12 *Ibid.*
13 Walter Duffield, b. 1816 (Great Baddow, Essex, U.K.), d. 5 November 1882 (Gawler, South Australia).
14 Jacob Hagen, b. 29 January 1809 (Bermondsey, London, U.K.), d. 24 January 1870 (Ropley, Hampshire, U.K.).
15 *Ibid.*
16 *The South Australian Register* (Adelaide), 19 February 1845, p. 2.
17 *The South Australian* (Adelaide), 4 March 1845, p. 2.
18 Tom and Elizabeth Holt to Mary Penfold, 21 March 1845, Personal papers of Christopher Rawson Penfold and Mary Penfold and family, SLSA, BRG 330/1.
19 *Ibid.*
20 *Ibid.*
21 *Ibid.*
22 *Ibid.*
23 Geoffrey C. Bishop, *The Vineyards of Adelaide*, Lynton Publications, 1977, p. 71.

24 Tom and Elizabeth Holt to Mary Penfold, 21 March 1845, Personal papers of Christopher Rawson Penfold and Mary Penfold and family, SLSA, BRG 330/1.
25 *Ibid.*
26 On 19 January 1846.
27 John Healey, S.A.'s Greats – The Men and Women of the North Terrace Plaques, Historical Society of South Australia Incorporated, 2001.
28 'Local Intelligence', *The Adelaide Observer*, 20 September 1845, p. 5.
29 Tom and Elizabeth Holt to Mary Penfold, 14 May 1845, Personal papers of Christopher Rawson Penfold and Mary Penfold and family, SLSA, BRG 330/1.
30 *Ibid.*
31 *Ibid.*
32 'Local Intelligence', *The Adelaide Observer*, 3 August 1844, p. 5.
33 Tom and Elizabeth Holt to Mary Penfold, 14 May 1845, Personal papers of Christopher Rawson Penfold and Mary Penfold and family, SLSA, BRG 330/1.
34 *Ibid.*
35 *Ibid.*
36 *Ibid.*
37 *Ibid.*

Chapter 16

1 'Vice Chancellor's Court, Penfold V. Penfold', *The Examiner* (London, U.K.), 28 June 1845, p. 11.
2 Richard Bethell, later 1st Baron Westbury, (30 June 1800 – 20 July 1873).
3 'Vice Chancellor's Court, Penfold V. Penfold', The Examiner (London, U.K.), 28 June 1845, p. 11.
4 *Ibid.*
5 *Ibid.*
6 *Ibid.*
7 Alexander Charles Kelly (1811–1877) b. 5 June 1811 (South Leith, Scotland) d. 9 October 1877 (Norwood, Adelaide, South Australia).
8 *The Examiner* (Adelaide), 19 November 1842, p. 1.
9 *The South Australian* (Adelaide), 23 May 1845, p. 3.
10 Maro [William Macarthur] *Letters on the Culture of the Vine, Fermentation, and the Management of the Cellar*, Statham & Forster, 1844.
11 George McEwin, *South Australian Vigneron and Gardeners' Manual*, James Allen, 1843.

12 George Suttor, *The Culture of the Grape-vine and the Orange in Australia and New Zealand*, Smith, Elder & Co, 1843.
13 'Historical Timeline: Wine and Grape History in the Sydney Region', hawkesbury.net.au.
14 Sir Thomas Livingstone Mitchell, b. 15 June 1792 (Grangemouth, Scotland), d. 5 October 1855 (Darling Point, Sydney, New South Wales).
15 Stuart Read, 'Early vineyards and viticulture in the Sydney basin', Paper presented at the Australian Garden History Society seminar, Adelaide, 15 October 2015, gardenhistorysociety.org.au.
16 Lieut. Colonel Sir T. L. Mitchell, *Notes On The Cultivation Of The Vine And The Olive: Methods Of Making Wine And Oil, In The Southern Parts Of Spain*, D. L. Welch, 1849.
17 Gerald Walsh, The Wine Industry of Australia 1788–1979, Wine Talk, A.N.U. Canberra, 1979, artserve.anu.edu.au.
18 'Shipping intelligence', *The South Australian* (Adelaide), 17 October 1845, p. 2.

Chapter 17

1 London, England, Church of England Deaths and Burials, 1813–2003, All Souls Church 1845, p. 39, Burial Date: 7 November 1845.
2 *The South Australian Register* (Adelaide), 29 November 1845, p. 2.
3 *Ibid.*, 10 January 1846, p. 2.
4 'Quarterly Meeting of Magistrates', *The South Australian Register* (Adelaide), 10 December 1845, p. 3.
5 Thomas Gilbert, b. 1786 (The Tower Hamlets, Middlesex, England), d. 30 May 1873 (Adelaide).
6 Mary Langmead, nee Fisher, b. 1797 (near Great Torrington, Devon, England,), d. 27 December 1845 (Second Creek, now known as Norwood, Adelaide).
7 'Local Intelligence', *The South Australian Register* (Adelaide), 31 December 1845, p. 2.
8 *Ibid.*
9 'Death From the Bite of a Snake', *The South Australian* (Adelaide), 30 December 1845, p. 3.
10 James George Nash (1804–1879).
11 'Local Intelligence', *The South Australian Register* (Adelaide), 31 December 1845, p. 2.
12 'Government Gazette', *The South Australian* (Adelaide), 20 February 1846, p. 2.
13 *Ibid.*

14 'Wine', *The Adelaide Observer*, 28 February 1846, p. 6.
15 *Ibid.*
16 *Ibid.*
17 *Ibid.*
18 The school land was purchased in 1846. 'Magill Village, An historical overview', campbelltown.sa.gov.au
19 'Local News', *The South Australian Gazette and Colonial Register* (Adelaide), 31 October 1846, p. 2.
20 *Ibid.*, 23 January 1847, p. 2.
21 Tom and Elizabeth Holt to Mary Penfold, 21 March 1845, Personal papers of Christopher Rawson Penfold and Mary Penfold and family, SLSA, BRG 330/1.
22 'Magill Village, An historical overview', campbelltown.sa.gov.au
23 Frederic (Fred) Bayne, b. 20 August 1809 (London, U.K.), d. 5 August 1875 (Kyneton, Victoria).
24 *The Adelaide Observer*, 28 February 1846, p. 3.
25 Arthur Forbes Lloyd (1795–1866).
26 *The South Australian Gazette and Colonial Register* (Adelaide), 23 January 1847, p. 2.
27 'Family Notices', *The South Australian* (Adelaide), 26 January 1847, p. 4.
28 'History', barossa.com.
29 The name was changed to Bethany during the First World War in an attempt to remove all German place names from Australia. In 1917 the state government closed Bethany's German-language school, which had 60 students at the time.
30 William Jacob (1814–1902).
31 'Advertising', *The Evening Journal* (Adelaide), 24 March 1893, p. 4.
32 Joseph Gilbert, b. 1800 (Vale of Pewsey, Wiltshire, U.K.), d. 23 December 1881 (Pewsey Vale, South Australia).
33 Samuel Smith, b. 17 July 1812 (Wareham, Dorset, U.K.), d. 15 June 1889 (Angaston, South Australia).
34 'Supreme Court – Civil Side', *The Adelaide Observer*, 27 February 1847, p. 4.
35 'Advertising', *Ibid.*, 27 February 1847, p. 8.
36 'Law And Police Courts', *The South Australian Register* (Adelaide), 27 February 1847, p. 1.
37 *Ibid.*
38 'Family Notices', *The South Australian Gazette and Colonial Register* (Adelaide), 27 February 1847, p. 1.

Chapter 18
1. 'Family Notices', *The Evening Journal* (Adelaide), 29 January 1896, p. 2.
2. 'Bench Of Magistrates, Quarterly Licensing Meeting', *The Adelaide Times*, 10 June 1851, p. 3.
3. Augustus Short (1802–1883).
4. 'History: Discovering Faith, Sharing our Story', stgeorgesmagill.org.
5. 'Law And Police Courts', *The South Australian Register* (Adelaide), 3 March 1847, p. 2.
6. Ibid.
7. 'East Torrens Election', *The Adelaide Observer*, 24 June 1854, p. 11.
8. Geoffrey C. Bishop, *The Vineyards of Adelaide*, Lynton Publications, 1977, p. 45.
9. 'Death Of Mr. Penfold Hyland', *The Advertiser* (Adelaide), 7 May 1940, p. 16.
10. 'Orchard & Vineyard', *The Adelaide Observer*, 11 December 1886, p. 11.
11. 'Penfolds Wines', wineaustralia.com.
12. Geoffrey C. Bishop, *The Vineyards of Adelaide*, Lynton Publications, 1977, p. 45.
13. 'Penfolds Wines', wineaustralia.com.
14. Norrie, 'Wine And Health Through the Ages with Special Reference to Australia', p. 142.
15. *The South Australian Register* (Adelaide) 6 October 1847, p. 4.
16. *The Adelaide Observer*, 9 October 1847, p. 5.
17. 'Bench of Magistrates – Quarterly Issue of Licences', *The South Australian Register* (Adelaide), 10 June 1851, p. 3.
18. 'Old-Time Memories: Beautiful Magill', *The Adelaide Observer*, 8 August 1903, p. 3.
19. 'History: Discovering Faith, Sharing our Story', stgeorgesmagill.org.
20. *The South Australian Register* (Adelaide), 22 January 1848, p. 2.
21. 'Old-Time Memories: Beautiful Magill', *The Adelaide Observer*, 8 August 1903, p. 3.
22. 'Family Notices', *The South Australian Register* (Adelaide), 29 December 1847, p. 2.
23. *The South Australian Register* (Adelaide), 22 January 1848, p. 2.
24. Major-General Frederick Holt Robe (1801 – 4 April 1871).
25. Rev. William Norris, M.A., *Annals of the Diocese of Adelaide, Society for Promoting Christian Knowledge*, 1852, Chapter III, anglicanhistory.org.
26. Ibid.
27. Hebrews, Chapter XI, Verse 1, *The Holy Bible*, King James Version, biblegateway.com.
28. Bishop Augustus Short Diary 1848, 29 January 1847, State Library of South Australia, PRG 160/52.

29 Hebrews, Chapter XI, Verses 7–10, *The Holy Bible*, King James Version, biblegateway.com.
30 Bishop Augustus Short Diary 1848, 30 January 1847, SLSA, PRG 160/52.
31 *Ibid.*
32 Geoffrey C. Bishop, *The Vineyards of Adelaide*, p. 39.
33 *The South Australian* (Adelaide) 4 January 1848, p. 2.
34 Bishop Augustus Short Diary 1848, 2–15 February 1847, SLSA, PRG 160/52.
35 Rev. William Norris, M.A., *Annals of the Diocese of Adelaide, Society for Promoting Christian Knowledge*, 1852, Chapter III, anglicanhistory.org.

Chapter 19

1 Description by Bishop Augustus Short Rev. William Norris, M.A., *Annals of the Diocese of Adelaide, Society for Promoting Christian Knowledge*, 1852, Chapter III, anglicanhistory.org.
2 *Ibid.*
3 *Ibid.*
4 *The South Australian* (Adelaide), 7 March 1848, p. 1.
5 Johann Friedrich Carl Bayer, b. 1815 (Nürnberg, Bayern, Germany), d. 15 August 1867 (Adelaide, South Australia)
6 *The Adelaide Observer*, 2 October 1847, p. 2.
7 *The South Australian* (Adelaide), 7 March 1848, p. 1.
8 Benjamin Archer Kent (1808 – 25 November 1864).
9 'Frederick Charles Bayer, M.D.' *The South Australian Register* (Adelaide), 17 August 1867, p. 2.
10 *Ibid.*
11 'Dr Friedrich Bayer, surgeon for Adelaide's first operation under ether in 1847; builds biggest practice in city,' adelaideaz.com.
12 'Local Intelligence', *The Adelaide Observer*, 23 September 1848, p. 2.
13 To Isabel Yatala Mary Bayne on 23 October 1848.
14 *The South Australian Register* (Adelaide) 23 September 1848, p. 3.
15 *The Adelaide Times*, 25 August 1856, p. 2.
16 *The Kyneton Observer*, 7 August 1875, p. 2.
17 'John Jacob Astor, The American Millionaire', *The South Australian* (Adelaide), 3 October 1848, p. 4.
18 *The South Australian Register* (Adelaide), 16 December 1848, p. 3.
19 Henry George Grey, 3rd Earl Grey (28 December 1802 – 9 October 1894).
20 Thomas Charles Banfield (1795–1880).
21 Earl Grey to Sir Charles Fitz Roy, 1 November 1848, *Historical Records of Australia*, Series 1, vol. 26 (October 1847–December 1848), p.671.

22 *Ibid.*, p. 672.
23 *Ibid.*
24 'Ferguson Conservation Park Management Plan: Adelaide – South Australia', cdn.environment.sa.gov.au.
25 Mikaël Pierre, 'France of the southern hemisphere: transferring a European wine model to colonial Australia', History, Université Michel de Montaigne–Bordeaux III; University of Newcastle (Newcastle, Australia), 2020, theses. hal.science, p. 78.
26 George Suttor, *The Culture of Grape-vine, and the Orange, in Australia and New Zealand*, p. 129.
27 John Macarthur Senior to John Macarthur Junior, 24 January 1824, State Library of New South Wales, MLMSS A2899, pp. 94–95.
28 *Some Account of the Vineyards at Camden on the Nepean River, Forty Miles South West of Sydney, the Property of James and William Macarthur*, John Nichols, 1851, p. 3.
29 Sir Edward Macarthur, b. 16 March 1789 (Bath, U.K.), d. 4 January 1872 (London, U.K.).
30 *Ibid.*
31 'Colonial Wines', *The Adelaide Times*, 29 October 1849, p. 3.
32 *Ibid.*

Chapter 20
1 Thomas Hardy, b. 14 January 1830 (Gittisham, Devon, U.K.), d. 10 January 1912 (Adelaide).
2 Gerald Walsh, 'The Wine Industry of Australia 1788–1979', Third wine symposium, August 3–4, 1979, University House, Australian National University, from artserve.anu.edu.au.
3 *Some Account of the Vineyards at Camden on the Nepean River, Forty Miles South West of Sydney, the Property of James and William Macarthur*, John Nichols, 1851, p 10.
4 *Ibid.*, pp. 3–4.
5 *Ibid.*, pp. 7–9.
6 *Ibid.*, pp. 10–11.
7 *Ibid.*, p. 11
8 *The South Australian Register* (Adelaide), 27 June 1850, p. 2.
9 'Magill Village, An historical overview', campbelltown.sa.gov.au.
10 *The Adelaide Times*, 18 October 1850, p. 2.
11 *The South Australian Register* (Adelaide), 25 March 1851, p. 1.
12 *Ibid.*, 9 Sept 1851, p. 1.
13 'The Gold Fever', *The Bathurst Free Press*, 17 May 1851, p. 4.

14 Letter written by Richard Clode to his mother in England, 26 September 1852, SLSA, D 3105(L).
15 'The Gold Fever In New South Wales', *The South Australian Register* (Adelaide), 10 June 1851, p. 2.
16 Stuart Macintyre, *A Concise History of Australia*, Cambridge University Press, 2020, p. 95.
17 'Victorian gold rush and South Australia', State Library of South Australia, digital.collections.slsa.sa.gov.au.
18 'South Australia in Crisis', sbs.com.au.
19 On 13 September 1851.
20 *The Maitland Mercury and Hunter River General Advertiser*, 7 May 1853, p.4.
21 Joseph Best (1830–1887).
22 Henry Best (1832–1913).
23 Richard George Clode (abt. 1815–1892).
24 'Immigration', State Library of South Australia: Passenger Arrivals 'Royal Sovereign 1849'.
25 Letter written by Richard Clode to his mother in England, 26 September 1852, SLSA, D 3105(L).
26 *Ibid*.
27 *Ibid*.
28 *Ibid*.
29 'Ferguson Conservation Park Management Plan: Adelaide – South Australia', cdn.environment.sa.gov.au.
30 'Latest News from the Victoria Diggings', *The South Australian Register* (Adelaide), 15 January 1853, p. 3.
31 *Ibid*.

Chapter 21

1 Kym Anderson, *Growth and Cycles in Australia's Wine Industry, A Statistical Compendium, 1843 to 2013*, The University of Adelaide, 2015, p. 25.
2 H. E. Laffer, *The Wine Industry of Australia*, Australian Wine Board, 1949, pp. 123–5.
3 Gerald Walsh, The Wine Industry of Australia 1788–1979, Wine Talk, A.N.U. Canberra, 1979, artserve.anu.edu.au.
4 Paul Frederic de Castella, b. 22 May 1827 (Neuchatel, Switzerland), d. 14 March 1903 (Fairlie House, South Yarra, Melbourne).
5 'Shipping and Commercial Gazette', *The Port Phillip Gazette and Settler's Journal* (Melbourne), 29 November 1849, p. 2.
6 'A Short History of the House', chateauyering.com.au.
7 In 1863.

8   Charles Hubert de Castella, b. 27 March 1825 (Neuchatel, Switzerland), d. 30 October 1907 (Ivanhoe, Melbourne).
9   Hubert de Castella's great-grandson is the Australian marathon champion Robert de Castella.
10 Hubert de Castella, *Extracts from an English Book on Wine*, Still and Knight, 1877, p. 10. De Castella was quoting Robert Druitt, *Report on the Cheap Wines from France, Germany, Italy, Austria, Greece, Hungary, and Australia: their use in diet and medicine*, H. Renshaw, 1873, p. 86.
11 Hubert de Castella, *Extracts from an English Book on Wine*, Still and Knight, 1877, pp. 12–14.
12 *The South Australian Register* (Adelaide), 6 November 1854, p. 3; 14 November 1854, p. 3.
13 *Ibid*.
14 *Ibid*., 13 December 1854, p. 3.
15 Dr Geoffrey Bishop, 'Mary Penfold and Joseph Gillard Jr: A different view of the Penfolds Wines', Burnside Library, South Australia, 374 T.
16 'East Torrens', *The Adelaide Observer*, 5 May 1855, p. 8.
17 'Reynella – New Township,' *The South Australian Register* (Adelaide), 21 February 1854, p. 4.
18 'Pioneer Vignerons: John Reynell: (1809–1873)', History Trust of South Australia, pir.sa.gov.au.
19 Edward Burton 'Paddy' Gleeson (1803 – 2 February 1870).
20 'Jesuits start the Clare Valley's first winery at Sevenhill in 1850s as part of the district's Catholic heritage', adelaideaz.com.
21 Edward John Peake (1822 – 23 March 1876).
22 Brian Andrews, 'Edward John Peake, artist', Design & Art Australia Online, daao.org.au.
23 'Paris Exhibition – Australian Contributions', *The Sydney Morning Herald*, 9 October 1855, p. 4.
24 William Macarthur to James Macarthur, 12 August 1855, Macarthur Papers, Vol. 38, SLNSW, MLMSS A2934, pp. 98–104.
25 *Ibid*.
26 *Ibid*.
27 *Ibid*.
28 William Macarthur to James Macarthur, 1 September 1855, SLNSW, MLMSS A2934, pp. 120–122.
29 'Paris Exhibition of Arts, Industry, and Science of All Nations', *The Empire* (Sydney, NSW), 28 December 1855, p. 2.
30 'From the Times', *The Sydney Morning Herald*, 4 December 1855, p. 4.

31 'Julie McIntyre', 'Camden to London and Paris: The Role of the Macarthur Family in the Early New South Wales Wine Industry', *History Compass*, Blackwell Publishing, 2007, p. 434, newcastle.edu.au.
32 'Bush Fire', *The South Australian Register* (Adelaide), 24 December 1855, p. 3.
33 *The South Australian Weekly Chronicle* (Adelaide), 1 January 1859, p. 4.
34 'Bush Fire', *The South Australian Register* (Adelaide), 24 December 1855, p. 3.
35 'Inquest on Fires Near Magill', *The Adelaide Observer*, 5 January 1856, p. 3.

Chapter 22
1 *The South Australian Register* (Adelaide) 9 October 1856, p. 3.
2 *The Adelaide Observer*, 11 October 1856, p. 8.
3 *The South Australian Register* (Adelaide), 25 November 1856, p. 4.
4 *Ibid.* 6 January 1857, p. 2.
5 *The Sun* (London), 18 May 1857.
6 Georgina Frances Penfold, b. 14 July 1859 (Bouverie Place, Mt Radford, Exeter, Devon, U.K.), d. June 1871 (Steyning, Sussex, U.K.).
7 'Burnside', *The Adelaide Observer*, 23 August 1856, p. 4.
8 The plaque commemorating the Green Gate Inn is at 450 Greenhill Road, Linden Park.
9 *The South Australian Register* (Adelaide) 25 August 1856, p. 1.
10 *Ibid.*, 13 December 1856, p. 2.
11 *Ibid.*
12 *Ibid.*, 20 June 1857, p. 3.
13 Diary of tours on the continent of Europe, October 1855–September 1856, Macarthur family papers, SLNSW, A2951.
14 Mikaël Pierre, '"France of the southern hemisphere": transferring a European wine model to colonial Australia', History, Université Michel de Montaigne–Bordeaux III; University of Newcastle (Newcastle, Australia), 2020, p. 81.
15 Receipt from Michel Claverie in Paris, 31 December 1860, Macarthur papers, SLNSW, A2969.
16 'Australian Wines – From New South Wales', *The Times*, 20 July 1857.
17 *Ibid.*
18 Death certificate for Ellen Timbrell, Births, Deaths and Marriages Registration Office, Adelaide, 1857/2050.
19 'Family Notices', *The South Australian Register* (Adelaide), 16 September 1857, p. 2.
20 Edwin Arnold, *The Light of Asia, or The Great Renunciation (Mahâbhinishkramana)*, A.L. Burt, 1879.

21 Eve Jolly, The Penfold Cottage Magill, State Library of South Australia, 663.20092 P397.
22 *Ibid.*
23 *Ibid.*
24 *Ibid.*
25 Craig Cook 'South Australia 1858–1890: The boom and bust years that shaped our state', adelaidenow.com.au, 2 July 2018.
26 *The Adelaide Observer*, 6 March 1858, p. 1.
27 'Municipal Corporation', *The South Australian Advertiser* (Adelaide), 7 September 1858, p. 3.
28 *The British Journal*, Aylott & Jones, 1853, p. 143.
29 'Statistics of the Colony of Victoria', 1850 and 1860, Australian Bureau of Statistics, abs.gov.au.
30 *The Adelaide Observer*, 6 March 1858, p. 1.
31 'Shipping Intelligence', *The Argus* (Melbourne), 15 October 1858, p. 4.
32 'Books, Stationery, &c', *The South Australian Advertiser* (Adelaide), 1 January 1859, p. 4.
33 *The South Australian Weekly Chronicle* (Adelaide), 1 January 1859, p. 4.
34 *Ibid.*
35 *The South Australian Register* (Adelaide), 10 February 1859, p. 4.
36 'Shipping Intelligence', *The Argus* (Melbourne), 21 February 1859.
37 'List of Legally Qualified Medical Practitioners 1859,' *The Geelong Advertiser*, 4 February 1859, p. 6.

Chapter 23

1 Christopher Rawson Penfold, Victoria, Australia, Rate Books, 1855–1963, Public Record Office Victoria; North Melbourne, Australia; Series Title: 2336/P Microfilm copy of Rate Books, City of Fitzroy [copy of VPRS 4301] [1858–1901].
2 *The Age* (Melbourne), 26 March 1859, p. 7.
3 'Melbourne panorama', National Museum of Australia, nma.gov.au.
4 *Ibid.*, 18 June 1859, p. 5.
5 'History of the Smallpox Vaccine', World Health Organization, who.int.
6 *Ibid.*
7 'Smallpox Epidemics in Victoria', collections.museumsvictoria.com.au.
8 'A Man Killed At A Wrestling Match', *The Argus* (Melbourne), 26 December 1859, p. 5.
9 'Melbourne Criminal Sessions', *The Age* (Melbourne), 23 February 1860, p. 6.

10 David Packham (9 April 1832 – 4 April 1912). He was a member of the South Australian House of Assembly from 1894 to 1896 representing East Torrens.
11 The South Australian Register (Adelaide), 10 September 1890, p. 4.
12 *The Victorian Farmers Journal and Gardeners Chronicle* (Melbourne), 27 October 1860, p. 6.
13 *The South Australian Register* (Adelaide), 19 September 1861, p. 4.
14 'Australian wine,' *The South Australian Register* (Adelaide), 24 January 1862, p. 3; 'Sale Of Colonial Wine', *The Adelaide Observer*, 1 February 1862, p. 7.
15 François de Castella, 'Early Victorian Winegrowing,' *The Victorian Historical Magazine*, no. 4, 1942, p. 19.
16 François Robert de Castella, 16 January 1867 (South Yarra, Victoria), d. 12 May 1953 (Heidelberg, Melbourne).
17 François de Castella, 'Early Victorian Winegrowing,' *The Victorian Historical Magazine*, no. 4, 1942, p. 146.
18 Craig Cook 'South Australia 1858–1890: The boom and bust years that shaped our state', adelaidenow.com.au, 2 July 2018.
19 A. C. Kelly, *The Vine in Australia*, Sands and Kenny, 1861.
20 Alex C. Kelly, *Wine-growing in Australia: And the Teachings of Modern Writers on Vine-culture and Wine-making*, E.S. Wigg, 1867.
21 Thomas and Alexander Lang Elder, Samuel Davenport, Robert Barr Smith and Edward Stirling.
22 Thomas Francis Hyland, b. December 1831 (Ballynilard, Co. Tipperary, Ireland), d. 1 March 1920 (Moorabbin House, Were St, Brighton, Melbourne, Victoria).
23 'Public Buildings Precinct – HO273', glenelg.vic.gov.au
24 Records of St Michaels Roman Catholic Church Tipperary, Cashel and Emly Tipperary 1822–1833, Ireland, Catholic Parish Registers, 1655–1915.
25 The Australasian (Melbourne), 6 January 1883, p. 19.
26 'The Penal Hulks of Williamstown', *Williamstown Historical Society Newsletter*, No.5, 6 October 1971.
27 Francis McNeiss McNeil McCallum (Captain Melville) (c. 1823 – 10 August 1857).
28 'Criminal Sessions', *The Age* (Melbourne), 20 November 1856, p. 7.
29 'Melville's Defence and Charges Against the Convict Superintendent', *The Perth Gazette and Independent Journal of Politics and News*, 30 January 1857, p. 4.
30 'Melbourne Criminal Sessions', *The Age* (Melbourne), 27 November 1856, p. 5.
31 *The Courier* (Hobart) 27 Nov 1856, p. 2.

32 'Suicide Of Melville', *The Bendigo Advertiser*, 14 Aug 1857, p. 2.
33 'Pentridge Stockade', *The Age* (Melbourne), 6 January 1857, p. 5.
34 'The Williamstown Tragedy', *The Age* (Melbourne), 30 March 1857, p. 5.
35 'The Murder Of Mr. Price', *Mount Alexander Mail* (Victoria), Wednesday 1 April 1857, p. 2.
36 'Funeral Of Mr. Price', *The Age* (Melbourne), 31 Mar 1857, p. 5.
37 'News of the Day', *The Age* (Melbourne), 31 Mar 1857, p. 5.
38 *Ibid.*
39 'Local and General News', *The Ararat and Mount Pleasant Creek Advertiser and Chronicle for the District of the Wimmera* (Victoria), 4 October 1861, p. 2.

Chapter 24

1 'Family Notices', *The Argus* (Melbourne), 27 September 1862, p. 4.
2 Henry Hewett Paulet Handfield, b. 12 December 1828, (Hermitage House, near Dublin, Ireland), d. 8 August 1900 (St Peter's vicarage, Eastern Hill, Melbourne).
3 Victoria, Australia, St. Peter's Eastern Hill, Marriages, Series 03, Certificates 1862.
4 *Ibid.*
5 It wasn't until 1894 that all South Australian women gained the same voting rights as men.
6 Bishop, *The Vineyards of Adelaide*, p. 77.
7 'The Stonyfell Story', stonyfellwines.com.au.
8 Dr Philip Norrie, 'Wine and Health Through the Ages with Special Reference to Australia', p. 147.
9 In 1865.
10 George Marsden Waterhouse, b. 6 April 1824 (Penzance, Cornwall, U.K.), d. 6 August 1906 (Torquay, Devonshire, U.K.)
11 Bishop, *The Vineyards of Adelaide*, p. 21.
12 The site now houses London's Natural History Museum and the Science Museum.
13 Bishop, *The Vineyards of Adelaide*, p. 85.
14 'Our Vineyards and Orchards', *The South Australian Advertiser* (Adelaide), 26 December 1861, p. 4.
15 'Burnside', *The South Australian Advertiser* (Adelaide, SA : 1858–1889), 30 January 1863, p. 3.
16 'The South Australian Vintage of 1875', *The Adelaide Observer*, 19 June 1875, p. 9.
17 *The Adelaide Observer*, 18 April 1863, p. 7.

18 'Shipping News', *The South Australian Weekly Chronicle* (Adelaide), 8 August 1863, p. 2.
19 Inez Kathleen Hyland, b. 16 August 1863 (Portland, Victoria), d. 11 January 1892 (The Grange, Magill, South Australia).
20 'Family Notices', *The Portland Guardian and Normanby General Advertiser* (Victoria), 20 August 1863, p. 2.
21 Dr Geoffrey Bishop, 'Mary Penfold and Joseph Gillard Jr: A different view of the Penfolds Wines', Burnside Library, 374 T.
22 *The South Australian Register* (Adelaide), 22 December 1864, p. 4.
23 'Family Notices', *The South Australian Register* (Adelaide), 11 August 1864, p. 2.
24 The Magill Institute was finally built in 1901 and is at 611 Magill Road.
25 'Family Notices', *The Australasian* (Melbourne), 20 May 1865, p. 8.
26 Deposition of Mary Penfold, Proceedings of Inquest upon the body of Imogene Olivia Ethel Hyland, 12 June 1865, Coroner Inquest Deposition Files, 1840–1925. VPRS 24, Public Record Office Victoria, North Melbourne, Victoria.
27 *Ibid.*
28 Deposition of Thomas Hyland, *Ibid.*
29 *Ibid.*

Chapter 25

1 The South Australian Weekly Chronicle (Adelaide), 3 March 1866, p. 2.
2 Louis Pasteur, Études Sur Le Vin [Wine Studies], A L'imprimerie Impériale, 1866.
3 'Pioneer Vignerons: John Reynell', adelaidia.sa.gov.au.
4 'Pioneer Vignerons: Thomas Hardy', adelaidia.sa.gov.au.
5 George Francis Morris, b. 1834 (Warrington, Lancashire, U.K.), d. 8 January 1910 (Toorak, Melbourne).
6 'Dr. Lindeman', *The Maitland Mercury and Hunter River General Advertiser*, 24 May 1873, p. 2.
7 Henry Lindeman, *The Sydney Morning Herald*, 25 December 1867, p. 2.
8 Gerald Walsh, 'The Wine Industry of Australia 1788–1979', Third wine symposium, August 3–4 1979, University House, Australian National University, from artserve.anu.edu.au.
9 Joseph Ernst Seppelt, b. 1813 (Wüstewaltersdorf, Prussia), d. 29 January 1868 (Seppeltsfield, South Australia).
10 John Roberts Sr (12 June 1823 – 27 March 1893).
11 'The Champion Billiard Matches', *The South Australian Advertiser* (Adelaide), 10 March 1865, p. 3.

12 *The Express and Telegraph* (Adelaide), 26 Aug 1867, p. 1.
13 'Death Of Dr. Bayer', *The South Australian Register* (Adelaide), 28 August 1867, p. 2.
14 'Melbourne: Intercolonial Exhibition of Australasia 1866–67', guides.slv.vic.gov.au.
15 'Intercolonial Exhibition 1866: official catalogue', guides.slv.vic.gov.au.
16 Joseph Gillard Sr, b. 24 December 1820 (Belstone, Devon, U.K.), d. 11 January 1897 (Clarendon, South Australia).
17 'Death Of An Old Colonist', *The Advertiser* (Adelaide), 12 January 1897, p. 6.
18 'Royal Visit And Colonial Loyalty', *The South Australian Register* (Adelaide), 1 November 1867, p. 2.
19 'The Illuminations', *The South Australian Advertiser* (Adelaide), 1 November 1867, p. 2.
20 'Visit of H.R.H. The Duke of Edinburgh', *The South Australian Weekly Chronicle* (Adelaide), 16 November 1867, p. 6.
21 'The Protestant Hall Outrage', *The Age* (Melbourne), 19 December 1867, p. 5.
22 'The Duke of Edinburgh in Melbourne', *The Argus* (Melbourne), 29 November 1867, p. 5.
23 *Ibid.*
24 'Sandhurst In Mourning', *The Age* (Melbourne) 23 December 1867, p. 6.
25 Henry James O'Farrell (1833 – 21 April 1868).
26 Intercolonial Exhibition 1866–67: Official Record, Published by the Exhibition Commissioners, 1867, p. 273.
27 *Ibid.*, p. 289.
28 *Ibid.*
29 *Ibid.*, p. 290.
30 *Ibid.*
31 John Ignatius Bleasdale, b. 1822 (Kirkham, Lancashire, U.K.), d. 28 June 1884 (San Francisco, U.S.A.).
32 J.I. Bleasdale. 'On colonial wines', *Transactions and Proceedings of the Royal Society of Victoria* 1867, Vol. VIII, pp. 53–72.

Chapter 26
1 'Complimentary lunch to Dr. Bleasdale', *The South Australian Register* (Adelaide), 20 December 1867, p. 3.
2 *Ibid.*
3 *Ibid.*
4 *Ibid.*

5   K. T. H. Farrer, 'The Rev Dr J. I. Bleasdale and the Medical Society of Victoria', *Journal of the Royal Society of Medicine*, Volume 86, March 1993, p. 167.
6   *The Express and Telegraph* (Adelaide), 23 July 1868, p. 1.
7   *The South Australian Advertiser* (Adelaide), 14 July 1868, p. 2.
8   *The Express and Telegraph* (Adelaide), 23 July 1868, p. 1.
9   *Ibid.*
10 *Ibid.*, 3 April 1868, p. 2.
11 *The South Australian Register* (Adelaide), 22 June 1868, p. 2.
12 'Family Notices', *The Argus* (Melbourne) 26 August 1868, p. 4.
13 'Shipping News', The Express and Telegraph (Adelaide), 21 October 1868, p. 2.
14 Thomas Hyland to Mary Penfold, 9 May 1870, Penfolds Wines Property Records, State Library of South Australia, BRG 330/6.
15 Shipping News', *The Express and Telegraph* (Adelaide), 21 October 1868, 11 November 1868, p. 2.
16 *Ibid.*, 23 October 1868, p. 2.
17 Joseph Gillard Jr, b. 17 July 1846 (Devon, U.K.), d. 22 May 1927 (Magill, South Australia).
18 Fanny Gillard, nee Rose, b. 26 January 1846 (No. I Sheep Station On The Sturt, South Australia), d. 24 August 1931 (Magill, South Australia).
19 William George Gillard, b. 11 May 1869 (Magill, South Australia), d. 30 October 1949 (Norwood, South Australia).
20 'Death of an Old Colonist', *The Advertiser* (Adelaide), 12 January 1897, p. 6.
21 Geoffrey C. Bishop, *Myth And Fact In Penfold History*, Burnside Historical Society Inc, June 1987 Supplement, burnsidehistory.org.au.
22 *The Ballarat Star*, 15 January 1869, p. 2.
23 'The Castlemaine Gaol Is Hell', *The Tarrangower Times and Maldon, Newstead, Baringhup, Laancoorie and Muckleford Advertiser* (Victoria), 19 April 1890, p. 2.
24 *The Geelong Advertiser*, 1 January 1870, p. 2.
25 Hubert de Castella, *John Bull's Vineyard*, Sands & McDougall, 1886, p.170.
26 Gerald Walsh, 'The Wine Industry of Australia 1788–1979', Third wine symposium, August 3–4 1979, University House, Australian National University, from artserve.anu.edu.au.
27 *The Evening Journal* (Adelaide), 21 January 1870, p. 2.
28 'Adelaide Vignerons' Club', *The South Australian Advertiser*, 16 February 1870, p. 3.
29 'Family Notices', The Express and Telegraph (Adelaide), 28 March 1870, p. 2.

Chapter 27

1. *The Evening Journal* (Adelaide) 30 March 1870, p. 2.
2. *Ibid.*
3. Death certificate for Christopher Rawson Penfold, Births, Deaths and Marriages Registration Office, Adelaide, 1977/1870.
4. *The Evening Journal* (Adelaide) 30 March 1870, p. 2.
5. Eve Jolly, The Penfold Cottage Magill, State Library of South Australia, 663.20092 P397.
6. 'Shipping News', *The Adelaide Observer*, 22 September 1877, p. 2.
7. Bills and accounts, Penfolds Wines Property Records, State Library of South Australia, BRG 330/6.
8. Thomas Hyland to Mary Penfold, 9 May 1870, Penfolds Wines Property Records, State Library of South Australia, BRG 330/6.
9. *Ibid.*
10. *Ibid.*
11. 'Execution of Ah Pew', *The Argus* (Melbourne), 24 May 1870, p. 7.
12. *The Evening Journal* (Adelaide), 12 November 1870, p. 1.
13. Henry Lindeman, *New South Wales Medical Gazette*, July 1872, Lindeman (Holdings) Ltd. Papers, Z418/Box 157, Noel Butlin Archives Centre, Australian National University.
14. *Ibid.*
15. 'Family Notices', *The Age* (Melbourne), 21 June 1871, p. 2.
16. 'Family Notices', *The Argus* (Melbourne), 29 July 1871, p. 4.
17. Ann Margaret Bickford, nee Garrett, b. 11 February 1810 (London, England), d. 24 January 1877 (Brighton, South Australia).
18. *The Express and Telegraph* (Adelaide), 8 November 1871, p. 4.
19. 'Shipping Intelligence', *The South Australian Register* (Adelaide), 24 October 1872, p. 4.
20. Eve Jolly, The Penfold Cottage Magill, State Library of South Australia, 663.20092 P397.
21. *Ibid.*

Chapter 28

1. 'Mrs. Penfold's Wine Manufactory Magill' *The South Australian Register* (Adelaide), 4 June 1874, p. 3.
2. Peter Bond Burgoyne (11 February 1844 – 4 September 1929) .
3. *The Adelaide Observer*, 9 May 1874, p. 7.
4. 'A Model Prison', *The Age* (Melbourne), 4 May 1872, p. 6.
5. Eve Jolly, *The Penfold Cottage Magill*, State Library of South Australia, 663.20092 P397.

6 James Wilkie, on 20 May 1872 for a murder at Daylesford, and Samuel Wright on 11 March 1873, for attempted murder at Dead Horse Flat, near Eaglehawk.
7 Frank Astor Penfold Hyland, b. 4 March 1873 (Castlemaine, Victoria), d. 17 December 1948 (Sydney, New South Wales).
8 *The Express and Telegraph* (Adelaide), 26 February 1874, p. 4.
9 'Mrs. Penfold's Wine Manufactory Magill', *The South Australian Register* (Adelaide), 4 June 1874, p. 3.
10 *Ibid.*
11 *Ibid.*
12 *Ibid.*
13 *Ibid.*
14 *Ibid.*
15 'Australian Affairs In England', *The Adelaide Observer*, 27 June 1874, p. 4.
16 'The South Australian Vintage of 1875', *The Adelaide Observer*, 19 June 1875, p. 9.
17 *Ibid.*
18 *Ibid.*

Chapter 29

1 Herbert Leslie Penfold Hyland, b. 4 March 1875 (Castlemaine, Victoria), d. 7 May 1940 (Adelaide, South Australia).
2 Vivien Dolores Hyland, b. August 1877 (Castlemaine, Victoria), d. 12 December 1877 (Castlemaine, Victoria).
3 Births, Deaths and Marriages Victoria, 10426/1877.
4 'Family Notices', *Mount Alexander Mail* (Victoria), 27 December 1877, p. 2.
5 *The Argus* (Melbourne), 15 June 1876, p. 4.
6 *Ibid.*
7 'Execution of Duffus', *The Kyneton Guardian* (Victoria), 24 May 1876, p. 2.
8 'Previous Executioners in Victoria', *The Age* (Melbourne), 13 January 1894, p. 13.
9 Castieau diary, 30 December 1874, from Mark Finnane, ed., *The Difficulties Of My Position: The Diaries of Prison Governor John Buckley Castieau 1855–1884*, National Library of Australia, 2004, p. 276.
10 'Previous Executioners In Victoria', *The Age* (Melbourne), 13 January 1894, p. 13.
11 *Ibid.*
12 'Execution of Duffus', *The Kyneton Guardian* (Victoria), 24 May 1876, p. 2.
13 'Oidium Tuckeri', *The Adelaide Observer*, 15 January 1876, p. 6.

14 'The Vintage Of 1878', *The South Australian Register* (Adelaide), 10 July 1878, p. 6.
15 'The Year's Retrospect', *The South Australian Advertiser* (Adelaide), 1 January 1877, p. 5.
16 *Ibid.*
17 Cindie Smart, '125 years for Vinehealth Australia', vinehealth.com.au.
18 'The Vine Scourge In Australia', *The Argus* (Melbourne), 8 December 1877, p. 9.
19 Wally Boehm, *The Phylloxera Fight: Protecting South Australia from the Phylloxera Threat*, Winetitles, 1996, p. 14.
20 Samuel McWilliam, b. 15 April 1830 (Raloo, near Larne, County Antrim, Northern Ireland), d. 2 June 1902 (Sydney, N.S.W.).
21 Andrew Caillard, 'The Australian Ark: The storied history of Australia's pre-phylloxera grapevines', worldoffinewine.com.
22 'Lady's Letter', *Melbourne Punch*, 28 January 1892, p. 13.
23 'Shipping Summary For England', *The South Australian Advertiser* (Adelaide), 29 December 1877, p. 2.
24 'Advertising', *The South Australian Register* (Adelaide), 22 March 1878, p. 3.
25 *The Express and Telegraph* (Adelaide), 19 March 1878, p. 1.
26 'The Vintage Of 1878', *The South Australian Register* (Adelaide), 10 July 1878, p. 6.
27 *The Brisbane Courier*, 13 November 1878, p. 1.
28 *Ibid.*
29 'The Paris Exhibition', *The Adelaide Observer*, 9 November 1878, p. 19.
30 *The South Australian Register* (Adelaide), 2 January 1879, p. 2.
31 'The population census—a brief history', *Year Book Australia, 2005*, Australian Bureau of Statistics. 2005.
32 'Vinegrowing and Winemaking in South Australia. The Magill Vineyards. The Grange', *The Express and Telegraph* (Adelaide), 5 March 1879, p. 3.
33 *Ibid.*
34 *Ibid.*
35 *Ibid.*
36 *Ibid.*
37 *Ibid.*

Chapter 30
1 'Union Of The Southern Colonies Under A Governor-General', *The Southern Australian* (Adelaide), 10 June 1842, p. 3.
2 *The South Australian Advertiser* (Adelaide), 10 November 1879, p. 5.
3 *Ibid.*

4   Sir Robert Dalrymple Ross (1827–1887).
5   *The South Australian Advertiser* (Adelaide), 10 November 1879, p. 5.
6   'Orchard and Vineyard', *The Adelaide Observer*, 15 November 1879, p. 9.
7   *Ibid*.
8   'Deputations', *The South Australian Chronicle and Weekly Mail* (Adelaide), 6 December 1879, p. 2.
9   *Ibid*.
10 *Ibid*.
11 'The Vintage of 1880', *The South Australian Register* (Adelaide), 3 July 1880, Supplement p. 1.
12 'Burning of The Garden Palace', *Illustrated Sydney News*, 25 October 1882, p. 1.
13 £200,000 was enough to buy more than 200 Sydney houses at that time.
14 'South Australian Wines at the Sydney Exhibition', *The Adelaide Observer*, 28 February 1880, p. 32.
15 *The Advertiser* (Adelaide), 17 July 1893, p. 6.
16 'Mary Penfold', The Woman Who Dared To Do It Differently', penfolds.com.
17 *The Mount Alexander Mail* (Victoria), 26 May 1881, p. 2.
18 *Ibid*. 15 July 1881, p. 2.
19 *Ibid*., 21 July 1881, p. 2.
20 'An Old Time House', *The Argus* (Melbourne), 26 April 1924, p. 5.
21 *Ibid*.
22 'Historic Home', *The Herald* (Melbourne), 1 May 1924, p. 9.
23 'An Old Time House', *The Argus* (Melbourne), 26 April 1924, p. 5.
24 Agreement between Mary Penfold and Thomas Francis Hyland, Penfolds Wines Property Records, State Library of South Australia, BRG 330/6.
25 *Ibid*.
26 *Ibid*.

Chapter 31

1   Giffard Edmund Hampton Bannister, b. 1855 (St Helier, Jersey, Channel Islands), d. 1911 (Adelaide, South Australia).
2   'Railway Freight On Colonial Wine', *The Sydney Morning Herald*, 22 January 1884, p. 7.
3   *The Brisbane Courier*, 7 October 1884, p. 4.
4   'The Colonial and Indian Exhibition', *The Express and Telegraph* (Adelaide), 5 July 1886, p. 3.
5   *Ibid*., 21 July 1886, p. 6.
6   'South Australian Wines In England', *The South Australian Advertiser* (Adelaide), 30 July 1886, p. 6.

7   Sir Henry Ayers (1 May 1821 – 11 June 1897).
8   Sir Thomas Elder (5 August 1818 – 6 March 1897).
9   Sir Edwin Thomas Smith (1830–1919).
10 Vice Regal Visit to Penfold's Vineyards', *The Express and Telegraph* (Adelaide), 8 December 1886, p. 7.
11 *The Sydney Morning Herald*, 13 July 1946, p. 4.
12 Vice Regal Visit to Penfold's Vineyards', *The Express and Telegraph* (Adelaide), 8 December 1886, p. 7.
13 'Orchard & Vineyard', *The Adelaide Observer*, 11 December 1886, p. 11.
14 *Ibid.*
15 'Orchard & Vineyard', *The Adelaide Observer*, 11 December 1886, p. 11.
16 'Vice Regal Visit to Penfold's Vineyards', *The Express and Telegraph* (Adelaide), 8 December 1886, p. 7.
17 *Ibid.*
18 'Vice Regal Visit to Penfold's Vineyards', *The Express and Telegraph* (Adelaide), 8 December 1886, p. 7.
19 'Visit to Penfold's Vineyard', *The South Australian Advertiser* (Adelaide), 1 April 1887, p. 6.
20 *Ibid.*
21 'Anglo-Colonial Gossip', *The Evening Journal* (Adelaide), 14 February 1888, p. 2.
22 *The South Australian Police Gazette*, 25 July 1894, p. 119; The Daily News (Perth, WA), 7 October 1896, p. 3.
23 'Family Notices', *The Argus* (Melbourne), 24 August 1889, p. 1.
24 Major Royston Engleheart Knight, b. 30 September 1890 (Melbourne, Australia), d. 2 January 1973 (Bexley, Kent, U.K.).
25 Mary Penfold to Leslie Hyland, c. 1886, The Penfold Cottage Magill, State Library of South Australia, 663.20092.
26 *Ibid.*
27 'Passengers to and from Melbourne', *The South Australian Advertiser* (Adelaide), 17 January 1889, p. 5.
28 'The Eiffel Tower', *The Times*, 1 April 1889, p. 5.
29 *L'Exposition de 1889 et la tour Eiffel, d'après les documents officiels*. 1889. pp. 165–166.
30 'Our Wines at the Paris Exhibition', *The Express and Telegraph* (Adelaide), 15 August 1889, p. 3.
31 *Ibid.*
32 *Ibid.*
33 *Ibid.*
34 *Ibid.*

35 *The Advertiser* (Adelaide), 24 August 1889, p. 4.
36 'Visit To The Grange Vineyard, Magill', *The Australian Advertiser* (Albany, W.A.), 10 December 1890, p. 3.
37 William Thomas Angove (1854–1912).
38 'William Angove's Tea Tree Gully vineyard follows other Adelaide doctors Kelly, Penfold into making wine tonic', adelaideaz.com.
39 John Riddoch (27 October 1827 – 15 July 1901).
40 *The Advertiser* (Adelaide), 15 August 1891, p. 2.
41 'Pharoah Lives For Ever', *The Adelaide Observer*, 29 August 1891, p. 15.
42 'Dot Confides To A Friend', *Quiz and the Lantern* (Adelaide), 2 October 1891, p. 15.

Chapter 32
1 Death Certificate of Inez Kathleen Hyland, South Australia Births, Deaths and Marriages, 1892/393.
2 *Quiz and the Lantern* (Adelaide), 2 October 1891, 15 January 1892, p. 10.
3 *Melbourne Punch*, 28 January 1892, p. 13.
4 *Ibid*.
5 'Family Notices', The Evening Journal (Adelaide), 11 January 1892, p. 2.
6 'Obituary', *ibid.*, 13 January 1892, p. 2.
7 Death Certificate of Inez Kathleen Hyland, South Australian Births, Deaths and Marriages, 1892/393.
8 Headstone of Inez Hyland, St George's churchyard.
9 'Obituary', The Evening Journal (Adelaide), 13 January 1892, p. 2.
10 *Ibid.*, 4 July 1893, p. 2.
11 'A Lily's Shadow', Inez K. Hyland, *In Sunshine and in Shadow*, George Robertson and Company, 1893, p. 3.
12 *The South Australian Register* (Adelaide), 27 January 1892, p. 8.
13 *Ibid*.
14 Death Certificate of Mary Penfold, Victorian Births, Deaths and Marriages, 1896/3481.
15 'Obituary', *The Evening Journal* (Adelaide), 3 January 1896, p. 2.
16 'The Late Mrs. Mary Penfold', *The Advertiser* (Adelaide), 3 January 1896, p. 6.

Epilogue
1 Last Will and Testament of Mary Penfold, Wills and Probate Records, 1841–2009, Supreme Court of Victoria, 62/376.
2 'The Wine Industry', *The Inquirer and Commercial News* (Perth) 7 February 1896, p. 6.
3 Oswald Ziegler, *The Penfold Story*, p. 26

4   Their headstones hyphenate their names as Penfold-Hyland.
5   'The Victorian Golf Championship', *The Weekly Times* (Melbourne), 21 September 1901, p. 9.
6   Hermann Paul Leopold Büring (7 October 1876 – 29 September 1961).
7   'Historic Home: Moorabbin House To Be Demolished', *The Herald* (Melbourne), 1 May 1924, p. 9.
8   'Death Of Mr. Penfold', The Advertiser (Adelaide), 7 May 1940, p. 16.
9   Oswald Ziegler, *The Penfold Story*, p. 31.
10 Léon Edmond Mazure (1860–1939).
11 Gladys Penfold Hyland nee Lethbridge (1886–1974).
12 Rada Penfold Hyland (1922–1980).
13 Jeffrey Penfold Hyland OBE (1911–1990).
14 penfolds.com.
15 Max Schubert (9 February 1915 – 6 March 1994).
16 'Winery farewells foreman with 65 years' service', The Burnside News-Review, January 1959, p. 7.
17 Oswald Ziegler, *The Penfold Story*, p. 51.

Appendix
1   Penfold Family Tree, Personal papers of Christopher Rawson Penfold and Mary Penfold and family, SLSA, BRG 330/1.

Index

Note: MP = Mary Penfold. Page numbers in *italics* refer to images and captions.

Aboriginal Australians 21–2, 26, 89, 91, 122–4, 128, 166, 199, 307
Adelaide 91–2, 98–9, 108, 121–3, 125, 175–6, 273–4
Adelaide Hills 123, 125, 135, 219
Adelaide Hospital 156, 246
The Adelaide Observer 125, 141, 148, 150, 267, 280, 296
Adelaide Oval 3, 259
Adelaide, Queen 91
Adelaide School of Mines 308
Adelaide Steamship Company 307
Adelaide Vignerons' Club 251, 280–1
Admella (ship) 218
Adventure Bay 25–6
The Adventures of Priscilla, Queen of the Desert (film) 307
Africaine (ship) 135
The Age 226, 228, 261
Agricultural and Horticultural Exhibition (1845) 140–1, *142*
Agricultural and Horticultural Exhibition (1846) 162–4
Agricultural and Horticultural Society of South Australia 137, 143
Agricultural Society of New South Wales 62
Ah Pew 255–6
Albert, Prince 103, 162, 208
Albury 238
Alder, James 171–2
Alexander (ship) 17
Alfred, King 67
Alfred, Prince 239–41, *240*
Alice Brooks (ship) 107
Alice, Princess 105

A.M. Bickford & Sons 258
America, British colonies in 11–12
American Revolution (1776) 12–14, 28
Ancient Egypt 10, 296
Ancient Greece 10, 62
Ancient Rome 10–11, 62
Anderson, William Acland 222
Angas, George Fife 121–2, 167
Angaston 167, 178, 198
Anglican Church of St George 165, 170, 174–7, 179, 232, 252, 298, 302, 307
Angmering 69
Angove, William Thomas 296
Anstey, George 137, 162, 164, 231
anthracnose 28, 55
apothecaries 66
Apothecaries Act (1815) 66
Arabanoo (Eora man) 26
Ararat 198
Aristides (ship) 273
art 124
Arthur, George 60
Association for the Introduction of Vines to South Australia 101
Astor & Horwood 41
Astor, Elizabeth Dorothea (née Wright) (MP's grandmother) 12, 14, 23
Astor, George (MP's grandfather)
 as an instrument maker and seller 12, *13*, 14, 31–4, 40, 49, 113, 218
 becomes British subject 34
 becomes father of third daughter 23
 death 41
 gives painting of Jesus to children 49, 96
 moves to Cornhill Road 34
 moves to London from Germany 8–9
 reads of First Fleet 18
Astor, Johann Jakob 'John' (MP's great-uncle) 12, 14–15, 184–5

Astorhaus, Walldorf 32, 185
Astoria, in Queens, New York 185
aucerot 188, 207
Augustus Frederick, Prince 55–6, 67
Augustus (ship) 155, 159
Auld, Agnes 135
Auld, Eliza 135
Auld, Georgiana 135
Auld, Patrick 135, 209, 213, 231, 237, 260
Auld, William Patrick 135, 237
Auldana vineyard 135, 239, 306
Austen, Jane 20
Australian Agricultural Company 58
Australian National University 32
Australian Wine Company 260
Ayers, Henry 288–9

Baboo (ship) 156
Bacchus 11
Bach, Johann Christian 8
Ballarat 196–7
Balmain, William 17, 27
Bamford, William 255, 269
Banfield, T.C. 186–8
Banks, Sir Joseph 9–12, 16–18, 20, 27–30, 35–8, 44, 51, 58
Bankside vineyard 205, 214, 231, 239
Bannister, Gifford 287, 289–92
banns 80
Barkly Hotel, Carlton 221
Baroncelli, Catherine (née Penfold) (MP's sister-in-law) 75, 233
Baroncelli, Giovanni 76, 80–1, 153–5
Barossa Valley 146, 166–7, 178, 205, 238, 246, 306
Barrabool Hills 157, 243
Barrier Range 147
Barrossa Ridge, Andalusia 166
Bass, George 37
Bassett, Samuel 238
Bathurst 195
The Bathurst Free Press 195
Batman, John 87
Battle of Parramatta 36
Battle of the Basque Roads 41
Battle of Waterloo 42, 134
Baudin, Nicolas 88
Baulkham Hills 38
Bay of Biscay 119
Bayer, Friedrich 182–3, *183*, 184, 238–9
Bayne, Elizabeth 165, 177, 184
Bayne, Fred 165, 175, 177, 183–5
Becquerel, Antoine César 76
Bedford Square, London 68
Beethoven, Ludwig van 8
Belfast (ship) 86

Belmont, August 96
Belmont Stakes 96
Bendigo 196, 241, 271
Bennelong (Wangal man) 26–7, 35
Beresford, Gilbert 82
Berry, Graham 279
Best, Henry 198
Best, Joseph 198
Bethanien (Bethany) 166
Bethell, Richard 153–5
Bible 10
Bickford, Ann 258
black cluster 73, 100, 202
black frontignac 38
black Hamburg 63, 73, 100, 270
black muscat 192–3
black Portugal 63, 230, 275
black rot 52
Black, William 114–15, 117, 119–20, 144
Blaxland, Gregory 44–7, *45*, 55–6, 67, 87
Blaxland, John 46
Bleasdale, John 243–6, 248
Bleng (ship) 160
Bligh, William 25–6, 40, 45, 51, 58
blight 47, 53, 55
blood and bone 212
'the Bloody Code' 13
Blue Mountains 46, 195
Blumenbach, Johann Friedrich 35–6, 58
Board of Ordnance (UK) 117
body snatchers 77
Bonaparte, Napoleon 20, 41–2, 51
books, on winemaking 156–7, 223
Bordeaux wines 213
Borradaile & Co. 102
Botany Bay 11, 17, 21–2
Bounty (ship) 25
Bourke, Sir Richard 71
Box, Thomas 103
Bradley, William 25
brandy 11, 172–3, 192
Branxton 72
Breschet, Gilbert 76
Brewer, Henry Edward 235
Brighton, Adelaide 216
Brighton, England 64, 69, 74, 83–6, 93, 102–3, 105, 285
The Brighton Gazette 105
Brighton, Melbourne 284, 292, 301–2
Britain 8, 12–14, 16, 190, 202, 260
broadsides 89
Broadwood, John 8
Brobdignagian Falstaff (wine vat) 296
Bromley, Edward Foord 60
Bronte 187
Brontë, Charlotte 194

Brooks Brothers 96
Brooks, Mary Anne 70
Brooks, Thomas 68
Broughton, Bartholomew 59–62
Brown, Lindsey 237
Bruny Island 25
Brush Farm 45–6, 55
Buffalo (ship) 91
Bulbeck, Martha 94
Bulbeck, William 93–4
Bungaree Station 206
Bungil Creek 238
Buninyong 196
Burgoyne, P.B. 260, 288
Burgundy 214, 222, 309
burgundy wine 38, 47, 63, 142–3, 167, 187
Buring, Leo 306
Burke, William 77
Burnside Council 212
Burra 197
Busby, James 56–8, 57, 72, 101
bush remedies 152
bushfires 201, 209–10, 251

cabernet 205, 230, 291
cabernet sauvignon 188
Calcutta 81
Californian gold rush 196
Camden Park 51, 53, 57, 72, 88, 137, 142, 157, 189
Campbell, Charles 194
Campbellfield, Sydney 62
Canary Islands 18
Cape Jaffa 122
Cape of Good Hope 43–4, 136, 142, 190
Cape Town 19–20, 29–30, 110
Carcavelos wine 9
carignan 72
Carroll, Lewis 194
Carte Blanche (hock) 167
Casanova, Giacomo 20
Castlemaine 196, 251, 257, 284
Castlemaine Gaol 250, 255, 261–2, 268–70, 284
Cathedral of St Francis Xavier, Adelaide 206
Catholics 205–6, 241
Cawarra Estate 110, 197
cellars 230–1, 276
C.G. Gurr & Co. 301
Chambers Rosewood vineyard 237
Champagne Growers' Syndicate 295
chardonnay 72
Charlotte (ship) 20
chasselas 101
Château Haut-Brion 213

Château Lafite 222
Château Lafite Rothschild 213, 309
Château Latour 213, 309
Château Margaux 213, 309
Château Mouton Rothschild 213
chenin blanc 20
Chertsey 233
Chichester, Earl of 103
Chichester Gardens 99
Chiltern 237
cider 40
Clare 206
Clare Valley 205
Clarendon 136, 206, 231, 239, 244, 246, 286
claret 43, 167, 306–7
Clark, Henry 230
Clarke, Richard 250
climate 24, 42–3
climate change 7
Clode, Richard 198–201
clothes 49–50, 69, 85–6
Clunes 196
Cock, Robert 91–2, 95, 125
Collingwood Stockade 228
Collins, David 19–20, 22–3, 30, 35, 37
Colonial and Indian Exhibition, London (1886) 287–8
Colonial Land and Emigration Commission 112–13, 115
The Colonial Times and Tasmanian Advertiser 60–1
Colt, Samuel 194
The Commander in Chief Shiraz Cabernet 308
Constantia 19–20, 38, 46–7, 73, 142, 205
convicts 40, 71, 224–7
Cook, James 2, 9–11, 105–6
Coonawarra 296
copper mining 146, 197
corks 11
corkscrews 11
Coromandel Valley 124
Corowa 237, 272
Craigend Estate 157
Craigmoor vineyard 238
crime, in Britain 8, 13
Crimean War 208
Cruz, Christian 309
Crystal Palace, London 191
The Culture of the Grape-vine and the Orange in Australia and New Zealand (Suttor) 157
Curnew, William 185
Cuthmann, Saint 67

Daguerre, Louis 110
Dalry Station 203

Dalwood Estate 73, 306
Damascus 100
Daniels, Daniel 71
Darling, Ralph 88
Darling River 147
Darug people 28
Darwin, Charles 194
d'Auvergne, Jean 157
Davis, Abraham 101, 141–2
Davoren, John 307
de Castella, François 222
de Castella, Hubert 203–4, 222, 237, 250
de Castella, Paul 202–3, 222, 237
De Freitas, Ana 62
de Pury, Baron Guillaume 203, 237
de Pury, Samuel 203
de Riveau, Francois 38–40
death penalty 13
Delhi (ship) 136
Dempster, George 113, 129, 168
Derwent (ship) 176
Derwent River 37
Devine, Nicholas 40
diabetes 252
Dickens, Charles 20, 194, 217
Dionysus 10
distilled beverages 37, 39
District Council of East Torrens 204
'The Divine Fisherman' (painting) 49, 96
Doradilla 178, 230–1, 267
Douglas Park 157
douro 142
Duff, John Finlay 135, 163, 165
Duffield, Walter 143, 162–3, *163*, 164
Duffus, John 268–70
Dufour, John James 45, 51–2
Dutch East India Company 239
Dutch East Indies 43
duty *see* tariffs, on wine

earthquakes 116–17
East India Company 70, 105–6, 156, 161
East Torrens Hotel 206, 210, 248
Eastern Hill 230
Echunga 142, 162
Echunga Springs 99–100, *100*
Eden Valley 167, 178, 246
Edward, Prince of Wales 105
Eiffel, Gustave 293
Eiffel Tower 293–4, *294*
Elba 51
Elborne, Henry Goode 97
Elder, Thomas 288
Elizabeth Farm 34
Elizabeth Moore (ship) 102
Emu Wine Co. Ltd 260

Endeavour (ship) 1, 9–12, 16, 44
Eora people 21–2, 26, 307
Eremont Arms Hotel, Brighton 93
An Essay on the Making of Wine (Henderson) 157
Ethelwulf, King 67
Evening Journal 252, 298
Evington Cottage 164, 168–9
Ewell Farm 101, 178
The Examiner 154
Exeter (ship) 106
exploration 117, *127*, 127–8, 147–8
exporting 202, 205, 208, 260, 273
The Express and Telegraph 274, 290
Eyre Peninsula 137

Fairfield vineyard 237
Faraday, Michael 194
farming, in the early colony 30
Federation 305
Ferguson, William 91–2, 95, 125
fermentation 187, 236, 264
Field of Mars 36
Fifeshire, Scotland 92
fire, in land management 123
First Fleet 1, 17–23
FitzRoy, Sir Charles Augustus 186
Fletcher, Roby 296
Flinders, Matthew 26, 37, 88
food 80–1
fortified wines 18–19
Fortitude (ship) 135
Fortitude Valley, Queensland 135
Foster's Group 307
France 4, 41, 43, 51–2, 57–8, 114, 208, 214, 271, 281, 309
Franklin, Benjamin 14
free settlers 88–9
French Revolution 293
'From 1844 to Evermore' (advertising slogan) 289
frontignac 38, 164, 173, 192–3, 232, 266, 273, 275, 283, 291
Frost, John 116
Frost, Mary 116
Fulham 101
Fyansford 271

Galatea (ship) 239
Garden Palace, Sydney 282–3, *283*
Gately, Michael 269
Gawler, George 101, 120–2, 134
Gawler Place 173
Geelong 157, 200, 241, 243, 250, 271
Gehrigs vineyard 237
George III, King 12, 17, 49

George IV, King 49, 64, 84, 86
George and John Astor (company) 12
George Astor & Co. 31
George Robertson & Co. 299
George Washington (ship) 121
German migrants 121–2, 157, 167–8, 189–90, 205–6
German wine 43
Gilbert, Joseph 167
Gilbert, Thomas 161
Gill, Reverend Samuel 124
Gill, S.T. 124, 127, *127*, 135, 141, 197
Gillard, Joseph Jnr
  as vineyard manager 270, 275–6, 282
  begins working at The Grange 249–50, 258–9
  business partnership with MP and Hyland 285–6
  buys land at Rosslyn Park 290
  gives Governor tour of The Grange 289–91
  gives reporters tour of The Grange 263, 265
  taught winemaking by father 239
  uses sulphur to combat fungus 270
Gillard, Joseph Snr 239, 249, 270, 286
Gilles, Osmond 146
Gleeson, Paddy 205
Glen Osmond 122
Glen Osmond Union Mining Company 146
Glenelg 101, 178, 239
Glenelg River 199
gold rushes 195–201, 204, 217, 220
Goold, Archbishop James Alipius 284
Gooramadda vineyard 237
Gordon, Robert 20
Gosport 68
gouais 63, 73, 205
Gould, John 98–9
Government House, Adelaide 124
Government House, Sydney 25
Gramp, Johann 121, 166–7, *167*
Grampians 198
The Grange (cottage) 1, 131–2, *132*, 145
The Grange Estate
  as a playground for children 174
  Chris and Mary Penfold plant The Grange Vineyard 133–4
  Chris Penfold advertises sale of 217, 222
  development encroaches upon 274
  dispute over building work done at 168, 171–2
  expands as demand grows 173, 295–6
  locally sourced cuttings planted at 148
  MP as commander in chief of 256, 262

MP gives Governor tour of 289–90
MP gives reporters tour of 274–6
MP increases production at 258
MP oversees building work 254
MP sells off surplus land 258
Penfolds auction off animals and equipment 217
Penfolds rent out 221–2
potential for expansion of 201
process of winemaking at 264–6
Register publishes article on 262–6
vines still in use today 307
vineyard and winemaking operation 272
visit by John Bleasdale 244
visit by Sir William Robinson 288–91
The Grange (wine) 309
grapes 30, 100–1, 141–2, 187, 266
grave robbers 77
Gravesend 115, 117, 212
Great Exhibition, London (1851) 191–2, 194
Great Western region 198
Green Gate Inn 212
green malaga 73
grenache 72, 169, 178, 230–1, 267, 273–5, 283, 288, 291
Gresford 110
Grey, Earl 185–6
Grey, George 122, 127
Griffith 306
groendruif 20
Grose, Francis 37
Guardian (ship) 28–9
Guernsey 116
Guillod, Ann 113, 168, 171

Hack, John Barton 99–100, *100*
Haffner vineyard 237
Hagen, Jacob 143, 162
Hahndorf 122
Halifax 76, 78
Hall, George 'Captain' 116
Hallett, Alfred 117
Hallett, John 117
Hamburg 8
Hamilton, Henry 178
Hamilton Hill 87
Hamilton, Richard 101, 178
Hampshire (ship) 105–6
Handel, George 8
Handfield, Henry 230
Hardy, Thomas
  arrives in Adelaide 191
  exhibits wines at Sydney International Exhibition 283
  expands plantings 231
  fine reputation as a winemaker 270

John Reynell sells wine to 237
meets with South Australian treasurer 281
plants vines at Bankside 205
portrait of *205*
presides over first meeting of Vignerons' Club 251
produces first wine at Bankside 214
sends wines to London International Exhibition 260
works for John Reynell 191, *205*
works on goldfields 198
Hardy's 156
Hardy's Reynella Winery 137
Hare, William 77
Harper's Weekly Gazette 288
Hart, James 221
Harte, Bret 283, 292, 297
Harvey, William 65
Havilah (ship) 217
Haydn, Joseph 8
Hayler, James 71
Hebden, William 96–7
Heidelberg Tun 8
Henderson, Alexander 157
Henry IV, King 67
Henschke, Johann Christian 246
Henty, Thomas 87
Heritage 214
Heseltine, George 116, 135
Highercombe vineyard 137, 231, 244
Hindmarsh, John 91, 108, 122
The History of Ancient and Modern Wines (Henderson) 157
The Hobart Town Gazette 59
Hobson, Malvina 60
Hobsons Bay 225
hock 142–3, 162, 167
Hodges, Nathaniel 62
hoenpoten 20
Hoffman, Samuel 167
Holdfast Bay 108, 136
Holt, Alfred Astor (MP's brother) 41, 48–9, 79, 95–6, 110, 129, 146
Holt, Elizabeth (née Astor) (MP's mother)
  angry with Chris Penfold for leaving 128
  birth 23
  comfortable middle-class upbringing 31, 40–1
  death 152, 160
  gives birth to Alfred 41
  gives birth to George 41
  gives birth to MP 41–2
  health problems 144, 150
  heartbroken at MP's departure 112–13, 118–19, 149
  husband sends daguerreotype of to MP 145
  love for MP 64, 79–80
  travels to Gravesend to see MP 116–18
  worries about Ellen Timbrell 106
  worries about MP in Adelaide 128
  writes to Chris Penfold 147
  writes to MP 128–30, 144, 151–2
Holt, George William Astor (MP's brother) 41, 79, 110–11, 146
Holt, Thomas Glover (MP's grandfather) 41
Holt, Tom (MP's father)
  becomes father of MP 43
  buries his wife 160
  calls painting 'The Divine Fisherman' 49
  death 233
  failing health 117, 129–30, 150
  gives permission for MP to marry Chris Penfold 79
  heartbroken at MP's departure 112–13, 115–16, 118–19, 149
  love for MP 64
  marries Elizabeth Astor 41
  MP sends photo of daughter to 191
  uses wine in his medical practice 48
  worries about Ellen Timbrell 106
  worries about MP in Adelaide 128
  writes to MP from London 144–50
Home Park (property) 231
home remedies 69–70, 80–1, 98, 152
Hope Farm 205
Hopkins & Penfold 71
Horrocks, John 205
Horsnell, Elizabeth 158, *158*
Horsnell, John 133–4, 144, 158, *158*, 204, 251
Houghton, Richmond 87
Houghton winery 87
Hove 96
Howell, John 217
Howley, William 84–5
Hugh Crawford (ship) 61
'hulks' (floating prisons) 13
Hulme, Nathaniel 9
Hunter, John 19, 25, 37
Hunter Valley 56, 72–3, 110, 188, 238, 306
Hyland, Estelle Ianthe (MP's granddaughter) 248–9, 292
Hyland, Frank Astor (MP's grandson) 262, 301–2, 305–7
Hyland, Gladys (wife of Frank) 307
Hyland, Harold Francis (MP's grandson) 257–8
Hyland, Imogene Olivia Ethel (MP's granddaughter) 233–5
Hyland, Inez (MP's granddaughter)
  as a young girl 272
  birth 232

bond with MP 233–4, 260, 283
death 297–8
has poems published 296
lives with MP part of the year 259
MP buried with 302–3, 307
MP publishes poems of 299–300
MP writes obituary for 298–9
sends poems to local press 296
shows promise as a poet 283, 292
shy and reclusive nature of 292
visits grandfather in Adelaide 249
Hyland, Jeffrey Penfold (son of Leslie) 307, *308*
Hyland, Leslie (MP's grandson) 268, 292, 302, 305–8
Hyland, Mary Georgina Anne 'Georgina' (née Penfold) (MP's daughter)
allows daughter to live with MP 259
as a teenager 210
at school 164
death 306
early childhood 103–5, 112–15, 117, 126–7, 174
finishes education in Melbourne 221
gives birth to Estelle 248
gives birth to Frank 262
gives birth to Harold 257
gives birth to Imogene 233–4
gives birth to Inez 232
gives birth to Leslie 268
gives birth to Vivien 268
inherits MP's estate 305
learns to read and write 185
loses daughter Imogene 234–5
loses daughter Vivien 268
loses son Harold 257–8
marries Thomas Hyland 228–30
meets Thomas Hyland 223
moves to Brighton in Melbourne 284
MP sends photo of to father 191
tours Ireland and Europe 288
tries to convince MP to retire 285
voyage from London to Adelaide 2, 7
Hyland, Rada (daughter of Frank and Gladys) 307
Hyland, Thomas Francis (MP's son-in-law)
advises MP to retire 253, 285
allows daughter to live with MP 259
appoints Giffard Bannister as accountant 287
as a prison warden 223–8, 261–2, 268–70, 284
becomes a father to Frank 262
business acumen 285
contests railway freight charges 287
death 306

devotes himself to selling wine full-time 268–9
exports wine to London 273
forms business partnership with MP 254–6, 285–6
inherits MP's estate 305
leaves running of business to sons 305
loses daughter Imogene 234–5
loses daughter Vivien 268
markets wine to Victorian buyers 249–50, 255, 258, 267
marries Georgina Penfold 228–30
meets Georgina Penfold 223
moves to Brighton in Melbourne 284
portrait of *224*
promotes South Australian wine at London Exhibition 288
receives letter from Bret Harte 297
retires from civil service 287
sends Bannister on sales expedition to Britain 291–2
takes over running of the winemaking business 285–7
takes wine to Colonial and Indian Exhibition 287–8
taps markets in Tasmania and New Zealand 260
tires of prison work 254–5
tough temperament of 250
tours Ireland and Europe 288
writes to MP 261–2
Hyland, Vivien (MP's granddaughter) 268
Hythe 76

In Sunshine and in Shadow (Hyland) 299–300
Inchiquin Station 205
Indigenous Australians 21–2, 26, 89, 91, 122–4, 128, 166, 199, 307
inland sea, search for 148
Inman Valley 204
Intercolonial Exhibition of Australasia, Melbourne (1866) 239, 241–5
Intercolonial Express 292–3, 302
intercolonial trade 245–6, 250, 264, 267, 273, 278–81, 287, 290–1, 305
ipecacuanha wine 69
Ireland 288
Irene (ship) 212
Irish Catholics 241
Irrawang 207
Isle of Wight 68

Jacob, William 167
Jacobs Creek 167
Jamison, Sir John 62–3, 71–2
Jeffcott, Sir John 123–4

Jefferson, Thomas 31, 45
Jenner, Edward 220–1
Jesuits 205–6
John Hayes (ship) 121
Johnson, Richard 27

Kalimna vineyard 306
Kapunda 146, 197
Kaurna people 91, 122–3, 166
Kavel, August 122
Kellie Castle (ship) 156
Kelly, Alexander Charles 156, 223, 230–1, 244–5, 250–1, 260
Kelly, Ned 279
Kelly, Thomas 156
Kelman, William 72
Kemble, Adelaide 103
Kent, Benjamin Archer 182
Kerikeri 53
Kildea, Patrick 221
King, James 207
King, Philip Gidley 21–2, *28*, 37, 39–40, 49–50, 307
Kings Cross 157
Kirkton 72
Klemzig 122, 167
Klinkowstrom, Maximillian 205
Knabe, John 298
Knight, Charles 292
Koh-i-Noor diamond 194
Kranewitter, Aloysius 205
Kyneton 184

La Belle Assemblée 85
La Folk 192
La Trobe, Charles 157
Lady Juliana (ship) 29
Lady Penrhyn (ship) 19–21
Laennec, René 76
The Lancet 76
land grants 29, 36, 40, 56
L'Andre, Antoine 38–40
Langhorne Creek 91
Langmead, Emma 161
Langmead, Mary 161–2
Langmeil 178
Lawson, William 46
Legislative Council, South Australia 124
Leigh, William 136, 206
Letters on the Culture of the Vine, Fermentation, and the Management of the Cellar (Macarthur) 156–7
libraries 213, 217
The Light of Asia 215
Light, Colonel William 99, 166
Lilydale 157

Lindeman, Harriet 110
Lindeman, Henry 76, 110, 188–9, 197, *197*, 237, 256–7, 283
Lindrum, Friedrich 238, 261
Lindrum, Horace 238
Lindrum, Walter 238
Lisbon 187
Little Dorrit (Dickens) 217
Livingstone, David 217
Lloyd, Arthur Forbes 165–6
Lobethal 266
London 7–8, 13, 49, 68, 114
London International Exhibition (1862) 231
London International Exhibition (1873) 260–1
London International Exhibition (1874) 266
London Plague 62
Lord Eldon (ship) 52–3
Lord Hawkesbury (ship) 106
Lovelock, Elijah 134, 158, 204
Lowi, Ninian 87
Lucas, Mary 136
Ludwig I, King 186
Lutherans 122–3, 166, 205
Luttrell, Alfred 59
Luttrell, Edward 59
Luxembourg Gardens, Paris 58
Lyttleton, Lady 105

M. Penfold & Company
  exhibits wines at Sydney International Exhibition 283
  expands sales 273
  exports wine to Melbourne 249
  increases production 282
  MP sets up business as 254
  Tom Hyland markets wine in Victoria 249–50
  visit by Bleasdale 244
  wins bronze medal at Paris Exposition 273–4
Macarthur, Edward 30, 189–90
Macarthur, Elizabeth 30–1, 34, 45, 49
Macarthur, James 51–2, 57, 190, 214
Macarthur, John 30–1, 34–5, 37, 49–53, 58, 72, 189
Macarthur, William
  buys winemaking equipment 214
  co-finances Busby's trip to Europe 57
  collects cuttings in Europe 52
  cuttings of sent to Swan River colony 87
  employs German winemakers 157
  Kelly blames vine failure on 156
  McEwen sources cuttings from 101, 142
  plants new vineyard at Camden Park 189
  returns to England for schooling 51

sends wines to The Great Exhibition 191–3
shows wines at Paris Exposition 206–9, 213
tours Europe 214
MacKillop, Mary 223–4
Macombs Dam, Harlem River 96
Macquarie, Lachlan 46–7
Madeira 11, 29–30, 44, 53, 62, 110, 187, 192
madeira wine 9, 11–12, 63, 71, 101–2, 157, 266–7
Magill 236, 248
Magill Estate (originally Makgill Estate)
  bought by Cock and Ferguson 92
  cellars 4–5
  Cock and Ferguson sell parcel of 95
  MP and husband buy 4, 125–6
  still producing wine today 307
  tributes to long-time employees 308–9
  see also The Grange Estate
Magill Institute 213, 217, 233
Magill Village (originally Makgill Village) 95, 134–5, 194
Makgill, David Maitland 92
Malaga 187
malbee 205
Mamre vineyard 40
Mann, Charles 281
A Manual for the Cultivation of the Vine and the Olive in Western Australia (Nash) 157
A Manual of Plain Directions for Planting and Cultivating Vineyards and for Making Wine in New South Wales (Bubsy) 57
Maria (ship) 122
Marriage Act (1753) 79
Marsden, Samuel 40, 53–4, 81
Marsfield 36
Martin, Annie 230
Marx, Karl 194
Mary, Queen of Scots 62
Masson, Francis 20
Mataro 72, 230, 267, 273, 275, 283, 291
Matra, James 16–17
Mazure, Edmond 306–7
McEwin, George 101, 141–2, 157
McFaull, Charles 87
McLaren Vale 136, 223, 230, 306
McWilliam, Samuel 272
McWilliam's Wines 272
Mechanics' Institute 100
medical men, as vineyard owners 63
medical science, advances in 64–5, 76, 182–3
medicine, wine as 9, 21, 47–8, 62, 65, 69, 86, 155–6, 181, 188–9, 203, 231, 246
Médoc 214

Melbourne 88, 196, 217, 220
Melbourne Benevolent Asylum 246
Melbourne Cottage 100
Melbourne Cup 221
Melbourne General Cemetery 228
Melbourne Hospital 246
Melbourne, Viscount 64, 88
Melville, Francis 'Captain' 225–6
merino sheep 36, 51, 117
Messrs Solomon (law firm) 165
Metropolitan Museum of Art, New York 32
Meyer, F.A. 63
Middle Ages 11
migration, to Australia 87, *90*, 109
mildew 52
Miller's burgundy 47, 53
Milmenrura people 122
Minchinbury Estate 306
mining, in South Australia 146
Minto 48, 58
missionaries 123
Missionary Tales and Researches in Africa (Livingstone) 217
Mitchell, Thomas 157
Modbury vineyard 306
Molesworth, Robert 228
Monroe, James 40
Montpellier 58
Moorabbin House 284, 292, 301–2, 306
Moorabool River 271
Moore Farm 101, 142
Moorundie people 123
Morning Chronicle 33
Morning Herald 138
The Morning Post 98
Morphett, John 136
Morphett Vale 156, 223
Morris, George 237
Mount Barker 100, *100*
Mount Lofty Ranges 95, 176
Mount Radford 212
Mount Tambora, eruption of 43
Mozart, Wolfgang 8
Mudgee 238
Municipal Corporations Act (SA) 221
Murray River 88, 147, 271
Murray Valley vineyard 238
muscadine 38, 101, 273, 275, 291, 294
muscat 101, 173, 192–3, 207–8, 230, 266, 291
Muscat de Frontignan 20
muscat noir 46
muscat of Alexandria 20, 38
muscatel 20, 73, 178, 187, 231–2, 267
musical instruments 8, 12, *13*, 14–15, 18, 30–2

Naples 75
Napoleon III, Emperor 208, 214
Napoleonic Wars 41–3, 51
Nash, James George 162, 201
Nash, Richard West 157
National Museum of American History 32
Nelson, David 25
Nepean, Evan 17–18, 27
Neuchâtel Canton 157
New Silesia 166
New South Wales
  chosen as a convict colony 17–18
  Cook maps 11
  first settlement at Sydney Cove 22–3
  first wine made in 29, 36
  increase in vineyards by the 1820s 49
  new areas planted with vines 238
  Royal Society offers medal for best wine from 44
  rum trade 37
New South Wales Corps 34, 37
New South Wales Medical Gazette 256
New York 14, 82, 95–6, 129, 185
New York Public Library 185
New Zealand 53, 72, 260, 273
Newman, John 116
newspapers 89–91, 116
Newtown, Sydney 40
Ngadjuri people 166
Nicholson Street, Carlton 220
Norfolk Island 27, 30, 225
Norfolk Lodge 104
Norfolk (sloop) 37
Norman, Robert 116, 135
North Adelaide 99–100
North Carolina (ship) 14
North Para River 167
North-West Passage 105
Norwood 238–9, 270, 286
Nurioopta 306

oenotherapy 9
Oidium tuckeri 270–1, 275, 282
Old Botanic Garden, Adelaide 142
Old Cave cellar 137
Old Gum Tree, Glenelg North 91
Olive Farm 87
Oliver, Elizabeth 136
Oliver, William 136
Ophir 196
Oporto 63, 73, 142, 193
Orange Grove vineyard 40
Overland Expedition, of Sturt 127, 127
Overland Telegraph line 259

Packham, David 221
Pakistan 133
palomino 173, 232
Paris 206–8
Paris Exposition Universelle (1855) 206–9, *207*, 244
Paris Exposition Universelle (1867) 246
Paris Exposition Universelle (1878) 273
Paris Exposition Universelle (1889) 293–4, *294*
Parkhall (property) 157
Parramatta 28, *28*, 36
Parramatta River 29–30, 44
Pasteur, Louis 4, 236, 248
pasteurisation 236
Paterson, William 36–7, 50
Peake, Edward 206, 231, 244–5, *245*, 260
Pedro Ximénez 142, 178, 205, 273, 275, 291
Pemulwuy (Bidjigal man) 36
Penfold, Catherine (MP's sister-in-law) *see* Baroncelli, Catherine
Penfold, Charlotte (MP's sister-in-law) 75
Penfold, Charlotte Jane (MP's mother-in-law) 67–70, 79–83, 98, 112
Penfold, Christopher Rawson (MP's husband)
  appearance 65–6
  appointed local medical officer 236, 248
  approved to practice medicine in Victoria 218
  argues with brother over loan 160
  as a church warden 232
  as a medical student 63, 65, 76–7
  as chair of Burnside Council 212
  as Government Vaccinator 220–1, 230
  assists in amputation without anaesthetic 182
  attends Bleasdale's lecture 245
  auctions off animals and equipment 217
  borrows £200 from brother Tom 112, 126, 168
  buys land sight unseen 115
  buys Makgill Estate 4, 125–6
  childhood 68
  death 5, 251–2
  delivers his own daughter 104
  dissolves partnership with Watson 113
  downsizes to reduce workload 232–3
  dreams of own farm in South Australia 88
  encourages MP to make wine 5
  enters medical partnership 78
  examines drowning victim 97
  expands vineyard at Magill 231–2
  exports wine to Melbourne 249
  fights bushfire 209–10

financial difficulties 168, 171
founding member of Adelaide Vignerons' Club 251
founding promoter of South Australian Wine Company 246–7
gives mother medical potions 98
harvests first grapes at Makgill 172
hires Joe Gillard 249–50
hires John Horsnell and Elizabeth Smyth 133–4
invited to Grand Civic Banquet 240
knowledge of wine 71
lives in Brighton 86, 102–3
marries MP 75, 79, 81–2
medical partnership with W.S. Watson 104
meets MP 63, 66
moves into lodgings in Adelaide 124–5
moves into The Grange 131
moves into wooden house on Makgill 126–7
moves to Melbourne 217–18, 220
moves to Norfolk Lodge 104
named after Christopher Rawson 70
newspaper pays tribute to vineyard of 148
opens quarries 216–17
oversees inquiry into fire 210
parlous financial situation 112–13
pays off mortgage for The Grange 201
poor health of 233, 244, 251
practises medicine in Adelaide 139, 144, 155–6, 158, 161–2, 173, 181–2, 185, 210, 213, 248
practises medicine in Brighton 93–4, 97
practises medicine in Melbourne 221
prospers at Magill 173
prospers in Adelaide 158
puts down deposit for move to Adelaide 112–13, 115
qualifies as a doctor 66
reassures MP's parents 115
refuses request for road to be built 204
rents out The Grange 221–2
returns to The Grange 230
shows signs of ageing 215–16, 244
sources vine cuttings from France and Portugal 114
starts own medical practice 82–3, 86
suffers bad harvests 204
taken to court by his brother 165, 168
taken to court over building work 168, 171–2
takes up appointment in Melbourne 217–18
uses fortified wine in medical practice 181
visits Emma and Mary Penfold 169–70

voyage from London to Adelaide 2, 114–21
Penfold, Emma (MP's sister-in-law)
death 212
falls pregnant 169
gives birth to Emma Mary 138, 144
gives birth to Laura 165–6
gives birth to stillborn child 174–5
grief-stricken after loss of daughter 168–9
husband of takes family to court 129, 138
joyful disposition of 150–1
returns to London 211–12
sets off for Adelaide from Torquay 155
Penfold, Emma Mary (MP's niece) *see* Whitling, Emma Mary
Penfold, Fanny (MP's sister-in-law) 74–6, 78–9
Penfold, George Rawson Saxby (MP's brother-in-law) 70, 233
Penfold, Georgina Frances (MP's niece) 212
Penfold, Hugh (ancestor) 69
Penfold, James (MP's brother-in-law) 76, 78, 112
Penfold, John (MP's father-in-law) 67–8, 70, 75, 82, 103, 153–4
Penfold, Laura (MP's niece) 166, 168–9
Penfold, Mary
acknowledged as a winemaker 274, 276–7, 282, 284, 302, 308
advertises for grape-pickers 273
ambivalence about trip to Australia 113
approves daughter's marriage 230
as a grandmother 232–4, 248, 259, 262, 292–3
as a young woman 64
attends Bleasdale's lecture 245
auctions off animals and equipment 217
becomes more active in business 171, 173, 216
becomes more involved in winemaking 216
birth 7, 41, 43
bond with granddaughter Inez 233–4, 260, 283
buried in St George's Church 302–3
business acumen of 33, 256, 262
buys grapes from other vineyards 262–3
buys land sight unseen 115
city council delegation toasts health of 291
clothing of 85–6
comforts Emma Penfold 168–70
complains to mother about Ellen Timbrell 144, 150
contribution of overlooked 160, 171, 253
crestfallen at Emma Penfold's departure 211–12

death and funeral 302–3
devastated by granddaughter's death 297
early childhood 48–50
engages Strutton & Trapman as agents 273
exports wine to London 273
exports wine to Melbourne 249
faints at sight of Tom Penfold 159
feels absence of her husband 259
fights bushfire 209–10
forms business partnership with Tom Hyland 254–6
forms partnership with Hyland and Gillard 285–6
gives birth to Mary Georgina 103–5
gives Governor tour of The Grange 289–90
gives reporters tour of The Grange 274–6
harvests first grapes at Makgill 172
heartbroken at death of friend Ellen 215
hires Ellen Timbrell as an assistant 104–5
hires Joe Gillard 249–50
hires John Horsnell and Elizabeth Smyth 133–4
imperious presence of 1
increases trade with Victoria 267
keeps notes on produce 232
learns of great-uncle's death 184–5
leaves estate to daughter and son-in-law 305
leaves The Grange and moves to Melbourne 301–2
legacy of 305, 307–8
lives in Brighton 86, 102–3
lobbies for abolition of interstate tariffs 278–82
looks after granddaughter part of the year 259
loses husband 251–4
makes wine in small batches 210
marries Christopher Penfold 75, 79, 81–2
meets Christopher Penfold 63, 66
moves into lodgings in Adelaide 124–5
moves into The Grange 131
moves into wooden house on Makgill 126–7
moves to Melbourne 218–20
moves to Norfolk Lodge 104
offers advice on improving community 213
oversees expansion of business 5
pays off mortgage for The Grange 201
portrait of (1869) 3
pours energy into vineyard 236
prepares to leave The Grange 300
prospers at Magill 158, 173
publishes Inez Hyland's poems 299–300

refuses request for road to be built 204
renegotiates mortgage 188
retires from family wine business 287
returns to The Grange 230
rides around property on white mare 259
satisfaction with accomplishments 284
sells off effects at The Grange 301
sells off surplus land 258
sends photo of daughter to father 191
sends wine to London Exhibition (1874) 266
sends wine to Paris Exposition (1889) 294–5
sends wine to Sydney International Exhibition (1879) 282–3
suffers bad harvests 204
supervises workforce 232, 267
takes over winemaking business 253–4, 256, 262
teaches herself to make wine 2–4, 173, 185, 188, 191, 275–7
voyage from London to Adelaide 2, 7, 114–21
wins prizes at Sydney Exhibition 283
witnesses death of granddaughter 234–5
writes obituary for Inez Hyland 298–9
writes to grandson Leslie 292–3
writes to parents from Adelaide 128, 137–9
Penfold, Mary (MP's sister-in-law) 66
Penfold, Richard (brother of Christopher) 65, 69
Penfold, Richard (cousin-once-removed of Christopher) 71
Penfold Road 131
Penfold, Robert (brother of Christopher) 67
Penfold-Russell, Rebel (MP's great-granddaughter) 307
Penfold, Thomas Brooks (MP's brother-in-law)
  arrives in Adelaide 158
  as a church warden 174–5
  assumes title of Captain 170
  becomes a leading light in the community 174
  builds two-storey hotel 206
  buys estate in Mount Radford 212
  buys site along Makgill Road 164–5
  clashes with family over will 112, 153
  death 233
  decides to emigrate to Adelaide 150–2
  develops shopping centre in Magill 164–5, 194
  difficult temperament of 81, 129, 151, 170
  lends brother £200 112, 126, 168
  loses daughter 168

loses wife 212
MP faints at sight of 159
naval career with East India Company 70
returns to London 211–12
sends mother recipe for Indian pickle 81, 98
taken to court by own family 153–5
takes his brother to court 165, 168, 172
takes own family to court 129, 138
tasked with raising funds for church 165, 170, 174
throws weight around in Adelaide 161
voyage to Adelaide from London 155
wants brother to repay loan 128, 130, 160
wants cut of brother's wheat deal 161
Penfold v Bouch 138
Penfold v Penfold 168, 172
Penfold, William (MP's brother-in-law) 153–5
Penfolds and Co.
  acquires Lindeman from Phillip Morris 110
  beginning of 2
  bronze medal boosts reputation of 274
  exhibits at the London Colonial and India Exhibition 288
  expands market into Western Australia 305
  exports to overseas markets 3
  MP goes into partnership to form 285–6
  MP's grandsons expand business 306–7
  opens Sydney office 306
  ownership passes from family 307, *308*
  tributes to long-time employees 308–9
  see also The Grange Estate; M. Penfold & Company
Penfolds Magill Estate Shiraz 307
Penfolds Road 5, 274
Peninsular War 166
Pentridge Stockade 224
Penwortham 205
Penzance 79
Peramangk people 166
Pewsey Vale winery 167, 239, 244
Phillip, Arthur 17–28, 30–1, 35, 37, 185
photography 110–11, 116, 135, 146
phylloxera 271, 273, 281
pianos 8, *13*, 31–2
pinot gris 72
pinot meunier 47, 53
pinot noir 47, 72–3, 202
Pipeclay Creek 238
Pitman, Septimus 309
Pitt, William 16
Pius VII, Pope 41
Plague of London 62

Plato 10
Pliny 56
Pommard wines 222
pontac 20
Poole, James 148
population 202, 216, 273
Porpoise (ship) 38
port 9, 43, 142, 172–3, 291, 294
Port Adelaide 7, 106–7, 120–1, 134, 158, 259
Port Arthur 225
Port Phillip Bay 87
Port Phillip District 157
porter (beer) 35
Portland 232, 248, 250
Portland Bay 87
Portland, Duke of 38–9
Portland Gaol 223, 228, 233, 235
Portugal 4, 114
Portuguese wine 43, 193
Portuguese winegrowers 295
Potts, Frank 91
poverty 13
Preservation Creek 147–8
Price, John Giles 226–8
Prince of Wales Cove 37
prisons
  Castlemaine Gaol 250, 255, 261, 268–70, 284
  Collingwood Stockade 228
  Pentridge Stockade 224
  Portland Gaol 223, 228, 233, 235
Probus, Emperor 187
Prospect Farm, Hobart 59–60
protectionism *see* tariffs, on wine
Protestants 241
Putland, Mary 40
Pybus, William 170

quarantine, between states 272
Quarterly Meeting of Magistrates, Adelaide 161
Queensland 238, 273
Quiz and the Lantern (magazine) 296

rail gauges 278, 292
Rawson, Christopher 70, 74, 76, 78–9
Rawson, Mary Anne 74, 79
Rawson's Bank 70
red muscat 192
red muscatel 20
red Portugal 73
red wines 9–10
Redfern, William 47–8, 62–3
Regentville 62–3, 71
Revolutionary War (1776) 12–14, 28

Reynell, John 136, 191, 197, 204–5, 237, 239, 251
Reynell, Samuel 136
Reynella Farm 204–5
Reynella House 137
Reynella (township) 137
Rhine riesling 8
Rhine River 8, 29, 187, 192
Rhodes, Matilda 96
Rhône region 52, 114, 188, 208, 271
Riddoch, John 296
riesling 8, 110, 187, 192, 207, 267, 291
Rio de Janeiro 19, 29–30
River Torrens 99, 122, 142, 205
Robe, Frederick 175–6
Roberts, John 238
Robertson, Charles 299
Robinson, Sir William 288–9, 291
Roma 238
Rome 41
Ronalds, Hugh 38
Rooty Hill 306
Rose Hill 28, *28*, 29, 35, 58
Ross, Robert 27
Rosslyn Park 290
Roth, Adam 238
roussane 188
roussillon 205, 231
Royal Admiral (ship) 35, 38
Royal Agricultural and Horticultural Society of South Australia 136, 143
Royal Botanic Gardens, Sydney 72, 87, 142
Royal Free Hospital 81
Royal Navy 41
Royal Pavilion, Brighton 84, 86
Royal Society for the Encouragement of Arts, Manufacturers and Commerce 44, 162
Royal Society of Arts 44, 55–6, 67
Royal Society of Victoria 243
Royal tours 239–41, *240*
rum 37, 39
Rum Corps 37, 51
Rutherglen 237
Ryrie, Donald 202–3, 222
Ryrie, William 88, 202–3, 222

sack 62
Saint Helena 106
Salter, George 93–4
Sanders, Henry 78, 82
Sauternes 214
sauvignon blanc 230
Scarborough (ship) 17, 30
Schaffer, Elizabeth 28
Schaffer, Philip 28–9, 36

Schubert, Max 308–9
Schürmann, Clamor 123
scurvy 9, 19–20
Second Creek 161
semillon 20
Seppelt, Joseph 238, 283
Seppeltsfield vineyard 238–9
sercial 230
Serle, Ambrose 53–4
Serrao, Emmanuel 62
Seven Years War 8, 13
Shakespeare, William 11
sherry 9, 62–3, 142, 173, 232, 291
Shield, Mr (accident victim) 181–2
Shikarpur 133
shipwrecks 122
shiraz 72, 91, 110, 178, 188, 193, 230–1, 261, 267, 307, 309
Shoreham 103
Short, Bishop Augustus 170, 174–81, 252
Short, Caroline 177–9
Short, Millicent 177
Shudi & Broadwood 8
Shudi, Burkat 8
Silesian Lutherans 166, 205
silver-lead ore 146
Sirius (ship) 18–19, 31, 36
Slavery Abolition Act (1833) 64
slavery, abolition of 64
Sloane Square, London 78
smallpox 67, 217, 220–1
Smith, E.T. 288–9, 291
Smith, Samuel 167, 198
Smithsonian Institution 32
Smyth, Arthur Bowes 19–21
Smyth, Elizabeth 134
snakebites 161–2, 199–201
social justice 64–5
Society for the Extinction of the Slave Trade and for the Civilisation of Africa 103
Somerville, BNill 171–2
South Africa 101–2
South Australia
  Aboriginal Australians in 122–4
  advertising for migrants *90*
  early colony of 88–92, 98–9, 107–9
  exodus from to the goldfields 197
  first church consecrated in 170
  First Fleet to 135, 161
  gives franchise to women 221–2
  population 216, 273
  progressiveness of 230
  reputation as a wine-making colony 242–3
  sends wine to Intercolonial Exhibition 239, 242

South Australian wine praised at London Exhibition 260–1
visit of Prince Alfred 239–40, *240*
South Australia Act (1834) 89
South Australia Association 88–9
The South Australian 141, 143, 156, 178, 185
The South Australian Advertiser 270–1
South Australian Brewing 307
South Australian Company 121–2
South Australian Cordial Factory 258
The South Australian Gazette and Colonial Register (later called *South Australian Register*) 91, 100
South Australian House of Assembly 206
South Australian Institute 243, 245
South Australian Legislative Council 194
South Australian Mining Association 194
The South Australian Register 107–8, 142–3, 163, 174–5, 196, 215, 238–9, 262–6
South Australian Supreme Court 165, 168, 171
The South Australian Vigneron and Gardener's Manual (McEwin) 101, 157
South Australian Vineyard Association 231
South Australian Wine Company 246–8
South Guildford 87
Southcorp Wines 307
Spain 57–8
Spanish wine 43–4
The Spectator 69
St Andrew Holborn 75, 81–2
St Andrew's, Steyning 67, 75
St Bartholomew's Hospital ('Barts'), London 65, 76–7, 162
St Botolph-without-Bishopsgate 115
St George's Church, Woodforde 165, 170, 174–7, 179, 232, 252, 298, 302, 307
St Henri claret 306–7
St Hubert's vineyard 237
St James's Library and Reading Room 69
St Kilda, Melbourne 223
St Leonards vineyard 237
St Marys 40
St Marys Towers Catholic retreat 157
St Patrick's College, Melbourne 243
St Vincent Gulf 88, 107
Stanley, Edward 162
Stawell 198
Stein, Jacob 157
The Steine 85–6
Stevenson, George 91, 100, 141–3, 162–3
Steyning 66–7, 71, 83
Stony Hill vineyard 137
Stonyfell vineyard 230, 244
storage tanks 265–6

Stradbroke House 165, 177, 183
Strutton & Trapman 273
Stuart, John McDouall 127
Sturt, Charles 59, 88, 99, 101, 117, *127*, 127–8, 147–8
Success (ship) 225–6
Suez Canal 259
Surrey (ship) 47, 136
Surreyville (property) 137
Suttor, George 37–8, 157, 188–9
Swan River colony 87
sweetwater 53, 101, 202, 232
Swiss migrants 157
Switzerland 51–2, 157
Sydney Cove 22–4
Sydney Harbour 25
Sydney International Exhibition (1879) 282–3
Sydney, Lord 17
The Sydney Monitor 63
The Sydney Morning Herald 237
Sylvania vineyard 239, 249, 270, 286
Syon House 58, 142
syrah 188

Table Bay 105
Taglioni, Marie 114, 145
Taglioni (ship) 113–18, 120–1, 129, 136, 159
Tain-l'Hermitage 52
Tanunda 167
Taranga vineyard 136
tariffs, on wine 190, 245, 250, 264, 267, 273, 278–81, 287, 290–1, 305
Tarndanya (Adelaide) 91
Tasmania 260
  see also Van Diemen's Land
Taunton Castle (ship) 106
Taylor, Thomas 177
Tea Tree Gully 296
Teichelmann, Christian 123
telegraph 232, 259
Tench, Watkin 18, 26–7, 29–30
Tenerife 18, 29
Tennyson, Alfred 194
Thackeray, William Makepeace 194
Theatre Royal, Melbourne 184
Theresa (ship) 110
Third Creek 95, 204, 209
Thomas, Mary 108–9
Thomas, Robert 100, 108
Thornton, Robert 80
Thorpe's (wine merchant) 43
tic douloureux 98
Timbrell, Andrew 106
Timbrell, Elizabeth 81, 106

Timbrell, Ellen
   accompanies MP on voyage to Adelaide 113
   death from typhus fever 215
   early life 106
   friendship with MP 81
   harvests first grapes at Makgill 172
   helps MP with winemaking 191, 214
   keeps accounts for Chris Penfold 158
   learns of her brother's death 133
   moves into wooden house on Makgill 126
   MP complains to mother about 144, 150
   plants vines at Makgill 2
   suffers poor health 210
   works as MP's assistant 104–5
Timbrell, Harriet 81, 104
Timbrell, James 106
Timbrell, Thomas 105–6
Timbrell, William 133
The Times 31, 208
Tinta 63
Tintara 156, 244, 260
Tintara Vineyard Co. 223, 230
Toby (dog) 259
tokay 9, 38, 58, 101, 187, 208, 266–7, 273–5, 283, 288, 291, 294
Tooth and Co. 307
Torrens Valley 270
Tower Hotel 206
Townshend, George 110
Townson, Robert 58–9
transportation 64, 71
Treasury Wine Estates 307
A Treatise on the Culture of the Vine and the Art of Making Wine (Busby) 56
Treaty of Paris 14
Trevallyn station 110
Trimmer, Edward 125–6, 173, 188, 201
Trinity (house) 156, 223
Trocadéro Palace, Paris 273
True-Briton (ship) 106
Turnbull, Alexander 98
Twain, Mark 283
Tyler, John Chatfield 279
Tyrrell, Edward 238

Underdale 205
United States 12–14, 45

vaccinations 67, 220–1
Van Diemen's Land 25–6, 37, 59–61, 184
   see also Tasmania
Varro, Marcus Terentius 59
Varro Ville 59
verdelho 29–30, 91, 101, 110, 142, 188, 192, 205, 244, 266, 270, 275

Vice-Chancellor's Court 138, 153
Victoria
   gold rush 196–7, 217
   Henty plants first vines in 87
   makes vaccinations compulsory 221
   new areas planted with vines 237
   Penfolds market wines in 249–50
   settlement of Melbourne 87
   Swiss and German settlers plant vines in 157
   tariffs on South Australian wine 245, 250, 264, 267, 273, 278–81
   vines planted in Yarra Valley 88
Victoria Hall, Adelaide 296
Victoria Medical Association 243
Victoria, Queen 84–6, 102–3, 105, 143, 162, 208–9, 287
Vine Cottage 102
vine cuttings
   Adelaide group buys South African cuttings 101–2
   Anderson plants Château Lafite cuttings 222
   Auld plants vines at Makgill 135
   Banfield on care of vines 186
   Banks sends cuttings to Sydney 37–8
   Broughton plants first cuttings in Tasmania 59–61
   Busby collects cuttings from Europe 57–8, 72
   Chris Penfold sources cuttings from Europe 114
   cuttings planted at Rose Hill 28, *28*
   cuttings planted on Norfolk Island 27, 30
   disease 46–7, 270–1, 273
   early plantings at Magill Estate 133–4
   first cuttings planted in colony 24–5, 27–8, 30, 185
   first plantings in Victoria 87–8
   first plantings in Western Australia 87
   from France and Portugal 4
   Hack plants cuttings in Adelaide 99–100
   Hamilton expands plantings in Glenelg 178
   in the First Fleet 18, 20, 22–3
   increase in availability of 72
   Jamison plants vines at Regentville 62–3, 71–2
   Kelly plants cuttings at Morphett Vale 156
   Macarthur collects cuttings from Europe 51–2
   Macarthur collects cuttings in Madeira 53
   Macarthur's cuttings stolen 53
   McEwin sources cuttings for South Australia 101
   Penfolds plant more cuttings at The Grange 148

Redfern collects cuttings in Madeira 62
Reynell plants cuttings at Reynella 136–7
Spanish cuttings planted at Clarendon 136
The Vine in Australia (Kelly) 223
vine louse 271
Vinegrowers Association 249
The Vineyard 29, 36
voting rights, for women 221–2

Wakefield, Edward 88–9
Wakley, Thomas 76
Waldorf Astoria Hotel 185
Walker, John 74–5, 78
Walldorf 8, 185
Wallumettagal people 29
Ward, Ebenezer 231
Warner, Jim 308–9
Warrandyte 196
Washington, George 12, 20
Waterhouse, George 231
Waterhouse, Henry 36
Waters, Thomas 87
Watson, Henry 101–2
Watson, W.S. 104, 113
Wellington, Duke of 42
Wentworth, William Charles 46
Were, Jonathan Binns 284
Western Australia 87, 305
Westminster Hall, London 138
wheat 134, 159–61, 223
white frontignac 38
white gouais 63
White, John 17, 20, 22
white muscadine 38
white muscat 101, 192
white muscatel 20
white wines 9
Whitling, Emma Mary (née Penfold) (MP's niece) 138, 144, 150–1, 155, 169–70, 233
Whitmore, William 89
wildlife 125
William IV, King 64, 84, 91
William Harris & Co. 82
Williams, Thomas 227
Williamstown 224, 226
Willliam Pitt (ship) 44
Willunga 231
Wilson, Theodore Percival 177
wine
  as a medicine 9, 21, 47–8, 62, 65, 69, 86, 155–6, 181, 188–9, 203, 231, 246
  as a pillar of civilization 10
  as an elixir 256–7
  at the Agricultural Society Exhibition 141–3

at the Intercolonial Exhibition 239, 244
Auld sends wine to London Exhibition 231
Australian wine at the Paris Exposition 206–9, *207*, 244
Busby takes produce to Europe 57–8
exports to Britain 202, 205, 208
friction over naming of 295
high price of in London (1816) 43–4
Hyland takes wine to Colonial and Indian Exhibition 287–8
in Britain in the late 1700s 10
in history 10–11
in the new colony of New South Wales 17, 26
Lindeman extols virtues of 237
Lindrum wins International Gold Medal for 261
Macarthur lobbies for tariff reduction 190
Macarthurs send wine to Great Exhibition 191–2
MP sends wine to London Exhibition 266
MP sends wine to Sydney Exhibition 282–3
MP's port draws praise at Paris Exposition 294–5
on Cook's *Endeavour* 9
on the First Fleet 17–21
overshadowed by rum trade 37
Penfolds win bronze at Paris Exposition 273
Queen Victoria likes Duffield's wine 162
Royal Society offers medal for best wine 44
snobbery about 250–1
South Australian wine praised at London Exhibition 260–1
South Australian wine praised at Paris Exposition 246
Sydney pubs' lack of 251
uses of in Greco-Roman times 62
vines depicted in art 124
see also vine cuttings; winemaking
wine casks 4, 8, 265–6, 296
Wine-Growing in Australia (Kelly) 223
Wine Olympics, Paris (1971) 309
Wine Spectator 309
winemaking
  advances in science of 236
  at The Grange 263–6
  Banfield on 186–8
  Blaxland gains international acclaim 55–6
  Blaxland makes wine at Brush Farm 44–7
  books on 156–7, 223
  commerial production by the Macarthurs 191–2

efforts of L'Andre and de Riveau 38–40
expansion of in the colony 157
first wine made in Australia 29, 36
in Europe 51–2
in the Yarra Valley 202–3
increases in volume of production 237
labour shortage during gold rush 201
MP learns how to make wine 2–4, 173, 185, 188, 191, 275–7
Penfolds make first wine at Magill 172
Reynell establishes commercial vineyard 137
size of domestic market 250
South Australia's first commercial vineyard 137
state of the industry in 1844 16
Thomas Hardy makes first wine 214
vineyards threatened by fungus 270–1
women, voting rights for 221–2
Woodchester, Gloucestershire 206
Woodforde 135, 165
Woodforde Arms Hotel 194–5
Woodvale Farm 134, 204
wool industry 117, 137, 193, 202
Worgan, George 18–19, 22, 25, 30–1

World's End Inn 195
Worthing 71
Wright, Edmund W. 231, 281
Wright, Elizabeth Dorothea *see* Astor, Elizabeth (née Wright)
Wurundjeri people 87
Wyndham Estate 306
Wyndham, George 72–3, 110, 283

xeres 63

Yalumba 167, 198, 239, 244
Yare (ship) 121
Yarra Park, Melbourne 241
Yarra Valley 88, 202–3, 222, 237
Yatala 166
Year Without a Summer (1816) 215
Yemmerrawanne (Wangal man) 35
Yering Station 88, 202–3, 222, 237
Yeringberg vineyard 203, 237
Yorke Peninsula 137
Young Men's Christian Association 296
Yule, Thomas 87

zante currant 231